SECOND EDITION

21 DEBATED

ISSUES IN WORLD POLITICS

EDITORS

Gregory M. Scott

University of Central Oklahoma

Randall J. Jones, Jr.

University of Central Oklahoma

Louis S. Furmanski

University of Central Oklahoma

PEARSON

Prentice Hall

UPPER SADDLE RIVER, NEW JERSEY 07458

Library of Congress Cataloging-in-Publication Data

21 debated: issues in world politics/editors: Gregory M. Scott, Randall J. Jones, Jr.,
Louis S. Furmanski.—2nd ed.
  p. cm.
Includes bibliographical references.
  ISBN 0-13-045829-5
  1. World politics—1989–.   2. Globalization.   3. Islam and politics.
4. Terrorism.   I. Title: Twenty one debated.   II. Scott, Gregory M.   III. Jones,
Randall J.   IV. Furmanski, Louis S.
  D2009.A14   2004
  320.9'0511—dc22

                                                          2003014911

Editorial Director: Charlyce Jones Owen
Acquisitions Editor: Glenn Johnston
Assistant Editor: John Ragozzine
Editorial Assistant: Suzanne Remore
Director of Marketing: Beth Mejia
Marketing Assistant: Jennifer Bryant
Prepress and Manufacturing Buyer: Sherry Lewis
Interior Design: John P. Mazzola
Cover Design: Lisa Boylan
Cover Art: The Studio Dog/Getty Images, Inc.
Composition/Full-Service Project Management: Kari Callaghan Mazzola and John P.
  Mazzola
Printer/Binder: Courier Companies, Inc.
Cover Printer: Coral Graphics

This book was set in 10/12 Meridien.

Pearson Education LTD.   Pearson Education North Asia Ltd
Pearson Education Singapore, Pte. Ltd   Pearson Educación de Mexico, S.A. de C.V.
Pearson Education, Canada, Ltd   Pearson Education Malaysia, Pte. Ltd
Pearson Education–Japan   Pearson Education, Upper Saddle River, NJ
Pearson Education Australia PTY, Limited

10 9 8 7 6 5 4 3 2
ISBN 0-13-045829-5

CONTENTS

PREFACE

The thousands of topics available in world politics pose a challenge for anyone assembling a sample, as in this book. Problems in the Middle East and the "war on terror" would themselves be sufficient to fill many books. This book, therefore, is not comprehensive, but it does include a sample intended to whet your appetite for a lifetime of reading about world affairs.

If you are reading this preface, you are probably a college student taking a course in world politics, foreign policy, or international relations. You may already know a good deal about global politics, or you may not have paid much attention thus far. You may be unaware of how many important issues are currently shaping the global, political, and economic environment. As today's citizen of the world and perhaps tomorrow's leader, you have a role in determining how these issues shape your future.

In order to grasp the importance of some of these issues, imagine a day in the life of a U.S. president who has turned from pressing domestic concerns to problems that may have a significant long-term effect on the nation's future. A presidential meeting with the National Security Council might feature an agenda containing the following items:

- Plan to stop al Qaeda
- Discussion of nuclear weapons proliferation
- Proposal to allow Turkey to join the European Union
- Plan to guard against terrorist attacks on U.S. embassies
- Resolution to reduce opportunities for Americans to become mercenaries
- Resolution to impose a tax on imported computers
- Response to expansion of the European Monetary Union (EMU)
- Request to increase the U.S. allocation to the International Monetary Fund (IMF)

- Decision on how to proceed with Iraq
- Request for a study of the strategic implications of global warming
- Request for assistance to several African countries to help reduce the spread of AIDS

The items listed above would make for a full agenda, to be sure, but they would by no means exhaust the number of foreign-affairs concerns deserving attention. But where do you begin to grasp the complex web of issues that confront ambassadors, statesmen, international corporations, and non-governmental organizations (NGOs) every day? This book can be more than just a course requirement; it can, in fact, help you get started in your quest to become familiar with the world's problems and opportunities.

Obviously, this book does not cover all world issues, nor does it address all aspects of any particular issue. The length of the book imposes a further limitation: The text is presented in a debate format, with one author on each side of an issue, whereas, in reality, every major social and political issue is complex, and many sides may develop in the process of an issue's resolution. This book does, however, point you in the right direction by introducing you to twenty-one of the most controversial and important issues facing the world's governments today, which are discussed by some of the world's most thoughtful commentators. Although the debate format is most often used, sometimes two different perspectives and approaches to an issue are presented rather than two directly opposing viewpoints (e.g., Issue 1, globalization).

It is unlikely that any single article will allow you to resolve conclusively for yourself any particular issue, but that is not our purpose. As editors we have, from the start, had in mind three objectives: The first is to pique your interest in the issues themselves. You may have already heard so much discussion on some of the issues that you think that nothing of interest can still be said. If this is the case, we hope to surprise you with some creative thought and good writing. Our second objective is to provide you with some of the basic information that is needed to begin to develop your own informed opinions. The articles in this book provide a great many facts and findings, as well as interpretations. Our third objective is to raise questions in your mind. Good analysis often raises more questions than it answers. We hope that after you have read these articles, you will have a wide array of new questions and that you will be more eager to begin a lifelong search for the insight needed to make the world a better place in which to live. We wish you all the best.

This book is dedicated to Taya, Jessica, and Drew.

Greg Scott
Randy Jones
Lou Furmanski

PART I

GLOBALIZATION AND DEMOCRACY

ISSUE 1

GLOBALIZATION

Israeli political thinker Yaron Ezrahi has said that "the most arbitrary powers in history always hid under the claim of some impersonal logic—God, the laws of nature, the laws of the market. The same could happen with globalization." Whether or not the term *globalization* will fall into this category, there is no question of its having become a standard term to describe the political and economic forces current at the turn of the twentieth century.

Perhaps no term better symbolizes the forces affecting the course of international relations than does *globalization*. Everywhere we turn, we read or hear about its impact. The refrain goes something like this: We live in a global society, increasingly linked together by an ever more complex web of communications, economies, and other types of mutual dependencies. Thus, there seems to be no denying the term's relevance.

What is globalization? The answer to this question begins with a few simple assertions and then the subject rapidly becomes much more complex. The concept begins with the idea that the economic world is much less insular than it once was. Increasingly, for example, a machine part manufacturing plant in Indiana faces more competition from a similar operation in Indonesia than it does from a similar operation in California. Increasingly, using the Internet and other communications systems, people everywhere look beyond their national borders to buy what they need and sell what they have. One result is that competition increases for markets and resources and exchange in products and services is much more rapid.

Globalization is not optional. In the long run, globalization is not even controllable, that is, by the policies of any one nation working on its own, and perhaps not even by combinations of nations. The most that nations can do is to attempt to control their economies through an assortment of regulation,

1

investment, and trade policies, but in the end, the pressures of the market will likely defeat those that do not flow with the global tide.

Technology and transportation facilities make it possible and the natural demand for goods and services creates new dimensions of globalization daily. For the United States, like the other nations of the world, globalization has both positive and negative results. On the positive side, people everywhere often enjoy a larger selection of goods and services at lower prices. Indeed, an entrepreneur in Vermont with a new product and service has at her disposal contacts with buyers all over the world, not just New York or New Hampshire or Georgia. In some ways, the United States enjoys greater advantages from globalization than other countries. Because the United States has a lead in many areas of technology, our services and products have a competitive advantage.

On the negative side, when other nations can produce similar products more cheaply, some of our workers, sometimes substantial numbers, lose their jobs. Many areas of the world pay their laborers far less than American workers receive, and this affects American producers of everything from automobiles to shoes and from DVDs to clothing. Having to pay higher wages puts American producers at a competitive disadvantage in relation to foreign producers that are able to sell their products at a lower price. The result is increased importation of foreign goods. When America imports more from another nation than it sells to that nation, a *trade deficit* is created. Trade deficits mean that other nations receive more of our currency or credit than we receive of theirs. The flow of money is from us to them. Their production of goods increases as ours decreases, and as a result, they hire more workers while ours are laid off.

Other problems that are increased—if not caused—by globalization, are exploitation of workers and environmental degradation. In Asia, Africa, and South America in particular, people living in poverty are exploited because they are willing to work for pennies per hour while the manufacturers employing them enjoy large profits. When increased trade in products creates demand for resources, countries with weak or corrupt regulatory systems allow large corporations to extract minerals, lumber, and many other materials while doing great harm to the environment. In addition, new coal-burning power plants, constructed to provide power to manufacturing plants, pour hundreds of tons of pollutants into the atmosphere.

If globalization is a fact of life, can its negative effects be controlled or limited? That question is debated, more or less continuously, in Congress. The debate is not so much about whether or not to try to stop globalization as it is about how to mitigate its effects. In the speeches that follow, Senator Byron Dorgan (D-ND) and Representative John J. Duncan, Jr. (R-TN) focus on different aspects of the problem in a manner that is typical of the debate as a whole. Both congressmen are concerned about growing U.S. trade deficits and both believe U.S. policies should serve our own interest first.

While Senator Dorgan is concerned with humanitarian and environmental issues, however, Representative Duncan is concerned that environmentalists are a part of the illness rather than a part of the cure.

DISCUSSION QUESTIONS

As you read the speeches by Senator Dorgan and Representative Duncan, consider the following questions:

1. To what extent can the effects of globalization be controlled?
2. Are humanitarian concerns inherently opposed to the national interest? Environmental concerns?
3. To what extent should Americans offset the trade deficit by buying American goods?

KEY WEB SITES

For more information on this topic, visit the following Web sites:

Millennium Institute
http://www.igc.org/millennium

Economic Policy Institute
http://epinet.org/index.html

The Commission on Global Governance
http://www.cgg.ch

Meeting the Challenges of Globalization

Senator Byron Dorgan

U.S. Senate, Washington, D.C.
April 24, 2001

Mr. President, last week we were all witnesses to headlines in the newspapers about a meeting held in Quebec City, Canada. The newspaper headlines talked about tear gas, chain link fences, police lines, demonstrators, 30,000 people marching down streets. It also discussed anarchists.

What is this all about, 30,000 people demonstrating in the streets of a major city in our hemisphere? It is about international trade. The same sort of thing happened in Seattle a year and a half ago. The future WTO (World Trade Organization) ministerial meeting will be held not in a major city but in a place called Qatar. Why? Because no city wanted to host it, as I understand it. They will have to even bring in cruise ships for hotel rooms. They feel if the ministers of trade from around the world can hold a meeting in an isolated place, no one will show up to protest their closed-door meeting.

Last week's demonstrations in Quebec City underscored again that world leaders are not going to hold trade talks without attention being paid to the issues and concerns of the people and the problems related to global trade. It is not that global trade ought to be stopped. It is that global trade has marched relentlessly forward without the rules of trade keeping pace. There is a relentless accelerated march toward globalization. However our world leaders have not developed acceptable rules, so people demonstrate in the streets.

I want to make two points this morning: One, trade is very positive for our country when it occurs in circumstances where it is fair. It makes sense for us to do that which we do best and trade with others who in their comparative advantage are doing what they do best. That makes sense on the world stage. Our country has been a leader in world trade, a leader in expanded trade, and it does make sense to expand our trade opportunities as long as doing so represents the values that this country considers important in the development of our economy and in the development of our international relationships.

It is also the case that while all say that expanded trade is good for this country, it is also the case that we ought not allow the international corporations in this world to pole-vault over all the issues that relate to labor, the environment, and of production simply by saying: We are going to produce in Sri Lanka, Indonesia, Bangladesh, or China, and we will ship back into the United States. So what if they hire twelve-year-olds and pay them twelve cents an hour, working them twelve hours a day. So what. They would like us to think that is fair trade.

It is not fair trade. That is why people are marching in the streets. It is not fair trade when corporations are able to become international citizens and decide to circle the globe in their airplanes and evaluate where they can produce the cheapest, where they can employ kids, where they can dump pollution in the water and the air, where they can have factories without the barriers and problems of making them safe, and produce there, create a cheap product, and send it to a department store in Pittsburgh, Los Angeles, or Butte, Montana.

The question is, is it fair trade when that happens? This country has fought for a century over these issues. All of those fights were agonizing. Many occurred in this Chamber. The fight about whether we ought to be able to employ children, so we have child labor laws saying we don't want you to send twelve-year-olds into coal mines. We don't want twelve- and fourteen-year-olds put on a factory floor to work twelve hours a day. We have child labor laws.

The question of safe workplace, demanding that those who employ people employ them in safe workplaces that are not going to pose risks to the life and safety of workers. We have fought, and made laws to protect our people.

The issue of fair compensation, we have fought for a long while in this country about that issue. We have collective bargaining and the ability of employees to form and join unions. We have minimum wages. We fought about that and continue to fight about that from time to time in this country, but we have settled part of it. Now, some say that doesn't matter; we can go elsewhere. We can produce elsewhere, where people can't join a labor union, they are illegal. We can produce where we can hire a twelve-year-old child and pay sixteen cents an hour, and we can make a pair of shoes that has an hour and a quarter direct labor, with twenty cents labor costs in a pair of shoes, and ship that to New York City for a department store shelf because we are saying to the American consumer, this is better for you because it is cheaper for you.

So people demonstrate in the streets because they say that is not fair trade. That is not what we mean by expanding the opportunities of trade. . . .

In 1993, we had merchandise trade deficits of $132 billion. It is now $449 billion and growing. This trade deficit is mushrooming. If there are people who think it doesn't matter, think again. This is like the run-up of dot com companies in the stock market. Everybody thought NASDAQ would continue to increase forever. These values are perfectly understandable. We had people on Wall Street who made a lot of money that were justifying and explaining why the values made sense.

They didn't make sense. This doesn't make sense. This ballooning, mushrooming trade deficit will cause serious problems to this country unless it is addressed. This country must repay these trade deficits. With a budget deficit, you can make the case that it is a deficit, you owe it to yourself. You cannot do that with trade deficits. This is a deficit we owe to others.

Inevitably, they are repaid with a lower standard of living in this country. That is an action in economics that no one disputes. This is a very serious, growing, abiding problem.

With whom are our trade deficits? Our trade deficits are with Canada. We passed a U.S.–Canada trade agreement. We had a reasonably small trade deficit with Canada. We quickly doubled it, very quickly doubled our trade deficit with Canada. What an incompetent trade agreement. We ought to haul those negotiators to the well of the Senate to explain to us what they did in public and in secret to undercut this country's interests in the U.S.–Canada agreement. I could talk about some of those issues, but I don't have time today.

China, the China trade deficit, the trade deficit we now have with China is an $83 billion merchandise trade deficit, and growing rapidly; the European Union, $55 billion trade deficit, and growing; Japan, $81 billion trade deficit, and growing. And we have had a trade deficit with Japan of $50 billion a year plus now for a long time.

Mexico, by the way, prior to the U.S.–Canada and Mexico trade agreement, something called NAFTA, North American Free Trade Agreement, we had a surplus trade balance with Mexico. We had a surplus. It is now nearly a $25 billion deficit. Talk about colossal incompetence. The trade agreements we have negotiated in recent years have undercut this country's interests in fair trade. In every set of circumstance, our country bows to trade agreements that undercut our workers and our producers all in the name of free trade.

Quebec City hosted a big meeting last week. The President went to Quebec City and talked about the desire for expanded trade agreements. He said Congress must give him what is called trade promotion authority. That is just new language for fast track. What the President is saying is: I want fast-track trade authority.

To the extent I have the capability of involving myself in this, I will say to the President: You are not going to get fast-track trade authority. We wouldn't give it to President Clinton, and we won't give it to you. Your first job is not to create new trade agreements when every agreement in recent years has undercut this country's interests and resulted in larger and larger trade deficits.

Your first job is to fix the problems that have been created in the last decade and a half. Fix these problems, then come to us. Then we can talk about trade promotion authority.

Do you want to hear some problems? We have a huge, growing trade deficit with Japan. Do you know what the tariff is on a T-bone steak we send to Tokyo, American beef sent to Japan? There is nearly a 40-percent tariff on every single pound of American beef sent to Japan—40 percent. That would be declared a huge problem if the United States imposed a 40-percent tariff, but we will allow our allies to do that, our trading partners. Why? Because we are poor negotiators and we do not have backbone and we do not have the nerve and we do not have the will to stand up for this country's economic interests. So T-bones to Tokyo are just a small example, just one small example.

How about going from T-bones to apples? Try sending apples to Japan. Do you know what Japan will tell apple growers in this country? They say the apples that are shipped in Japan must be shipped from trees in the United States that are separated by at least 500 meters from the other trees in the orchard. Does it sound goofy to you? It does to me. How do they get by with it? They get by with it because we negotiate incompetent agreements, incompetent bilateral agreements with these countries. . . .

The question for this administration—and I have asked exactly the same question with the previous administrations—is: Are you going to stand up for this country's economic interests? President Bush went to Canada. He said at the outset that we have to recognize the issues of labor and the environment in trade agreements. Then later in the week he said: Trade agreements must be commercial—commercial interests, and, by the way, what I want is trade promotion authority—which, as I said, is a new term for fast track.

For those who do not know what fast-track authority is, it means our negotiators shall go negotiate an agreement with another country, bring it back as a treaty to this Senate, and the provisions under fast track would be we can debate it but cannot amend it; no Senator has the right to offer any amendments at any time under any circumstances.

It is fundamentally undemocratic. Had we had the opportunity to offer amendments to NAFTA, we would not be in this situation with Mexico and Canada, just as an example, with respect to our current trade agreement with our neighbors.

The big study on Mexico and Canada was the Hufbauer and Schott study, which everybody used. The Chamber of Commerce and all our colleagues used it. They said if we do this trade agreement, we will have 350,000 new jobs in this country. And they said here are the imports and exports between the United States and Mexico that we expect after this agreement.

It turns out they said the principal imports from Mexico would be imports of largely unskilled labor. What are the three largest imports from Mexico? The three largest imports are automobiles, automobile parts, and electronics, all of which come from skilled labor, all of which mean the Hufbauer and Schott study missed its mark. We didn't gain jobs, we lost jobs with that trade agreement and turned a surplus into a fairly large trade deficit.

Who is going to be called to account for that? Nobody. Because that is exactly what the international companies wanted. They do not get up in the morning and say the Pledge of Allegiance. They are international entrepreneurs, and they are interested in producing anywhere in the world where they can find the fewest impediments to production and the cheapest place to produce. They don't want to have to worry about the child labor laws, pollution, and the standards that countries impose in preventing companies from dumping into the air and water. They don't want to have to worry about worker safety. They don't want to have to worry about fair compensation. They had those fights and lost them in this country, and now they want to go elsewhere and say: We want to be able to ignore that.

The people in the streets are saying: Wait a second, there needs to be some basic set of standards. What does it mean when someone ships carpets to this country and the carpets are made by kids, ten- and twelve-year-old kids, some of whom have had gunpowder put on their fingertips to have them burned off so they have permanent scarring, so ten- and twelve-year-old kids can make carpets and run needles through the carpets, and when they stick the top of their fingers, it doesn't hurt them because they have already been scarred by burning.

That is part of the testimony before Congress about child labor. It is happening in this world. Is it fair trade for those carpets to come into our country and be on our store shelves? Would anybody be proud to buy from countries where the circumstances of production are represented by that kind of behavior? The answer is no.

What I want to say today is very simple. The example in Quebec City last week is an example that is going to continue. I do not support the anarchists and others who show up for those events to cause trouble, but I understand why protesters come to those events, peaceful protesters—and most of the 30,000 people who showed up were peaceful. I believe we should expand trade. I believe expanded trade is important for this country. But I also believe this country ought to be a world leader, promoting and standing up for the values for which we fought for over a century to protect. Those are the values of dealing thoughtfully with the rules of production dealing with the hiring of children, with safe workplaces, dealing with the environment, and controlling the emission of pollutants.

If this is, indeed, a global economy and if it matters little where people are producing, then you have to have some assurance, if they are going to close a plant in Toledo or Fargo and move to Guangzhou, they are not going to be able to do that because in Guangzhou they can hire kids and pollute the water and air and not have a safe workplace and produce a cheaper product and represent to the people of the world: We have done it all for you. That is not doing anybody a favor. That is a retreat from the standards for which we fought for a century in this country.

People will demonstrate in the streets on trade issues because they want the rules to keep pace with the relentless march of globalization. I want globalization to continue, but I want it done under rules that are fair. Coming from a small state in the northern part of this country, North Dakota, that borders a friendly nation, Canada, I know full well what happens when we are sold out and undercut by our trade negotiators. It happened to us with the trade negotiations with Canada. We sent a trade ambassador to Canada. They negotiated a trade agreement, and they essentially said to family farmers: Your interests are unimportant to us, so we will sell those interests out in order to get concessions for other industries. And we have family farmers going broke in my state because we have an avalanche of unfairly traded durum wheat coming into this country. We produce 80 percent of that in the state of North Dakota. Durum wheat is used to produce semolina flour which makes pasta, so most everyone has eaten semolina which comes from the fields of North Dakota in the form of our pasta. . . .

I hope it is not lost on this administration—I have said the same thing to previous administrations—that they should not hold trade agreements or trade negotiations, or trade conferences for that matter, in cities around the world without, in my judgment, opening the discussion for a lot of people who want to raise questions about what the fair rules are for international trade. Globalization will continue, and should. But it must be attended by rules of fair trade, and people ought to understand that and know that.

Second, finally, when we negotiate trade agreements, we ought not to be afraid to stand up for this country's economic interests. It is about time to be a bit hard-nosed, and have a backbone that serves to stand up for this country's interests.

Mr. President, I yield the floor.

Problems of Globalization

Representative John J. Duncan, Jr.

U.S. House of Representatives, Washington, D.C.
April 10, 2002

Mr. Speaker, yesterday in my hometown of Knoxville, Tennessee, the Levi Strauss Company announced that a plant was closing and 900 jobs would be moved out of this country. This follows on the heels over the past year of many other plants closing in east Tennessee and throughout this nation.

We have entered into some trade deals over the past several years that have not been good for American companies and American workers. They may have been good for big multinational companies, but they have resulted in millions of jobs going to other countries. I think that many, many people, in fact I think a great majority of the people in this nation, are sick and tired of all of these jobs going to other nations.

Our trade deficits have been running at almost unbelievable levels over the last couple of years, usually $25 billion to $30 billion a month, or even higher. Many economists say that we lose 20,000 jobs per billion, but even if the job loss is much smaller than that, it still means that we have been losing millions and millions of jobs over the last several years, and I just do not believe that we can sustain that kind of job loss indefinitely on into the future.

In the short run, we do benefit from being able to buy cheaper goods from overseas. In the long run, however, we have lost and continue to lose millions of jobs to other countries. These jobs will not be easy to replace.

Michael Kelly, a columnist for the *Washington Post*, wrote recently that "Globalization ultimately depends on driving manufacturing jobs out of the United States and results in the loss of real jobs for real people in, say, Akron, Ohio. More than that," Mr. Kelly continues, "it results in real costs to the Nation as a whole, and these costs are massive. When, as has happened all across the country, a factory shuts its doors and shatters a town, turning what had been a productive community into a ward of the State, what does that cost America? Over time, many, many millions, a price that globalists ignore. Finally, globalization results in the loss of a way of life," what was quaintly known as the American way of life.

This columnist, Michael Kelly for the *Washington Post*, continues by saying, "In the long run, global free trade may be, as its boosters say, to the greater good of all, but in the short and even medium run in any developed country, it is to the greater pain of many for the greater gain of a few. Those who do not understand this may be well-intentioned, but the people who live in globalism's growing number of ghost towns must consider them shockingly ill-informed."

Then, Mr. Speaker, just yesterday Paul Craig Roberts, writing in the *Washington Times*, wrote this. He said, "Today, free trade has come to mean opening U.S. markets to those who do not open their markets to us. To meet this competition, U.S. firms locate factories in low-wage countries in order to be able to compete in the American consumer market. Free-traders think this is fine so long as the American consumer is benefiting from a lower price. But, of course, if specialization and division of labor means shifting production to low-wage countries, the U.S. population will find itself specialized in selling and servicing imported goods."

He continues on, and he says, "Free-traders are out to lunch when they say things like 'Oh, let the Chinese have the low-wage textile jobs,' implying that the United States retains the high-tech jobs. The reality is that the United States has had a trade deficit with China even in advanced technology goods since 1995."

And then he ends his column by saying, "The United States already has the export profile of a Third World country. The massive influx of poor immigrants from the Third World and the outflow of advanced technology will complete the transformation of the United States from a superpower into a colony."

Mr. Speaker, this greatly concerns me. Already we have environmental extremists who protest any time anyone tries to cut any trees or dig for any coal or drill for any oil or produce any natural gas. They destroy jobs and drive up prices in the process and they hurt the poor and the lower income and the working people of this country. They always say, well, let us turn to tourism. But we cannot base the whole economy of this Nation on tourism.

Mr. Speaker, we need a trade policy, we need economic policies that put America first, once again, and that put American companies and American workers first, once again. The obligation of this Congress is not to foreign companies and foreign countries; it should be to the American people. If we do not wake up, this country is going to be in bad, bad trouble, because I am not sure that this economy is bouncing back as some of the experts say. I hope it is. But after what happened yesterday in Knoxville and what has happened over the last year or so, I have my doubts. I think we need to take another look at some of these trade deals and put our own people first, once again, in this country.

ISSUE 2

GLOBALIZATION
AND THE NATION-STATE

There is no doubt that a communications and information revolution has hit the world. Suppose that a modern-day Rip van Winkle woke up today after being asleep for twenty years. Can you imagine the shock he would experience? He would witness people walking down the street talking on tiny portable telephones—after being beeped on their pagers. He would see computers the size of notebooks that are more powerful than most mainframes that had been in use when he dozed off. And he would discover near-instantaneous access to a mind-boggling array of information on the Internet.

In the first article for this issue, Walter B. Wriston shows how these marvels in communications and information processing are limiting the ability of national governments to control what occurs within their territories. How can a dictatorship control the information that its people get when they can watch CNN? How can a government control the value of its currency when bankers move billions of dollars across the world electronically every day?

Is all of this electronic portability a threat to national sovereignty? Wriston thinks so and seems concerned about the possibility. But for him to come to that conclusion is a bit ironic. He was, after all, chief executive of Citicorp for seventeen years before his retirement in 1984. Under his leadership, that premier banking institution was in the forefront of applying information and communication technology to finance. Moreover, during Wriston's tenure, Citicorp was a major lender to Third World governments, whose sovereignty undoubtedly came into question when loans had to be rescheduled for fear of default.

The second article for this issue, by Anne-Marie Slaughter, notes that some observers, working from information like Wriston's, have come to the conclusion that the nation-state is dying or is already effectively dead. That bit of hyperbole is nothing new. Forty years before Wriston's article was published, political scientist John Herz came to the dire conclusion that nuclear weapons had effectively caused the demise of the nation-state. His main point was that protecting its territory is an essential function of the nation-state and that atomic weapons make it impossible for even the most powerful countries to ensure that their citizens can be free from fear of attack. Of course, Herz later recanted after watching many new nations come into being, with the nuclear stalemate between the big powers providing some security.

Slaughter, Dean of Woodrow Wilson School of Public and International Affairs at Princeton University, says that people today who argue that the nation-state is dying because of the information/communications revolution are overstating the situation. So are those who say that supra-national organizations—like the United Nations or the European Union—are becoming all-powerful. Slaughter proposes a middle ground between these extreme views.

DISCUSSION QUESTIONS

As you read the articles by Wriston and Slaughter, consider the following questions:

1. In what ways has near-instantaneous satellite communication affected the way that governments conduct their relations with one another? Does this phenomenon better promote peace and security in the world? Is it possible for diplomatic communication to be too easy, too frequent?

2. Some observers argue that quick and easy international communications can help empower ordinary citizens in dealing with repressive governments in these countries. How might this happen?

3. Some people believe that speedy communications cause economic or political problems within countries to become contagious, spreading quickly to other countries. Do you believe that this is a problem? If so, can anything be done to prevent it?

KEY WEB SITES

For more information on this topic, visit the following Web sites:

Report of the Defense Science Board Task Force on Information Warfare
http://www.cryptone.org/iwd.htm

Satellite photos of much of the United States, Europe, and Asia
http://terraserver.homeadvisor.msn.com

Global Positioning System for determining location and for navigation
http://www.colorado.edu/geography/gcraft/notes/gps.html

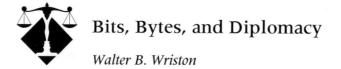

Bits, Bytes, and Diplomacy

Walter B. Wriston

An American historian once opined, "Peace is the mastery of great forces; it is not the solution of a problem."[1] Great new forces are at work in the world, and if we are to master them, the beginning of wisdom is to recognize that the world is changing dramatically and at unprecedented speed. We are in the midst of a revolution. A revolution by definition causes old power structures to crumble and new ones to rise. The catalyst—but not the cause—has always been technological change. Now, as in revolutions past, technology is profoundly affecting the sovereignty of governments, the world economy, and military strategy.

We are now living in the midst of the third great revolution in history. When the principle of the lever was applied to make a plow, the agricultural revolution was born, and the power of nomadic tribal chiefs declined. When centuries later, men substituted the power of water, steam, and electricity for animal muscle, the Industrial Revolution was born. Both of these massive changes took centuries to unfold. Each caused a shift in the power structure. Today, the marriage of computers and telecommunications has ushered in the Information Age, which is as different from the Industrial Age as that period was from the Agricultural Age. Information technology has demolished time and distance. Instead of validating Orwell's vision of Big Brother watching the citizen, the third revolution enables the citizen to watch Big Brother. And so the virus of freedom, for which there is no antidote, is spread by electronic networks to the four corners of the earth.

History is strewn with wonderful inventions. Most of them were designed to solve specific problems: the wheel to move things, engines to supply power, clocks and compasses to tell time and direction. The inventions that made possible the information revolution were different. They changed the way we solve problems. When Johann Gutenberg pioneered movable type in Europe in 1436, and when Intel designed the integrated circuit in the 1970s, the way we record, store, access, and peruse knowledge made quantum leaps forward and affected not only how we do our jobs, but what we do.

These two events were just as important as they sound. Gutenberg broke the monopoly of the monks who copied manuscripts by hand and guarded them jealously. They understood that knowledge was power and sometimes

Walter B. Wriston, former chairman and chief executive officer of Citicorp/Citibank, served as chairman of the Economic Policy Advisory Board in the Reagan administration.

This article is from *Foreign Affairs* 76, no. 5 (September/October 1997). Reprinted by permission of *Foreign Affairs*. Copyright 1997 by the Council on Foreign Relations, Inc.

chained books to the shelves. In *The Discoverers*, Daniel Boorstin cites a twelfth-century manuscript inscription: "This book belongs to the monastery of St. Mary of Robert's Bridge, who ever shall steal it from this house, or mutilate it let him be forever cursed. Amen." Contrast that mindset with the ability of a researcher anywhere in the world with a computer and a modem to tap into the entire database of the Library of Congress, the Bibliothèque de France, or the British Library. In today's parlance, this change constitutes a paradigm shift.

George Gilder explains that "the key to paradigm shifts is the collapse of formerly pivotal scarcities, the rise of new forms of abundance, and the onset of new scarcities. Successful innovators use these new forms of abundance to redress the emergent shortages."[2] The enormous use of timber for railroad ties and trestles as American railroads pushed west caused Theodore Roosevelt to declare a national shortage of timber, which was soon replaced by an abundance of concrete, iron, and steel. Shortly thereafter, electricity and steam power overcame looming shortages of labor and materials. The recent alleged shortage of broadcast frequencies caused electronic engineers to expand the spectrum's useful frequencies. This cycle has continued throughout history. In the three pillars of the order that resulted from the Industrial Revolution—national sovereignty, national economies, and military power—the information revolution has increased the power of individuals and outmoded old hierarchies.

A GLOBAL VILLAGE

Sovereignty, the power of a nation to stop others from interfering in its internal affairs, is rapidly eroding. When Woodrow Wilson went to Paris to negotiate the Treaty of Versailles, he ordered his postmaster-general to assume control over all transatlantic cable lines in order to censor the news from Europe. Today no one and no nation can block the flow of information across national borders.

During the Persian Gulf War, Saddam Hussein proposed what was viewed in Washington as a phony peace settlement. President Bush had to convey that judgment to the 26 nations in the coalition. As Marlin Fitzwater, former White House Press Secretary, remembers, the "quickest and most effective way was CNN, because all countries in the world had it and were watching it on a real-time basis . . . and 20 minutes after we got the proposal . . . I went on national television . . . to tell the 26 members—that the war was continuing." In this and many other instances, the elite foreign policy establishment and its government-to-government communications were bypassed. No highly trained foreign service officer meticulously drafted a note, no secretary of state signed it, and no American ambassadors called on foreign ministers to deliver the message. The United States entrusted a vital diplomatic message to a private television company seen by the whole world. Wilson's strategy was to control the flow of information by fiat, while Bush realized that since he could not beat the world information free market, he had better join it.

Today special interest groups of all kinds, from terrorists to human rights activists, bypass government-based communications channels. In *The News Media in National and International Conflicts*, Andrew Arno explains that when relations sour between two countries "it is often more a matter of strained relations between centers of interest than whole countries." We have seen these forces at work from South Africa to Korea as one pressure group after another steps around national governments to further its own crusade.

The convergence of computers and telecommunications has made us into a global community, ready or not. For the first time in history, rich and poor, north and south, east and west, city and countryside are linked in a global electronic network of shared images in real time. Ideas move across borders as if they did not exist. Indeed, time zones are becoming more important than borders.

Small villages are known as efficient marketplaces of ideas. A village quickly shares news of any innovation, and if anyone gets a raise or new privileges, everyone similarly situated will soon be pressing for the same. And why not? These people are just like me, the villagers say. Why should I not have what they have? The Internet carries conversations between millions of people without regard to gender, race, or color. The impact of the global conversation, like that of a village conversation, is enormous—and it is multiplied many times.

A global village will have global customs. Denying people human rights or democratic freedoms no longer means denying them an abstraction they have never experienced, but violating the established customs of the village. It hardly matters that only a minority of the world's people enjoy such freedoms or the prosperity that goes with them; these are now the benchmarks. More and more people around the globe are demanding more say in their own destiny. Once people are convinced that this is possible, an enormous burden of proof falls on those who would deny them.

The global conversation puts pressure on sovereign governments that over time will influence political processes all over the world. The information revolution is thus profoundly threatening to the power structures of the world, and with good reason. In Prague in 1988 the first protesters in the streets looked into CNN cameras and chanted at the riot police, "The world sees you." And it did. It was an anomaly of history that other Eastern Europeans watched the revolution on CNN relayed by a Russian satellite and mustered the courage to rebel against their own sovereigns. All this has confirmed Abraham Lincoln's sentiment, expressed on his way to his first inauguration, that the American Declaration of Independence "gave liberty not alone to the people of this country, but hope to all the world, for all future time." At the time Lincoln spoke, his words were heard by only a handful of people. It is a testament to his prescience that changes he could not have imagined have brought his words, and freedom itself, to unprecedented portions of humanity.

A New Source of Wealth

The flood of real-time data has also transformed the international economy. The depth of the global market renders economic theory based on national markets suspect. In the world's financial markets, sovereign governments have lost the ability to influence the price others will pay for their currency on anything but a momentary basis. When I started in the banking business, the total foreign exchange market in New York was only about $50 million. If the Federal Reserve called Citibank or Chase and instructed them to sell $10 million, an order that size could move the market. Today, the market is $1 trillion, and central bank intervention in foreign exchange becomes an expensive exercise in futility. The market is a giant voting machine that records in real time the judgment of traders all over the world about American diplomatic, fiscal, and monetary policies. It has created an information standard that is far more rapid and draconian than the gold standard ever was. Moments after a president announces a policy in the Rose Garden, the market's judgment is reflected in the price of the dollar.

Information technology has also produced a new source of wealth that is not material; it is information—knowledge applied to work to create value. When we apply knowledge to ongoing tasks, we increase productivity. When we apply it to new tasks, we create innovation. The pursuit of wealth is now largely the pursuit of information and its application to the means of production. The rules, customs, skills, and talents necessary to uncover, capture, produce, preserve, and exploit information are now humankind's most important. The competition for the best information has replaced the competition for the best farmland or coal fields. In fact, the appetite to annex territory has already attenuated, and major powers have withdrawn from previously occupied territories.

The new economic powerhouses are masters not of huge material resources, but of ideas and technology. The way the market values companies is instructive: It now places a higher value on intellectual capital than on hard assets like bricks and mortar. Microsoft, with only a relatively small amount of fixed assets, now has a market capitalization well in excess of Ford, General Motors, and Chrysler combined, all of which have huge bases. The powerful economies of Singapore and Hong Kong, countries with virtually no physical assets, demonstrate the growing irrelevance of territory to wealth. This shift requires a different management structure and mindset, and affects not only individual companies, but entire nations.

The changing perception of what constitutes an asset poses huge problems in expanding or even maintaining the power of government. Unlike land or industrial plants, information resources are not bound to geography or easily taxed and controlled by governments. In an economy that consists largely of information products, the government's power to tax and regulate erodes rapidly. Our laws and systems of measurement are becoming artifacts of another age. Bill Gates, with the skills to write and market a complex software system that can produce $1 billion of revenue, can walk past a customs officer anywhere in the world with nothing of "value" to declare, but his wife might have to pay duty on her new ring. Bad data produces bad decisions and leaves us puzzled as to why old policies no longer work. The measures of the industrial society, which count the number of railroad brakemen but do not record the number of computer programmers, highlight a growing problem in setting policy. As DNA research reveals more precise understandings about the way a living organism functions than gross observations of developed biological structures, so we need more precise measures of how nations and companies function in our new environment.

INFORMATION DOMINANCE

These changes affect not only the civilian production machine on which our economic strength rests, but also our military capabilities. In science, there used to be two ways to proceed: The first was to construct a theory, and the second was to conduct a physical experiment. Today we have a third: computer simulation. In the Persian Gulf War, for example, young, basically inexperienced Americans defeated Iraq's feared Republican Guards. A retired colonel asked one commander: "How do you account for your dramatic success, when not a single officer or man in your entire outfit ever had combat experience?" "But we were experienced," said the commander. "We had fought such engagements six times before in complete battle simulation at the National Training Center and in Germany."[3] The U.S. military today is a spectacular example of the replacement of physical assets by information. Information, to be sure, has often made the difference between victory and defeat. Where is the enemy located? How many troops are involved? How are they armed? What is new is the ease and accuracy with which such questions can be answered.

Military intelligence has become much more complex and even has a new name: "information dominance." Today Apache helicopters flying over Bosnia upload detailed pictures of action on the ground to a satellite, record them with a video camera, or beam them directly to local headquarters. Videos taken from the air verify the Dayton accords. Major General William Nash observed that in Bosnia, "We don't have arguments. We hand them pictures, and they move their tanks." This is a long way from 1943, when analysts were hunting through the stacks of the Library of Congress for maps and photographs of possible German targets for Allied bombers since few, if any, were available in the War Department. Today even the ground troops on patrol are equipped with night vision goggles and use a hand-held Global Positioning System device to pinpoint their exact position from satellites. Because the soil is strewn with mines, knowing exactly where you are is a matter of life and death even when there is no fighting. Mines that have been located by an airborne mine detection system are exploded by remotely controlled drone Panther tanks. And so in the military as in civilian life, information in all its forms is replacing hard assets.

|Reliance on information technology also has dangerous downsides. The American information infrastructure, in the words of the recent Report of the Defense Science Board Task Force on Information Warfare, is "vulnerable to attack" and "creates a tunnel of vulnerability previously unrealized in the history of conflict."| Rogue states and groups can conduct information warfare even though they do not command a large military establishment. Today we are witnessing guerrilla warfare, ethnic conflicts, and active terrorist groups. As the Task Force notes:

> Offensive information warfare is attractive to many because it is cheap in relation to the cost of developing, maintaining, and using advanced military capabilities. It may cost little to suborn an insider, create false information, manipulate information, or launch malicious logic-based weapons against an information system connected to the globally shared telecommunications infrastructure. The latter is particularly attractive; the latest information on how to exploit many of the design attributes and security flaws of commercial computer software is freely available on the Internet.

|Adversaries, both real and potential, have a lot to work with since the Department of Defense has over two million computers, over 10,000 local-area networks, and over 100 long-distance networks that coordinate and implement every element of its missions, from weapons design to battlefield management| During the calendar year 1995, up to 200,000 intrusions may have been made into the DOD's unclassified computers. These intruders "have modified, stolen and destroyed data and software and shut down computers and networks." Effective diplomacy at critical junctures in any age is backed by the knowledge that if all else fails, military force can be used to attain national goals.

Therefore, vulnerability to an attack on information infrastructure is attracting the attention of a presidential commission and numerous task forces. But with about 90 percent of our military traffic moving over public computer networks, it is increasingly hard to tell the military from the civilian infrastructure. The bureaucratic distinctions between intelligence and law enforcement, between permitted surveillance at home and abroad, may be unsuited for information warfare. There are no borders in cyberspace to mandate these distinctions. The smallest nation, terrorist group, or drug cartel could hire a computer programmer to plant a Trojan horse virus in software, take down a vital network, or cause a missile to misfire. Voltaire said: "God is always for the big battalions." In this new world he may be wrong. The increasing U.S. reliance on massive networks may make the United States more, not less vulnerable.

It may even be unclear what constitutes an act of war. If U.S. satellites suddenly go blind and the telephone network on the eastern seaboard goes down, it is possible that the United States could not even identify the enemy. Its strategic stockpile of weapons would be of little use. There would be no big factory to bomb—only a person somewhere writing software. The possibility of an electronic Pearl Harbor has sparked a debate on how to counter the threat. The Commission on Critical Infrastructure Protection established by President Clinton's executive order is a step in the right direction and has been described in Senate testimony "as the equivalent of the Manhattan Project." It will work at the crossroads of the First Amendment and national security, at the vortex of personal privacy through encryption and the National Security Agency's desire to breach it, and at the frontier of what Sun Tzu two millennia ago described as "vanquishing the enemy without fighting."

VIRTUAL LEADERSHIP

We live in revolutionary times, as did the Founding Fathers. They exhibited a keen interest in technology—provision for copyright and patent protection was written into the Constitution itself. This provision was implemented by an act of Congress in 1790 creating a patent board consisting of the secretary of state, the secretary of war, and the attorney general. It was a prestigious group: Thomas Jefferson, Henry Knox, and Edmund Randolph. That board is long gone and the schism between the diplomat and the scientist has grown wider at the very time it is becoming more and more important that the two understand each other. Because so much change in the current revolution is driven by technology, our task in mastering these new forces is made more complex by the difficulty of communicating across disciplines. Diplomats, trained in the humanities, often tend to validate C. P. Snow's famous lecture on "Two Cultures," in which he argued that scientists and humanists are ignorant of each other's knowledge and are content to stay that way. Many diplomatic historians have minimized or even ignored the impact of scientific discoveries on the course of history, preferring instead to follow the great man theory or look for the historical tides that carry the world along. Indeed, the indexes of many standard texts on diplomatic history do not even include the words "technology" or "economics."

An expert is a person with great knowledge about a legacy system—indeed there are no experts on the future. Henry Kissinger observed in *Diplomacy* that "most foreign policies that history has marked highly, in whatever country, have been originated by leaders who were opposed by experts. It is, after all, the responsibility of the expert to operate the familiar and that of the leader to transcend it." During World War I, an aide-de-camp to British Field Marshal Douglas Haig, after seeing a tank demonstration, commented, "The idea that cavalry will be replaced by these iron coaches is absurd. It is little short of treasonous." In the United States, the ridicule and court-martial of

Brigadier General Billy Mitchell, when he postulated the importance of air power by offering to sink a battleship, is instructive. Secretary of War Newton D. Baker thought so little of the idea that he was "willing to stand on the bridge of a battleship while that nitwit tries to hit it from the air." Indeed this recurring phenomenon was encapsulated in Arthur Clarke's First Law, cited in his *Profiles of the Future*: "When a distinguished but elderly scientist states that something is possible he is almost certainly right. When he states that something is impossible, he is very probably wrong." In the case of U.S. national security, a refusal to take note of real change in the world is a recipe for disaster.

The new technology will not go away—it will only get better in accordance with Moore's law, which postulates that microchips will double in density and speed every 18 months. Bandwidth will grow even faster. The third technological revolution has brought about immense global prosperity. Contrary to the doomsayers who postulated that the world would run out of resources by the year 2000, it is difficult to find a single commodity that is worth more in real terms today than it was ten years ago. Knowledge, once an ornament displayed by the rich and powerful at conferences, now combines with management skills to produce wealth. The vast increase of knowledge has brought with it a huge increase in the ability to manipulate matter, increasing its value by the power of the mind and generating new products and substances unknown in nature and undreamed of only a few years ago. In the past, when the method of creating wealth changed, old power structures lost influence, new ones arose, and every facet of society was affected. As we can already see the beginning of that process in this revolution, one can postulate that in the next few decades the attraction and management of intellectual capital will determine which institutions and nations will survive and prosper, and which will not.

But despite all of the advances of science and the ways in which it is changing the world, science does not remake the human mind or alter the power of the human spirit. There is still no substitute for courage and leadership in confronting the new problems and opportunities that our world presents. What has changed dramatically is the amount of information available to our policymakers. One hopes that the data processed by the minds of trained diplomats will produce real knowledge, and with enough experience, wisdom. Wisdom has always been in short supply, but it will be sorely needed in the days and years ahead, because in the words of former President Richard Nixon, "Only people can solve problems people create."

NOTES

1. Henry M. Wriston, *Prepare for Peace* (New York: Harper & Bros., 1941), p. 237.
2. George Gilder, "Over the Paradigm Cliff," *ASAP*, February 1997, p. 29.
3. Kevin Kelly, *Out of Control: The Rise of a Neo-Biological Civilization* (Reading, MA: Addison-Wesley, 1994), p. 246.

The Real New World Order

Anne-Marie Slaughter

Many thought that the new world order proclaimed by George Bush was the promise of 1945 fulfilled, a world in which international institutions, led by the United Nations, guaranteed international peace and security with the active support of the world's major powers. That world order is a chimera. Even as a liberal internationalist ideal, it is infeasible at best and dangerous at worst. It requires a centralized rule-making authority, a hierarchy of institutions, and universal membership. Equally to the point, efforts to create such an order have failed. The United Nations cannot function effectively independent of the major powers that compose it, nor will those nations cede their power and sovereignty to an international institution. Efforts to expand supra-national authority, whether by the UN secretary-general's office, the European Commission, or the World Trade Organization (WTO), have consistently produced a backlash among member states.

The leading alternative to liberal internationalism is "the new medievalism," a back-to-the-future model of the twenty-first century. Where liberal internationalists see a need for international rules and institutions to solve states' problems, the new medievalists proclaim the end of the nation-state. Less hyperbolically, in her article, "Power Shift," in the January/February 1997 *Foreign Affairs*, Jessica T. Mathews describes a shift away from the state—up, down, and sideways—to supra-state, sub-state, and, above all, non-state actors. These new players have multiple allegiances and global reach.

Mathews attributes this power shift to a change in the structure of organizations: from hierarchies to networks, from centralized compulsion to voluntary association. The engine of this transformation is the information technology revolution, a radically expanded communications capacity that empowers individuals and groups while diminishing traditional authority. The result is not world government, but global governance. If government denotes the formal exercise of power by established institutions, governance denotes cooperative problem-solving by a changing and often uncertain cast. The result is a world order in which global governance networks link Microsoft, the Roman Catholic Church, and Amnesty International to the European Union, the United Nations, and Catalonia.

Anne-Marie Slaughter is Dean of Woodrow Wilson School of Public and International Affairs at Princeton University.

This article is from *Foreign Affairs* 76, no. 5 (September/October 1997). Reprinted by permission of *Foreign Affairs*. Copyright 1997 by the Council on Foreign Relations, Inc.

The new medievalists miss two central points. First, private power is still no substitute for state power. Consumer boycotts of transnational corporations destroying rain forests or exploiting child labor may have an impact on the margin, but most environmentalists or labor activists would prefer national legislation mandating control of foreign subsidiaries. Second, the power shift is not a zero-sum game. A gain in power by non-state actors does not necessarily translate into a loss of power for the state. On the contrary, many of these nongovernmental organizations (NGOs) network with their foreign counterparts to apply additional pressure on the traditional levers of domestic politics.

A new world order is emerging, with less fanfare but more substance than either the liberal internationalist or new medievalist visions. The state is not disappearing, it is disaggregating into its separate, functionally distinct parts. These parts—courts, regulatory agencies, executives, and even legislatures—are networking with their counterparts abroad, creating a dense web of relations that constitutes a new, transgovernmental order. Today's international problems—terrorism, organized crime, environmental degradation, money laundering, bank failure, and securities fraud—created and sustain these relations. Government institutions have formed networks of their own, ranging from the Basle Committee of Central Bankers to informal ties between law enforcement agencies to legal networks that make foreign judicial decisions more and more familiar. While political scientists Robert Keohane and Joseph Nye first observed its emergence in the 1970s, today transgovernmentalism is rapidly becoming the most widespread and effective mode of international governance.

Compared to the lofty ideals of liberal internationalism and the exuberant possibilities of the new medievalism, transgovernmentalism seems mundane. Meetings between securities regulators, antitrust or environmental officials, judges, or legislators lack the drama of high politics. But for the internationalists of the 1990s—bankers, lawyers, businesspeople, public-interest activists, and criminals—transnational government networks are a reality. Wall Street looks to the Basle Committee rather than the World Bank. Human rights lawyers are more likely to develop transnational litigation strategies for domestic courts than to petition the UN Committee on Human Rights.

Moreover, transgovernmentalism has many virtues. It is a key element of a bipartisan foreign policy, simultaneously assuaging conservative fears of a loss of sovereignty to international institutions and liberal fears of a loss of regulatory power in a globalized economy. While presidential candidate Pat Buchanan and Senator Jesse Helms (R-NC) demonize the UN and the WTO as supra-national bureaucracies that seek to dictate to national governments, Senators Ted Kennedy (D-MA) and [the late] Paul Wellstone (D-MN) inveigh against international capital mobility as the catalyst of a global "race to the bottom" in regulatory standards. Networks of bureaucrats responding to international crises and planning to prevent future problems are more flexible than international institutions and expand the regulatory reach of all participating nations. This combination of flexibility and effectiveness offers something for both sides of the aisle.

Transgovernmentalism also offers promising new mechanisms for the Clinton administration's "enlargement" policy, aiming to expand the community of liberal democracies. Contrary to Samuel Huntington's gloomy predictions in *The Clash of Civilizations and the New World Order* (1996), existing government networks span civilizations, drawing in courts from Argentina to Zimbabwe and financial regulators from Japan to Saudi Arabia. The dominant institutions in these networks remain concentrated in North America and Western Europe, but their impact can be felt in every corner of the globe. Moreover, disaggregating the state makes it possible to assess the quality of specific judicial, administrative, and legislative institutions, whether or not the governments are liberal democracies. Regular interaction with foreign colleagues offers new channels for spreading democratic accountability, governmental integrity, and the rule of law.

An offspring of an increasingly borderless world, transgovernmentalism is a world order ideal in its own right, one that is more effective and potentially more accountable than either of the current alternatives. Liberal internationalism poses the prospect of a supra-national bureaucracy answerable to no one. The new medievalist vision appeals equally to states' rights enthusiasts and supra-nationalists, but could easily reflect the worst of both worlds. Transgovernmentalism, by contrast, leaves the control of government institutions in the hands of national citizens, who must hold their governments as accountable for their transnational activities as for their domestic duties.

JUDICIAL FOREIGN POLICY

Judges are building a global community of law. They share values and interests based on their belief in the law as distinct but not divorced from politics and their view of themselves as professionals who must be insulated from direct political influence. At its best, this global community reminds each participant that his or her professional performance is being monitored and supported by a larger audience.

National and international judges are networking, becoming increasingly aware of one another and of their stake in a common enterprise. The most informal level of transnational judicial contact is knowledge of foreign and international judicial decisions and a corresponding willingness to cite them. The Israeli Supreme Court and the German and Canadian constitutional courts have long researched U.S. Supreme Court precedents in reaching their own conclusions on questions like freedom of speech, privacy rights, and due process. Fledgling constitutional courts in Central and Eastern Europe and in Russia are eagerly following suit. In 1995, the South African Supreme Court, finding the death penalty unconstitutional under the national constitution, referred to decisions from national and supranational courts around the world, including ones in Hungary, India, Tanzania, Canada, Germany, and the European Court of Human Rights. The U.S. Supreme Court has typically been more of a giver than a receiver in this exchange, but Justice Sandra Day O'Connor recently chided American lawyers and judges for their insularity in ignoring foreign law and predicted that she and her fellow justices would find themselves "looking more frequently to the decisions of other constitutional courts."

Why should a court in Israel or South Africa cite a decision by the U.S. Supreme Court in reaching its own conclusion? Decisions rendered by outside courts can have no authoritative value. They carry weight only because of their intrinsic logical power or because the court invoking them seeks to gain legitimacy by linking itself to a larger community of courts considering similar issues. National courts have become increasingly aware that they and their foreign counterparts are often engaged in a common effort to delimit the boundaries of individual rights in the face of an apparently overriding public interest. Thus, the British House of Lords recently rebuked the U.S. Supreme Court for its decision to uphold the kidnapping of a Mexican doctor by U.S. officials determined to bring him to trial in the United States.

Judges also cooperate in resolving transnational or international disputes. In cases involving citizens of two different states, courts have long been willing to acknowledge each other's potential interest and to defer to one another when such deference is not too costly. U.S. courts now recognize that they may become involved in a sustained dialogue with a foreign court. For instance, Judge Guido Calabresi of the Second Circuit recently allowed a French litigant to invoke U.S. discovery provisions without exhausting discovery options in France, reasoning that it was up to the French courts to identify and protest any infringements of French sovereignty. U.S. courts would then respond to such protests.

Judicial communication is not always harmonious, as in a recent squabble between a U.S. judge and a Hong Kong judge over an insider trading case. The U.S. judge refused to decline jurisdiction in favor of the Hong Kong court on grounds that "in Hong Kong they practically give you a medal for doing this sort of thing [insider trading]." In response, the Hong Kong judge stiffly defended the adequacy of Hong Kong law and asserted his willingness to apply it. He also chided his American counterpart, pointing out that any conflict "should be approached in the spirit of judicial comity rather than judicial competitiveness." Such conflict is to be expected among diplomats, but what is striking here is the two courts' view of themselves as quasi-autonomous foreign policy actors doing battle against international securities fraud.

The most advanced form of judicial cooperation is a partnership between national courts and a supra-national tribunal. In the European Union (EU), the European Court of Justice works with national courts when questions of European law overlap national law. National courts refer cases up to the

European Court, which issues an opinion and sends the case back to national courts; the supra-national recommendation guides the national court's decision. This cooperation marshals the power of domestic courts behind the judgment of a supra-national tribunal. While the Treaty of Rome provides for this reference procedure, it is the courts that have transformed it into a judicial partnership.

Finally, judges are talking face to face. The judges of the supreme courts of Western Europe began meeting every three years in 1978. Since then they have become more aware of one another's decisions, particularly with regard to each other's willingness to accept the decisions handed down by the European Court of Justice. Meetings between U.S. Supreme Court justices and their counterparts on the European Court have been sponsored by private groups, as have meetings of U.S. judges with judges from the supreme courts of Central and Eastern Europe and Russia.

The most formal initiative aimed at bringing judges together is the recently inaugurated Organization of the Supreme Courts of the Americas. Twenty-five supreme court justices or their designees met in Washington in October 1995 and drafted the OCSA charter, dedicating the organization to "promot[ing] and strengthen[ing] judicial independence and the rule of law among the members, as well as the proper constitutional treatment of the judiciary as a fundamental branch of the state." The charter calls for triennial meetings and envisages a permanent secretariat. It required ratification by 15 supreme courts, achieved in spring 1996. An initiative by judges, for judges, it is not a stretch to say that the OCSA is the product of judicial foreign policy.

Champions of a global rule of law have most frequently envisioned one rule for all, a unified legal system topped by a world court. The global community of law emerging from judicial networks will more likely encompass many rules of law, each established in a specific state or region. No high court would hand down definitive global rules. National courts would interact with one another and with supra-national tribunals in ways that would accommodate differences but acknowledge and reinforce common values.

THE REGULATORY WEB

The densest area of transgovernmental activity is among national regulators. Bureaucrats charged with the administration of antitrust policy, securities regulation, environmental policy, criminal law enforcement, banking and insurance supervision—in short, all the agents of the modern regulatory state—regularly collaborate with their foreign counterparts.

National regulators track their quarry through cooperation. While frequently ad hoc, such cooperation is increasingly cemented by bilateral and multilateral agreements. The most formal of these are mutual legal assistance treaties, whereby two states lay out a protocol governing cooperation between their law enforcement agencies and courts. However, the preferred instrument of cooperation is the memorandum of understanding, in which two or more regulatory agencies set forth and initial terms for an ongoing relationship. Such memorandums are not treaties; they do not engage the executive or the legislature in negotiations, deliberation, or signature. Rather, they are good-faith agreements, affirming ties between regulatory agencies based on their like-minded commitment to getting results.

"Positive comity," a concept developed by the U.S. Department of Justice, epitomizes the changing nature of transgovernmental relations. Comity of nations, an archaic and notoriously vague term beloved by diplomats and international lawyers, has traditionally signified the deference one nation grants another in recognition of their mutual sovereignty. For instance, a state will recognize another state's laws or judicial judgments based on comity. Positive comity requires more active cooperation. As worked out by the Antitrust Division of the U.S. Department of Justice and the EU's European Commission, the regulatory authorities of both states alert one another to violations within their jurisdiction, with the understanding that the responsible authority will take action. Positive comity is a principle of enduring cooperation between government agencies.

In 1988 the central bankers of the world's major financial powers adopted capital adequacy requirements for all banks under their supervision—a significant reform of the international banking system. It was not the International Monetary Fund, or even the Group of Seven that took this step. Rather, the forum was the Basle Committee on Banking Supervision, an organization composed of 12 central bank governors. The Basle Committee was created by a simple agreement among the governors themselves. Its members meet four times a year and follow their own rules. Decisions are made by consensus and are not formally binding; however, members do implement these decisions within their own systems. The Basle Committee's authority is often cited as an argument for taking domestic action.

National securities commissioners and insurance regulators have followed the Basle Committee's example. Incorporated by a private bill of the Quebec National Assembly, the International Organization of Securities Commissioners has no formal charter or founding treaty. Its primary purpose is to solve problems affecting international securities markets by creating a consensus for enactment of national legislation. Its members have also entered into information-sharing agreements on their own initiative. The International Association of Insurance Supervisors follows a similar model, as does the newly created Tripartite Group, an international coalition of banking, insurance, and securities regulators the Basle Committee created to improve the supervision of financial conglomerates.

Pat Buchanan would have had a field day with the Tripartite Group, denouncing it as a prime example of bureaucrats taking power out of the hands of American voters. In fact, unlike the international bogeymen of demagogic fantasy, transnational regulatory organizations do not aspire to exercise power in the international system independent of their members. Indeed, their main purpose is to help regulators apprehend those who would harm the interests of American voters. Transgovernmental networks often promulgate their own rules, but the purpose of those rules is to enhance the enforcement of national law.

Traditional international law requires states to implement the international obligations they incur through their own law. Thus, if states agree to a 12-mile territorial sea, they must change their domestic legislation concerning the interdiction of vessels in territorial waters accordingly. But this legislation is unlikely to overlap with domestic law, as national legislatures do not usually seek to regulate global commons issues and interstate relations.

Transgovernmental regulation, by contrast, produces rules concerning issues that each nation already regulates within its borders: crime, securities fraud, pollution, tax evasion. The advances in technology and transportation that have fueled globalization have made it more difficult to enforce national law. Regulators benefit from coordinating their enforcement efforts with those of their foreign counterparts and from ensuring that other nations adopt similar approaches.

The result is the nationalization of international law. Regulatory agreements between states are pledges of good faith that are self-enforcing, in the sense that each nation will be better able to enforce its national law by implementing the agreement if other nations do likewise. Laws are binding or coercive only at the national level. Uniformity of result and diversity of means go hand in hand, and the makers and enforcers of rules are national leaders who are accountable to the people.

BIPARTISAN GLOBALIZATION

Secretary of State Madeleine Albright seeks to revive the bipartisan foreign policy consensus of the late 1940s. Deputy Secretary of State Strobe Talbott argues that promoting democracy worldwide satisfies the American need for idealpolitik as well as realpolitik. President Clinton, in his second inaugural address, called for a "new government for a new century," abroad as well as at home. But bipartisanship is threatened by divergent responses to globalization, democratization is a tricky business, and Vice President Al Gore's efforts to "reinvent government" have focused on domestic rather than international institutions. Transgovernmentalism can address all these problems.

Globalization implies the erosion of national boundaries. Consequently, regulators' power to implement national regulations within those boundaries declines both because people can easily flee their jurisdiction and because the flows of capital, pollution, pathogens, and weapons are too great and sudden for any one regulator to control. The liberal internationalist response to these assaults on state regulatory power is to build a larger international apparatus. Globalization thus leads to internationalization, or the transfer of regulatory authority from the national level to an international institution. The best example is not the WTO itself, but rather the stream of proposals to expand the WTO's jurisdiction to global competition policy, intellectual property regulation, and other trade-related issues. Liberals are likely to support expanding the power of international institutions to guard against the global dismantling of the regulatory state.

Here's the rub. Conservatives are more likely to favor the expansion of globalized markets without the internationalization that goes with it, since internationalization, from their perspective, equals a loss of sovereignty. According to Buchanan, the U.S. foreign policy establishment "want[s] to move America into a New World Order where the World Court decides quarrels between nations; the WTO writes the rules for trade and settles all disputes; the IMF and World Bank order wealth transfers from continent to continent and country to country; the Law of the Sea Treaty tells us what we may and may not do on the high seas and ocean floor, and the United Nations decides where U.S. military forces may and may not intervene." The rhetoric is deliberately inflammatory, but echoes resound across the Republican spectrum.

Transgovernmental initiatives are a compromise that could command bipartisan support. Regulatory loopholes caused by global forces require a coordinated response beyond the reach of any one country. But this coordination need not come from building more international institutions. It can be achieved through transgovernmental cooperation, involving the same officials who make and implement policy at the national level. The transgovernmental alternative is fast, flexible, and effective.

A leading example of transgovernmentalism in action that demonstrates its bipartisan appeal is a State Department initiative christened the New Transatlantic Agenda. Launched in 1991 under the Bush administration and reinvigorated by Secretary of State Warren Christopher in 1995, the initiative structures the relationship between the United States and the EU, fostering cooperation in areas ranging from opening markets to fighting terrorism, drug trafficking, and infectious disease. It is an umbrella for ongoing projects between U.S. officials and their European counterparts. It reaches ordinary citizens, embracing efforts like the Transatlantic Business Dialogue and engaging individuals through people-to-people exchanges and expanded communication through the Internet.

DEMOCRATIZATION, STEP BY STEP

Transgovernmental networks are concentrated among liberal democracies but are not limited to them. Some nondemocratic states have institutions capable of cooperating with their foreign counterparts, such as committed and effective regulatory agencies or relatively independent judiciaries. Transgovernmental ties can strengthen institutions in ways that will help them resist political domination, corruption, and incompetence and build democratic institutions in their countries, step by step. The Organization of Supreme Courts of the Americas, for instance, actively seeks to strengthen norms of judicial independence among its members, many of whom must fend off powerful political forces.

Individuals and groups in nondemocratic countries may also "borrow" government institutions of democratic states to achieve a measure of justice they cannot obtain in their own countries. The court or regulatory agency of one state may be able to perform judicial or regulatory functions for the people of another. Victims of human rights violations, for example, in countries such as Argentina, Ethiopia, Haiti, and the Philippines have sued for redress in the courts of the United States. U.S. courts accepted these cases, often over the objections of the executive branch, using a broad interpretation of a moribund statute dating back to 1789. Under this interpretation, aliens may sue in U.S. courts to seek damages from foreign government officials accused of torture, even if the torture allegedly took place in the foreign country. More generally, a nongovernmental organization seeking to prevent human rights violations can often circumvent their own government's corrupt legislature and politicized court by publicizing the plight of victims abroad and mobilizing a foreign court, legislature, or executive to take action.

Responding to calls for a coherent U.S. foreign policy and seeking to strengthen the community of democratic nations, President Clinton substituted the concept of "enlargement" for the Cold War principle of "containment." Expanding transgovernmental outreach to include institutions from nondemocratic states would help expand the circle of democracies one institution at a time.

A New World Order Ideal

Transgovernmentalism offers its own world order ideal, less dramatic but more compelling than either liberal internationalism or the new medievalism. It harnesses the state's power to find and implement solutions to global problems. International institutions have a lackluster record on such problem-solving; indeed, NGOs exist largely to compensate for their inadequacies. Doing away with the state, however, is hardly the answer. The new medievalist mantra of global governance is "governance without government." But governance without government is governance without power, and government without power rarely works. Many pressing international and domestic problems result from states' insufficient power to establish order, build infrastructure, and provide minimum social services. Private actors may take up some slack, but there is no substitute for the state.

Transgovernmental networks allow governments to benefit from the flexibility and decentralization of non-state actors. Jessica T. Mathews argues that "businesses, citizens' organizations, ethnic groups, and crime cartels have all readily adopted the network model," while governments "are quintessential hierarchies, wedded to an organizational form incompatible with all that the new technologies make possible." Not so. Disaggregating the state into its functional components makes it possible to create networks of institutions engaged in a common enterprise even as they represent distinct national interests. Moreover, they can work with their subnational and supra-national counterparts, creating a genuinely new world order in which networked institutions perform the functions of a world government—legislation, administration, and adjudication—without the form.

These globe-spanning networks will strengthen the state as the primary player in the international system. The state's defining attribute has traditionally been sovereignty, conceived as absolute power in domestic affairs and autonomy in relations with other states. But as Abram and Antonia Chayes observe in *The New Sovereignty* (1995), sovereignty is actually "status—the vindication of the state's existence in the international system." More importantly, they demonstrate that in contemporary international relations, sovereignty has been redefined to mean "membership . . . in the regimes that make up the substance of international life." Disaggregating the state permits the disaggregation of sovereignty as well, ensuring that specific state institutions derive strength and status from participation in a transgovernmental order.

Transgovernmental networks will increasingly provide an important anchor for international organizations and non-state actors alike. UN officials have already learned a lesson about the limits of supra-national authority; mandated cuts in the international bureaucracy will further tip the balance of power toward national regulators. The next generation of international institutions is also likely to look more like the Basle Committee, or, more formally, the Organization of Economic Cooperation and Development, dedicated to providing a forum for transnational problem-solving and the harmonization of national law. The disaggregation of the state creates opportunities for domestic institutions, particularly courts, to make common cause with their supra-national counterparts against their fellow branches of government. Non-state actors will lobby and litigate wherever they think they will have the most effect. Many already realize that corporate self-regulation and states' promises to comply with vague international agreements are no substitute for national law.

The spread of transgovernmental networks will depend more on political and professional convergence than on civilizational boundaries. Trust and awareness of a common enterprise are more vulnerable to differing political ideologies and corruption than to cultural differences. Government networks transcend the traditional divide between high and low politics. National militaries, for instance, network as extensively as central bankers with their counterparts in friendly states. Judicial and regulatory networks can help achieve gradual political convergence, but are unlikely to be of much help in the face of a serious economic or military threat. If the coming conflict with China is indeed coming, transgovernmentalism will not stop it.

The strength of transgovernmental networks and of transgovernmental-ism as a world order ideal will ultimately depend on their accountability to the world's peoples. To many, the prospect of transnational government by judges and bureaucrats looks more like technocracy than democracy. Critics contend that government institutions engaged in policy coordination with their foreign counterparts will be barely visible, much less accountable, to voters still largely tied to national territory.

Citizens of liberal democracies will not accept any form of international regulation they cannot control. But checking unelected officials is a familiar problem in domestic politics. As national legislators become increasingly aware of transgovernmental networks, they will expand their oversight capacities and develop networks of their own. Transnational NGO networks will de-velop a similar monitoring capacity. It will be harder to monitor themselves.

Transgovernmentalism offers answers to the most important challenges facing advanced industrial countries: loss of regulatory power with econom-ic globalization, perceptions of a "democratic deficit" as international insti-tutions step in to fill the regulatory gap, and the difficulties of engaging nondemocratic states. Moreover, it provides a powerful alternative to a lib-eral internationalism that has reached its limits and to a new medievalism that, like the old Marxism, sees the state slowly fading away. The new medieval-ists are right to emphasize the dawn of a new era, in which information tech-nology will transform the globe. But government networks are government for the information age. They offer the world a blueprint for the international architecture of the twenty-first century.

ISSUE 3

THE FUTURE OF DEMOCRACY

What is the future of democracy in a world increasingly torn by ethnic and religious strife, and one in which the strains of globalization, rather than bringing a greater sense of oneness amongst the world's diverse peoples, are throwing up barriers to increasing economic and political integration?

To further consolidate the spread of democratic institutions after the end of the Cold War, the United States, in conjunction with the governments of Poland, the Czech Republic, Chile, India, the Republic of Korea, and Mali sponsored a ministerial meeting on June 26–27, 2000, in Warsaw to exchange ideas and proposals to strengthen and preserve the advances democratic governance made over the past decade. A follow-up ministerial meeting of The Community of Democracies was held on November 10–12, 2002, in Seoul, Korea. Recognizing the heightened threat to democratic government in the post–September 11 global environment, this meeting sought to reaffirm the commitment of the participant states to promoting the values of democratic government, and to produce a Plan of Action to help foster its goals. "A Case for Consolidating Democracy" is the title of the discussion paper produced by the governments of Poland and the United States, which sought to outline the challenges democracy faces, as well as a strategy for further promoting its spread. This document, which appears as the first article for Issue 3, addresses the existence of a "spreading democratic malaise," and highlights actions that, if undertaken, would help to further consolidate established democracies, as well as promote the spread of democratic government.

The second article for Issue 3, which is written by Arthur M. Schlesinger, Jr., is more cautious in its assessment of the prospect for the spread of democracy, pointing out that democracy has always been threatened by a wide array of political, social, and economic forces that question its long-term viability. Schlesinger maintains that religious, racial, and ethnic differences continuously undermine democratic states. The dissolution of the former Soviet Union and the wars in and among the new states of the former Yugoslavia indeed posed some of the most serious challenges to the stability of the international community at the end of the twentieth century. But are these conflicts challenges to democracy or to certain types of nationalism? If we examine Schlesinger's argument more carefully, perhaps we shall conclude that democracy is defective. It simply does not solve all the problems it was meant to solve. After all, when James Madison wrote his defense of the U.S. Constitution in *Federalist Papers 10* and *51*, he claimed that democracy alone could not resolve the number one threat to stability in society: "the violence of faction." According to Madison, the division of rich and poor in society leads everywhere and always to a division of interests that normally results in violence. In order to avoid the violence of faction, a nation must have a republic with a government with divided powers among competing groups. Only checks and balances could assure freedom. It is not the participation inherent in democracy, therefore, but the limitations on power imposed by a republican framework that guarantees order and freedom. If we agree with Madison, we must look to republican representational forms of government to secure democratic freedoms, and it is precisely these republican forms that governments across the world have such difficulty in instituting.

Discussion Questions

As you read the articles by the Co-Chairs of the Round Table I and Schlesinger, consider the following questions:

1. What is democracy?
2. Of the generic problems of democratic governance mentioned in the Round Table I Discussion Paper and in Schlesinger's article, which one is the most likely to pose the most difficult challenge in the near-term, and in the long-term?
3. What plan of action would you advocate to consolidate and spread the values of democratic governance?

Key Web Sites

For more information on this topic, visit the following Web sites:

National Endowment for Democracy
http://www.ned.org

The Second Ministerial Conference of the Communities of Democracies
http://www.cd2002.go.kr

Center for the Study of Democracy
http://www.democ.uci.edu/demo

A Case for Consolidating Democracy

Co-Chairs of the Round Table I of the Second Ministerial Conference of the Community of Democracies

For many years, democracy was viewed as a luxury, not a necessity, next to urgent quests for development. Increasingly, however, scholars, policy analysts, and people themselves in many countries recognize that democracy is not only a critical human rights component that allows for the full protection of fundamental freedoms and human rights but also an important condition for development. It cannot be only a privilege of the rich.

Improvements in physical infrastructure, public health, and education are crucial to development. But they are not the most crucial factors. Indeed, no amount of spending or public investment can compensate for bad governance. Corrupt, wasteful, abusive, incompetent governance undermines basic economic development. Where governance is endemically bad, leaders do not use public resources effectively, nor is private sector growth allowed to prosper smoothly and efficiently. Such a situation can also seriously inhibit democracy.

While good governance and democracy are not synonymous, democracy helps foster good governance. Truly democratic elections can remove bad, corrupt, or merely ineffectual leaders. Free and fair elections also provide an incentive for political leaders to govern more effectively in the public interest. A strong body of law and a system of effective checks and balances— with an independent judiciary and a network of countercorruption, audit, and other oversight agencies—can deter abuse of power. A free press and civil society help to consolidate democratic institutions and processes, and can expose wrongdoing and hold government officials accountable before society and the law.

BUILDING STABLE DEMOCRACY

Democracies are consolidated where there is a widespread and deeply ingrained commitment to the legitimacy of democracy among all major societal groups, and where major democratic institutions have such strength, depth, and predictability that there is no prospect of a breakdown of democracy. Many of the new democracies that have emerged in the past two decades have not yet reached this level of stability. The global quest for democracy has

This Round Table I "Consolidating Democratic Institutions" Discussion Paper, generated at The Second Ministerial Conference of the Community of Democracies in Seoul (November 10–12, 2002), was prepared by the Co-Chairs of the Round Table I (Poland, the United States).

generated some important lessons for many new, developing democracies and also for seasoned democracies:

1. Human rights—including the right of citizens to choose their government in free, fair, and periodic elections—and the rule of law are ends in themselves. Yet even many electoral democracies fall seriously short of their obligations to foster and protect the human rights and fundamental freedoms of their citizens.

2. There is a strong association between the quality and the legitimacy of democracy in the mind of the public: Citizen support for democracy is more robust and democracy is more stable when there is respect for individual liberties, a system of justice and accountability, and transparency in governmental decision making.

3. Underlying this relationship is the strong connection between the quality of governance and the stability of democracy. Where democracy is restricted, governance is poorer—more corrupt, wasteful, incompetent, and unresponsive. This entrenches poverty, obstructs economic development, opens the country up to recurrent crises, and prevents effective use of international assistance.

4. The good governance that fosters development therefore requires not just representative democracy, but democracy that is transparent, accountable, bound by the rule of law, and provides protection for human rights and fundamental freedoms.

GENERIC PROBLEMS OF DEMOCRATIC GOVERNANCE

Since the mid-1990s, two global trends have been colliding. One trend has been the surprisingly robust and resilient wave of democratization, producing a record number of electoral democracies. The other trend has been a spreading democratic malaise in many parts of the world. Several generic problems of governance underlie this malaise and must be urgently confronted.

Weakness of the Rule of Law   The most urgent and pervasive obstacle is the weakness or, in some cases, decay of the rule of law. Widespread corruption undermines the legitimacy of government, alienates citizens from their leaders, and threatens political stability and economic development. The more endemic the problem of corruption, the more likely it is to be accompanied by other serious deficiencies in the rule of law: smuggling, drug trafficking, criminal violence, abuse of power, and human rights abuses.

In both newer and established democracies, political corruption scandals threaten to erode public faith in democracy and thereby to destabilize the entire system. This is particularly so where corruption is part of a more general syndrome involving the spread of organized crime with political connections, the misuse of executive and police powers to punish political opposition, and the politicization of key institutions of "horizontal accountability," such as the judiciary, the audit agency, and even the electoral commission. It is necessary for political leaders to provide sufficient democratic commitment—the political will—to build or maintain institutions that constrain their own power.

An important ingredient in all democracies is the political will of the nation's leaders to improve the quality of governance. At its most resilient, political will involves a broad consensus among ruling elites, across political parties and sectors of government, in favor of democratic and good governance reforms.

Attenuation of Civil Society and the Environment Conducive to Democracy   Particular attention must be focused on the need to preserve and consolidate the political, social, and economic environments rendering the development of democracy possible, environments which are threatened by steady fragmentation of societies due to political and economic factors. We must pay attention to depreciation of the value of humans and their fundamental rights. We must also pay attention to the economic conditions of persons, determined by ineffective economic policies incompatible with the principles of sustained development. Many developments underlie the growing crisis of confidence in some countries in state institutions, in the democratic order, in political parties, in respect for the principles of constitutionally guaranteed justice as well as in mutual trust. These include concerns about the perception that global free markets and political liberalism have not led to prosperity; irresponsible, unprofessional media; corrupt practices and inadequate mechanisms to deal with corruption; and the lack of transparency in decision-making processes.

In certain cases there has been the rise of the veneer of democracy with a formally working representative system, periodic elections and the rule of law but where the major decisions are made behind the back of all representative bodies. The result is often the decreased civic engagement in public affairs and exclusion of democratically oriented political figures. The withering of, and in many cases the absence of, democratic habits of citizens and politicians, combined with increased threats of terrorism or extremism, account for the fact that democratic institutions in many countries are seriously threatened. For all these reasons it is necessary to focus efforts on the promotion of a culture of democracy and strict observance of human rights, both civic and political, social, economic, and cultural. They all constitute principal components of an environment conducive to democracy.

Economic Malaise as a Threat to Democracy   In many emerging democracies, economic reforms have not yet generated rapid, sustainable economic growth. This can cause the public to question the benefits of having an open, democratic system. There have been success stories in which rapid or modest growth has accompanied democratic development. However, in many new and troubled democracies, economic growth has not met public expectations, and large segments of the population remain in poverty. In some cases these lower than expected results are the result of a failure to control corruption and a lack of genuine rule of law. If countries embrace growth-oriented policies and fiscal prudence and are open to privatizing previously state-run enterprises they will likely attract adequate foreign investment and stimulate their own economic climate. Investors—foreign and domestic—are attracted to secure property rights and low transaction costs.

Transnational corporations have been accused of contributing to the atrophy of democratic institutions. They should be encouraged to cooperate in order to promote an environment conducive to the development of both democratic structures and a culture of democracy. A role of its own would be played by the promotion of the new UN Global Compact on Corporate Social Responsibility.

Managing Ethnic, Regional, and Religious Differences Cultural diversity is not an insurmountable obstacle to stable democracy. Countries in Asia, Africa, the Americas, and Europe have learned to manage diversity through federalist arrangements to devolve power, assimilation of immigrants, and complex mixes of laws and customs designed to include, not exclude, those from different cultures. The problem arises when one ethnic or religious group seeks hegemony over others, or when some minorities perceive that they are being permanently and completely excluded from power, including any meaningful control of their own affairs. Identifying, then implementing, the kinds of policies and institutional arrangements by which minorities can be protected and all citizens can feel they have a stake and say in the political system helps secure stable democracy.

Media In the era of information and television society, where media can contribute to the discourse on and development of democratic values, special attention must be paid to the primacy of the freedom of speech in regard to common and direct access to the media. The development of an environment conducive to democracy and consolidation of democratic institutions is supported by professional, responsible, and accurate media. It is indeed necessary to appreciate the role that public media have to play in this respect.

These three challenges of governance intensify and reinforce one another. Highly visible corruption accentuates the sense of injustice and grievance associated with poverty, unemployment, and economic hardship. Corruption has also been a major obstacle to the successful implementation of economic reforms, especially privatization. Poverty and economic stagnation reinforce the sense of discrimination and powerlessness that many religious and ethnic minorities and indigenous populations feel. Corruption aggravates societal conflict by raising the premium on control of the state and rendering politics a more desperate, zero-sum struggle for control of economic opportunity. The weakness of the rule of law makes it easier for leaders of different ethnic and sectarian groups to mobilize violence at the grass roots as part of their efforts to win power for themselves. It also facilitates electoral fraud and violence.

Underlying all of these problems in many countries is a lack of commitment to the rule of law, transparency, and accountability. With the construction of effective institutions to control corruption and secure the rule of law, democracy can be stable and development can be sustainable.

STRATEGIC PRIORITIES FOR CONSOLIDATING DEMOCRATIC INSTITUTIONS

The political will for reform is the most important prerequisite for consolidating democracy. Consolidated established democracies, as well as international organizations, can provide invaluable assistance, experience, and guidance. International and regional organizations play a crucial role in promoting and supporting the development of democratic institutions. Reforms to improve and deepen democracy require leadership from within the country. As countries take steps to consolidate democracy, the following areas are priorities:

- controlling corruption and improving the entire apparatus of accountability, from the legal framework to the audit and countercorruption agencies, and from free media to nongovernmental organizations;
- strengthening the rule of law, not only through a trained and independent judiciary but also through functioning, more professional and ethical law enforcement bodies;
- strengthening and democratizing political parties, and deepening their roots in society;
- involving prodemocracy, development, and good-governance NGOs, as well as representative interest groups, in the design and implementation of reforms to deepen democracy; and
- developing stronger, more professional and capable states that are better able to manage their economies and respond to rising societal demands for better governance.

CONCLUSIONS

The past quarter century has seen a remarkable global transformation. Today, most countries are electoral democracies, and people in every part of the world want civil and political freedoms, both for their intrinsic worth and for the better society they can produce. Democracy is the best system for securing freedom, good governance, and a decent, humane society. But democratic electoral competition does not ensure these other important ends. That requires reform to deepen, strengthen, and consolidate democracy—to build a rule of law and a culture of governance in which public resources are used for the public good. Countries that cannot mobilize the will for reform face bleak prospects for political stability and economic development. However, democracies that prove serious about governance will attract the productive investment, increased international assistance, and societal support that will help them to prosper.

Has Democracy a Future?

Arthur M. Schlesinger, Jr.

The twentieth century has no doubt been, as Isaiah Berlin has said, "the most terrible century in Western history." But this terrible century has—or appears to be having—a happy ending. As in melodramas of old, the maiden democracy, bound by villains to the railroad track, is rescued in the nick of time from the onrushing train. As the century draws to a close, both major villains have perished, fascism with a bang, communism with a whimper.

A season of triumphalism has followed. Two centuries ago Kant argued in his *Idea for a Universal History* that the republican form of government was destined to supersede all others. At last the prophecy seemed on the way to fulfillment. Savants hailed "the end of history." "For the first time in all history," President Clinton declared in his second inaugural address, "more people on this planet live under democracy than dictatorship." The *New York Times*, after careful checking, approved: 3.1 billion people live in democracies, 2.66 billion do not. According to end-of-history doctrine as expounded by its prophet, the minority can look forward to "the universalization of Western liberal democracy as the final form of human government."

For historians, this euphoria rang a bell of memory. Did not the same radiant hope accompany the transition from the nineteenth to the twentieth century? This most terrible hundred years in Western history started out in an atmosphere of optimism and high expectations. People of good will in 1900 believed in the inevitability of democracy, the invincibility of progress, the decency of human nature, and the coming reign of reason and peace. David Starr Jordan, the president of Stanford University, expressed the mood in his turn-of-the-century book *The Call of the Twentieth Century*. "The man of the Twentieth Century," Jordan predicted, "will be a hopeful man. He will love the world and the world will love him."

Looking back, we recall a century marked a good deal less by love than by hate, irrationality, and atrocity, one that for a long dark passage inspired the gravest forebodings about the very survival of the human race. Democracy, striding confidently into the 1900s, found itself almost at once on the defensive. The Great War, exposing the pretension that democracy would guarantee peace, shattered old structures of security and order and unleashed

Arthur M. Schlesinger, Jr. is an award-winning historian, writer, and former special assistant to President John F. Kennedy.

This article is from *Foreign Affairs* 76, no. 5 (September/October 1997). Reprinted by permission of *Foreign Affairs*. Copyright 1997 by the Council on Foreign Relations, Inc.

angry energies of revolution—revolution not for democracy but against it. Bolshevism in Russia, Fascism in Italy, Nazism in Germany, militarism in Japan all despised, denounced, and, wherever they could, destroyed individual rights and the processes of self-government.

In another decade the Great Depression came along to expose the pretension that democracy would guarantee prosperity. A third of the way into the century, democracy seemed a helpless thing, spiritless, paralyzed, doomed. Contempt for democracy spread among elites and masses alike: contempt for parliamentary dithering, for "talking-shops," for liberties of expression and opposition, for bourgeois civility and cowardice, for pragmatic muddling through.

In another decade the Second World War threatened to administer the coup de grâce. Liberal society, its back to the wall, fought for its life. There was considerable defeatism in the West. The title of Anne Morrow Lindbergh's 1940 bestseller proclaimed totalitarianism *The Wave of the Future*. It was, she wrote, a "new, and perhaps even ultimately good, conception of humanity trying to come to birth." Hitlerism and Stalinism were merely "scum on the wave of the future. . . . The wave of the future is coming and there is no fighting it." By 1941 only about a dozen democracies were left on the planet.

The political, economic, and moral failures of democracy had handed the initiative to totalitarianism. Something like this could happen again. If liberal democracy fails in the twenty-first century, as it failed in the twentieth, to construct a humane, prosperous, and peaceful world, it will invite the rise of alternative creeds apt to be based, like fascism and communism, on flight from freedom and surrender to authority.

After all, democracy in its modern version—representative government, party competition, the secret ballot, all founded on guarantees of individual rights and freedoms—is at most 200 years old. A majority of the world's inhabitants may be living under democracy in 1997, but democratic hegemony is a mere flash in the long vistas of recorded history. One wonders how deeply democracy has sunk roots in previously democratic countries in the years since the collapse of the totalitarian challenges. Now the democratic adventure must confront tremendous pent-up energies that threaten to blow it off course and even drive it onto the rocks.

The Law of Acceleration

Much of this energy is pent up within democracy itself. The most fateful source in the United States is race. "The problem of the twentieth century," W. E. B. Du Bois observed in 1900, "is the problem of the color line." His prediction will come to full flower in the twenty-first century. Minorities seek full membership in the larger American society. Doors slammed in their faces drive them to protest. The revolt against racism has taken time to gather strength. White America belatedly awakens to the cruelties long practiced against nonwhite peoples, and the revolt intensifies. As Tocqueville explained long ago, "Patiently endured so long as it seemed beyond redress, a grievance comes to appear intolerable once the possibility of removing it crosses men's minds. For the mere fact that certain abuses have been remedied draws attention to others, and they now appear more galling; people may suffer less, but their sensibility is exacerbated."

There are other pent-up energies. Modern democracy itself is the political offspring of technology and capitalism, the two most dynamic—that is to say, destabilizing—forces loose in the world today. Both are driven ever onward by self-generated momentum that strains the bonds of social control and of political sovereignty.

Technology created the clock, the printing press, the compass, the steam engine, the power loom, and the other innovations that laid the foundation for capitalism and that in time generated rationalism, individualism, and democracy. At first technological advance was unsystematic and intermittent. Soon it was institutionalized. "The greatest invention of the nineteenth century," said Alfred North Whitehead, "was the invention of the method of invention."

In the twentieth century, scientific and technological innovation increased at an exponential rate. Henry Adams, the most brilliant of American historians, meditated on the acceleration of history. "The world did not double or treble its movement between 1800 and 1900," Adams wrote in 1909, "but, measured by any standard . . . the tension and vibration and volume and so-called progression of society were fully a thousand times greater in 1900 than in 1800;—the force had doubled ten times over, and the speed, when measured by electrical standards as in telegraphy, approached infinity, and had annihilated both space and time." Nothing, Adams thought, could slow this process, for "the law of acceleration . . . cannot be supposed to relax its energy to suit the convenience of man."

The law of acceleration now hurtles us into a new age. The shift from a factory-based to a computer-based economy is more traumatic even than our great-grandparents' shift from a farm-based to a factory-based economy. The Industrial Revolution extended over generations and allowed time for human and institutional adjustment. The Computer Revolution is far swifter, more concentrated, and more drastic in its impact.

HYPERINTERACTIVE STATE

The computerized world poses problems for democracy. Where the Industrial Revolution created more jobs than it destroyed, the Computer Revolution threatens to destroy more jobs than it creates. It also threatens to erect new and rigid class barriers, especially between the well-educated and the ill-educated. Economic inequality has already grown in the United States to the point where disparities are greater in egalitarian America than in the class-ridden societies of Europe. Felix Rohatyn, the investment banker and rescuer of a bankrupt New York City, speaks of the "huge transfers of wealth from lower-skilled middle-class workers to the owners of capital assets and to a new technological aristocracy." Those who skip or flunk the computer will fall into the Blade Runner proletariat, a snarling, embittered, violent underclass.

The computer will also affect the procedures of democratic politics. James Madison in *The Federalist Papers* distinguished between "pure democracy," by which he meant a system in which citizens assemble and administer the government in person, and a republic, by which he meant a system in which the majority expresses its will through "a scheme of representation." For most of American history, "pure democracy" was necessarily limited to town meetings in small villages. Now the interactivity introduced by the Computer Revolution makes "pure democracy," technically feasible on a national scale.

Brian Beedham in an article in the December 21, 1996, *Economist* applauds this development, claiming representative democracy is "a half-finished thing." Every citizen, Beedham argues, is entitled to an equal say in the conduct of public affairs. The rise of public opinion polls, focus groups, and referendums suggests popular demand for a finished democracy. With a nation of computers plugged into information and communication networks, "full democracy" is just around the corner. Full democracy, pure democracy, plebiscitary democracy, direct democracy, cyberdemocracy, the electronic town hall: Under whatever name, is this a desirable prospect?

Perhaps not. Interactivity encourages instant responses, discourages second thoughts, and offers outlets for demagoguery, egomania, insult, and hate. Listen to talk radio! In too interactive a polity, a "common passion," as Madison thought, could sweep through a people and lead to emotional and ill-judged actions. Remembering the explosion of popular indignation when President Truman fired General Douglas MacArthur, one is grateful that the electronic town hall was not running the country in 1951. The Internet has done little thus far to foster the reasoned exchanges that in Madison's words "refine and enlarge the public views."

UNBRIDLED CAPITALISM

While the onrush of technology creates new substantive problems and promises to revise the political system through which we deal with them, the onrush of capitalism may have even more disruptive consequences. Let us understand the relationship between capitalism and democracy. Democracy is impossible without private ownership because private property—resources beyond the arbitrary reach of the state—provides the only secure basis for political opposition and intellectual freedom. But the capitalist market is no guarantee of democracy, as Deng Xiaoping, Lee Kuan Yew, Pinochet, and Franco, not to mention Hitler and Mussolini, have amply demonstrated. Democracy requires capitalism, but capitalism does not require democracy, at least in the short run.

Capitalism has proved itself the supreme engine of innovation, production, and distribution. But its method, as it careens ahead, heedless of little beyond its own profits, is what Joseph Schumpeter called "creative destruction." In its economic theory, capitalism rests on the concept of equilibrium. In practice, its very virtues drive it toward disequilibrium. This is the dilemma of contemporary conservatism. The unfettered market that conservatives worship undermines the values—stability, morality, family, community, work, discipline, delayed gratification—that conservatives avow. The glitter of the marketplace, the greed, the short-termism, the exploitation of prurient appetites, the ease of fraud, the devil-take-the-hindmost ethos—all these are at war with purported conservative ideals. "Stationary capitalism," as Schumpeter said, "is a contradiction in terms."

Even premier capitalists are appalled by what runaway capitalism has wrought. If understanding of capitalism can be measured by success in making money out of it, no one understands contemporary capitalism better than the financier and philanthropist George Soros. "Although I have made a fortune in the financial markets," Soros writes, "I now fear that the untrammeled intensification of laissez-faire capitalism and the spread of market values into all areas of life is endangering our open and democratic society." The "uninhibited pursuit of self-interest," Soros continues, results in "intolerable inequities and instability."

The Computer Revolution offers wondrous, new possibilities for creative destruction. One goal of capitalist creativity is the globalized economy. One—unplanned—candidate for capitalist destruction is the nation-state, the traditional site of democracy. The computer turns the untrammeled market into a global juggernaut crashing across frontiers, enfeebling national powers of taxation and regulation, undercutting national management of interest rates and exchange rates, widening disparities of wealth both within and between nations, dragging down labor standards, degrading the environment, denying nations the shaping of their own economic destiny, accountable to no one, creating a world economy without a world polity. Cyberspace is beyond national control. No authorities exist to provide international control. Where is democracy now?

The Asian Shift

The end of the Eurocentric era raises further problems for democracy. Self-government, individual rights, equality before the law are European inventions. Now the age of the Pacific is upon us. The breakthrough of Japan in the century coming to an end heralds the breakthrough of China and India in the century ahead. The economic magnetism of Asia is already altering the contours of the global economy, and foreshadows historic shifts in the planetary balance of power.

I am not greatly concerned about the "clash of civilizations" that worries some thoughtful analysts. Civilizations are rarely unified. Countries within the same civilization are more likely to fight with each other than to join in monolithic assaults on other civilizations. But the impact of the rise of Asia on the future of democracy is worth consideration. The Asian tradition, we are told, values the group more than the individual, order more than argument, authority more than liberty, solidarity more than freedom. Some Asian leaders, notably Lee Kuan Yew of Singapore and Mahathir bin Mohamad of Malaysia, love to contrast Asian discipline and stability with the disorder and decadence they impute to the individualistic West. They denounce the attempt to hold Asian countries to Western democratic standards as the new form of Western imperialism.

Nevertheless, both India and Japan are functioning democracies. If the claim that human rights are universal is proof of Western arrogance, the restriction of those rights to Europe and the Americas brands non-Western peoples as lesser breeds incapable of appreciating personal liberty and self-government, and that is surely Western arrogance too. In fact, many Asians fight for human rights, and at the risk of their freedom and their lives. "Why do we assume," asks Christopher Patten, the last British governor of Hong Kong, "that Lee Kuan Yew is the embodiment of Asian values rather than Daw Aung San Suu Kyi," the courageous opposition leader under prolonged house arrest in Burma? A pre-Tiananmen Square wall poster in Beijing proclaimed: "We cannot tolerate that human rights and democracy are only slogans of the Western bourgeoisie and the Eastern proletariat only needs dictatorship." In the words of the Indian economist Amartya Sen, "The so-called Asian values that are invoked to justify authoritarianism are not especially Asian in any significant sense." Chris Patten concludes, "I think the Asian value debate is piffle. What are these Asian values? When you home in on what one or two Asian leaders mean by them, what they actually mean is that anyone who disagrees with me should shut up."

Still, the new salience of Asia on the world scene, the absence of historical predilections for democracy, and the self-interest of rulers who see democracy as a threat to their power suggest a period of Asian resistance to the spread of the democratic idea.

CULTURE LASHES BACK

That resistance will be reinforced by the defensive reaction around the planet to relentless globalization—a reaction that takes the form of withdrawal from modernity. The world today is torn in opposite directions. Globalization is in the saddle and rides mankind, but at the same time drives people to seek refuge from its powerful forces beyond their control and comprehension. They retreat into familiar, intelligible, protective units. They crave the politics of identity. The faster the world integrates, the more people will huddle in their religious or ethnic or tribal enclaves. Integration and disintegration feed on each other.

A militant expression of what Samuel Huntington calls cultural backlash is the upsurge of religious fundamentalism. Islamic fundamentalism seems especially hostile to freedom of expression, to women's rights, and, contrary to historical Islam, to other religions. Nor is the fundamentalist revival confined to the Third World. Many people living lives of quiet desperation in modern societies hunger for transcendent meaning and turn to inerrant faith for solace and support.

According to a 1995 Gallup poll, more than a third of American adults claim that God speaks to them directly. One hopes it is the God of love rather than the God of wrath on the other end of the line. Fundamentalism, carried too far, has ominous implications for democracy. Those who believe they are executing the will of the Almighty are notably harsh on nonbelievers. A fanatic, as the Irish-American wit Finley Peter Dunne's Mr. Dooley once observed, "does what he thinks th' Lord wud do if He only knew th' facts in th' case." Fanaticism is the mortal enemy of democracy.

Back to the question: Has democracy a future? Yes, Virginia, it does, but not the glorious future predicted in the triumphalist moment. Democracy has survived the twentieth century by the skin of its teeth. It will not enjoy a free ride through the century to come.

In America, democracy must run a gauntlet of challenges. The most crucial is still Du Bois' color line. Much depends on the availability of jobs, especially in the inner city. If employment remains high, political action will mitigate racial tensions, particularly when minorities understand that in the longer run, ethnic gerrymandering will reduce, not increase, their influence. Tension will be mitigated even more by intermarriage. Sex—and love—between people of different creeds and colors can probably be counted on to arrest the disuniting of America.

The national capacity to absorb and assimilate newcomers will remain powerful. The call of the mainstream will appeal far more than linguistic or ethnic ghettos, above all to the young. English will continue as the dominant language. Indeed, in essentials the national character will be recognizably much as it has been for a couple of centuries. People seeking clues to the American mystery will still read, and quote, Tocqueville.

Technology will rush on according to Adams' law of acceleration. But for all the temptations of interactivity and all the unpopularity of elected officials, I doubt that Americans will sanction the degradation of representative democracy into a system of plebiscites. Capitalism too will career on, through downs as well as ups, but laissez-faire ideology will probably wane as capitalists discover the range of troubles the unfettered market cannot solve, or makes worse. Unbridled capitalism, with low wages, long hours, and exploited workers, excites social resentment, revives class warfare, and infuses Marxism with new life. To move along constructive lines, capitalism must subordinate short-term plans and profits to such long-term social necessities as investment in education, research and development, environmental protection, the extension of health care, the rehabilitation of infrastructure, the redemption of the city. Capitalists are not likely to do this by themselves. Long-term perspectives demand public leadership and affirmative government.

In the world at large, can capitalism, once loose from national moorings, be held to social accountability? Will international institutions acquire the authority to impose, for example, a global SEC? This won't happen next week, but continuing abuse of power will build a constituency for reform. Wars will still disturb the tenor of life, but where in the past they generally arose from aggression across national frontiers, the wars of the twenty-first century will more likely be between ethnic, religious, ideological, or tribal factions within the same country. Such wars are harder to define and to control. Let us pray that no factional zealot gets hold of an atomic bomb.

Nation-states will continue to decline as effective power units: too small for the big problems, as the sociologist Daniel Bell has said, and too big for the small problems. Despite this decline, nationalism will persist as the most potent of political emotions. Whether democracy, a Western creation, can be transplanted to parts of the world with different cultures and traditions is far from certain. Yet I would expect a gradual expansion of democratic institutions and ideals. It is hard to believe that the instinct for political and intellectual freedom is limited to a happy few around the North Atlantic littoral.

Democracy in the twenty-first century must manage the pressures of race, of technology, and of capitalism, and it must cope with the spiritual frustrations and yearnings generated in the vast anonymity of global society. The great strength of democracy is its capacity for self-correction. Intelligent diagnosis and guidance are essential. "Perhaps no form of government," said the historian and diplomat Lord Bryce, "needs great leaders so much as democracy." Yet even the greatest of democratic leaders lack the talent to cajole violent, retrograde, and intractable humankind into utopia. Still, with the failures of democracy in the twentieth century at the back of their minds, leaders in the century to come may do a better job than we have done of making the world safe for democracy.

PART II

THE MIDDLE EAST AND THE WAR ON TERROR

ISSUE 4

U.S. UNILATERALISM AND IRAQ

June 1, 2002, was a happy day at the U.S. Military Academy. The senior class at West Point was graduating, and the president of the United States had come to join the celebration. As the corps applauded, President Bush humorously announced: "As Commander-in-Chief, I hereby grant amnesty to all cadets who are on restriction for minor conduct offenses." However, the President quickly moved to the main purpose of his speech: announcing a major change in U.S. defense strategy.

Throughout the forty-plus years of the Cold War, deterrence was the fundamental American strategy for defending itself and its Western European allies in the North Atlantic Treaty Organization (NATO). A Soviet attack against the West would be forcefully countered by the United States, possibly even with nuclear weapons. It was assumed that the Soviets would be rational and, therefore, not launch such an attack.

At West Point, President Bush argued that in an era of irrational terrorism deterrence is no longer an adequate strategy. He announced that, instead, the United States would take "preemptive action"—that is, strike first—when necessary. The clear implication was that the United States would do so unilaterally. That is, the world's only superpower would act alone if need be. (An excerpt from that speech is the first selection presented for Issue 4.)

Several months later, on September 12, 2002, the president addressed the General Assembly of the United Nations. In this speech (the second selection for Issue 4) he made it clear that the United States would apply this strategy against Iraq—acting alone in taking preemptive action—if the UN did not force Iraq to abide by previous UN resolutions and rid itself of weapons of mass destruction.

Shortly before President Bush spoke at the United Nations, the UN Secretary General, Kofi Annan, went before the General Assembly, pleading for a "multilateral" approach to solving international problems that involved the world community. (That speech is the third selection for Issue 4.) Later the United States did agree to work through the UN in attempting to disarm Iraq, while still claiming the right to act alone, preemptively, outside the UN framework.

DISCUSSION QUESTIONS

As you read the speeches by President Bush and UN Secretary-General Annan, consider the following questions:

1. To date, what has been the outcome of the American policy asserting the right to preemptive action against Iraq?
2. The UN Charter states that nations may act alone in using force only in self-defense. Is an American attack on Iraq justifiable as self-defense?
3. Do you believe that the strategy of deterrence is no longer relevant to world conditions?

KEY WEB SITES

For more information on this topic, visit the following Web sites:

Council on Foreign Relations (page on Iraq weapons issue)
http://www.cfr.org/background/background_iraq.php

Stockholm (Sweden) International Peace Research Institute (page on "Iraq and Arms Control: A SIPRI Archive")
http://editors.sipri.org/pubs/Iraq_AC.html

Center for Strategic and International Studies
http://www.csis.org

Addresses to West Point and the United Nations

President George W. Bush

Graduation Exercise of the U.S. Military Academy, West Point, New York
June 1, 2002

Thank you very much, General Lennox. Mr. Secretary, Governor Pataki, members of the U.S. Congress, Academy staff and faculty, distinguished guests, proud family members, and graduates: I want to thank you for your welcome. Laura and I are especially honored to visit this great institution in your bicentennial year.

In every corner of America, the words "West Point" command immediate respect. This place where the Hudson River bends is more than a fine institution of learning. The U.S. Military Academy is the guardian of values that have shaped the soldiers who have shaped the history of the world.

A few of you have followed in the path of the perfect West Point graduate, Robert E. Lee, who never received a single demerit in four years. Some of you followed in the path of the imperfect graduate, Ulysses S. Grant, who had his fair share of demerits, and said the happiest day of his life was "the day I left West Point." During my college years I guess you could say I was a Grant man.

You walk in the tradition of Eisenhower and MacArthur, Patton and Bradley—the commanders who saved a civilization. And you walk in the tradition of second lieutenants who did the same, by fighting and dying on distant battlefields.

Graduates of this academy have brought creativity and courage to every field of endeavor. West Point produced the chief engineer of the Panama Canal, the mind behind the Manhattan Project, the first American to walk in space. This fine institution gave us the man they say invented baseball, and other young men over the years who perfected the game of football.

You know this, but many in America don't—George C. Marshall, a VMI graduate, is said to have given this order: "I want an officer for a secret and dangerous mission. I want a West Point football player."

As you leave here today, I know there's one thing you'll never miss about this place: being a plebe. But even a plebe at West Point is made to feel he or she has some standing in the world. I'm told that plebes, when asked whom they outrank, are required to answer this: "Sir, the Superintendent's dog, the Commandant's cat, and all the admirals in the whole damn Navy." I probably won't be sharing that with the Secretary of the Navy.

West Point is guided by tradition, and in honor of the "Golden Children of the Corps," I will observe one of the traditions you cherish most. As the Commander-in-Chief, I hereby grant amnesty to all cadets who are on restriction for minor conduct offenses. Those of you in the end zone might have cheered a little early. Because, you see, I'm going to let General Lennox define exactly what "minor" means.

Every West Point class is commissioned to the Armed Forces. Some West Point classes are also commissioned by history, to take part in a great new calling for their country. Speaking here to the class of 1942—six months after Pearl Harbor—General Marshall said, "We're determined that before the sun sets on this terrible struggle, our flag will be recognized throughout the world as a symbol of freedom on the one hand, and of overwhelming power on the other."

Officers graduating that year helped fulfill that mission, defeating Japan and Germany, and then reconstructing those nations as allies. West Point graduates of the 1940s saw the rise of a deadly new challenge—the challenge of imperial communism—and opposed it from Korea to Berlin, to Vietnam, and in the Cold War, from beginning to end. And as the sun set on their struggle, many of those West Point officers lived to see a world transformed.

History has also issued its call to your generation. In your last year, America was attacked by a ruthless and resourceful enemy. You graduate from this Academy in a time of war, taking your place in an American military that is powerful and is honorable. Our war on terror is only begun, but in Afghanistan it was begun well.

I am proud of the men and women who have fought on my orders. America is profoundly grateful for all who serve the cause of freedom, and for all who have given their lives in its defense. This nation respects and trusts our military, and we are confident in your victories to come.

This war will take many turns we cannot predict. Yet I am certain of this: Wherever we carry it, the American flag will stand not only for our power, but for freedom. Our nation's cause has always been larger than our nation's defense. We fight, as we always fight, for a just peace—a peace that favors human liberty. We will defend the peace against threats from terrorists and tyrants. We will preserve the peace by building good relations among the great powers. And we will extend the peace by encouraging free and open societies on every continent.

Building this just peace is America's opportunity, and America's duty. From this day forward, it is your challenge, as well, and we will meet this challenge together. You will wear the uniform of a great and unique country. America has no empire to extend or utopia to establish. We wish for others only what we wish for ourselves—safety from violence, the rewards of liberty, and the hope for a better life.

In defending the peace, we face a threat with no precedent. Enemies in the past needed great armies and great industrial capabilities to endanger the American people and our nation. The attacks of September 11 required a few hundred thousand dollars in the hands of a few dozen evil and deluded men. All of the chaos and suffering they caused came at much less than the cost of a single tank. The dangers have not passed. This government and the American people are on watch, we are ready, because we know the terrorists have more money and more men and more plans.

The gravest danger to freedom lies at the perilous crossroads of radicalism and technology. When the spread of chemical and biological and nuclear weapons, along with ballistic missile technology—when that occurs, even weak states and small groups could attain a catastrophic power to strike great nations. Our enemies have declared this very intention, and have been caught seeking these terrible weapons. They want the capability to blackmail us, or to harm us, or to harm our friends—and we will oppose them with all our power.

For much of the past century, America's defense relied on the Cold War doctrines of deterrence and containment. In some cases, those strategies still apply. But new threats also require new thinking. Deterrence—the promise of massive retaliation against nations—means nothing against shadowy terrorist networks with no nation or citizens to defend. Containment is not possible when unbalanced dictators with weapons of mass destruction can deliver those weapons on missiles or secretly provide them to terrorist allies.

We cannot defend America and our friends by hoping for the best. We cannot put our faith in the word of tyrants, who solemnly sign nonproliferation treaties, and then systemically break them. If we wait for threats to fully materialize, we will have waited too long.

Homeland defense and missile defense are part of stronger security, and they're essential priorities for America. Yet the war on terror will not be won on the defensive. We must take the battle to the enemy, disrupt his plans, and confront the worst threats before they emerge. In the world we have entered, the only path to safety is the path of action. And this nation will act.

Our security will require the best intelligence, to reveal threats hidden in caves and growing in laboratories. Our security will require modernizing domestic agencies such as the FBI, so they're prepared to act, and act quickly, against danger. Our security will require transforming the military you will lead—a military that must be ready to strike at a moment's notice in any dark corner of the world. And our security will require all Americans to be forward-looking and resolute, to be ready for preemptive action when necessary to defend our liberty and to defend our lives.

The work ahead is difficult. The choices we will face are complex. We must uncover terror cells in sixty or more countries, using every tool of finance, intelligence, and law enforcement. Along with our friends and allies, we must oppose proliferation and confront regimes that sponsor terror, as each case requires. Some nations need military training to fight terror, and we'll provide it. Other nations oppose terror, but tolerate the hatred that leads to terror—and that must change. We will send diplomats where they are needed, and we will send you, our soldiers, where you're needed.

All nations that decide for aggression and terror will pay a price. We will not leave the safety of America and the peace of the planet at the mercy of a few mad terrorists and tyrants. We will lift this dark threat from our country and from the world.

Because the war on terror will require resolve and patience, it will also require firm moral purpose. In this way our struggle is similar to the Cold War. Now, as then, our enemies are totalitarians, holding a creed of power with no place for human dignity. Now, as then, they seek to impose a joyless conformity, to control every life and all of life.

America confronted imperial communism in many different ways—diplomatic, economic, and military. Yet moral clarity was essential to our victory in the Cold War. When leaders like John F. Kennedy and Ronald Reagan refused to gloss over the brutality of tyrants, they gave hope to prisoners and dissidents and exiles, and rallied free nations to a great cause.

Some worry that it is somehow undiplomatic or impolite to speak the language of right and wrong. I disagree. Different circumstances require different methods, but not different moralities. Moral truth is the same in every culture, in every time, and in every place. Targeting innocent civilians for murder is always and everywhere wrong. Brutality against women is always and everywhere wrong. There can be no neutrality between justice and cruelty, between the innocent and the guilty. We are in a conflict between good and evil, and America will call evil by its name. By confronting evil and lawless regimes, we do not create a problem, we reveal a problem. And we will lead the world in opposing it.

As we defend the peace, we also have an historic opportunity to preserve the peace. We have our best chance since the rise of the nation-state in the seventeenth century to build a world where the great powers compete in peace instead of prepare for war. The history of the past century, in particular, was dominated by a series of destructive national rivalries that left battlefields and graveyards across the Earth. Germany fought France, the Axis fought the Allies, and then the East fought the West, in proxy wars and tense standoffs, against a backdrop of nuclear Armageddon.

Competition between great nations is inevitable, but armed conflict in our world is not. More and more, civilized nations find ourselves on the same side—united by common dangers of terrorist violence and chaos. America has, and intends to keep, military strengths beyond challenge, thereby making the destabilizing arms races of other eras pointless, and limiting rivalries to trade and other pursuits of peace.

Today the great powers are also increasingly united by common values, instead of divided by conflicting ideologies. The United States, Japan and our Pacific friends, and now all of Europe, share a deep commitment to human freedom, embodied in strong alliances such as NATO. And the tide of liberty is rising in many other nations.

Generations of West Point officers planned and practiced for battles with Soviet Russia. I've just returned from a new Russia, now a country reaching toward democracy, and our partner in the war against terror. Even in China, leaders are discovering that economic freedom is the only lasting source of national wealth. In time, they will find that social and political freedom is the only true source of national greatness.

When the great powers share common values, we are better able to confront serious regional conflicts together, better able to cooperate in preventing the spread of violence or economic chaos. In the past, great power rivals took sides in difficult regional problems, making divisions deeper and more complicated. Today, from the Middle East to South Asia, we are gathering broad international coalitions to increase the pressure for peace. We must build strong and great power relations when times are good; to help manage crisis when times are bad. America needs partners to preserve the peace, and we will work with every nation that shares this noble goal.

And finally, America stands for more than the absence of war. We have a great opportunity to extend a just peace, by replacing poverty, repression, and resentment around the world with hope of a better day. Through most of history, poverty was persistent, inescapable, and almost universal. In the last few decades, we've seen nations from Chile to South Korea build modern economies and freer societies, lifting millions of people out of despair and want. And there's no mystery to this achievement.

The twentieth century ended with a single surviving model of human progress, based on nonnegotiable demands of human dignity, the rule of law, limits on the power of the state, respect for women and private property and free speech and equal justice and religious tolerance. America cannot impose this vision—yet we can support and reward governments that make the right choices for their own people. In our development aid, in our diplomatic efforts, in our international broadcasting, and in our educational assistance, the United States will promote moderation and tolerance and human rights. And we will defend the peace that makes all progress possible.

When it comes to the common rights and needs of men and women, there is no clash of civilizations. The requirements of freedom apply fully to Africa and Latin America and the entire Islamic world. The peoples of the Islamic nations want and deserve the same freedoms and opportunities as people in every nation. And their governments should listen to their hopes.

A truly strong nation will permit legal avenues of dissent for all groups that pursue their aspirations without violence. An advancing nation will pursue economic reform, to unleash the great entrepreneurial energy of its people. A thriving nation will respect the rights of women, because no society can prosper while denying opportunity to half its citizens. Mothers and fathers and children across the Islamic world, and all the world, share the same fears and aspirations. In poverty, they struggle. In tyranny, they suffer. And as we saw in Afghanistan, in liberation they celebrate.

America has a greater objective than controlling threats and containing resentment. We will work for a just and peaceful world beyond the war on terror.

The bicentennial class of West Point now enters this drama. With all in the U.S. Army, you will stand between your fellow citizens and grave danger. You will help establish a peace that allows millions around the world to live in liberty and to grow in prosperity. You will face times of calm, and times of crisis. And every test will find you prepared—because you're the men and women of West Point. You leave here marked by the character of this Academy, carrying with you the highest ideals of our nation.

Toward the end of his life, Dwight Eisenhower recalled the first day he stood on the plain at West Point. "The feeling came over me," he said, "that the expression 'the United States of America' would now and henceforth mean something different than it had ever before. From here on, it would be the nation I would be serving, not myself."

Today, your last day at West Point, you begin a life of service in a career unlike any other. You've answered a calling to hardship and purpose, to risk and honor. At the end of every day you will know that you have faithfully done your duty. May you always bring to that duty the high standards of this great American institution. May you always be worthy of the long gray line that stretches two centuries behind you.

On behalf of the nation, I congratulate each one of you for the commission you've earned and for the credit you bring to the United States of America. May God bless you all.

United Nations General Assembly, New York
September 12, 2002

Mr. Secretary General, Mr. President, distinguished delegates, and ladies and gentlemen: We meet one year and one day after a terrorist attack brought grief to my country, and brought grief to many citizens of our world. Yesterday, we remembered the innocent lives taken that terrible morning. Today, we turn to the urgent duty of protecting other lives, without illusion and without fear.

We've accomplished much in the last year—in Afghanistan and beyond. We have much yet to do—in Afghanistan and beyond. Many nations represented here have joined in the fight against global terror, and the people of the United States are grateful.

The United Nations was born in the hope that survived a world war—the hope of a world moving toward justice, escaping old patterns of conflict and fear. The founding members resolved that the peace of the world must never again be destroyed by the will and wickedness of any man. We created the United Nations Security Council, so that, unlike the League of Nations, our deliberations would be more than talk, our resolutions would be more than wishes. After generations of deceitful dictators and broken treaties and squandered lives, we dedicated ourselves to standards of human dignity shared by all, and to a system of security defended by all.

Today, these standards, and this security, are challenged. Our commitment to human dignity is challenged by persistent poverty and raging disease. The suffering is great, and our responsibilities are clear. The United States is joining with the world to supply aid where it reaches people and lifts up lives, to extend trade and the prosperity it brings, and to bring medical care where it is desperately needed.

As a symbol of our commitment to human dignity, the United States will return to UNESCO. This organization has been reformed and America will participate fully in its mission to advance human rights and tolerance and learning.

Our common security is challenged by regional conflicts—ethnic and religious strife that is ancient, but not inevitable. In the Middle East, there can be no peace for either side without freedom for both sides. America stands committed to an independent and democratic Palestine, living side by side with Israel in peace and security. Like all other people, Palestinians deserve a government that serves their interests and listens to their voices. My nation will continue to encourage all parties to step up to their responsibilities as we seek a just and comprehensive settlement to the conflict.

Above all, our principles and our security are challenged today by outlaw groups and regimes that accept no law of morality and have no limit to their violent ambitions. In the attacks on America a year ago, we saw the destructive intentions of our enemies. This threat hides within many nations, including my own. In cells and camps, terrorists are plotting further destruction, and building new bases for their war against civilization. And our greatest fear is that terrorists will find a shortcut to their mad ambitions when an outlaw regime supplies them with the technologies to kill on a massive scale.

In one place—in one regime—we find all these dangers, in their most lethal and aggressive forms, exactly the kind of aggressive threat the United Nations was born to confront.

Twelve years ago, Iraq invaded Kuwait without provocation. And the regime's forces were poised to continue their march to seize other countries and their resources. Had Saddam Hussein been appeased instead of stopped, he would have endangered the peace and stability of the world. Yet this aggression was stopped—by the might of coalition forces and the will of the United Nations.

To suspend hostilities, to spare himself, Iraq's dictator accepted a series of commitments. The terms were clear, to him and to all. And he agreed to prove he is complying with every one of those obligations.

He has proven instead only his contempt for the United Nations, and for all his pledges. By breaking every pledge—by his deceptions, and by his cruelties—Saddam Hussein has made the case against himself.

In 1991, Security Council Resolution 688 demanded that the Iraqi regime cease at once the repression of its own people, including the systematic repression of minorities—which, the Council said, threatened international peace and security in the region. This demand goes ignored.

Last year, the UN Commission on Human Rights found that Iraq continues to commit extremely grave violations of human rights, and that the regime's repression is all pervasive. Tens of thousands of political opponents and ordinary citizens have been subjected to arbitrary arrest and imprisonment, summary execution, and torture by beating and burning, electric shock, starvation, mutilation, and rape. Wives are tortured in front of their husbands, children in the presence of their parents—and all of these horrors concealed from the world by the apparatus of a totalitarian state.

In 1991, the UN Security Council, through Resolutions 686 and 687, demanded that Iraq return all prisoners from Kuwait and other lands. Iraq's regime agreed. It broke its promise. Last year the Secretary General's high-level coordinator for this issue reported that Kuwaiti, Saudi, Indian, Syrian, Lebanese, Iranian, Egyptian, Bahraini, and Omani nationals remain unaccounted for—more than 600 people. One American pilot is among them.

In 1991, the UN Security Council, through Resolution 687, demanded that Iraq renounce all involvement with terrorism, and permit no terrorist organizations to operate in Iraq. Iraq's regime agreed. It broke this promise. In violation of Security Council Resolution 1373, Iraq continues to shelter and support terrorist organizations that direct violence against Iran, Israel, and Western governments. Iraqi dissidents abroad are targeted for murder. In 1993, Iraq attempted to assassinate the emir of Kuwait and a former American president. Iraq's government openly praised the attacks of September 11. And al Qaeda terrorists escaped from Afghanistan and are known to be in Iraq.

In 1991, the Iraqi regime agreed to destroy and stop developing all weapons of mass destruction and long-range missiles, and to prove to the world it has done so by complying with rigorous inspections. Iraq has broken every aspect of this fundamental pledge.

From 1991 to 1995, the Iraqi regime said it had no biological weapons. After a senior official in its weapons program defected and exposed this lie, the regime admitted to producing tens of thousands of liters of anthrax and other deadly biological agents for use with Scud warheads, aerial bombs, and aircraft spray tanks. UN inspectors believe Iraq has produced two to four times the amount of biological agents it declared, and has failed to account for more than three metric tons of material that could be used to produce biological weapons. Right now, Iraq is expanding and improving facilities that were used for the production of biological weapons.

United Nations' inspections also revealed that Iraq likely maintains stockpiles of VX, mustard, and other chemical agents, and that the regime is rebuilding and expanding facilities capable of producing chemical weapons.

And in 1995, after four years of deception, Iraq finally admitted it had a crash nuclear weapons program prior to the Gulf War. We know now, were it not for that war, the regime in Iraq would likely have possessed a nuclear weapon no later than 1993.

Today, Iraq continues to withhold important information about its nuclear program—weapons design, procurement logs, experiment data, an accounting of nuclear materials and documentation of foreign assistance. Iraq employs capable nuclear scientists and technicians. It retains physical infrastructure needed to build a nuclear weapon. Iraq has made several attempts to buy high-strength aluminum tubes used to enrich uranium for a nuclear weapon. Should Iraq acquire fissile material, it would be able to build a nuclear weapon within a year. And Iraq's state-controlled media has reported numerous meetings between Saddam Hussein and his nuclear scientists, leaving little doubt about his continued appetite for these weapons.

Iraq also possesses a force of Scud-type missiles with ranges beyond the 150 kilometers permitted by the UN. Work at testing and production facilities shows that Iraq is building more long-range missiles that can inflict mass death throughout the region.

In 1990, after Iraq's invasion of Kuwait, the world imposed economic sanctions on Iraq. Those sanctions were maintained after the war to compel the regime's compliance with Security Council resolutions. In time, Iraq was allowed to use oil revenues to buy food. Saddam Hussein has subverted this program, working around the sanctions to buy missile technology and military materials. He blames the suffering of Iraq's people on the United Nations, even as he uses his oil wealth to build lavish palaces for himself, and to buy arms for his country. By refusing to comply with his own agreements, he bears full guilt for the hunger and misery of innocent Iraqi citizens.

In 1991, Iraq promised UN inspectors immediate and unrestricted access to verify Iraq's commitment to rid itself of weapons of mass destruction and long-range missiles. Iraq broke this promise, spending seven years deceiving, evading, and harassing UN inspectors before ceasing cooperation entirely. Just months after the 1991 cease-fire, the Security Council twice renewed its demand that the Iraqi regime cooperate fully with inspectors, condemning Iraq's serious violations of its obligations. The Security Council again renewed that demand in 1994, and twice more in 1996, deploring Iraq's clear violations of its obligations. The Security Council renewed its demand three more times in 1997, citing flagrant violations; and three more times in 1998, calling Iraq's behavior totally unacceptable. And in 1999, the demand was renewed yet again.

As we meet today, it's been almost four years since the last UN inspectors set foot in Iraq, four years for the Iraqi regime to plan, and to build, and to test behind the cloak of secrecy.

We know that Saddam Hussein pursued weapons of mass murder even when inspectors were in his country. Are we to assume that he stopped when they left? The history, the logic, and the facts lead to one conclusion: Saddam

Hussein's regime is a grave and gathering danger. To suggest otherwise is to hope against the evidence. To assume this regime's good faith is to bet the lives of millions and the peace of the world in a reckless gamble. And this is a risk we must not take.

Delegates to the General Assembly, we have been more than patient. We've tried sanctions. We've tried the carrot of oil for food, and the stick of coalition military strikes. But Saddam Hussein has defied all these efforts and continues to develop weapons of mass destruction. The first time we may be completely certain he has a nuclear weapon is when, God forbid, he uses one. We owe it to all our citizens to do everything in our power to prevent that day from coming.

The conduct of the Iraqi regime is a threat to the authority of the United Nations, and a threat to peace. Iraq has answered a decade of UN demands with a decade of defiance. All the world now faces a test, and the United Nations a difficult and defining moment. Are Security Council resolutions to be honored and enforced, or cast aside without consequence? Will the United Nations serve the purpose of its founding, or will it be irrelevant?

The United States helped found the United Nations. We want the United Nations to be effective, and respectful, and successful. We want the resolutions of the world's most important multilateral body to be enforced. And right now those resolutions are being unilaterally subverted by the Iraqi regime. Our partnership of nations can meet the test before us, by making clear what we now expect of the Iraqi regime.

If the Iraqi regime wishes peace, it will immediately and unconditionally forswear, disclose, and remove or destroy all weapons of mass destruction, long-range missiles, and all related material.

If the Iraqi regime wishes peace, it will immediately end all support for terrorism and act to suppress it, as all states are required to do by UN Security Council resolutions.

If the Iraqi regime wishes peace, it will cease persecution of its civilian population, including Shi'a, Sunnis, Kurds, Turkomans, and others, again as required by Security Council resolutions.

If the Iraqi regime wishes peace, it will release or account for all Gulf War personnel whose fate is still unknown. It will return the remains of any who are deceased, return stolen property, accept liability for losses resulting from the invasion of Kuwait, and fully cooperate with international efforts to resolve these issues, as required by Security Council resolutions.

If the Iraqi regime wishes peace, it will immediately end all illicit trade outside the oil-for-food program. It will accept UN administration of funds from that program, to ensure that the money is used fairly and promptly for the benefit of the Iraqi people.

If all these steps are taken, it will signal a new openness and accountability in Iraq. And it could open the prospect of the United Nations helping to build a government that represents all Iraqis—a government based on respect for human rights, economic liberty, and internationally supervised elections.

The United States has no quarrel with the Iraqi people; they've suffered too long in silent captivity. Liberty for the Iraqi people is a great moral cause, and a great strategic goal. The people of Iraq deserve it; the security of all nations requires it. Free societies do not intimidate through cruelty and conquest, and open societies do not threaten the world with mass murder. The United States supports political and economic liberty in a unified Iraq.

We can harbor no illusions—and that's important today to remember. Saddam Hussein attacked Iran in 1980 and Kuwait in 1990. He's fired ballistic missiles at Iran and Saudi Arabia, Bahrain, and Israel. His regime once ordered the killing of every person between the ages of fifteen and seventy in certain Kurdish villages in northern Iraq. He has gassed many Iranians, and forty Iraqi villages.

My nation will work with the UN Security Council to meet our common challenge. If Iraq's regime defies us again, the world must move deliberately, decisively to hold Iraq to account. We will work with the UN Security Council for the necessary resolutions. But the purposes of the United States should not be doubted. The Security Council resolutions will be enforced—the just demands of peace and security will be met—or action will be unavoidable. And a regime that has lost its legitimacy will also lose its power.

Events can turn in one of two ways: If we fail to act in the face of danger, the people of Iraq will continue to live in brutal submission. The regime will have new power to bully and dominate and conquer its neighbors, condemning the Middle East to more years of bloodshed and fear. The regime will remain unstable—the region will remain unstable, with little hope of freedom, and isolated from the progress of our times. With every step the Iraqi regime takes toward gaining and deploying the most terrible weapons, our own options to confront that regime will narrow. And if an emboldened regime were to supply these weapons to terrorist allies, then the attacks of September 11 would be a prelude to far greater horrors.

If we meet our responsibilities, if we overcome this danger, we can arrive at a very different future. The people of Iraq can shake off their captivity. They can one day join a democratic Afghanistan and a democratic Palestine, inspiring reforms throughout the Muslim world. These nations can show by their example that honest government, and respect for women, and the great Islamic tradition of learning can triumph in the Middle East and beyond. And we will show that the promise of the United Nations can be fulfilled in our time.

Neither of these outcomes is certain. Both have been set before us. We must choose between a world of fear and a world of progress. We cannot stand by and do nothing while dangers gather. We must stand up for our security, and for the permanent rights and the hopes of mankind. By heritage and by choice, the United States of America will make that stand. And, delegates to the United Nations, you have the power to make that stand, as well.

Thank you very much.

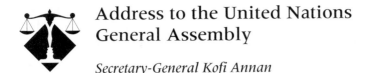

Address to the United Nations General Assembly

Secretary-General Kofi Annan

United Nations, New York
September 12, 2002

Mr. President, Distinguished Heads of State and Government, Excellencies, Ladies and Gentlemen: We cannot begin today without reflecting on yesterday's anniversary—on the criminal challenge so brutally thrown in our faces on 11 September 2001.

The terrorist attacks of that day were not an isolated event. They were an extreme example of a global scourge, which requires a broad, sustained, and global response.

Broad, because terrorism can be defeated only if all nations unite against it.

Sustained, because the battle against terrorism will not be won easily, or overnight. It requires patience and persistence.

And *global*, because terrorism is a widespread and complex phenomenon, with many deep roots and exacerbating factors.

Mr. President, I believe that such a response can only succeed if we make full use of *multilateral* institutions.

I stand before you today as a multilateralist—by precedent, by principle, by Charter and by duty.

I also believe that every government that is committed to the rule of law at home, must be committed also to the rule of law *abroad*. All States have a clear *interest*, as well as a clear *responsibility*, to uphold international law and maintain international order.

Our founding fathers, the statesmen of 1945, had learnt that lesson from the bitter experience of two world wars and a great depression.

They recognised that international security is not a zero-sum game. Peace, security, and freedom are not finite commodities—like land, oil, or gold—which one State can acquire at another's expense. On the contrary, the more peace, security, and freedom any one State has, the more its neighbours are likely to have.

And they recognised that, by agreeing to exercise sovereignty *together*, they could gain a hold over problems that would defeat any one of them acting separately.

If those lessons were clear in 1945, should they not be much more so today, in the age of globalisation?

On almost no item on our agenda does anyone seriously contend that each nation, or any nation, can fend for itself. Even the most powerful countries know that they need to work with others, in multilateral institutions, to achieve their aims.

Only by multilateral action can we ensure that open markets offer benefits and opportunities to all.

Only by multilateral action can we give people in the least developed countries the chance to escape the ugly misery of poverty, ignorance, and disease.

Only by multilateral action can we protect ourselves from acid rain, or global warming; from the spread of HIV/AIDS, the illicit trade in drugs, or the odious traffic in human beings.

That applies even more to the prevention of *terrorism*. Individual States may defend themselves, by striking back at terrorist groups and the countries that harbour or support them. But only concerted vigilance and cooperation among *all* States, with constant, systematic exchange of information, offers any real hope of denying terrorists their opportunities.

On all these matters, for any one State—large or small—choosing to follow or reject the multilateral path must not be a simple matter of political convenience. It has consequences far beyond the immediate context.

When countries work together in multilateral institutions—developing, respecting, and when necessary, enforcing international law—they also develop mutual *trust*, and more effective cooperation on other issues.

The more a country makes use of multilateral institutions—thereby respecting shared values, and accepting the obligations and restraints inherent in those values—the more others will trust and respect it, and the stronger its chance to exercise true *leadership*.

And among multilateral institutions, *this universal Organisation* has a special place.

Any State, if attacked, retains the inherent right of self-defence under Article 51 of the Charter. But beyond that, when States decide to use force to deal with broader threats to international peace and security, there is no substitute for the unique legitimacy provided by the United Nations.

Member States attach fundamental importance to such legitimacy and to the international rule of law. They have shown—notably in the action to liberate Kuwait, twelve years ago—that they are willing to take actions under the authority of the Security Council, which they would *not* be willing to take without it.

The existence of an *effective* international security system depends on the Council's authority—and therefore on the Council having the political will to act, even in the most difficult cases, when agreement seems elusive at the outset. The primary criterion for putting an issue on the Council's agenda should not be the receptiveness of the parties, but the existence of a grave threat to world peace.

Mr. President, let me now turn to four current threats to world peace, where true leadership and effective action are badly needed.

First, the Israeli–Palestinian conflict. Many of us have recently been struggling to reconcile Israel's legitimate security concerns with Palestinian humanitarian needs.

But these limited objectives cannot be achieved in isolation from the wider political context. We must return to the search for a just and *comprehensive* solution, which alone can bring security and prosperity to both peoples, and indeed to the whole region.

The ultimate shape of a Middle East peace settlement is well known. It was defined long ago in Security Council Resolutions 242 and 338, and its Israeli–Palestinian components were spelt out even more clearly in Resolution 1397: land for peace; an end to terror and to occupation; two States, Israel and Palestine, living side by side within secure and recognized borders.

Both parties accept this vision. But we can reach it only if we move rapidly and in parallel on *all* fronts. The so-called "sequential" approach has failed.

As we agreed at the Quartet meeting in Washington last May, an international peace conference is needed without delay, to set out a road map of parallel steps: steps to strengthen Israel's security, steps to strengthen Palestinian economic and political institutions, and steps to settle the details of the final peace agreement. Meanwhile, humanitarian steps to relieve Palestinian suffering must be intensified. The need is urgent.

Second, the leadership of *Iraq* continues to defy mandatory resolutions adopted by the Security Council under Chapter VII of the Charter.

I have engaged Iraq in an in-depth discussion on a range of issues, including the need for arms inspectors to return, in accordance with the relevant Security Council Resolutions.

Efforts to obtain Iraq's compliance with the Council's resolutions must continue. I appeal to all who have influence with Iraq's leaders to impress on them the vital importance of accepting the weapons inspections. This is the indispensable first step toward assuring the world that all Iraq's weapons of mass destruction have indeed been eliminated, and—let me stress—toward the suspension and eventual ending of the sanctions that are causing so many hardships for the Iraqi people.

I urge Iraq to comply with its obligations—for the sake of its own people, and for the sake of world order. If Iraq's defiance continues, the Security Council must face its responsibilities.

Third, permit me to press all of you, as leaders of the international community, to maintain your commitment to *Afghanistan*.

I know I speak for all in welcoming President Karzai to this Assembly, and congratulating him on his escape from last week's vicious assassination attempt—a graphic reminder of how hard it is to uproot the remnants of terrorism in any country where it has taken root. It was the international community's shameful neglect of Afghanistan in the 1990s that allowed that country to slide into chaos, providing a fertile breeding ground for Al-Qaeda.

Today, Afghanistan urgently needs help in two areas. The government must be helped to extend its authority throughout the country. Without this, all else may fail. And donors must follow through on their commitments to help with rehabilitation, reconstruction, and development. Otherwise the Afghan people will lose hope—and desperation, we know, breeds violence.

Fourth, and finally, in *South Asia* the world has recently come closer than for many years past to a direct conflict between two nuclear weapon capable countries. The situation may now have calmed a little, but it remains perilous. The underlying causes must be addressed. If a fresh crisis erupts, the international community might have a role to play; though I gladly acknowledge—indeed, strongly welcome—the efforts made by well-placed Member States to help the two leaders find a solution.

Excellencies, let me conclude by reminding you of your pledge two years ago, at the Millennium Summit, "to make the United Nations a more effective instrument" in the service of the world's peoples.

Today I ask all of you to honour that pledge.

Let us all recognise, from now on—in each of our capitals, in every nation, large and small—that the global interest *is* our national interest.

Thank you very much.

ISSUE 5

GLOBAL ACTIVISM

Should the United States, the world's sole remaining superpower, intervene militarily in disputes abroad? This question is especially pertinent in view of American-led intervention by NATO (the North Atlantic Treaty Organization) air forces in the conflict in Serbia. Haunting pictures of forlorn Kosovo refugees, who were driven from their homes into neighboring countries, captured the world's attention. The NATO campaign of air bombardment was aimed at punishing the Serbs and stopping their policy of "ethnic cleansing" of Muslims from Kosovo. From a longer-term perspective, this conflict was yet another expression of long-standing animosity between the dominant Christian Orthodox Serbs and the Islamic Kosovars of Albanian descent.

If the Serb–Kosovar conflict is deeply rooted in history, so is the inclination of the United States to intervene in such disputes. The latter point is clear in the first selection for Issue 5, by former State Department official Robert Kagan. As Kagan notes, although Americans often have expressed considerable reticence to become embroiled in foreign disputes, in the end the United States has usually intervened out of necessity.

Kagan supports a policy of intervention, even in relatively minor disputes, arguing that "the way one handles the small threats is likely to determine the way one handles the larger threats." Moreover, he contends that "once appeasing adversaries and wishing away problems becomes a habit, it becomes a hard habit to break." In essence, Kagan takes the psychological concept of habitual learning—a characteristic of individuals—and applies it to a nation, the United States.

The second selection for Issue 5 is a speech by Justin Raimondo, editorial director of the Web site <Antiwar.com>. Raimondo's polemical exposition posits a scenario in which the intervention–isolation controversy is waged by two adversaries, a war party and a peace party. Raimondo clearly conceptualizes the issues in a manner very different from that of Kagan.

DISCUSSION QUESTIONS

As you read the article by Kagan and the speech by Raimondo, consider the following questions:

1. Whose conceptualization of the intervention–isolation controversy is more accurate, Kagan's or Raimondo's?
2. In this post–Cold War world, under what circumstances should the United States intervene militarily in other countries? Should critical American national interests always be at stake? Suppose, for example, the goal is to feed starving people in an area where the United States has no national interests. Can military intervention be justified then?
3. Suppose that Russia were still a strong superpower. Would the United States be as likely to intervene abroad as it has in recent years? Why or why not?

KEY WEB SITES

For more information on this topic, visit the following Web sites:

Weatherhead Center for International Affairs at Harvard University
http://www.wcfia.harvard.edu

The Center for Strategic and International Studies in Washington
http://www.csis.org

Sweden's Stockholm International Peace Research Institute
http://www.sipri.se

The Case for Global Activism

Robert Kagan

Future historians will record—perhaps in astonishment—that the demise of the Soviet Union ushered in an era of American worldwide engagement and armed intervention unprecedented in scope and frequency. Despite a widespread conviction that, in a post–Cold War world, the American role would diminish, in a brief four years the United States has: launched a massive counteroffensive against the world's fourth largest army in the Middle East; invaded, occupied, and supervised elections in a Latin American country; intervened with force to provide food to starving peoples in Africa; and conducted punitive bombing raids in the Balkans.

Nor is this all. The United States has sent troops on another humanitarian mission in Africa, and volunteered troops to serve as peacekeeping forces in the Middle East and in the former Yugoslavia. It has worked in the UN Security Council to enact punitive sanctions against at least a half-dozen international scofflaws. It has seriously considered extending military protection to several important nations of Eastern Europe that have never before been part of an alliance with the United States. And it has interceded in disputes among the former republics of the Soviet Union.

How is this increased activity to be explained? The answer is rather easily found in the new relations of power in the post–Cold War world. The fall of the Soviet Union removed restraints on foreign leaders unhappy with the order imposed by the Cold War and unleashed new struggles for power in areas hitherto under the former superpower's thumb. Some would-be challengers of the old order were encouraged by the belief that the United States would not step in. The United States, however, itself freed from the restraints of the Cold War, began to fill the gap left by the absence of Soviet global power and continued a historical tradition of using its influence to promote a world order consistent with its material needs and philosophical predilections.

But if the course America has followed has been natural enough, to many American strategists, policymakers, and politicians it seems also to have been unexpected—and unwelcome. Today, a scant two years after the intervention in Somalia, three years after the Gulf War, and four years since the invasion

Robert Kagan, who served in the State Department from 1984 to 1988, is the author of *Of Paradise and Power: America and Europe in the New World Order*.

This article is from *Commentary* 98, no. 3 (September 1994). Reprinted by permission of Robert Kagan.

of Panama, foreign-policy theorists continue to write of the need for a "global retrenchment" of American power. Before and after each venture abroad, they have argued that such high levels of American engagement cannot be sustained, politically or economically, and that a failure to be more selective in the application of American power will either bankrupt the country or drive the American public further toward the isolationism into which, they warn, it is already beginning to slip.

This political judgment has found intellectual buttressing in the so-called "realist" approach to foreign policy, which asserts that the United States should limit itself to defending its "core" national interests and abandon costly and unpopular efforts to solve the many problems on the "periphery." During the Cold War, realists fought against efforts by presidents from Truman to Kennedy to Reagan to equate American interests with the advancement of a democratic world order. In the post–Cold War era, they have gained new prominence by again recommending a retreat from such ambitions and the definition of a far more limited set of foreign-policy goals.

Yet the realist view remains inadequate, both as a description, precisely, of reality—of the way the world really works—and as a recommendation for defending America's interests, either on the "periphery" or at the "core." When Americans have exercised their power in pursuit of a broad definition of interests—in pursuit, that is, of a more decent world order—they have succeeded in defending their "vital" interests as well. When they have sought to evade the dangers of global involvement, they have found themselves unexpectedly in a fight for national survival.

Throughout this century, the United States has faced the problem of its expanding power—and has responded with ambivalence. Americans are perhaps more suspicious of power than most people on earth, but just like others they have nonetheless sought it, guarded it, and enjoyed its benefits. As products of a modern, nonmartial republic, Americans have always tended to cherish the lives of their young more than the glories to be won on the battlefield; yet they have sacrificed their young for the sake of honor, interest, and principle as frequently as any nation in the world over the past 200 years. Again, as the products of a revolution against an imperial master, Americans have always abhorred imperialism; yet where their power was preponderant, they have assumed hegemony and have been unwilling to relinquish it.

The common view of American foreign policy as endlessly vacillating between isolationism and interventionism is wrong: Americans in this century have never ceased expanding their sphere of interests across the globe, but they have tried to evade the responsibility of defending those interests, until they had no choice but to fight a war for which they were unprepared. The American conception of interest, moreover, has always gone beyond narrow security concerns to include the promotion of a world order consistent with American economic, political, and ideological aspirations.

It was Theodore Roosevelt, paradoxically a president admired by realists for his shrewd understanding of power politics, who first grafted principled ends to the exercise of power. Roosevelt insisted that it was America's duty to "assume an attitude of protection and regulation in regard to all these little states" in the Western hemisphere, to help them acquire the "capacity for self-government," to assist their progress "up out of the discord and turmoil of continual revolution into a general public sense of justice and determination to maintain order."

For Roosevelt, American stewardship in the Western hemisphere was more than a defensive response to European meddling there; it was proof that the United States had arrived as a world power, with responsibilities to shape a decent order in its own region. When Woodrow Wilson, the quintessential "utopian" president, took office later, his policies in the hemisphere were little more than a variation on Roosevelt's theme.

The same mix of motives followed the United States as it reached out into the wider world, especially Europe and Asia. Growing power expanded American interests, but also expanded the risks of protecting them against the ambitions of others. After the 1880s, America's navy grew from a size comparable to Chile's to become one of the three great navies of the world. That increase in power alone made America a potential arbiter of overseas conflicts in a way it had never been in the eighteenth and nineteenth centuries. Greater power meant that if a general European war broke out, the United States would no longer have to sit back and accept dictation of its trade routes. It also meant, however, that the United States could not sit back without accepting a diminished role in world affairs.

Nor could Americans escape choosing sides. Although German and Irish Americans disagreed, most Americans in the 1910s preferred the British-run world order with which they were familiar to a prospective German one. Wilson's pro-British neutrality made conflict with Germany almost inevitable, and America's new great-power status made it equally inevitable that when the German challenge came, the United States would not back down.

It was the growth of American power, not Wilsonian idealism and not national interest narrowly conceived, that led the United States into its first European war. A weak nineteenth-century America could not have conceived of intervening in Europe; a strong twentieth-century America, because it could intervene, found that it had an interest in doing so.

After World War I, Americans recoiled from the new responsibilities and dangers which their power had brought. But they did not really abandon their new, broader conception of the national interest. Throughout the "isolationist" years, the United States still sought, however half-heartedly and ineffectually, to preserve its expanded influence and the world order it had fought for.

Although they refused to assume military obligations, presidents from Harding to Franklin Roosevelt tried to maintain balance and order in Europe and in Asia through economic and political agreements. In Central America and the Caribbean, the Republican presidents found themselves endlessly intervening, occupying, and supervising elections only so that they might eventually withdraw. (Only FDR decided that the best way to be a "good neighbor" in the hemisphere was to allow dictatorship to flourish.)

Americans, then, did not shun international involvement in the interwar years. Rather, they tried to enjoy the benefits of such involvement while hoping to avoid its inevitable costs. They resisted Japanese attempts to swallow China, but they did not believe the national interest required them to fight in Asia. They were unwilling to see France and England defeated by an increasingly dangerous Germany, but they did not see an interest in risking American lives in Europe. Through arms control and the theoretical banning of war, the United States sought ever more utopian mechanisms for pursuing its interests without risk. In the end, of course, this refusal to acknowledge the need to defend its expanded interests helped make war inevitable. Americans allowed the world order to collapse only to realize that this was a result they could not afford.

But if World War II marked the destruction of the old world order, it also extended the reach of American power beyond Theodore Roosevelt's capacity to imagine. And it offered American leaders another chance to confront the new responsibilities which the expansion of power had created.

We often forget that the plan for world order devised by American leaders in the last years of the war was not intended to contain the Soviet Union. Their purpose was to build a more stable international system than that which had exploded in 1939. They hoped that the new system, embodied in the United Nations, would eventually become a self-regulating mechanism, protecting American interests without requiring the constant exercise of American power. But they also understood that American power had become the keystone in the arch of any world order.

The threat to the new system which soon emerged in the form of the Soviet Union quickly changed Americans' sense of what the United States was trying to accomplish. The original goal of promoting and defending a decent world order became conflated with the goal of meeting the challenge of Soviet power—and in the minds of many people it remains so to this day.

Thus, all the policies that the United States would have continued to pursue without the existence of a Soviet Union—seeking a stable international economic system, exercising dominant influence in the Western hemisphere, insisting on an ever-increasing role in Europe, Asia, and the Middle East, demanding adherence to international agreements, preferring dictatorship to disorder but also preferring democracy to dictatorship—became associated with the strategy of containment. This had the effect, unfortunate in retrospect, of obscuring the essential continuities in American foreign policy since the beginning of the century.

The fact is that America was simultaneously pursuing two goals during the Cold War—promotion of a world order and defense against the biggest threat to it. Characteristically, each of them was beset by ambivalence. There is a common presumption today that the choices of that era were somehow easier, that there was a broad consensus about at least a few basic certainties. Nostalgia for these alleged "certainties" obscures from memory the long, bitter debates over the proper definition of American interests during the Cold War. But it is worth remembering that even the now-hallowed doctrine of containment was denounced as dangerous and impossibly ambitious by clearheaded "realists" of the time. (Walter Lippmann, for example, called containment a "strategic monstrosity" because it seemed to require an American response to every conceivable Soviet thrust anywhere in the world.)

There were, as it happens, few certainties in the Cold War. The gray areas in which the hardest decisions had to be made were much like the gray areas of today. The two major American wars of that era were fought in regions and involved conflicts—Korea and Vietnam—where the direct interests of the United States were at least debatable. Throughout the Cold War, indeed, fighting took place almost entirely on the "periphery," and was often conducted in the name of universal ideals that transcended the strategic importance of the plot of ground being contested.

The end of the Cold War has required the United States once again to face the old dilemmas. As in the aftermath of World War II, the areas of the world where America exerts influence have expanded, not contracted. So, too, have the burdens of promoting and sustaining a world order that serves American material and spiritual needs.

The demise of the Soviet Union has not eliminated the threat to that order; it has only changed its form. Instead of arising from a single, large adversary, the threat has devolved into a large number of smaller but collectively serious challenges. As in the past, many experts have come forward to argue that resources are lacking for a globally active policy designed to meet those challenges, that the American public would be unwilling to support it, and even that American power is declining.

The evidence does not support these claims.

The percentage of the American economy devoted to military spending has dropped to the small digits. This is too low to allow the United States to carry out the many new tasks it will face in the post–Cold War era, but the increases that will be necessary will hardly bankrupt the country.

Nor is the assumption warranted that the American public does not support the overseas commitments and interventions undertaken in these past four years, or opposes further commitments today. Americans have rarely been enthusiastic about extensive overseas involvements, but the public has clearly been more willing to support them in the 1990s than it was in the '70s and '80s, as is demonstrated by the popularity of successful actions in such places as the Persian Gulf and Panama. Even in Bosnia and Somalia, ordinary

Americans have complained not about action, but about confused and half-hearted policies and weak and incompetent execution.

We have also learned that the use of force need not be tied to unmistakable and narrowly defined security interests in order to win public support. A Latin American dictator cancels elections and helps Colombian drug dealers sell cocaine; a Middle Eastern despot invades a tiny neighboring country in order to control its oil wells; an African country dissolves into civil war and chaos, and famine threatens millions with starvation; one ethnic group tries to drive another ethnic group off its land and commits atrocities; an unfriendly Asian power develops nuclear weapons in violation of international agreements. Among these various events, only the Iraqi invasion of Kuwait qualified as a direct threat to American economic interests. In general, the issues that have invited an American response—aggression, political illegitimacy, genocide, mass starvation, nuclear proliferation, violations of international agreements—are all matters that fall under the general heading of threats to the kind of world order Americans value.

Can we sustain a policy of active response? Henry Kissinger has recently argued that, contrary to appearances, American power is actually in decline relative to other nations. While he admits that it "will remain unrivaled for the foreseeable future," nevertheless, because all power in the world has become more "diffuse," America's ability "to shape the rest of the world has actually decreased."

But surely the same level of American power applied to a world where opposing power is more diffuse should be more, not less, effective. America's problem today is not that its power is in relative decline but, on the contrary, that the places where it can exert potentially decisive influence have increased in number, and so have the choices we must confront.

Do "losses" on the periphery matter? Indeed, can there even be American "losses" on the periphery if America does not choose to become involved? Should America resist all those who oppose its view of world order? Or should the United States keep its powder dry for the really serious threats to its existence—the dominance of Europe or Asia, for instance, by a single power? Such is the nature of the questions Americans have faced throughout this century, and have answered in two different and historically instructive ways.

It would seem to make sense to heed the realists' assertion that a nation may become distracted, or exhaust itself by lesser endeavors, and thus fail to guard that which is most important. But this in fact is the path the United States followed in the 1930s, and lived to regret. First it failed to respond to the peripheral Italian invasion of Ethiopia, the peripheral Spanish Civil War, and the peripheral Japanese conquest of Manchuria, and then it failed to respond as well when the big threat to "core" interests did finally emerge in the figure of Hitler's Germany. The big threats and vital interests, as it turned out, were no less debatable than the small threats and lesser interests.

American policy during the Cold War provides an interesting contrast. Despite a terrible debacle on the periphery, the United States did not lose sight of the core. On the contrary, concern about the core and concern about the periphery seem to have been mutually reinforcing. The "lesson of Munich," which dominated Cold War thinking until its temporary replacement by the "lesson of Vietnam," taught that a failure of will on small matters eventually led to a failure of will on more vital matters as well. This proved to be a sound strategy for defending American interests, both large and small, and it was this strategy that made possible a peaceful victory in the Cold War.

There is no certainty that we can correctly distinguish between high-stakes issues and small-stakes issues in time to sound the alarm. In the past we did not know for sure whether an invasion of Ethiopia was merely the whim of an Italian despot in an irrelevant part of Africa or the harbinger of fascist aggression in Europe, whether a North Vietnamese victory was a signal of national reunification or the prelude to a hostile takeover of Southeast Asia. So today we do not know whether Serbian aggression is "ethnic turmoil" or the first step in the breakdown of European order.

But the way one handles the small threats is likely to determine the way one handles the larger threats. It does not take much imagination to envision what those larger threats may be: the rise of militant anti-American Muslim fundamentalism in North Africa and the Middle East, a rearmed Germany in a chaotic Europe, a revitalized Russia, a rearmed Japan in a scramble for power with China in a volatile East Asia. If the goal is a United States capable of meeting these more serious threats when they do arise, then the best policy is one that seeks involvement rather than shuns it. Once appeasing adversaries and wishing away problems becomes a habit, it becomes a hard habit to break. Confrontation with the next Nazi Germany or Soviet empire, the tests of American strength, character, and endurance, essential to the preservation of a more stable world order, will continue to come in such unlikely places as Bosnia, Haiti, Somalia, and Korea. If we cannot plug every breach in the world order, we also cannot allow potential challengers of that order to act in the confidence that the United States will stand aside.

The post–Cold War era is a time of readjustment. Relationships of power change constantly, but how Americans respond to crises, even small ones, in this time of transition will affect the nature of the changes yet to come. Only if it is ready to engage its power when and as needed can the United States hope to shape the character and direction of the forces of change rather than be overwhelmed by them.

Finally, a political question that needs to be asked: Who among us, Democrat or Republican, is prepared to rise to the challenge and follow the demanding (if in the long run safer) course of global activism?

On the Democratic side, even those Clinton-administration officials who appear willing to assert American leadership find it hard to overcome the instinctive aversion to the use of power which still burdens them twenty years after Vietnam. They seek the fruits of American intervention, yet seem incapable of doing what is necessary to secure them. Democrats today are paying the price for their years of opposition to Republican assertions of American strength abroad.

Since the Vietnam War, indeed, only the Republican party has had the understanding and the confidence to use American power in defense of the nation's interests. Yet the Republican party itself is now teetering on the edge of a historic transformation. Increasing numbers of Republican politicians, policymakers, and intellectuals agree with Minority Whip Newt Gingrich's judgment that the United States is now "overextended around the world." There are fewer Republican calls for increases in the defense budget, and more Republican calls for decreases in overseas commitments. The Republican party is less and less recognizable as the party of Ronald Reagan or the George Bush who sent troops to Panama and the Persian Gulf.

In the same way, seventy-five years ago the Republicans transformed themselves from the party of the internationalist Theodore Roosevelt into the party of the isolationist Senator William Borah. In defeating Woodrow Wilson's brand of utopian internationalism, Republicans also killed the more practical internationalism of men like Henry Cabot Lodge, who believed American power had a critical role to play in preventing another war in Europe. When that disaster finally loomed, it was not Lodge but Borah who spoke for the party.

Victory in the Cold War came when Republicans vehemently rejected the idea that the United States had to accept a diminished capacity to shape the world and adjust to the increasing power of its strategic and ideological adversaries. Such a prescription is as disastrous today as it was then, and shows the same lack of faith in the American people and their acceptance of responsibility. It took confidence and determination to take the United States safely through the end of the Cold War. It will take no less confidence and determination to move America through this next, dangerous phase of history.

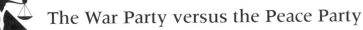

The War Party versus the Peace Party

Justin Raimondo

"Beyond Left and Right: The New Face of the Antiwar Movement" is the theme of this conference. It's a catchy phrase—but what does it mean?

November 9, 1989 marked the end of the old politics and the old alignments. On that day, as the Berlin Wall fell, so too did the political categories and alliances of half a century. The end of the Cold War meant a lot more than the end of communism as a viable ideology, more than the implosion of the Soviet Empire and the breakup of the old USSR. Here in the United States, it meant the end of anticommunism as a viable ideology, and the implosion of the old conservative coalition that governed America in the eighties. It meant the breakup of the right as well as the left—since both had largely defined themselves in relation to something that no longer existed.

Of course, this process did not happen immediately; it took a while, and is still working itself out. But the great realignment has progressed far enough that we can begin to see the shape, or at least the broad outlines, of the new political landscape. I often refer to what I call the "War Party," shorthand for that complex of social, political, and economic forces that constitutes a permanent and powerful lobby on behalf of imperialism and militarism. In my very first column for Antiwar.com, I described the War Party as "the war propaganda apparatus maintained by the interventionist lobby. Well-funded and well-connected, the War Party is such a varied and complex phenomenon that a detailed description of its activities, and its vast system of interlocking directorates and special interests, both foreign and domestic, would fill the pages of a good-sized book." I solved the problem of presenting this material in the form of a daily column by focusing on specific individuals, the biggest and most vocal supporters of the Kosovo war, from Madeleine Albright to Vanessa Redgrave and all the way round to Jeanne Kirkpatrick. These three Harpies of the Apocalypse pretty much represented the ideological contours of the War Party during the Kosovo conflict: Clintonian Democrats, hard leftists, and neoconservatives.

Justin Raimondo is editorial director of <Antiwar.com>, for which he writes an on-line column three times a week. His books include *Reclaiming the American Right: The Lost Legacy of the Conservative Movement* (1993) and *An Enemy of the State: The Life of Murray N. Rothbard* (2000).

Raimondo delivered this speech at the "Beyond Left and Right" conference (March 24–26, 2000, in San Mateo, California) sponsored by <Antiwar.com>. This transcription of Raimondo's speech is from *Whole Earth* 101 (Summer 2000). Copyright © 2000 Whole Earth. Reprinted by permission.

Many hard leftists naturally rallied round the flag when Clinton declared that this was a war against "racism" and for "diversity." The Clintonians, for their part, were glad enough to divert attention away from the fact that their leader had turned the White House into the heterosexual equivalent of a gay bathhouse. But the neoconservatives—that merry little band of ex-lefties who left the Democratic Party in the 1970s and '80s over its lack of enthusiasm for the Cold War—were the most bloodthirsty of the whole sorry lot. Bill Kristol, the editor of the *Weekly Standard*, openly called for "crushing Serb skulls" in a famous editorial a full year before the bombs began to fall on Belgrade. Opportunists like John McCain sought to climb on the "kill the Serbs" bandwagon out of their instinct for the main chance, but the real hardcore ideologues of the War Party were the neocons. While the Clintonians served up some rhetorical hash consisting of bromides about "humanitarianism" and "diversity" to justify the war, this was at most a half-hearted effort: After all, if you're bombing television stations and raining death on a civilian population, it becomes increasingly hard to pass yourself off as Mother Teresa.

Only the neocons had a clear ideological agenda, and Kristol's remark about "crushing Serb skulls" pretty much expresses what it means in practice. In theory, however, it is much more high-sounding, and I must admire Kristol and his coauthor Robert Kagan for their effort to dress up what is basically the most barbaric doctrine ever enunciated in language that sounds almost like it might have been written by a civilized human being. In their article for the Summer, 1996, issue of Foreign Affairs, Kristol and Kagan enunciate the outlines of what they call a "neo-Reaganite" foreign policy. Conservatives, it seems, had been "adrift" in the realm of foreign policy since the end of the Cold War. Until November 9, 1989, the role of the United States in world affairs was defined by the alleged threat posed by the Soviet Union. Now that the Soviets were gone, the question arose: "What should that role be?" Kristol and Kagan had an answer, and I quote:

> Benevolent global hegemony. Having defeated the "evil empire," the United States enjoys strategic and ideological predominance. The first objective of U.S. foreign policy should be to preserve and enhance that predominance by strengthening America's security, supporting its friends, advancing its interests, and standing up for its principles around the world. The aspiration to benevolent hegemony might strike some as either hubristic or morally suspect. But a hegemon is nothing more or less than a leader with preponderant influence and authority over all others in its domain. That is America's position in the world today. The leaders of Russia and China understand this. At their April summit meeting, Boris Yeltsin and Jiang Zemin joined in denouncing "hegemonism" in the post–Cold War world. They meant this as a complaint about the United States. It should be taken as a compliment and a guide to action.

BEYOND HUBRIS

This vision of world domination goes way, way beyond hubris, and crosses the border into outright megalomania. It reminds me of all those terrible science-fiction movies, where the goal of the mad scientist or the evil space-beings is always to conquer the world. For the authors of this manifesto of empire, however, what most normal people would consider villainous is, instead, virtuous. As the great architects of "national greatness conservatism," Kristol and his cabal naturally want to export that "greatness" to the rest of the world. It is the old Marxism turned inside out, in which the "democratic revolution" must be exported to the far corners of the globe.

While the neocon theoretician Francis Fukuyama deploys Hegelian dialectic to show that history has ended in the birth of what he calls the "universal homogeneous state," the *Weekly Standard* and the cadre of neocon columnists and editorial writers beat the war drums continuously and ever more loudly: They want an all-out war against Serbia, Iraq, Russia, China, North Korea, and who knows how many other so-called "rogue states." I think Austria may very well be next. Of course, by the neocon definition, any state that does not recognize American supremacy, that doesn't kowtow and surrender its sovereignty to the West, is a "rogue state." Neoconservatism is an ideology that has to mean perpetual war.

The War Party is not a unitary party; it is riven into various factions, with ostensibly "left" and "right" wings. Some members, like Kristol and Kagan, want the United States to assume a frankly imperial stance, and to act unilaterally to achieve global dominance. Others, the "left" imperialists, see the United States acting through the United Nations or some other multilateral institution. Both see the emergence of a global state, centered in the West, as inevitable and desirable. Their only argument is the means to bring this about, and their differences are almost purely stylistic. (There are other differences, such as the regional preferences each wing has for the enemies it chooses, with the "left" wing of the War Party concentrating on Europe while the "right" wing has always been focused on the Asian theater of operations. But that is a whole other subject, which we don't have sufficient space to explore here.) Suffice it to say that we are talking about two versions of essentially the same poison. The dwarfish Bill Kristol likes to affect a macho stance, and is enraptured by his vision of "crushing Serb skulls," while Clinton and his enablers pose as great "humanitarians"—even as they bomb one of the oldest cities in Europe from the cowardly height of 15,000 feet.

And so we have a War Party that spans the very narrow spectrum of the politically permissible, from the neoliberal "left" to the neoconservative "right"—with anything and everything that falls outside of these parameters exiled to the so-called "fringe." Of course, when the mainstream is defined so narrowly, we get to the point where millions of Americans are considered to be "fringe elements." This is the great dream of the neocons: to lop off the fringes and institute the rule of the Eternal Center, where dissent is nonexistent, especially in the realm of foreign policy.

Mobilizing for Peace

It's very clever how they've gone about it, in a deliberate campaign to marginalize any opposition to the globalist idea. But any attempt to suppress opposition is bound, instead, to stimulate it. That is the reason for this conference, and all the conferences to come: to mobilize the party of peace. The first step of that mobilization is to recognize who we are, and where we're coming from. The "Peace Party," though less organized—and far less generously funded—than the War Party, represents a far greater number of Americans, most of whom are instinctual isolationists. The American people have had to be dragged, kicking and screaming, into virtually every war in their history, and the post–Cold War trend has been to encourage this natural isolationism.

But this opposition to foreign adventurism is normally activated only after we actually go to war. Active opposition to *interventionism* in between wars is therefore limited to the "far" left and the "far" right. We have the remnants of the Old Left, whose best elements are represented by a man like Alexander Cockburn—and whose worst aspects are exemplified by the neoStalinist robots of the Workers World Party, whose "International Action Center" has marginalized the opposition to the Kosovo war as a wacko sideshow far better than the War Party ever could.

It is on the right, however, that the most interesting developments have taken place, for until the end of the Cold War there were very few antiwar rightists. Up until recently, the long tradition of anti-imperialism on the right was completely forgotten, especially by conservatives. Yet it was the old America First Committee, founded by rock-ribbed conservatives and opponents of Franklin Delano Roosevelt in 1940, that was the biggest and best-organized antiwar movement in American history. The fight to keep us out of the European war was led by such Roosevelt-haters as John T. Flynn, and such editorial bastions of Midwestern middle Americanism as the *Chicago Tribune* and the *Saturday Evening Post*. Their analysis that we would win the war against National Socialism in the trenches, but lose the battle for liberty on the home front, was largely borne out by events. Garet Garrett, chief editorial writer for the *Saturday Evening Post*, warned in 1950 that "we have crossed the boundary that lies between Republic and Empire"—but by then not many were listening. Only a few, notably Murray N. Rothbard, the libertarian economist and theoretician, carried on the Old Right tradition. By the midsixties the so-called "New Right" of William F. Buckley, Jr. and the National Review had taken over the conservative movement almost completely—along with a crew of ex-leftists such as James Burnham (a former leader of the Fourth International) and a whole coven of ex-Commies of one sort or another, who were hell-bent on destroying their ex-comrades in the Kremlin.

PARALLEL HISTORY

If we look at the parallel histories of the War Party and the party of peace, we can see a whole series of such realignments, starting with the First World War and its aftermath. The crusading spirit of the War Party of 1917 was animated by Wilsonian liberalism, a militant internationalism of the left. These same liberals, however, were cruelly disillusioned by the vengeance of Versailles and the subsequent redivision of Europe by the Great Powers. This great betrayal gave rise to a new, noninterventionist liberalism, which found political expression in the Midwestern populists of both parties (but primarily the Republicans). Exemplified by Senator William C. Borah, the great orator known as the "Lion of Idaho," this group constituted the Midwestern leadership of the antiwar movement of the 1930s. These progressive Republicans were initially friendly to Franklin Roosevelt, but were alienated by the Mussolini-esque National Recovery Act, horrified by the court-packing scheme, and bitterly opposed to getting into the European war, which they saw as a war between empires in which the republican United States had no interest and no stake. U.S. intervention in the war, they saw, was a scheme by the president to increase his power, and to plant his foot firmly on the neck of the nation.

In this suspicion they had plenty of company in conservative businessmen such as Colonel Robert E. Wood, the head of Sears, Roebuck & Co., and a group of Yale undergraduates led by R. Douglas Stuart, the son of the first vice president of the Quaker Oats Company. This working alliance, based on opposition to a common enemy, soon evolved a common analysis of America in the 1930s: that Roosevelt was a warmongering would-be dictator who was taking the country down the path to perdition. While opposition to the president's domestic policies formed some basis for the alliance, the real catalyst of the 1930s realignment was the war question—as it has been throughout American history.

Over on the left, another sort of realignment was taking place, with the formerly antiwar Communist Party turning on a dime. The signing of the Hitler–Stalin Pact had motivated their opposition to intervention, but when Hitler turned on his twin brother in the Kremlin, Stalin's American agents changed their line in mid-sentence—without missing a beat. Suddenly, the Commies were the biggest warmongers on the block, stridently demanding that the United States open up a "second front" and save the Soviet Union, and demanding that all opponents of the war be jailed as "traitors"—this from a party funded and directly controlled by a foreign power, a party that now billed communism as being the living incarnation of "twentieth century Americanism"!

The Communists had been on the outs with their liberal friends and potential fellow travelers on the war question, but just as soon as the Commies were pro-war they were let into the government and the seats of power without question. The Communists hailed the passage of the Smith Act, which criminalized opposition to the war, and cheered when Roosevelt jailed some thirty members of the Socialist Workers Party, which opposed the war. A few years later, the same law was used to jail leaders of the Communist Party—demonstrating how karma operates in history.

The War Party, as we have seen, has worn many guises throughout American history. Sometimes it is left wing, at other times it is a creature of the right. The party of peace is likewise prone to switch polarities. If you live long enough, you can start out your life as a liberal and wind up a right-wing reactionary without undergoing any fundamental change of views. That is what happened to H. L. Mencken, who was considered the guru of the freethinking "flaming youth" of the 1920s and early '30s—and later consigned to the fever swamps of "right-wing extremism" for his opposition to the war and his visceral hatred of Roosevelt. The same was true of Albert Jay Nock, and John T. Flynn: Their views did not change so much as others' perception of them did. Opposition to war, imperialism, and the centralized state was "left" at the turn of the century and "right" by the 1930s. In the 1960s it was considered "radical"—that is, radical left—to oppose our policy of global intervention, whereas the noninterventionist of today is far more likely to be a conservative Republican or a member of the Reform Party than a liberal Democrat.

The idea of an alliance between the antiwar left and the anti-imperialist right is a concept rooted in more than just the opposition to war. Out of the struggle against the empire will arise a whole new way of looking at the world, a common analysis of how the few use the state to rule the many. Naturally, there will be disagreements, and competing analyses, and a lot of initial confusion. But over the long haul, the two sides in the battle for hearts and minds in the postmillennial world will sort themselves out. A movement in opposition to imperialism must, in this day and age, necessarily become a struggle against globalism, against the idea of a world state. In the era of enforced globalization, the Peace Party is the greatest defender of national sovereignty as a bulwark of resistance to the emerging transnational tyranny, while the War Party is the great champion of a world without borders (or, indeed, any place to evade the long arm of the Global Hegemon). Now that the epic battle between communism and capitalism has been decisively decided in favor of the latter, a new struggle of "isms" is breaking out, this time between globalism and nationalism. Kosovo was just the beginning.

POSTSCRIPT

This year's conference was an attempt to bridge the gap between left and right, to bring the first fight against war and globalism to a higher level—and to begin to organize the first real opposition to the War Party since the 1960s.

There were many voices of protest at this year's gathering, from Tom Fleming and Srdja Trikovic, editors of the paleoconservative magazine *Chronicles*, to old-fashioned Marxists like Alexander Cockburn . . . and virtually everything in between. As the rule of the acronyms (WTO, NATO, EU, UN) replaces the self-rule of sovereign nations, a broad opposition is sure to arise. Who can say whether it is "right" or "left"—and in the end, what does it matter? Such labels no longer describe anything meaningful—and that, really, is the whole point.

ISSUE 6

SANCTIONS

Sometimes a nation may prohibit its citizens from having contact with persons in another nation. Trade, financial transactions, foreign investment, communication, travel, and other ties may be prohibited. The goal in imposing these penalties, or sanctions, may be to influence the other government, to punish it for objectionable actions previously taken, to encourage an overthrow of the regime, or even to curry favor with influential domestic groups.

Sanctions are most effective if the country applying them is strong and if the target country is significantly dependent on the sanctioning country. No doubt this is one reason why sanctions have been a favored technique of influence among American leaders. The basic U.S. sanctions law, still on the books, is the 1917 Trading with the Enemy Act. That law makes it illegal for any person in the United States to trade with an "enemy" of the United States, defined as any person in a designated hostile country. In the years since 1917, Congress has added prohibitions against economic transactions other than trade, as well as restrictions on travel and cultural contacts. Various countries that are now on the U.S. enemies list include Iran, Iraq, Libya, Sudan, and, of course, Cuba.

A strong proponent of U.S. sanctions, especially against Cuba, is the colorful former Chairman of the Senate Foreign Relations Committee, Jesse Helms. In 1995, Senator Helms authored legislation that extended the reach of U.S. sanctions to foreign companies that do business with Cuba, if they own assets there that had originally been seized from U.S. companies by the Castro government. In his irrepressible style, Senator Helms said: "Well, you cannot do business with Castro just as you could not do business with Adolph Hitler. . . . Cuba is controlled by the same Communist tyrant who has inflicted so much death and mayhem upon the Cuban people since he took over years ago. . . . We have condoned Fidel Castro long enough. It is time to get him out."

Fellow committee member Senator Paul Simon took an opposing position, arguing in favor of trade and contacts with Cuba:

> If you take a look at how we handle[d] the Soviet Union, we really had two courses; one by those who just wanted to isolate the Soviet Union completely, and the other by those who said, "Let us trade, let us have business back and forth, let us get them exposed to what democracy is all about." And that view prevailed and it, I do not need to tell you, was successful. I think we face the same two choices with Cuba. And my feeling is that what we ought to be doing is trading, exchanging visits, opening Cuba up, giving people of Cuba, like we gave people of the Soviet Union, a chance to see what things are like on the outside.

Do sanctions work, even when imposed by a country as powerful as the United States? Are they successful in causing policy changes by the targeted government or a change in the regime? And what are the costs of sanctions for a country's own companies that lose business in target countries—and for ordinary people in those countries who are deprived of needed imports?

In the articles that follow, David E. Weekman makes the argument for sanctions, while Richard N. Haass, president of the Council on Foreign Relations, contends that sanctions are ill-advised.

DISCUSSION QUESTIONS

As you read the articles by Weekman and Haass, consider the following questions:

1. Now that you have read opinions on both sides of the sanctions issue, where do you stand? On balance, are sanctions a useful foreign policy tool or not?
2. The U.S. government usually seems more interested in imposing economic sanctions than do America's European allies. Why?
3. Suppose that you accept the proposition that sanctions could, at least potentially, be useful instruments of U.S. policy. How would you change the American approach to sanctions to make them more effective?

KEY WEB SITES

For more information on this topic, visit the following Web sites:

Office of Foreign Assets Control of U.S. Treasury Department
http://www.treas.gov/ofac

James Orr Associates (lists national, state, and local trade-sanctions laws)
http://www.sanctions.net

USA Engage (a coalition that opposes U.S. trade sanctions)
http://www.usaengage.com

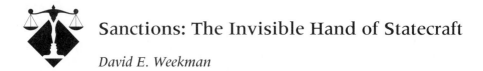

Sanctions: The Invisible Hand of Statecraft

David E. Weekman

Sanctions, when implemented as a result of an emerging U.S. foreign policy crisis, are usually evaluated in the public domain when the government is in a transitory phase somewhere between diplomacy and war. Analysis in the spotlight often drives the publicity-seeking politicians, pundits, and other sanctions "experts" to focus solely on the adverse impact of the sanctions and whether or not the sanctions have, to date, achieved the foreign policy objective. In most cases, the conclusion is that sanctions have "failed."

Similarly, in the aftermath of conflict, experts are usually quick to focus on the critical role that military force—or its threatened use—played in resolving the crisis. Thus, oftentimes, little attention is devoted seriously to examining the true role that sanctions played in helping to resolve—or at least manage—that crisis. The role that sanctions played in the 1994 Haitian crisis brings into question the conventional wisdom of those who claim the Haitian sanctions "failed." It can be argued that sanctions played a prominent, if not a key role in forcing the junta to depart Haiti.

While this article is specifically about the 1994 intervention in Haiti, it is possible—and the author asks readers to consider the possibility—that the type of analytical approach taken here (e.g., viewing sanctions as one tool in the toolbox of statecraft, as opposed to viewing sanctions as the primary weapon employed) may be useful in further understanding the true role that sanctions are playing in the U.S. and UN quest to contain Saddam Hussein and eliminate his weapons of mass destruction program. That, however, is the subject of another article.

THE UN SANCTIONS

After close to thirty years of dictatorship, democracy in Haiti prevailed for the first time in 1990 with the election of Jean-Bertrand Aristide, a Roman Catholic priest, as president. The Haitian experience with democracy was short-lived, however. Aristide was ousted on September 30, 1991, by a military coup. The junta was led by Lt. Gen. Raoul Cedras, Commander in Chief of Haitian Armed Forces, Brig. Gen. Phillippe Biamby, Army Chief of Staff, and Lt. Col. Michael François, Chief of Police.

David E. Weekman is a Foreign Affairs Specialist with the U.S. Arms Control and Disarmament Agency.

This article is from *Strategic Review* (winter 1998), a former MIT publication. Reprinted by permission.

The Organization of American States (OAS) imposed trade sanctions on Haiti in November 1991 in an attempt to punish the coup leaders and restore President Aristide to power. In May 1993, the United Nations Security Council (UNSC) enacted UN Resolution 841, which made the OAS trade embargo universal and imposed mandatory arms, oil, and financial embargoes on Haiti.[1] The junta on July 3, 1993, agreed to the Governor's Island Accord (GIA), which called for the return of President Aristide to Haiti by October 30, 1993. In return, on August 27, 1993, the UNSC under Resolution 861 suspended the oil and arms embargo. However, after the Haitian generals were found to be in "serious and consistent noncompliance" with the GIA, the UNSC, under Resolution 873, reimposed the oil and arms embargo on October 13, 1993. Following the assassination of Justice Minister François-Guy Malary on October 14, the UNSC further tightened the embargo on October 16, 1993 under Resolution 875.[2]

However, President Clinton became increasingly frustrated with his inability to restore democracy to Haiti and by the increased reports from Haiti of judicial killings, arbitrary arrests, abductions, and rapes. As a result, the UNSC, acting on U.S. leadership, passed Resolution 917 on May 6, 1994, which was the strictest set of sanctions passed to date and designed to "tighten the noose" around the necks of the junta and their inner circle of support.

Then, on July 22, 1994, the United States announced that it would push for a UN resolution to use "all necessary means" to restore exiled President Aristide to power.[3] On July 31, the UNSC passed Resolution 940 granting the United States that authority.

SANCTIONS IN ACTION

Prior to the embargo, the Haitian economy was driven by an export-based assembly industry, which produced baseballs, electronic goods, fishing lures, and clothing. These low-wage, low-skill assembly jobs, coupled with the fact that most Haitians farmed for sustenance, made Haiti one of the poorest countries in the Western Hemisphere. The plethora of sanctions imposed on Haiti from 1991 through 1994 had a devastating effect on the Haitian countryside, economy, and people.

International relief workers in Haiti observed that the most devastating impact of the embargo was a sharp increase in the price of propane gas, commonly used for cooking. The inability of most Haitians to afford propane drove up the demand for charcoal, the only readily available fuel substitute, which accelerated widespread deforestation and led to severe soil erosion.[4]

During the OAS embargo from 1991 to 1993, Haiti is said to have lost an estimated 150,000 jobs in the assembly sector. Unemployment estimates were as high as 70 percent. The government's deficit increased, trade fell, and Haitian currency plummeted. Real gross domestic product declined by 14.8 percent in 1992, 5.2 percent in 1993, and 13.2 percent in 1994. Inflation for

1993 and 1994 was close to 50 percent.[5] A study that received a great deal of press during the embargo of Haiti was a 1993 report issued by the Harvard Center for Population and Development Studies that found that the deaths of 1,000 children per month in Haiti could be attributed to the sanctions.[6] Journalists never lacked anecdotal evidence detailing the devastating impact that the sanctions were having on the civilian population of Haiti, while the inner circle of the de facto government and its leaders apparently remained unaffected by the embargo, thus concluding that the sanctions were "failing." The reports often detailed incidents of malnutrition and starvation, while the wealthy elites and the generals sipped French champagne and ate salmon fillets and imported cheeses. The civilian population could not afford $10 for a gallon of gasoline, while Cedras and his ilk had full tanks in their land cruisers and access to all the fuel they needed. To pretend that the effects of sanctions against Haiti should be measured in strictly economic statistics, particularly with regard to the populace, is misleading and misses the point. To state that the sanctions had very little to do with the psychological, political, and diplomatic isolation of the junta is to misconstrue the intended and actual effects of the sanctions. Imposing the sanctions on Haiti was a political act designed to have political effects. Furthermore, as an authority on economic sanctions, David Baldwin argues one must always be careful to recognize and acknowledge the degree of difficulty at hand—trying to dislodge a de facto government from power being one of the hardest.[7]

Sanctions, especially negative ones, are often believed to be, and frequently are viewed as instruments of coercion. Did the sanctions imposed by A result in B doing X? This begs the question for a yes (success) or no (failure) response. The literature on economic sanctions tends to be permeated with this school of thought.[8] Success in international politics, however, is usually a matter of degree. For instance, Baldwin has written that the costs of noncompliance with regard to X constitutes influence even though no change occurs in the policies of the target country.[9] Baldwin continues that not all influence is manifest in terms of changes in policy; changes in the cost of noncompliance also constitute influence. This increased cost of noncompliance can be a significant factor in the target government making some movement toward X. According to Baldwin, the relevant question is not whether economic measures were "decisive"—whatever that may mean—but whether they had a significant effect on the length, outcome, or intensity of the crisis.[10]

The pressure on Haiti's de facto government was dramatically increased in May 1994 with the passage of UNSC Resolution 917, which banned all travel to and from Haiti, denied visas to military, police, and other coup supporters, placed a total trade embargo on Haiti for nonhumanitarian goods, and strongly urged all governments to freeze the financial resources of the coup leaders and their supporters.

Soon thereafter, the United States banned all financial transactions between the United States and Haiti and froze the assets, subject to U.S. jurisdiction, of 600 military leaders and other supporters of the Cedras regime. In June, the Clinton administration expanded the assets freeze to include all Haitian citizens. The implementation of Resolution 917 by various states increased the costs to the junta for noncompliance with the terms of the GIA. Essentially, the regime had become internationally isolated. The de facto Haitian leaders, their families, and key supporters, accustomed to an opulent and aristocratic lifestyle, could no longer freely travel, found a sizable amount of their assets seized, and essentially were shunned by the international community. This last round of sanctions appeared to have the de facto authorities on the verge of buckling. Throughout the embargo, the border between the Dominican Republic and Haiti was very porous. Gasoline was a much needed commodity, and millions of gallons flowed freely into Haiti. Since the junta's inner circle owned all the gas stations, trucks, and pumping stations, they experienced no shortage of fuel, even at exorbitant prices. They not only survived but prospered. Joaquin Balaguer, president of the Dominican Republic, repeatedly claimed that his country was enforcing the embargo, despite evidence to the contrary.

On May 16, 1994, there was a hotly disputed presidential election in the Dominican Republic. This event, seemingly unrelated to the Haitian situation, did make a direct impact on the Haitian junta and dramatically increased their costs for noncompliance with the sanctions. The election was marked by widespread accusations of fraud by international observers. The United States brokered a deal with Mr. Balaguer to achieve an understanding whereby the United States would not make an issue of the election irregularities, if President Balaguer would cooperate in "seriously" enforcing the embargo by sealing the Dominican border with Haiti.[11] Evidence exists that this understanding largely succeeded in having the Dominican armed forces deploy nearly half of the nation's army, shutting down a substantial number of once bustling smuggling centers along the border. The fuel supply of the de facto government began to dry up and this put increased pressure on the junta.

In June, press reports began to surface of a split within and between the junta and their wealthy supporters, who urged Cedras to resign, as well as reports which amazingly foretold the outcome of the crisis, stating that Cedras had agreed to resign as commander of the Haitian Armed Forces when his term expired in October 1994.[12] It appears reasonable to conclude that the sanctions, rather than "failing," must have played some role in forcing the hand of Cedras to at least begin discussing and apparently deciding upon a retirement date—progress not evident before the imposition of sanctions.

THE THEORY OF SANCTIONS

"In discussing the role of sanctions . . . the pens often slip toward negative sanctions and almost never slip toward positive sanctions."—David A. Baldwin.[13]

Sanctions come in two forms, negative and positive. Negative sanctions can be defined as actual or threatened punishments to B; positive sanctions can be defined as actual or promised rewards to B. David Baldwin has observed that few analysts make a distinction between positive and negative sanctions because all threats imply promises and all promises imply threats; they are simply different ways of describing the same conditional influence attempt. In other words, a threat to punish B for noncompliance must imply a promise not to punish for compliance. Likewise, a promise to reward if B complies must imply a threat not to reward if B fails to comply.[14]

Baldwin moves beyond this "traditional" paradigm of positive sanctions and argues that in order to distinguish rewards from punishments, one must establish B's baseline of expectations at the moment A's influence attempt begins.[15] Positive sanctions then are actual or promised improvements in B's value position relative to his baseline of expectations. In other words, if A offers B $100 for doing X, and B is expecting to receive that $100, then this cannot be considered a reward. Whereas, if B is not expecting anything for doing X and suddenly A offers B $100 for doing X, then this can be considered a reward. In both episodes, B is operating from a different baseline of expectations—perhaps leading to a different outcome and a different time frame within which that outcome occurs.

Baldwin, drawing upon Thomas Schelling's discussion of "compellent threats" to describe A's use of the stick to shift B's expectations, explains that A uses a negative sanction (the punishment) to lay the groundwork for the subsequent use of positive sanctions (the promise to withdraw the punishment if B complies).[16] Taking it a step further, if B's expectations are so low as a result of the negative sanctions imposed, A may gain increased leverage, and shorten the time frame in getting B to comply with X, by not only promising to withdraw the punishment, but by offering additional rewards for compliance.

Purchase, as an instrument of positive sanctions, is an often underused and frequently misunderstood form of economic statecraft. In *Economic Statecraft*, Baldwin argues that direct monetary payment is one of the most common ways for some people to get other people to do things they would not otherwise do.[17] The purchase of B by A to do X translates into a cost—perhaps, in some instances, a significant monetary expenditure. However, as Baldwin points out in his discussion on monetary costs, the cost of one instrument of statecraft must be carefully weighed against the costs and benefits of using other forms of statecraft to achieve that foreign policy goal.[18] Compared to military statecraft, economic statecraft is almost always cheaper. While a statesman using the power of positive sanctions risks being perceived by domestic audiences as soft, weak, or lacking in toughness for "buying one's way out of a fight," only unimaginative statesmen would need-lessly take their country to war if the foreign policy objective could be achieved by other means.

THE ENDGAME

Harold Lasswell has written that there are four types of statecraft: propagan-da, diplomacy, military force, and economic statecraft.[19] Diplomacy and mil-itary force, or the threat of force, can be very powerful instruments of statecraft on the international stage, especially when employed at critical junctures of the crisis and when functioning in synergistic fashion. Policy-makers tend not to give credit to, or publicly acknowledge, the role that other instruments may have played in solving a foreign policy problem. Even in the planning stages of a crisis, policymakers tend to focus exclusively on diplo-macy and military force. The problem that the United States encountered in Haiti with these two levers of statecraft, at least up until the endgame, was that the threat to employ military force was not credible, thus weakening the hand of diplomacy. The United States lacked credibility on the threat to em-ploy military force due largely to President Clinton's October 12, 1993 deci-sion to withdraw the USS Harlan County from Port-au-Prince after mobs of gun-toting thugs demonstrated against the arrival of U.S. and Canadian mil-itary advisors.

The United States made no secret of its intent to return President Aris-tide to power by any means necessary. In testimony before the House Foreign Affairs Committee on June 8, 1994, William H. Gray III, President Clinton's Special Representative to Haiti, repeatedly refused to rule out military inter-vention as the means for restoring Aristide to power. Gray testified that "fur-ther steps will be taken in the coming days and weeks. No operations have been excluded. Democracy in Haiti will prevail."[20]

On September 15, 1994, in an Oval Office address, President Clinton stat-ed, "Your time is up. Leave now or we will force you from power. . . . Our mis-sion in Haiti, as it was in Panama and Grenada, will be limited and specific . . . we will remove the dictators from power. . . ."[21]

During a meeting at the White House two days prior to the planned in-vasion, the twenty-four-nation Multination Force Coalition on Haiti issued a joint statement: "The dictators have . . . run out of time. . . . The Haitian mil-itary leaders should have absolutely no doubt about our resolve. We will show them that the international community stands by its word."[22]

Meanwhile, President Clinton dispatched a team, consisting of former Joint Chiefs of Staff Chairman General Colin Powell, former President Jimmy Carter, and former U.S. Senator Sam Nunn, to Haiti for face-to-face negotiations with the junta. General Powell, in his memoirs, recounts his meetings with Haitian leaders and his perception of the effectiveness of the sanctions: "Our party retired to the Hotel Villa Creole in the hills above the city for a courtesy meeting with the Haitian parliamentarians. Later, we had dinner with prominent business leaders. What struck me was how sleek, well-fed, and well-dressed these men looked after almost three years of economic embargo had impoverished the rest of their countrymen. So much for sanctions."[23]

In discussions with General Cedras hours before the invasion, General Powell was unable to convince the junta that the United States was ready to employ military force. Powell stated: "Let me make sure you understand what you are facing. Two aircraft carriers, two and a half infantry divisions, 20,000 troops, helicopter gunships, tanks and artillery."[24] General Cedras responded, "We used to be the weakest nation in the Hemisphere. After this, we'll be the strongest."[25]

The breakthrough came just as Carter, Powell, and Nunn were deadlocked with the junta. Powell explains that General Biamby burst into the room and announced "the invasion is coming." Biamby had just been tipped off by a source at Fort Bragg. As Powell recounts, it was shortly thereafter that Haitian President Emile Jonassaint agreed to resign, which cleared the way for the resignation of Generals Cedras and Biamby.[26]

It is clear that the mission of the American troika, coupled with the departure of sixty-one planes from Fort Bragg bound for Haiti, were important factors in getting the junta to step down.[27] It was a classic synergistic coupling of diplomacy and military force, well timed, and designed to achieve the desired foreign policy outcome.

The negative sanctions appeared, at the very least, to fracture the cohesiveness of the junta and apparently even resulted in General Cedras deciding on a date to retire. At the very least, the junta was made more vulnerable to outside persuasion than they may otherwise have been. Furthermore, the Carter mission, coupled with the dispatch of the 82nd Airborne, only resulted in reaching an agreement, in principle, for the generals to step down on or before October 15, 1994.[28] This was an outcome that was no different than that apparently achieved by the severe negative sanctions. Moreover, this "coercive diplomacy" did not physically force the junta to leave Haiti. Therefore, what did force them to depart the country? Perhaps it was the U.S. military sitting off the coast ready to invade at a moment's notice, or perhaps it is worth considering that positive sanctions, at least in part, also played a role in forcing the junta to depart Haiti.

In the days preceding and following Cedras' departure from Haiti, a number of stories emerged, subsequently confirmed by the White House.[29] Reports indicated that General Cedras and other officials received a "golden parachute" from the United States in exchange for their departure from Haiti.[30] These reports suggest that there were several components to the deal.

1. Generals Cedras and Biamby gained immediate access to their share of the $79 million frozen in U.S. banks as a result of the sanctions.[31] Bank secrecy laws have prohibited the Treasury Department from saying exactly how much of the $79 million belonged to the two generals.

2. An agreement was reached whereby the United States would lease three rental properties in Haiti from Cedras, estimated to provide him with $60,000 paid one year in advance.[32]

3. Twenty-three of Cedras' relatives and associates were provided with safe passage to the United States, plus transportation, housing, and living expenses.[33]

4. Cedras, Biamby, and five others were provided with safe passage to Panama, plus transportation, housing, and living expenses.[34]

5. In Panama, Cedras was provided with a beachside villa (believed to be at the Contadora Island Resort, which housed the exiled Shah of Iran), its rent paid one year in advance by the United States.[35]

6. Moving expenses for Cedras and his entourage are available, if he chooses to leave Panama (most likely to Spain, where he owns two homes).[36]

When the United States negotiated with Cedras on the terms of the golden parachute, Cedras was probably not expecting to be compensated for his departure. The severity of the sanctions under Resolution 917, the ever-increasing size of the U.S. military offshore, the fracturing of the junta and the subsequent passage of Resolution 940, authorizing a U.S.-led international invasion of Haiti, all led to a low and ever-decreasing baseline of expectations. The inducements to depart Haiti, in the eyes of Cedras, truly were a golden parachute, compensation, or a reward for fleeing the country. Furthermore, the negative sanctions (e.g., the freezing of assets and denial of visas) became a positive sanction (their removal as a reward).

Clearly, the U.S. purchase of the junta incurred a monetary cost to force their departure from Haiti. But, so what? As Baldwin would ask, "Would war have been cheaper?" The cost of fuel, spare parts, ammunition, food and medicine, equipment depreciation and replacement, combat pay—let alone the loss of human life to support a military intervention—would have far outweighed what the United States paid General Cedras for his departure from Haiti.

Lessons for the Future

In the analysis of sanctions during a major foreign policy crisis, one must be careful not to become too enamored with analysis performed under a political spotlight. The Haitian sanctions did inflict tremendous pain on the Haitian population (as a military invasion would have as well), but that does not automatically translate into "failure." The negative sanctions, particularly those imposed under Resolution 917, resulted in severe discomfort to the junta, if not an outright fracturing of the alliance, and apparently did help motivate Cedras to plan to resign in October 1994. If sanctions did not bring this about, what did?

The golden parachute deal received a fair amount of negative press.[37] The image of General Cedras living a pampered life in exile makes it understandable how one could believe that Cedras "won" (thus implying a U.S. loss) because he walked away with "silver rather than full of lead." As Baldwin reminds us, however, power is not a zero-sum game.[38] If the adversary gains, the United States does not necessarily lose; such thinking impedes fruitful thinking about economic statecraft. Cedras and other international thugs can win, as long as the United States wins bigger. In the future, when policymakers jump to reap the political capital of a foreign policy victory, and as scholars and others write their postmortems, it is hoped that they will view sanctions through Baldwin's lens rather than through General Powell's and let their pens slip toward positive sanctions and a more favorable view of negative sanctions.

Moreover, when future scholars review the history of the UN sanctions on Iraq (both pre– and post–Desert Storm), one hopes that they will critically examine the actual role that sanctions may have played in that crisis and not just arbitrarily conclude that sanctions "failed" because they did not oust Saddam Hussein from power.

Ejecting a government or dictator from power is no easy task, not even when military force is employed; witness the 1989 U.S. invasion of Panama and the 1993 U.S. intervention in Mogadishu, Somalia. For instance, it would be interesting to know what role sanctions played in impeding Saddam Hussein's ability to fight the coalition forces during Desert Storm (e.g., denial of spare parts, tank treads, and tires). Likewise, how robust would Saddam Hussein's military and weapons of mass destruction program be if there was no international oil embargo to deny him hard currency? What if there was no UN trade embargo on dual-use equipment, technologies, and chemicals? When viewed from this perspective, it would appear difficult to conclude that the sanctions on Iraq "failed."

NOTES

1. United Nations Security Council, Resolution 841, June 16, 1993, paragraphs 5 & 8.

2. "Attaining Democracy: A Lengthy and Difficult Task," *UN Chronicle* (December 1993), pp. 20–22.

3. Daniel Williams and Julia Preston, "U.S. Requests Open-ended Resolution from UN Backing Invasion of Haiti," *Washington Post*, 22 July 1994.

4. Lee Hockstader, "Embargo Translates into Ecological Disaster for Haiti," *Washington Post*, 31 May 1992, p. Al.

5. Haiti Country Profile, 1995–1996 (London: Economic Intelligence Unit, 1995), pp. 38–40.

6. World Disaster Report, 1995 (Geneva: International Federation of Red Cross and Red Crescent Societies, 1995), p. 24.

7. David A. Baldwin, *Economic Statecraft* (Princeton: Princeton University Press, 1985), p. 372.

8. See, for instance, Makio Miyagawa, *Do Economic Sanctions Work?* (New York: St. Martin's Press, 1992); Gary Clyde Hufbauer, Jeffrey J. Schott, Kimberly Ann Elliott, *Economic Sanctions Reconsidered: History and Current Policy*, 2nd ed. (Washington, D.C.: Institute for International Economics, 1990); Hufbauer, Schott, Elliott,

Economic Sanctions Reconsidered: Supplemental Case Histories, 2nd ed. (Washington, D.C.: Institute for International Economics, 1990); Lisa L. Martin, *Coercive Cooperation: Explaining Multilateral Economic Sanctions* (Princeton: Princeton University Press, 1992); Gunnar Adler-Karlsson, "The U.S. Embargo: Inefficient and Counterproductive," *Aussenwirtschaft* XXXV, June 1980, pp. 170–187; Peter A. G. Van Bergeijk, "Success and Failure of Economic Sanctions," *Kyklos*, 42 (1989), pp. 385–403; Howard M. Fish, "The Problems with Sanctions," *Foreign Service Journal* (November 1990), p. 24; *Economic Sanctions* (U.S. General Accounting Office, NSIAD92-106, February 19, 1992).

9. Baldwin, *Economic Statecraft*, pp. 132–133.
10. Ibid., p. 143.
11. See "Haiti: Tightening the Stranglehold," *The Economist*, 6 August 1994, p. 35; John Kifner, "Effort Is Begun by Dominicans to Seal Border," *Washington Post*, 1 June 1994, p. Al; Douglas Farah, "Balaguer Bars Cutting off Haiti," *Washington Post*, 16 May 1994; Robert S. Greenberger, "U.S. Policy on Haiti May Be Affected by Recent Vote in Dominican Republic," *Wall Street Journal*, 27 June 1994.
12. Douglas Farah, "Power in the Shadows in Haiti," *Washington Post*, 20 June 1994; Howard W. French, "Split Reported in Haiti's Army with Chief Urged to Quit," *New York Times*, 27 June 1994, p. A2. Also see Gary Pierre-Pierre, "Haiti Strongman Reported to Set Retirement Date," *New York Times*, 28 June 1994, p. A6.
13. David A. Baldwin, "The Power of Positive Sanctions," *World Politics*, vol. XXIV, no. 1, October 1971, p. 22.
14. Ibid., p. 25.
15. Ibid., p. 23.
16. Ibid., pp. 24–25.
17. Baldwin, *Economic Statecraft*, p. 42.
18. Ibid., "Costs? Compared to What?" p. 140.
19. Harold D. Lasswell, *World Politics Faces Economics* (New York: McGraw Hill, 1945), p. 9.
20. "Give Sanctions Time to Bite, Gray Tells Lawmakers," *Congressional Quarterly*, 11 June 1994, p. 1540.
21. U.S. Department of State Dispatch, vol. 5, no. 38, 19 September 1994, pp. 605, 607.
22. Ibid., pp. 607–608.
23. Colin L. Powell, with Joseph E. Persico, *My American Journey* (New York: Random House, 1995), p. 599.
24. Ibid., p. 600.
25. Ibid., p. 601.
26. Ibid., pp. 601–602.
27. Ibid., p. 612.
28. Assessment Mission to Haiti, December 11–14, 1994 (Atlanta: The Carter Center of Emory University, 1995), Appendix 1.
29. Doyle McManus, "White House Defends Cedras Deal," *Los Angeles Times*, 15 October 1994, p. Al. Personal correspondence dated November 22, 1995, with Doron Bard, Desk Officer, Haiti Working Group, U.S. Department of State verified that an "arrangement" was made between the United States and Gen. Cedras.
30. The U.S. Department of State verified that ". . . all arrangements for Gen. Cedras' departure were made after the Carter Agreement was negotiated, immediately prior to Gen. Cedras' departure." See Note 29.
31. Douglas Jehl, "Haiti Generals Regain Access to $79 Million," *New York Times*, 14 October 1994, p. Al.
32. Douglas Farah, "U.S. Assists Dictators' Luxury Exile," *Washington Post*, 14 October 1994, p. Al. Kenneth Freed, "U.S. Gives Cedras a Lucrative Deal to Get Out

of Haiti," *Los Angeles Times*, 14 October 1994, p. Al. This point was verified by the U.S. Department of State and negotiated ". . . on the eve of Gen. Cedras' departure from Haiti" (see Note 29).

33. Ibid., *Los Angeles Times*. The U.S. Department of State verified that the United States did fly Gen. Cedras and his family out of Haiti (see Note 29).
34. Ibid., *Los Angeles Times*.
35. "Not-so-pampered in exile," *The Economist*, 22 October 1994, p. 56. The U.S. Department of State denied that prepaid rental housing awaited Gen. Cedras in Panama ". . . as far as the U.S. Government is concerned. We are unaware of any such arrangements in Panama" (see Note 29).
36. Ibid.
37. See for instance, Art Buchwald, "It Pays to Be a U.S. Enemy Nowadays," *Los Angeles Times*, 18 October 1994, p. E2; "Why Reward These Thugs? Payoff to Cedras Is a Blot on American Honor," *Los Angeles Times*, 15 October 1994, p. B7.
38. Baldwin, *Economic Statecraft*, p. 22.

Sanctioning Madness

Richard N. Haass

A ROTTEN CORE

Economic sanctions are fast becoming the U.S. policy tool of choice. A 1997 study by the National Association of Manufacturers listed thirty-five countries targeted by new American sanctions from 1993 to 1996 alone. What is noteworthy, however, is not just the frequency with which sanctions are used but their centrality; economic sanctions are increasingly at the core of U.S. foreign policy.

Sanctions—predominantly economic but also political and military penalties aimed at states or other entities so as to alter unacceptable political or military behavior—are employed for a wide range of purposes. The United States, far more than any other country, uses them to discourage the proliferation of weapons of mass destruction and ballistic missiles, promote human rights, end support for terrorism, thwart drug trafficking, discourage armed aggression, protect the environment, and oust governments.[1] To accomplish these ends, sanctions may take the form of arms embargoes, foreign assistance reductions and cutoffs, export and import limitations, asset freezes, tariff increases, import quota decreases, revocation of most favored nation (MFN) trade status, votes in international organizations, withdrawal of diplomatic relations, visa denials, cancellation of air links, and credit, financing, and investment prohibitions. Even U.S. state and local governments are introducing economic sanctions. Dozens have adopted "selective purchasing laws" that prohibit public agencies from purchasing goods and services from companies doing business with such countries as Burma and Indonesia.

With a few exceptions, the growing use of economic sanctions to promote foreign policy objectives is deplorable. This is not simply because sanctions are expensive, although they are. Nor is it strictly a matter of whether sanctions "work"; the answer to that question invariably depends on how demanding a task is set for a particular sanction. Rather, the problem with economic sanctions is that they frequently contribute little to American foreign policy goals while being costly and even counterproductive. A recent study by the Institute for International Economics concluded that in 1995 alone,

Richard N. Haass is the president of the Council on Foreign Relations. Formerly he was director of Foreign Policy Studies at the Brookings Institution.
This article is from *Foreign Affairs* 76, no. 6 (November/December 1997). Reprinted by permission of *Foreign Affairs*. Copyright 1997 by the Council on Foreign Relations, Inc.

sanctions cost U.S. companies between $15 billion and $19 billion and affected some 200,000 workers. Secondary sanctions, levelled against third-party states that do not support a particular sanctions regime, add to this cost by jeopardizing U.S. trade relations. Thus, policymakers need to give more serious consideration to the impact of a sanction and weigh alternative policies more carefully.

THE SANCTIONS BOOM

Economic sanctions are popular because they offer what appears to be a proportional response to challenges in which the interests at stake are less than vital. They are also a form of expression, a way to signal official displeasure with a behavior or action. They thus satisfy a domestic political need to do something and reinforce a commitment to a norm, such as respect for human rights or opposition to weapons proliferation. Reluctance to use military force is another motivation. As the National Conference of Catholic Bishops points out, "Sanctions can offer a nonmilitary alternative to the terrible options of war or indifference when confronted with aggression or injustice."

The frequency with which the United States uses sanctions is also a result of the increased influence, especially on Congress, of single-issue constituencies, notably those promoting human rights, environmentalism, or ethnic, religious, or racially oriented causes. The media, too, plays a part. The so-called CNN effect can increase the visibility of problems in another country and stimulate Americans' desire to respond. Sanctions offer a popular and seemingly cost-free way of acting. The end of the Cold War and the demise of the Soviet Union have also contributed to the sanctions boom. Sanctions can now usually be introduced without opposition from Moscow, which in the past meant a veto in the UN Security Council or a Soviet subsidy for a target of U.S. sanctions.

Some evidence supports the efficacy of economic sanctions. One influential study concludes from analysis of more than 100 cases that economic sanctions have worked to some extent about a third of the time.[2] Other advocates are more selective in their views of history. For groups on the left, it is an article of faith that sanctions helped dismantle apartheid, just as the right argues that sanctions played a major role in the demise of the "evil empire."

Under the right circumstances, sanctions can achieve, or help achieve, various foreign policy goals ranging from the modest to the fairly significant. Sanctions introduced against Iraq after the Persian Gulf War have increased Iraqi compliance with UN resolutions calling for the elimination of its weapons of mass destruction. They have also diminished Baghdad's ability to import weapons and related technology. Iraq today is considerably weaker militarily and economically than it would have been without these sanctions.

Sanctions were one reason for the Serbs' decision to accept the Dayton agreement in August 1995 ending the fighting in Bosnia. The threat of sanctions may have also deterred several European firms from investing in Iran's oil and gas industry. Sanctions have burdened the economies of Iran, Cuba, and Libya, and may eventually contribute to change in those societies or in their behavior. U.S. sanctions against Pakistan, while having little discernible effect on that country's nuclear weapons program, have hurt Islamabad both economically and militarily, possibly influencing Pakistan's future actions as well as those of other would-be proliferators.

More Harm than Good

The limitations of sanctions are more pronounced than their accomplishments. Sanctions alone are unlikely to achieve results if the aims are large or time is short. Even though they were comprehensive and enjoyed almost universal international backing for nearly six months, sanctions failed to compel Saddam Hussein to withdraw from Kuwait in 1990. In the end, it took nothing less than Operation Desert Storm.

Other sanctions have also fallen short of their stated purposes. Despite sanctions against Iran, Tehran remains defiant in its support of terrorism, its subversion of its neighbors, its opposition to the Middle East peace process, and its pursuit of nuclear weapons. Fidel Castro still commands an authoritarian political system and a statist economy. Pakistan's nuclear program is well advanced; it now has enough material for at least a dozen bombs. Libya has refused to hand over the two individuals accused of destroying Pan Am Flight 103 over Lockerbie, Scotland. Sanctions did not persuade Haiti's junta to honor the results of the 1990 election that brought Jean Bertrand Aristide to power, nor did they convince Serbia and the Bosnian Serbs for several years to call off their military aggression. Unilateral sanctions are particularly ineffective. In a global economy, unilateral sanctions impose higher costs on American firms than on the target country, which can usually find substitute sources of supply and financing. Unilateral sanctions did, however, prove more costly for Haiti and Cuba, which were heavily dependent on trade with the United States. They also hurt Pakistan, which had been receiving substantial U.S. military and economic aid. Such cases are the exception, though; most unilateral sanctions will be little more than costly expressions of opposition except in those instances in which the ties between the United States and the target are so extensive that the latter cannot adjust to an American cutoff.

Generating international support for sanctions is often extremely difficult. In most instances, other governments prefer minimal sanctions, or none at all. They tend to value commercial interaction more than the United States does and are less willing to forfeit it. In addition, the argument that economic interaction is desirable because it promotes more open political and economic systems normally has more resonance in other capitals, although it has been used successfully by both the Bush and Clinton administrations to defeat Congress's attempts to revoke China's MFN status. Such thinking makes achieving multilateral support for sanctions more difficult for the United States. It usually takes something truly egregious, like Saddam Hussein's occupation of Kuwait, to overcome this antisanctions bias. Even with Iraq, generous compensation for third-party states affected by the sanctions, including Egypt and Turkey, was a prerequisite for their support.

Trying to compel others to join a sanctions regime by threatening secondary sanctions can seriously harm U.S. foreign policy interests. Congress is increasingly turning to secondary sanctions to bolster ineffective unilateral sanctions regimes, as with Cuba, Iran, and Libya; in all three instances, sanctions now apply to overseas firms that violate the terms of U.S. legislation like the Iran-Libya Sanctions Act and Helms-Burton Act. This threat appears to have deterred some individuals and firms from entering into proscribed business activities, but it has increased anti-American sentiment, threatened the future of the World Trade Organization (WTO), distracted attention from the provocative behavior of the target governments, and made Europeans less likely to work with the United States in shaping policies to contend with post–Cold War challenges.

MISSING THE TARGET

Sanctions often produce unintended and undesirable consequences. Haiti is a prime example. Sanctions exacerbated the island's economic distress, causing a massive exodus of Haitians to the United States that proved life-threatening for them and expensive and disruptive for Florida. In Bosnia, the arms embargo weakened the Muslims, since Bosnia's Serbs and Croats had larger stores of military supplies and greater access to outside sources. This military imbalance contributed to the fighting and to the disproportionate Muslim suffering. Military sanctions against Pakistan may actually have increased Islamabad's reliance on a nuclear option because they cut off its access to U.S. weaponry and dramatically weakened Pakistan's confidence in Washington.

All this demonstrates that sanctions can be a blunt instrument. Most sanctions do not discriminate within the target country. There is a rationale for this: Funds and goods can easily be moved around, and governments can often command what is in the hands of others. The problem with such a broad-brush approach is that sanctions tend to affect the general population, while those in the government and the military are able to skirt the sanctions.

Thus, the tendency to see economic sanctions as "below" the use of military force on some imagined ladder of foreign policy escalation must be revised. Sanctions can be a powerful and deadly form of intervention. The danger inherent in broad sanctions—beyond missing the true target—is both moral, in that innocents are affected, and practical, in that sanctions that harm the general population can bring about undesired effects, including strengthening the regime, triggering large-scale emigration, and retarding the emergence of a middle class and a civil society. Mass hardship can also weaken domestic and international support for sanctions, as with Iraq, despite the fact that those sanctions have included from the outset a provision allowing Iraq to import humanitarian goods and services.

"NOT-SO-SMART" SANCTIONS

"Smart" or "designer" sanctions, which penalize leaders while sparing the general public, are only a partial solution. It is possible that Haiti's military leaders were bothered by the fact their families could no longer shop in Florida. And executives who risk being denied access to the United States under the 1996 Helms-Burton Act may think twice before entering into proscribed business deals. But opportunities to employ effective sanctions with precision are rare. Gathering the necessary information about assets, and then moving quickly enough to freeze them, can often prove impossible. Leaders and governments have many ways to insulate themselves, and designing "smart" sanctions to target only them is extraordinarily difficult, especially with a totalitarian or authoritarian state run by a few people.

In addition, authoritarian, statist societies are often able to hunker down and withstand the effects of sanctions. There are several possible reasons: Sanctions sometimes trigger a "rally around the flag" nationalist reaction; by creating scarcity, they enable governments to better control the distribution of goods; and they create a general sense of siege that governments can exploit to maintain political control. This conclusion is consistent with literature suggesting that market economic reform reinforces the development of civil society; by reducing the scope for independent action, sanctions can work against forces promoting political pluralism.

Last, but far from least, sanctions can be expensive for American business. There is a tendency to overlook or underestimate the direct costs of sanctions, perhaps because, unlike the costs of military intervention, they do not show up in U.S. government budget tables. Sanctions do, however, affect the economy by reducing revenues of U.S. companies and individuals. Moreover, this cost is difficult to measure because it includes not only lost sales but also forfeited opportunities: Governments and overseas companies can elect not to do business with the United States for fear that sanctions might one day be introduced, wreaking havoc with normal commercial relations.

TAKING SANCTIONS SERIOUSLY

A fundamental change in thinking and attitude is required. Economic sanctions are a serious instrument of foreign policy and should be employed only after consideration no less rigorous than for other forms of intervention, including the use of military force. The likely benefits of a particular sanction to U.S. foreign policy should be greater than the anticipated costs to the U.S. government and the American economy. Moreover, the sanction's likely effect on U.S. interests should compare favorably to the projected consequences of all other options, including military intervention, covert action, public and private diplomacy, or simply doing nothing. Broad sanctions should not be used as a means of expression. Foreign policy is not therapy; its purpose is not to make us feel good but to do good. The same holds for sanctions.

For pragmatic more than normative reasons, multilateral support for economic sanctions should typically be a prerequisite for the U.S. imposition of them. Such support need not be simultaneous, but it should be all but certain to follow. Except when the United States is in a unique position to exert leverage based on its economic relationship with the target, unilateral sanctions should be avoided. Building international support will require intense, often high-level diplomatic efforts and even then may not succeed. Policy-makers must then consider whether some alternative would not be better than weaker or unilateral sanctions.

International compliance with sanctions regimes can be increased by providing assistance to third parties to offset the economic cost of implementing sanctions. Greater use should be made of Article 50 of the UN Charter, which allows such states to approach the Security Council for redress. In addition, a fund for this purpose should be established within the U.S. foreign assistance budget. The cost would be more than offset by the benefits of multilateral cooperation.

By contrast, secondary sanctions are not a desirable means of securing multilateral support. They are not only an admission of diplomatic failure but they are also expensive. The costs to U.S. foreign policy, including the damage to relations with major partners and U.S. efforts to build an effective WTO, almost always outweigh the potential benefits of coercing unwilling friends to join sanctions regimes.

Sanctions should focus, as far as possible, on those responsible for the offending behavior and on limiting penalties to the particular area of dispute. Such limited sanctions would avoid jeopardizing other interests or an entire bilateral relationship. They would cause less collateral damage to innocents, and make it easier to garner multinational support. Sanctions designed to stem the proliferation of weapons of mass destruction are a prime example. Where there are transgressions, the United States should direct any sanctions toward nuclear- or weapons-related activity, for example by cutting off associated technological cooperation or trade. Similarly, political responses such as event boycotts and visa denials might be the best way to signal opposition to objectionable behavior when no appropriate economic or military sanction is available or as a complement to something as specific as freezing an individual's assets. Political sanctions should not, however, extend to breaking diplomatic relations or canceling high-level meetings. Such interactions help the United States as much as the targeted party.

Sanctions should not hold major or complex bilateral relationships hostage to one or two issues. This is especially true with a country like China, where the United States has to balance interests that include maintaining stability on the Korean peninsula, discouraging any support for "rogue" states' weapons of mass destruction or ballistic missile programs, managing the Taiwan–China situation, and promoting trade, market reform, and human rights. Similarly, the United States has a range of interests with Pakistan that go well beyond nuclear matters, including promoting democracy, economic development, and regional stability. The principal alternative to broad sanctions in such instances is sanctions that are narrow and germane to the issue at hand. With Pakistan, for example, sanctions could focus on specific defense articles and technologies but exempt all economic assistance and military education and training.

Humanitarian exceptions should be part of any comprehensive sanctions regime. In part, this is a moral judgment, that innocents should not be made to suffer any more than is absolutely necessary. But it is also pragmatic, since it is easier to generate and sustain domestic and international support for sanctions that allow the importation of food and medicine. Sanctions, however, should not necessarily be suspended if the humanitarian harm is the direct result of cynical government policy, such as Iraq's, that creates shortages among the general population in order to garner international sympathy.

Any imposition of sanctions should be swift. As with other forms of intervention, including military action, gradual escalation allows the target to adapt and adjust. Such an approach forfeits shock value and allows asset shifting, hoarding, and other arrangements to circumvent sanctions—as Libya and Iran found. This recommendation is easier said than done, since gaining international support for sanctions will in many cases require that the United States move slowly and gradually, further limiting the potential effectiveness of economic sanctions in today's world.

GETTING IT RIGHT

Policymakers should be required to prepare and send to Congress a policy statement similar to the reports prepared and forwarded under the 1973 War Powers Act before or soon after a sanction is put in place. Such statements should clearly explain the sanction's purpose, the legal or political authority supporting its use, the expected impact on the target, retaliatory steps the target or third parties may take, the probable humanitarian consequences and what is being done to minimize them, the expected costs to the United States, prospects for enforcement, the expected degree of international support or opposition, and an exit strategy, including the criteria for lifting the sanction. In addition, policymakers should be able to explain why a particular sanction was selected over other sanctions or policies. If necessary, portions of this report could be classified to avoid providing information that would be useful to the target. Any sanction Congress initiates should be approved only after the relevant committees have carefully considered the matter;

members being asked to vote on the proposal would then be able to refer to a report that addresses their questions.

All sanctions embedded in legislation should allow the president to suspend or terminate them in the interest of national security. Beyond being consistent with the Constitution's bias in favor of executive primacy in foreign affairs, such latitude is needed if relationships are not to fall hostage to one interest and if the executive is to have the flexibility to explore whether limited incentives could bring about a desired policy result. The benefits of this latitude outweigh any diminution of automatic sanctions' deterrent power. Current legislation that mandates sanctions in specific circumstances should be repealed or modified.

The federal government, together with affected firms, should challenge in court states' and municipalities' right to institute economic sanctions against companies and individuals operating in their jurisdiction. This practice is eliciting protests not just from the targeted countries but from the European Union, which argues convincingly that such sanctions violate commitments made by the U.S. government to the World Trade Organization. The Constitution may not settle the struggle between the executive and legislative branches in foreign affairs, but it limits it to the federal branch of government.[3] State and local sanctions undermine the flexibility necessary for the executive branch to effectively carry out foreign policy. To paraphrase Justice Louis Brandeis, states may be laboratories of democracy, but not of diplomacy. Unfortunately, the Clinton administration—like the Reagan administration, which never challenged the more than 100 state and local sanctions targeting firms involved with South Africa—has chosen not to confront this issue. Beyond using the legal system, companies might consider deploying their economic power and avoid investing in states that have a history of supporting sanctions. Firms would also be wise to build broader coalitions (including labor unions) that would have a stake in opposing certain state and local sanctions.

Any sanction should be the subject of an annual impact statement, prepared by the executive branch and submitted in unclassified form to Congress, which would provide far more information and analysis than the pro forma documents written to justify many current sanctions. Like the report that would accompany a new sanction, the annual statement would introduce much-needed rigor into the sanction's decision-making process. A more careful calculation of economic costs would also provide a basis for determining payments to workers and companies being asked to bear a disproportionate share of the sanctions burden. Such seriousness has not been the hallmark of the American embrace of sanctions, which are often imposed and maintained with only cursory analysis of likely or actual effects.

The consequences of what is recommended here—less frequent and more modest use of economic sanctions—would risk creating something of a policy vacuum. In Washington it is difficult to beat something with nothing. So how does one beat economic sanctions?

Sometimes military force will be required. This was the lesson of Desert Storm and Bosnia. In Cuba, for example, instead of tightening sanctions—which increased the misery of the Cuban people—and going along with Congress's introduction of secondary sanctions against U.S. allies, the Clinton administration might have been wiser to launch a cruise missile salvo or use stealth aircraft to take out the MiGs that in 1996 shot down the unarmed plane flown by Cuban exiles from the group Brothers to the Rescue.

In other instances, focused sanctions could be useful. A more appropriate response to Pakistan's nuclear program would have been export controls designed to slow missile and nuclear bomb development. With Haiti, narrow sanctions aimed at the illegitimate leadership would not have triggered the human exodus that pressured the administration into an armed intervention that could well have proved far more costly than it did. China was stung by the U.S. decision to oppose Beijing's bid to host the Olympic games in the year 2000 and is bothered by being singled out in various international bodies for its treatment of its citizens.

The principal alternative to economic sanctions is best described as constructive or conditional engagement. Such an approach, involving a mix of narrow sanctions and limited political and economic interactions that are conditioned on specified behavioral changes, might be preferable, especially if the goal is to weaken the near-monopoly of an authoritarian leadership over a country like Cuba, Iran, or China. Such an approach is not as simple as imposing economic sanctions; nor does it yield as dramatic a sound bite. Its principal advantage is that it might have a more desirable impact at less cost to Americans and American foreign policy.

NOTES

1. Excluded here are sanctions introduced to ensure market access or compliance with trade pacts. Economic sanctions for economic purposes tend to be used pursuant to the rules that guide trade. By contrast, economic sanctions for political purposes work in the absence of any agreed-on political or legal framework.
2. Gary Clyde Hufbauer, Jeffrey J. Schott, and Kimberly Ann Elliott, *Economic Sanctions Reconsidered: History and Current Policy*, 2nd ed. (Washington, D.C.: Institute for International Economics, 1990). This relatively positive assessment is hotly disputed on the grounds that the authors were overly generous in judging what constitutes "success" and in not properly disaggregating the effects of sanctions from the impact of the threat or use of military force. See Robert A. Pape, "Why Economic Sanctions Still Do Not Work," *International Security* (fall 1997), pp. 90–136.
3. David Schmahmann and James Finch, "The Unconstitutionality of State and Local Enactments in the United States Restricting Business Ties with Burma (Myanmar)," *Vanderbilt Journal of Transnational Law* (March 1997), pp. 175–207.

ISSUE 7

ISRAEL AND PALESTINE

Deeply enmeshed with America's war on terrorism is the conflict between Israel and the Palestinians that Israel displaced. In 1948, with substantial support from the United States, Great Britain, and other European countries, Jews from around the world established the state of Israel in territory formerly occupied by Palestinians. More than a half century and several wars later, the Palestinians are still struggling, some to regain their homeland, and some to eliminate Israel altogether. Although every American president since Truman has been concerned with various conflicts related to Israel in the Middle East, every president since Jimmy Carter has exerted considerable effort to resolve the conflict between the Israelis and Palestinians. Although these efforts have helped to continue a dialogue between the two parties, the Israeli–Palestinian conflict seems as intractable as ever. Unremitting conflict has resumed after the hopes of the July 2000 Camp David meetings floundered on the shoals of mutual suspicions and recriminations.

Israel lays the blame for the "Terror Intifada" squarely on the shoulders of the Palestinian Authority for its refusal to fully commit itself to a negotiated peace process. Charging that the Palestinian Authority has pursued violence as a political tool, the Israeli government accuses the PA of allowing the recent violence in order to cover up its failure to negotiate in good faith.

Chairman Arafat's speech to the Davos meetings (economic summit) charged that Israel's continuing "policy of economic strangulation" has sowed the seeds of the current conflict. This despair, when coupled with Arafat's additional accusation that Israel has backed away from the positions it took in the Oslo Accords of 1993, explains the continuing frustration of the Palestinian people, and their heightened suspicion of the commitment of Israel to an equitable settlement.

In view of this conflict, what should America do? Should we give continued strong support to Israel, or should we be more sensitive to the needs of the Palestinians?

In the following speeches, Representatives Michael Pence (R-IN) and Barney Frank (D-MA) first explain why the United States should support Israel. Senator Charles Hagel (R-NE) then warns us that justice for the Palestinians is not only merited by the treatment they have received, but also is in the interest of the United States.

DISCUSSION QUESTIONS

As you read the speeches by Representatives Pence and Frank and Senator Hagel, consider the following questions:

1. Is a Palestinian state the only reasonable solution to the Israeli–Palestinian conflict?
2. Should the United States apply more pressure on Israel to come to an agreement with the PLO?
3. Should the United States be providing more aid to the Palestinians?

KEY WEB SITES

For more information on this topic, visit the following Web sites:

Official U.S. State Department Web site for the Sharm El-Sheikh Fact-Finding Committee (the Mitchell Committee)

http://usinfo.state.gov/regional/nea/mitchell.htm

Official Web site of the Israel Ministry of Foreign Affairs

http://www.israel.org/mfa/home.asp

Official Web site of the Palestinian Liberation Organization—Negotiations Affairs Department

http://www.nad-plo.org

Support for Israel

Representative Michael Pence / Representative Barney Frank

U.S. House of Representatives, Washington, D.C.
December 4, 2001
Representative Michael Pence

Mr. Speaker, I rise today after a harrowing set of days, explosions, fire, innocent civilians running in panic through the streets; and I do not refer to life in America, New York City, or in the environs of the Pentagon on September 11; but I speak of Jerusalem and Israel. I speak of a nation that in the last week and past several days has grievously lost husbands and fathers, wives and mothers, sons and daughters, grandsons and granddaughters to the scourge of political terror.

I rise today humbly to speak of Israel and of the precious relationship that does and must continue to exist between the Government of the United States and the government of that great and historic people. As an American, a Christian, and a Hoosier, it is my firm belief now more than ever that it is my duty to insist that the United States of America never waver in protecting and defending the interests of the State of Israel in its battle for survival in this dangerous part of the world, and in its efforts now to open up, as the President's press secretary spoke yesterday, of the second front of the war on terrorism.

Mr. Speaker, many of these things may seem obvious, but many in the media are having a hard time figuring out who is right in the current conflict and how to best stop, we are told, the cycle of violence in order to help the parties get back to the negotiating table so they can iron out differences and misunderstandings. While I will say I am the first to admit that I know less than most of my colleagues do about Israel and its importance to America, let me say what I think this conflict is about and see whether my colleagues might agree.

Mr. Speaker, first I want to assert that I do not think that there is anything current about this conflict. I believe it is part of a continuing struggle being waged by many in the Arab world of extremists' views to do nothing other than to destroy the State of Israel, period. It is the historic aim of many in the terrorist organizations of Palestine and elsewhere, and the conflict today is simply an extension of that.

As to the question of who is right, that is simple. Mr. Speaker, it has ever been the policy of the United States of America and the people of this country since 1948 that Israel is right, believing as I do, as millions of Americans do, that He will still bless those who bless Israel, and so we stand with her.

A cycle of violence, I reject the term. When terrorists blow up a school bus or explode bombs in a mall killing children and innocent men and women, this is their aim. When Israel defense forces strike back, as they are at this hour and have in the last twenty-four hours, killing known terrorists and neutralizing terrorist assets, Mr. Speaker, this is not a cycle of violence; it is Israel performing her own self-defense.

As to returning to negotiations, one might ask what is there left to negotiate. Last summer at Camp David former Prime Minister Barak offered Yasser Arafat virtually everything. And how did Arafat respond? By launching a nine-month guerrilla war culminating this weekend, targeting women and children, some of whom were born in this country, and even in my State of Indiana. No, Yasser Arafat is not an effective negotiating partner. He is a terrorist, and it is time America stood strongly by Israel and said to Yasser Arafat, it is time that the terrorists and their capabilities are secured within the Palestinian Authority or else.

U.S. House of Representatives, Washington, D.C.
May 20, 2002
Representative Barney Frank

Mr. Speaker, I apologize to the hard-working members of our staff for keeping them here at this hour. I do not often indulge in long speeches at this time of night, but I do feel an obligation to talk about the situation in the Middle East, particularly the security of Israel and the position of Israel vis-à-vis the United States, for two reasons.

First, it is a subject both very important and very emotional. A large number of people in my district, as in every other, care deeply about this. I believe the people who feel the most strongly and the largest number are people who, like myself, have both an emotional attachment to Israel and also a strong intellectual degree of support for it. There are others who are troubled by what is happening in the Middle East and are somewhat critical or harshly critical of the Israeli government.

I think it is an obligation of those of us in elected office when an issue is of this importance to explain ourselves, and I find here, given the complexity of the issue, I think it is an essentially simple one. I believe that simplicity consists of the fact that for more than fifty years, until maybe recently, and we still do not know this, there has been an unwillingness on the part of the Arab community in the Middle East to allow Israel to exist.

The troubles began when the UN voted in a resolution, UN resolutions have become the currency in the Middle East of late, but the most important UN resolution, the one which said that there should be two states, Israel and

Palestine, was not only disregarded by the Arab world at that time, but became the occasion for violent attack, and it always ought to be remembered if the Arab world had abided by UN resolutions fifty-some years ago, we would have the two-state solution which so many, including myself, think is the best ultimate answer, without a lot of killing and without a lot of misery and pain. But while there is essential simplicity to the issue, there are, when things have been going on for fifty-five years, a great deal of complexity, and that needs to be addressed.

But I also want to talk about it precisely because I do believe very strongly that the continued existence of Israel as a free, democratic society, with secure boundaries, is important morally for the world, as well as in our interests as a country. I worry that some people, particularly within Israel, may have misinterpreted recent events in the United States.

I think there continues to be very strong support for Israel's right to exist and for its right to have secure boundaries. I think there is a great deal of admiration, as there should be, for what Israel has accomplished economically and socially and politically in the broadest sense, that is, maintaining a democracy.

The excuse we often hear from violators of human rights, people who disregard democratic procedures, is that democracy is kind of a luxury for a nation that is at peace, but we are often told when a nation is at war, it really cannot afford to be democratic, it cannot afford such luxuries as electing a government and then throwing it out of office by open means, a freely critical parliament, open press, free speech.

In fact, Israel, from the moment of its existence, was under siege; indeed, people were attacking it before it existed as a sovereign nation. It has been in a war-like state, unfortunately, I think not through its own choice, for its entire existence, and, despite that, has brought forward one of the most flourishing democracies in the world and, sadly, the only democracy of any consistency in that part of the world. So I am grateful to the people of Israel for showing that democracy is not a source of weakness, not something to be put aside when things are tough, but a source of great strength.

That respect for Israel, that admiration for it, that understanding that it has played a very important role as an ally of America, all contribute to a great deal of American support for Israel, as does the fact that it is, as we know, the successor state to that horror, the Holocaust, in which an organized state tried to wipe out a people, and came closer than anyone would have thought before could have been done.

Yes, there is a moral obligation to the remnants of the Holocaust and they were given a safe haven. As we know, had there been such a place during the time of the Holocaust, many who died, many who escaped only to be sent back because no one would take them, would still be alive.

So there is legitimately a great deal of support for Israel. What I fear, however, is that some within Israel will assume that that support is there, here in America, no matter what, despite policy decisions Israel might take.

Now, Israel is a democracy, as I said, and people will say, you know, a democracy has a right to make its own choices. Of course it does. The people of Israel have a right to elect governments, advocate positions, as any democracy does. I will note that there is a certain inconsistency from some who now say that because when Ehud Barak was prime minister and trying very hard with the support of former President Clinton to reach a reasonable peace, some of those who now tell me that it is inappropriate to differ with the government of Israel were much less reluctant to do that under Prime Minister Barak or under the martyred Prime Minister Yitzak Rabin. But Israel has a right to make decisions.

On the other hand, it is also the case that the United States is a democracy and it has a right to make decisions.

Now, American support at a very high level is essential, I believe, for Israel to be able to survive as a free and secure society. It is a small population. They have done wonders. But they are so heavily outnumbered, they are devoid of the kind of resources that many of their historic enemies have had, and there has been, for reasons that do the rest of the world no credit, a great deal of unfair criticism, I think, of Israel, so Israel has really found itself consistently bereft of friends in many cases when it counted, with the consistent exception of the United States.

It is entirely valid for the United States, in my judgment, to provide a degree of military assistance to Israel. This is a nation which is forced to survive to spend a very high percentage of its own income on the military. I think America plays a very useful role in helping them deal with that.

It is a nation which has had a policy of taking in people from the former Soviet Union, from Ethiopia, from Arab countries who were driven out, Yemen, Morocco, and elsewhere. It is very important that they be able to play that role, and I think the money we provide is helpful.

We should note, of course, Israel is the number one recipient of American foreign aid, and Egypt is the second largest recipient of foreign aid, and that is probably because twenty-five years ago the leaders of Egypt and Israel, Menachem Begin and Anwar Sadat, took great risks for peace and engaged in a great transfer of land, really a somewhat extraordinary example in history, where the victorious nation, Israel, gave back to the defeated nation a very large piece of land, the Sinai desert, so that you could begin to have peace.

While there have been problems and difficulties, peace has in fact survived there, and I think the work of Menachem Begin and Anwar Sadat was vindicated. People should note that Menachem Begin, who was one of the intellectual and political founders of the current conservative movement in Israel, not only made peace with Egypt, not only gave back land, but presided over the dismantlement of a settlement, a Jewish settlement, in the Sinai, so that it could be given back. I think that is a very important precedent that I will get back to.

But we should understand that the United States gives high levels of aid to Israel and Egypt in part because of a perception that these are allies, in part because of the great admiration we have for Israeli society, but also since 1977–78 because these two nations undertook that peace agreement, and I think it was an entirely constructive policy begun in the Carter administration and carried through Presidents Reagan and Bush and Clinton, and now President Bush again, to say that if countries in an area that is very important to America take risks for peace and try very hard to overcome these difficulties, the United States will try to help out. That was an entirely fitting situation and people should understand.

That is the biggest single reason why there was this ongoing degree of aid. So I think that is entirely appropriate. I look forward to continuing to support a level of aid appropriate to Israel until and unless there is a peace; and if and when peace is achieved, yes, it will be possible to reduce the level of aid. . . .

Now, I have a question for those who say, well, what we really need is a two-state solution. Why did the Arab world not implement one fifty-four years ago? The UN called for a two-state solution, Palestine and Israel. The Arabs attacked and tried to prevent that from happening. The nation that became Israel was able to defend itself. At that point, there was an Israel. Also at this point, the lands that we now refer to as being occupied by Israel, the Gaza Strip and the West Bank, were under the control of Arabs. Jordan controlled the West Bank, including eastern Jerusalem, the Old City. Egypt controlled the Gaza Strip.

From 1948 to 1967, the Gaza Strip, the West Bank in east Jerusalem, were controlled by Arab nations. Why, and I really think this is a valid question not often enough asked, why did they not create a Palestine then? If the Arab world genuinely believes in a two-state solution, why did they not implement one when they had the chance? There was certainly a period when Israel did not have the strength, even if it had the interest, in trying to prevent that from happening. I do not understand why the Egyptians and Jordanians did not get together and create that two-state solution. They talk about how much of the West Bank they had; they had it all, by definition, before 1967.

The reason, I am afraid, is, and this is very relevant and continues to be, the reason the Arab world did not implement the two-state solution is that they were not for a two-state solution. They were for a one-state solution. Palestine, no Israel. They did not use their ability to implement an Arab nation of Palestine in the Gaza Strip and the West Bank from 1948 to 1967 because to do so would have meant accepting the reality of Israel, and they were not ready to do that. Instead, what they did was to use the Gaza Strip and the West Bank and the Golan Heights of Syria and other lands as a basis for continuing to attack Israel. There was a continuing effort to undo Israel's existence militarily.

So in 1967, I believe entirely in self-defense, Israel moved into those adjacent areas, which had been used as places from which Israel was attacked. That is when Israel moved into the Gaza Strip and the West Bank, after the Arab nations, for nineteen years, declined to create a state there and, instead, preferred to use them as bases to attack Israel. Israel wound up with the Sinai Peninsula from Egypt, the Gaza Strip, the West Bank, and the Golan Heights.

Since that time, the Israelis and, obviously, a lot of history goes back to the 1973 war, which was more of a standoff, although it was again an effort by the Arabs to destroy Israel, the 1973 war was the Arabs taking another chance, as they did in 1948, of trying to dismantle Israel and they made some gains at first but were ultimately unable to do that with some help from the Nixon administration; the Israelis were able to defend themselves and maintain that status quo. Then ensued a period of people feeling each other out.

The next thing that happened was that Menachem Begin met with Anwar Sadat; Menachem Begin, the leader of the right in Israel and the man who undid the previously uninterrupted rule of the left in Israel politically, and what he did was to proceed to give the Sinai Peninsula back to Egypt, not for any material gain, but remember what the deal was. Israel gave back the Sinai Peninsula and dismantled a settlement of Jews in that peninsula solely for Egypt's recognition of Israel's right to exist. Until then, that did not exist. It is a nation which has had a policy of taking in people from the former Soviet Union, from Ethiopia, from Arab countries who were driven out, Yemen, Morocco and elsewhere. It is very important that they be able to play that role, and I think the money we provide is helpful.

Guarantee a Palestinian Homeland

Senator Charles Hagel

U.S. Senate, Washington, D.C.
June 14, 2002

Mr. President, I rise today to address an issue of urgent concern for American foreign policy: the situation in the Middle East and its implications for our war on terrorism.

Yesterday the majority leader offered three principles to guide our policy in the Middle East. I share his concern about the gravity of the situation we face and his affirmation of American support for Israel, and the imperative of American leadership in helping bring about a lasting peace in the region.

Time is not on our side. In April, I spoke before this body in support of President Bush's leadership in bringing a diplomatic resolution to this conflict. I applaud the President and his team for their progress so far in assembling the pieces of a potentially historic agreement and coalition for peace. But we are still only at the beginning of a long and difficult process.

What happens in the Middle East cannot be separated from our interests in the war on terrorism. If we fail in peacemaking between Israel and her neighbors, there will be grave consequences for the United States, Israel, and the world. We will further empower the terrorists and extremists, those who thrive, find refuge, and recruit in conditions of poverty, violence, and despair. We must help secure a vision of hope for the people of the Middle East in order to reclaim the peace initiative.

It is time to put the endgame up front in the Israeli–Palestinian conflict. The Palestinians must have a state, with contiguous and secure borders, and Israel must have a state without terrorism and with secure borders. President Bush endorsed the concept of a Palestinian state in a historic speech to the United Nations last year. If we do not address this, the core political issue of this conflict, we will allow the extremists on both sides to win. And then we will all lose: Palestinians, Israelis, Arabs, Americans, the world.

Strong, engaged, steady, and visionary American leadership is a predicate for the future of the Middle East. The Arab League peace proposal, at the initiative of Crown Prince Abdullah of Saudi Arabia, calls for normal relations between Israel and the Arab world and presents a unique and historic opportunity for peace. The Bush administration may be considering recognizing a transitional or provisional Palestinian state, with the specific details to be worked out over time, an idea similar to the Peres-Abu Ala agreement of last year. The so-called "Quartet"—US, Russia, the EU, and the UN—provides an international context for this possibility and a revived diplomatic track.

The pieces may be in place, the image of an idea for peace forming on the horizon, although the work ahead will be difficult. There are no easy answers or risk-free options. We can no longer defer the tough decisions on Israeli settlements, Palestinian refugees, borders, and the status of Jerusalem. The time for a step-by-step sequential process has come and gone. We are close to reaching a line of demarcation, where only bold and courageous leadership on all sides can show the way to a resolution.

Israel must make some hard choices for peace. It knows that military means alone will not end terrorism. Settlements in the occupied West Bank and Gaza must end.

Israel should withdraw its military from the Palestinian towns it has reoccupied, as soon as the security situation allows. The emphasis for Israel must be on developing a coalition of common interests including our Arab allies and the United States to form the core of a peace coalition. Israel should move closer to this coalition and away from isolation and reliance on only the military option to ending the crisis.

The Israeli people have suffered too much and too long from terrorism. It must end. America will continue to stand by our friend and do what we must to help secure a peace and Israel's survival. But America's support of Israel should not be at the expense or exclusion of our relationships with our Arab friends and the Palestinian people. It need not be. America is against terrorists, America is not against Arabs or Palestinians. We are and can be a friend and supporter of all sides. We must be, or there will be no hope and no peace.

This also means that we will not retreat from our support of democratic principles, values, and expectations. We will not trade friendship and freedom for expediency and peace.

The other Arab leaders of the region must play a major role in this revived peace process. They have serious responsibilities and significant self-interests in helping end terrorism and resolving this conflict. There is no longer room for ambiguity or criticism from the sidelines. Abdication of responsibility or subtlety is no longer an option.

Crown Prince Abdullah, King Abdullah of Jordan, and President Mubarak of Egypt and other Arab leaders clearly understand the high stakes and are willing to take risks for peace. The prospects for getting a peace process back on track is best served when the risks are shared.

The Palestinian leadership must respond to the challenge and opportunity before it. Terrorism does an injustice to the Palestinian struggle for self-determination. A Palestinian state cannot be born from and committed to terrorism and hostility toward its neighbor.

It is a tragedy that the Palestinian people have been linked in the minds of many people—many Americans, to the methods of terrorists and extremists who represent only darkness and hatred, not the aspirations of most Palestinians for statehood and a life of hope and peace.

Real reform and change within the Palestinian Authority has become a condition of any peace agreement. This must happen—and happen now. The present Palestinian government must stand up and show a leadership that has been lacking for too long. The current Palestinian leaders must be accountable and take responsibility for the future of the Palestinian people. Terrorism and violence are not the means to statehood and legitimacy.

American and Israeli pressure and intervention, however, cannot be the final determinants of a new Palestinian leadership. An alternative Palestinian leadership, as Foreign Minister Shimon Peres told me a couple of months ago, may be either too weak to make peace or too radical to even consider it. This will certainly be the case if alternative leadership is perceived as primarily the result of American or Israeli collaboration.

There are those in the Palestinian movement that have been speaking out for democracy and against corruption in the Palestinian Authority for some time. Hanan Ashrawi and Mustafa Barghouti, as well as many others, have been taking risks for democracy for Palestinians and transparency in Palestinian governance long before it became a condition for a renewed peace process.

Leaders of the Arab world must take more responsibility for Palestinian leadership. They cannot look away. It is now far too dangerous for them to allow further drift in the Middle East.

In considering the difficult road ahead, I understand the political constraints and risks that Israel and our Arab friends face in moving forward with peace. But it is better to share the risk than leave the field to the terrorists and extremists who will fill the leadership vacuum.

The problems in the Middle East affect and influence all aspects of our foreign policy, including our leadership in the war on terrorism. The Arab–Israeli conflict cannot be separated from America's foreign policy. Actions in the Middle East have immense consequences for our other policies and interests in the world. We are limited in dealing with other conflicts until this conflict is on a path to resolution.

America's policy and role in the Middle East, and the perception of our policies and role across the globe, affects our policies and interests in Afghanistan, South Asia, Indonesia, and all parts of the world. We cannot defeat terrorism without the active support of our friends and allies around the world. This will require an enhancement of our relationships, not an enhancement of our power. It will require America's reaching out to other nations. It will require a wider lens in our foreign policy with a new emphasis on humanitarian, economic, and trade issues as well as military and intelligence relationships.

We need the active support and involvement of Egypt, Saudi Arabia, Jordan, and the other states of the Middle East to defeat terrorism. The potential for isolating them on one side, with the United States and Israel on the other, is the wrong path. The alternative to developing coalitions of common interest in the Middle East and our war on terrorism is a region afire with radicalism and rage directed at Israel and the United States. We cannot wait. We cannot defer the peace timetable to the perfect time for peace. There is no perfect time for peace or perfect set of dynamics for peace. It will happen because we make it happen. We must seize the time we have, with all its imperfections.

The perception of American power becomes the reality of American power. If we fail in our diplomatic efforts to help bring peace to Israel and her neighbors, and isolate ourselves and Israel in the process, our security and Israel's security will become more vulnerable and the world more dangerous.

We need to keep our eye on the objectives: peace between Israel and its neighbors and victory in our war on terrorism. I close by joining my colleague, the majority leader, in encouraging President Bush not to risk unraveling the progress we have made so far in the Middle East by allowing a period of inattention and inaction to drag us all back into a dark abyss of despair and danger. A conference or some tangible relevant framework for peace must be announced and organized soon. The stakes have rarely been so high, the opportunities so great, and the margins for error so small.

ISSUE 8

POLITICAL ISLAM AND DEMOCRACY

Just as the Cold War was driven by the competing clash of ideologies, it is not uncommonly thought that the post–Cold War future will be driven by the competing clash of civilizations. Many theorists who entertain this scenario believe that, if a clash is to occur, it is most likely to happen between the West and the Islamic world.

This argument is predicated on the assumption that Islamic culture is incompatible with Western democratic values—an assumption that is vigorously denied by both of the authors for Issue 8. Ali A. Mazrui's argument is proactive in defense of Islamic civilization. His points are well made, such as when he argues that "of all the value systems in the world, Islam has been the most resistant to the leading destructive forces of the twentieth century" or "while Islam may generate more political violence than Western culture, Western culture generates more street violence than Islam." David G. Kibble cites the Islamic scholar Aziz Al-Azmeh, who regards Islamic fundamentalism as a transitory phase in a highly conflictual process of evolutionary change in the Islamic world toward freer and more democratic societies.

DISCUSSION QUESTIONS

As you read the articles by Mazrui and Kibble, consider the following questions:

1. Is fundamentalism, Islamic or otherwise, a reaction to westernization or to modernization?
2. Is Islam incompatible with democracy? With capitalism?
3. Does Islam place too high a premium on community and consensus? Are these not important democratic values as well?

4. Will the driving force of twenty-first-century international politics be clashes between civilizations?

KEY WEB SITES

For more information on this topic, visit the following Web sites:

Middle East Association of North America
http://www.mesa.arizona.edu

Islamic Texts and Resources Metapage
http://www.wings.buffalo.edu/sa/muslim/isl/isl.html

Middle East Institute
http://www.mideasti.org

Islamic and Western Values

Ali A. Mazrui

DEMOCRACY AND THE HUMANE LIFE

Westerners tend to think of Islamic societies as backward-looking, oppressed by religion, and inhumanely governed, comparing them to their own enlightened, secular democracies. But measurement of the cultural distance between the West and Islam is a complex undertaking, and that distance is narrower than they assume. Islam is not just a religion, and certainly not just a fundamentalist political movement. It is a civilization, and a way of life that varies from one Muslim country to another but is animated by a common spirit far more humane than most Westerners realize. Nor do those in the West always recognize how their own societies have failed to live up to their liberal mythology. Moreover, aspects of Islamic culture that Westerners regard as medieval may have prevailed in their own culture until fairly recently; in many cases, Islamic societies may be only a few decades behind socially and technologically advanced Western ones. In the end, the question is what path leads to the highest quality of life for the average citizen, while avoiding the worst abuses. The path of the West does not provide all the answers; Islamic values deserve serious consideration.

THE WAY IT RECENTLY WAS

Mores and values have changed rapidly in the West in the last several decades as revolutions in technology and society progressed. Islamic countries, which are now experiencing many of the same changes, may well follow suit. Premarital sex, for example, was strongly disapproved of in the West until after World War II. There were laws against sex outside marriage, some of which are still on the books, if rarely enforced. Today sex before marriage, with parental consent, is common.

Homosexual acts between males were a crime in Great Britain until the 1960s (although lesbianism was not outlawed). Now such acts between consenting adults, male or female, are legal in much of the West, although they remain illegal in most other countries. Half the Western world, in fact, would say that laws against homosexual sex are a violation of gays' and lesbians' human rights.

Ali A. Mazrui is Director of the Institute of Global Cultural Studies at the State University of New York at Binghamton.

This article is from *Foreign Affairs* 76, no. 5 (September/October 1997). Reprinted by permission of *Foreign Affairs*. Copyright 1997 by the Council on Foreign Relations, Inc.

Even within the West, one sees cultural lag. Although capital punishment has been abolished almost everywhere in the Western world, the United States is currently increasing the number of capital offenses and executing more death row inmates than it has in years. But death penalty opponents, including Human Rights Watch and the Roman Catholic Church, continue to protest the practice in the United States, and one day capital punishment will almost certainly be regarded in America as a violation of human rights.

Westerners regard Muslim societies as unenlightened when it comes to the status of women, and it is true that the gender question is still troublesome in Muslim countries. Islamic rules on sexual modesty have often resulted in excessive segregation of the sexes in public places, sometimes bringing about the marginalization of women in public affairs more generally. British women, however, were granted the right to own property independent of their husbands only in 1870, while Muslim women have always had that right. Indeed, Islam is the only world religion founded by a businessman in commercial partnership with his wife. While in many Western cultures daughters could not inherit anything if there were sons in the family, Islamic law has always allocated shares from every inheritance to both daughters and sons. Primogeniture has been illegal under the *sharia* for fourteen centuries.

The historical distance between the West and Islam in the treatment of women may be a matter of decades rather than centuries. Recall that in almost all Western countries except for New Zealand, women did not gain the right to vote until the twentieth century. Great Britain extended the vote to women in two stages, in 1918 and 1928, and the United States enfranchised them by constitutional amendment in 1920. France followed as recently as 1944. Switzerland did not permit women to vote in national elections until 1971—decades after Muslim women in Afghanistan, Iran, Iraq, and Pakistan had been casting ballots.

Furthermore, the United States, the largest and most influential Western nation, has never had a female president. In contrast, two of the most populous Muslim countries, Pakistan and Bangladesh, have had women prime ministers: Benazir Bhutto headed two governments in Pakistan, and Khaleda Zia and Hasina Wajed served consecutively in Bangladesh. Turkey has had Prime Minister Tansu Ciller. Muslim countries are ahead in female empowerment, though still behind in female liberation.

CONCEPTS OF THE SACRED

Censorship is one issue on which the cultural divide between the West and Islam turns out to be less wide than Westerners ordinarily assume. The most celebrated case of the last decade—that of Salman Rushdie's novel *The Satanic Verses*, published in Britain in 1988 but banned in most Muslim countries—brought the Western world and the Muslim world in conflict, but also uncovered some surprising similarities and large helpings of Western hypocrisy. Further scrutiny reveals widespread censorship in the West, if imposed by different forces than in Muslim societies.

As their civilization has become more secular, Westerners have looked for new abodes of the sacred. By the late twentieth century, the freedom of the artist—in this case, Salman Rushdie—was more sacred to them than religion. But many Muslims saw Rushdie's novel as holding Islam up to ridicule. The novel suggests that Islam's holy scripture, the Koran, is filled with inventions of the Prophet Muhammad or is, in fact, the work of the devil rather than communications from Allah, and implies, moreover, that the religion's founder was not very intelligent. Rushdie also puts women characters bearing the names of the Prophet's wives in a whorehouse, where the clients find the blasphemy arousing.

Many devout Muslims felt that Rushdie had no right to poke fun at and twist into obscenity some of the most sacred symbols of Islam. Most Muslim countries banned the novel because officials there considered it morally repugnant.[1] Western intellectuals argued that as an artist, Rushdie had the sacred right and even duty to go wherever his imagination led him in his writing. Yet until the 1960s *Lady Chatterley's Lover* was regarded as morally repugnant under British law for daring to depict an affair between a married member of the gentry and a worker on the estate. For a long time after Oscar Wilde's conviction for homosexual acts, *The Picture of Dorian Gray* was regarded as morally repugnant. Today other gay writers are up against a wall of prejudice.

The Satanic Verses was banned in some places because of fears that it would cause riots. Indian officials explained that they were banning the novel because it would inflame religious passions in the country, already aroused by Kashmiri separatism. The United States has a legal standard for preventive action when negative consequences are feared—"clear and present danger." But the West was less than sympathetic to India's warnings that the book was inflammatory. Rushdie's London publisher, Jonathan Cape, went ahead, and the book's publication even in far-off Britain resulted in civil disturbances in Bombay, Islamabad, and Karachi in which some fifteen people were killed and dozens more injured.

Distinguished Western publishers, however, have been known to reject a manuscript because of fears for the safety of their own. Last year Cambridge University Press turned down *Fields of Wheat, Rivers of Blood* by Anastasia Karakasidou, a sociological study on ethnicity in the Greek province of Macedonia, publicly acknowledging that it did so because of worries about the safety of its employees in Greece. If Jonathan Cape had cared as much about South Asian lives as it said it cared about freedom of expression, or as Cambridge University Press cared about its staff members in Greece, less blood would have been spilled.

Targets, sources, and methods of censorship differ, but censorship is just as much a fact of life in Western societies as in the Muslim world. Censorship in the latter is often crude, imposed by governments, mullahs and imams, and, more recently, militant Islamic movements. Censorship in the West, on the other hand, is more polished and decentralized. Its practitioners are financial backers of cultural activity and entertainment, advertisers who buy time on commercial television, subscribers of the Public Broadcasting System (PBS), influential interest groups including ethnic pressure groups, and editors, publishers, and other controllers of the means of communication.[2] In Europe, governments, too, sometimes get into the business of censorship.

CENSORING AMERICA

The threat to free speech in the United States comes not from the law and the Constitution but from outside the government. PBS, legally invulnerable on the issue of free speech, capitulated to other forces when faced with the metaphorical description in my 1986 television series "The Africans" of Karl Marx as "the last of the great Jewish prophets." The British version had included the phrase, but the American producing station, WETA, a PBS affiliate in Washington, deleted it without authorial permission so as not to risk offending Jewish Americans.

On one issue of censorship WETA did consult me. Station officials were unhappy I had not injected more negativity into the series' three-minute segment on Libya's leader, Muammar Qaddafi. First they asked for extra commentary on allegations that Libya sponsored terrorism. When I refused, they suggested changing the pictures instead—deleting one sequence that humanized Qaddafi by showing him visiting a hospital and substituting a shot of the Rome airport after a terrorist bombing. After much debate I managed to save the hospital scene but surrendered on the Rome airport addition, on condition that neither I nor the written caption implied that Libya was responsible for the bombing. But, ideally, WETA would have preferred to cut the whole segment.

WETA in those days had more in common with the censors in Libya than either side realized. Although the Libyans broadcast an Arabic version and seemed pleased with the series as a whole, they cut the Qaddafi sequence. The segment also offended Lynne Cheney, chair of the National Endowment for the Humanities, who demanded that the endowment's name be removed from the series credits. After she stepped down from her post, she called for the NEH to be abolished, citing "The Africans" as an example of the objectionable liberal projects that, she said, the endowment had tended to fund.

In another case of decentralized censorship that affected my own work, Westview Press in Boulder, Colorado, was about to go to press with my book *Cultural Forces in World Politics* when editors there announced they wanted to delete three chapters: one discussing *The Satanic Verses* as a case of cultural treason, another comparing the Palestinian intifada with Chinese students' 1989 rebellion in Tiananmen Square, and a third comparing the South African apartheid doctrine of separate homelands for blacks and whites with the Zionist doctrine of separate states for Jews and Arabs. Suspecting that I would have similar problems with most other major U.S. publishers, I decided that the book would be published exclusively by James Currey, my British publisher, and Heinemann Educational Books, the American offshoot of another British house, which brought it out in 1990. Not even universities in the United States, supposed bastions of intellectual freedom, have been free from censorship. Until recently the greatest danger to one's chances of getting tenure lay in espousing Marxism or criticizing Israel or Zionism.

The positive aspect of decentralized censorship in the West, at least with regard to books, is that what is unacceptable to one publisher may be acceptable to another; what is almost unpublishable in the United States may be easily publishable in Britain or the Netherlands. With national television, the choices are more restricted. Many points of view are banned from the screen, with the possibility of a hearing only on the public access stations with the weakest signals.

In Western societies as in Muslim ones, only a few points of view have access to the national broadcast media and publishing industry or even to university faculties. In both civilizations, certain points of view are excluded from the center and marginalized. The source of the censorship may be different, but censorship is the result in the West just as surely as in the Islamic world.

LIFE AMONG THE BELIEVERS

Many of the above issues are bound up with religion. Westerners consider many problems or flaws of the Muslim world products of Islam and pride their societies and their governments on their purported secularism. But when it comes to separation of church and state, how long and wide is the distance between the two cultures?

A central question is whether a theocracy can ever be democratized. British history since Henry VIII's establishment of the Church of England in 1531 proves that it can be. The English theocracy was democratized first by making democracy stronger and later by making the theocracy weaker. The major democratic changes had to wait until the nineteenth and twentieth centuries, when the vote was extended to new social classes and finally to women.[3] The Islamic Republic of Iran is less than two decades old, but already there seem to be signs of softening theocracy and the beginnings of liberalization. Nor must we forget Muslim monarchies that have taken initial steps toward liberalization. Jordan has gone further than most others in legalizing opposition groups. But even Saudi Arabia and the smaller Gulf states have begun to use the Islamic concept of shura (consultative assembly) as a guide to democracy.

The West has sought to protect minority religions through secularism. It has not always worked. The Holocaust in secular Germany was the worst case. And even today, anti-Semitism in Eastern Europe is disturbing, as are anti-Muslim trends in France.

The United States has had separation of church and state under the Constitution for over 200 years, but American politics is hardly completely secular. Only once has the electorate chosen a non-Protestant president—and the Roman Catholic John F. Kennedy won by such a narrow margin, amid such allegations of electoral fraud, that we will never know for certain whether a majority of Americans actually voted for him. Jews have distinguished themselves in many fields, but they have so far avoided competing for the White House, and there is still a fear of unleashing the demon of anti-Semitism among Christian fundamentalists. There are now more Muslims—an estimated six million—than Jews in the United States, yet anti-Muslim feeling and the success of appeals to Christian sentiment among voters make it extremely unlikely that Americans will elect a Muslim head of state anytime in the foreseeable future. Even the appointment of a Muslim secretary of commerce, let alone an attorney general, is no more than a distant conjecture because of the political fallout that all administrations fear. When First Lady Hillary Rodham Clinton entertained Muslim leaders at the White House last year to mark a special Islamic festival, a *Wall Street Journal* article cited that as evidence that friends of *Hamas* had penetrated the White House. In Western Europe, too, there are now millions of Muslims, but history is still awaiting the appointment of the first to a cabinet position in Britain, France, or Germany. Islam, on the other hand, has tried to protect minority religions through ecumenicalism throughout its history. Jews and Christians had special status as People of the Book—a fraternity of monotheists. Other religious minorities were later also accorded the status of protected minorities (*dhimmis*). The approach has had its successes. Jewish scholars rose to high positions in Muslim Spain. During the Ottoman Empire, Christians sometimes attained high political office: Suleiman I (1520–1566) had Christian ministers in his government, as did Selim III (1789–1807). The Moghul Empire integrated Hindus and Muslims into a consolidated Indian state; Emperor Akbar (1556–1605) carried furthest the Moghul policy of bringing Hindus into the government. In the 1990s Iraq has had a Chaldean Christian deputy prime minister, Tariq Aziz. And Boutros Boutros-ghali, a Coptic Christian, would never have been appointed secretary-general of the United Nations if not for his long and distinguished service in the foreign ministry of an otherwise Muslim government in Egypt.

The Republic of Senegal in West Africa, which is nearly 95 percent Muslim, had a Roman Catholic president for two decades (1960–1980). In his years presiding over that relatively open society, Leopold Sedar Senghor never once had to deal with anti-Christian disturbances in the streets of Dakar. His political opponents called him a wide range of derogatory names—hypocrite, stooge of the French, dictator, political prostitute—but virtually never taunted him for being a *kafir* (infidel).

When Senghor became the first African head of state to retire voluntarily from office, Abdou Diouf, a Muslim, succeeded him, and he remains president today. But the ecumenical story of Senegal did not end there; the first lady is Catholic. Can one imagine an American presidential candidate confessing on Larry King Live, "Incidentally, my wife is a Shiite Muslim"? That would almost certainly mark the end of his hopes for the White House.

One conclusion to be drawn from all this is that Westerners are far less secular in their political behavior than they think they are. Another is that Muslim societies historically have been more ecumenical, and therefore more humane, than their Western critics have recognized. Islamic ecumenicalism has sometimes protected religious minorities more effectively than Western secularism.

BETWEEN THE DAZZLING AND THE DEPRAVED

Cultures should be judged not merely by the heights of achievement to which they have ascended but by the depths of brutality to which they have descended. The measure of cultures is not only their virtues but also their vices.

In the twentieth century, Islam has not often proved fertile ground for democracy and its virtues. On the other hand, Islamic culture has not been hospitable to Nazism, fascism, or communism, unlike Christian culture (as in Germany, Italy, Russia, Czechoslovakia), Buddhist culture (Japan before and during World War II, Pol Pot's Cambodia, Vietnam, North Korea), or Confucian culture (Mao's China). The Muslim world has never yet given rise to systematic fascism and its organized brutalities. Hafiz al-Assad's Syria and Saddam Hussein's Iraq have been guilty of large-scale violence, but fascism also requires an ideology of repression that has been absent in the two countries. And apart from the dubious case of Albania, communism has never independently taken hold in a Muslim culture.

Muslims are often criticized for not producing the best, but they are seldom congratulated for an ethic that has averted the worst. There are no Muslim equivalents of Nazi extermination camps; nor Muslim conquests by genocide on the scale perpetrated by Europeans in the Americas and Australia, nor Muslim equivalents of Stalinist terror, Pol Pot's killing fields, or the starvation and uprooting of tens of millions in the name of Five Year Plans. Nor are there Muslim versions of apartheid like that once approved by the South African Dutch Reformed Church, or of the ferocious racism of Japan before 1945, or of the racist culture of the Old South in the United States with its lynchings and brutalization of black people.

Islam brings to the calculus of universal justice some protection from the abyss of human depravity. Historically, the religion and the civilization have been resistant to forces that contributed to the worst aspects of the twentieth century's interludes of barbarism: racism, genocide, and violence within society.

First, Islam has been relatively resistant to racism. The Koran confronts the issue of national and ethnic differences head on. The standard of excellence it sets has nothing to do with race, but is instead moral and religious worth—what the Koran calls "piety" and what Martin Luther King, Jr., called "the content of one's character." An oft-quoted verse of the Koran reads:

> O people! We have created you from a male and a female, and have made you nations and tribes so that you may know one another. The noblest among you is the most pious. Allah is all-knowing.

In his farewell address, delivered on his last pilgrimage to Mecca in A.D. 632, Muhammad declared: "There is no superiority of an Arab over a non-Arab, and indeed, no superiority of a red man over a black man except through piety and fear of God . . . Let those who are present convey this message to those who are absent."

Unlike Christian churches, the mosque has never been segregated by race. One of Muhammad's most beloved companions was an Ethiopian, Bilal Rabah, a freed slave who rose to great prominence in early Islam. Under Arab lineage systems and kinship traditions, racial intermarriage was not discouraged and the children were considered Arab regardless of who the mother was. These Arab ways influenced Muslim societies elsewhere. Of the four presidents of Egypt since the revolution of 1952, two had black African ancestors—Muhammad Nagib and Anwar al-Sadat.[4]

Islam has a doctrine of Chosen Language (Arabic) but no Chosen People. Since the conversion of the Roman Emperor Constantine I in A.D. 313, Christianity has been led if not dominated by Europeans. But the leadership of the Muslim world has changed hands several times: from the mainly Arab Umayyad dynasty (661–750) to the multiethnic Abbasid dynasty (750–1258) to the Ottoman Empire (1453–1922), dominated by the Turks. And this history is quite apart from such flourishing Muslim dynasties as the Moghuls of India and the Safavids of Persia or the sub-Saharan empires of Mali and Songhai. The diversification of Muslim leadership—in contrast to the Europeanization of Christian leadership—helped the cause of relative racial equality in Islamic culture.

Partly because of Islam's relatively nonracial nature, Islamic history has been free of systematic efforts to obliterate a people. Islam conquered by co-optation, intermarriage, and conversion rather than by genocide. Incidents in Muslim history, it is true, have caused large-scale loss of life. During Turkey's attempt in 1915 to deport the entire Armenian population of about 1,750,000 to Syria and Palestine, hundreds of thousands of people, perhaps up to a million, died of starvation or were murdered on the way. But—though this does not exonerate Turkey of its responsibility for the deaths—Armenians had provoked Turkey by organizing volunteer battalions to help Russia fight against it in World War I. Nor is the expulsion of a people from a territory, however disastrous its consequences, equivalent to the Nazi Holocaust, which systematically took the lives of six million Jews and members of other despised groups. Movement of people between India and Pakistan after partition in 1947 also resulted in thousands of deaths en route.

Saddam Hussein's use of poison gas against Kurdish villages in Iraq in 1988 is more clearly comparable to Nazi behavior. But Saddam's action was the use of an illegitimate weapon in a civil war rather than a planned program to destroy the Kurdish people; it was an evil incident rather than a program of genocide. Many people feel that President Harry S Truman's dropping of atomic bombs on Hiroshima and Nagasaki was also an evil episode. There is a difference between massacre and genocide. Massacres have been perpetrated in almost every country on earth, but only a few cultures have been guilty of genocide.

Nor did Islam ever spawn an Inquisition in which the burning of heretics at the stake was sanctioned. Cultures that had condemned human beings to burn and celebrated as they died in the flames, even hundreds of years before, were more likely to tolerate the herding of a whole people of another faith into gas chambers. Islam has been a shield against such excesses of evil.

THE ORDER OF ISLAM

Against Western claims that Islamic "fundamentalism" feeds terrorism, one powerful paradox of the twentieth century is often overlooked. While Islam may generate more political violence than Western culture, Western culture generates more street violence than Islam. Islam does indeed produce a disproportionate share of *mujahideen*, but Western culture produces a disproportionate share of muggers. The largest Muslim city in Africa is Cairo. The largest westernized city is Johannesburg. Cairo is much more populous than Johannesburg, but street violence is only a fraction of what it is in the South African city. Does Islam help pacify Cairo? I, along with many others, believe that it does. The high premium Islam places on *umma* (community) and *ijma* (consensus) has made for a Pax Islamica in day-to-day life.

In terms of quality of life, is the average citizen better off under the excesses of the Islamic state or the excesses of the liberal state, where political tension may be low but social violence has reached crisis proportions? Tehran, the capital of the Islamic Republic of Iran, is a city of some ten million. Families with small children picnic in public parks at 11 P.M. or midnight. Residents of the capital and other cities stroll late at night, seemingly unafraid of mugging, rape, or murder. This is a society that has known large-scale political violence in war and revolution, but one in which petty interpersonal violence is much rarer than in Washington or New York. Iranians are more subject to their government than Americans, but they are less at risk from the depredations of their fellow citizens. Nor is dictatorial government the explanation for the safe streets of Tehran—otherwise, Lagos would be as peaceful as the Iranian capital.

The Iranian solution is mainly in the moral sphere. As an approach to the problems of modernity, some Muslim societies are attempting a return to premodernism, to indigenous traditional disciplines and values. Aside from Iran, countries such as Sudan and Saudi Arabia have revived Islamic legal systems and other features of the Islamic way of life, aspects of which go back fourteen centuries. Islamic movements in countries like Algeria, Egypt, and Afghanistan are also seeking revivalist goals. A similar sacred nostalgia is evident in other religions, such as the born-again Christian sects in the United States and Africa.

Of all the value systems in the world, Islam has been the most resistant to the leading destructive forces of the twentieth century—including AIDS. Lower levels of prostitution and of hard drug use in conservative Muslim cultures compared with other cultures have, so far, contributed to lower-than-average HIV infection rates.[5] If societies closer to the *sharia* are also more distant from the human immunodeficiency virus, should the rest of the world take a closer look?

One can escape modernity by striving to transcend it as well as by retreating from it into the past. Perhaps the Muslim world should explore this path, searching for postmodern solutions to its political tensions and economic woes, and pursuing the positive aspects of globalization without falling victim to the negative aspects of westernization.

The Dialectic of Culture

Western Liberal democracy has enabled societies to enjoy openness, government accountability, popular participation, and high economic productivity, but Western pluralism has also been a breeding ground for racism, fascism, exploitation, and genocide. If history is to end in arrival at the ultimate political order, it will require more than the West's message on how to maximize the best in human nature. Humankind must also consult Islam about how to check the worst in human nature—from alcoholism to racism, materialism to Nazism, drug addiction to Marxism as the opiate of the intellectuals.

One must distinguish between democratic principles and humane principles. In some humane principles—including stabilizing the family, security from social violence, and the relatively nonracial nature of religious institutions—the Muslim world may be ahead of the West.

Turkey is a prime example of the dilemma of balancing humane principles with democratic principles. In times of peace, the Ottoman Empire was more humane in its treatment of religious minorities than the Turkish Republic after 1923 under the westernizing influence of Mustafa Kemal Atatürk. The Turkish Republic, on the other hand, gradually moved toward a policy of cultural assimilation. While the Ottoman Empire tolerated the Kurdish language, the Turkish Republic outlawed its use for a considerable period. When not at war, the empire was more humane than the Turkish Republic, but less democratic.

At bottom, democracy is a system for selecting one's rulers; humane governance is a system for treating citizens. Ottoman rule at its best was humane governance; the Turkish Republic at its best has been a quest for democratic values. In the final years of the twentieth century, Turkey may be engaged in reconciling the greater humaneness of the Ottoman Empire with the greater democracy of the Republic. The current Islamic revival in the country may be the beginning of a fundamental review of the Kemalist revolution, which inaugurated Turkish secularism. In England since Henry VIII, a theocracy has been democratized. In Turkey, might a democracy be theocratized? Although the Turkish army is trying to stop it, electoral support for Islamic revivalism is growing in the country. There has been increased speculation that secularism may be pushed back, in spite of the resignation in June, under political pressure from the generals, of Prime Minister Necmettin Erbakan, the leader of the Islamist Welfare Party. Is Erbakan nevertheless destined to play in the Kemalist revolution the role that Mikhail Gorbachev or Boris Yeltsin played in the Leninist revolution? Or is Erbakan a forerunner of change? It is too early to be sure. The dialectic of history continues its conversation with the dialectic of culture within the wider rhythms of relativity in human experience.

NOTES

1. In citing the Rushdie case as evidence of Islamic society's repressive nature, Westerners point to the 1989 *fatwa*, or legal ruling, by the Ayatollah Khomeini of Iran indicting Rushdie for blasphemy and the capital crime of apostasy and sentencing him to death in absentia. Iran, however, was the only Muslim country to decree the death penalty for Rushdie. Bangladesh said that Rushdie's crime, if proved, was a capital offense, but that he would have to be tried in a Muslim country to ascertain his guilt. There is a broad consensus that the book is blasphemous (even the Vatican agrees that it is), but Iran stands alone with the *fatwa*.

2. American writers such as Carl Bernstein, Howard Fast, Erica Jong, and Peter Maas have spoken of both overt and covert censorship; see Midge Decter, "The Rushdiad," *Commentary*, vol. 87, no. 6 (June 1989), pp. 20–21.

3. See Leonard Binder, *Islamic Liberalism: A Critique of Development Ideologies* (Chicago: University of Chicago Press, 1988), especially Chapter 9, "Conclusion: The Prospects for Liberal Government in the Middle East," pp. 336–60.

4. Like most other religions and civilizations, Islam tolerated the ownership and trade of slaves for centuries. But slavery among Muslims was almost race-neutral. In contrast to the racially polarized transatlantic slave system—white masters, black slaves—slaves in the Islamic world could be white, black, brown, or other, and so could masters. Moreover, slavery among Muslims allowed for great upward social mobility. Both Muslim India and Muslim Egypt produced slave dynasties; the former slaves who became Mamluk rulers of Egypt dominated the country from 1250 to 1517.

5. Studies by researchers in Ivory Coast of Muslim countries in Africa have shown that approximately half as many Muslims as non-Muslims are likely to be infected with HIV. See Catherine Tastemain and Peter Coles, "Can a Culture Stop AIDS in Its Tracks?" *New Scientist* (London), vol. 139, no. 1890.

Islamic Fundamentalism: A Transitory Threat?

David G. Kibble

Islamic fundamentalism is never far from the news. A portrayal of what Islamic fundamentalism can mean in practice was provided by the graphic media accounts of life in Kabul after it was overrun by the Taliban Militia in October 1996. Public transport was ordered to halt five times a day to allow people to report to the mosque for prayer. Kabul radio announced, "All drivers of taxis, buses and lorries are asked to park their vehicles at the nearest mosque and to offer congregational prayers along with their passengers."[1] Women were banished from the workplace, girls' schools closed and women doctors sent home. Soccer was declared to be against Islam. Even chess was forbidden! Men were given six weeks to grow a beard, while women were asked to cover themselves in strict Islamic dress so that no part of the face could be seen. A spokesman for the Taliban commented: "We will punish all those who do not follow Islamic teachings, whether educated or uneducated."[2] Even Iran complained that the Taliban were going far beyond what Islam required.[3]

Other events keep Islamic fundamentalism in the news. In the summer of 1996 there was an abortive coup in Bahrain by a fundamentalist group calling themselves *Hezbollah Bahrain*. In June of the same year 19 U.S. servicemen were killed and 386 wounded in an attack on a military complex in Dhahran, Saudi Arabia. It is assumed that a fundamentalist group carried out the attack. Shortly after the victory of the Taliban Militia in Afghanistan, there was an attack in December on the Paris Metro, killing four. This was assumed to be an act of the GIA, the *Groupe Islamique Armée*, following on from the Algerian government's victory in a referendum which outlawed political parties based on religion.

In 1997, 250 people were killed in January by the GIA in Algiers, and 3 people were killed and 42 were injured in March in Tel Aviv as a result of a *Hamas* suicide bombing. In July, 2 further *Hamas* suicide bombers killed 15 people and wounded 170 in an attack on the Mahane Yehuda food market in Jerusalem, while more than 300 people died in attacks by the GIA in and around Algiers in one week at the end of August. Attacks in Algeria continued with 400 killed

David G. Kibble, a theology graduate of Edinburgh University, is a Deputy Headteacher at Huntington School in York, England. A former Naval Reservist and Commanding Officer of HMS *Ceres*, he has written on both sides of the Atlantic on defense issues, particularly on the Islamic background to problems in the Middle East and on the ethics of nuclear deterrence.
This article is from *Strategic Review* XXVI, no. 2 (spring 1998), a former MIT publication. Reprinted by permission.

in December 1997 and over 10 massacred in Relizone province at the beginning of 1998. The year 1997 also saw the Egyptian fundamentalist terrorist group, *Gama al-Islamiya*, murdering 58 tourists at Luxor.

At the beginning of 1998, Muslim fundamentalist Ramzi Ahmed Yousef was sentenced to 240 years in prison for masterminding the 1993 bombing of the World Trade Center in New York and an unsuccessful plot to blow up a dozen U.S. planes in Asia. He went to jail defiantly proclaiming, "I am a terrorist and I am proud of it."

Yet, while Islamic fundamentalism may regularly hit the newspaper headlines, it is only a temporary phenomenon. Its internal contradictions and weaknesses combined with its passage into the new millennium cannot but ensure its demise in the longer term. Islamic fundamentalism may therefore be said to be "here today, gone tomorrow."

FUNDAMENTALIST ISLAM

Islam, like any other faith or political party, has many different hues. Islam contains people of many different nations and backgrounds and of many different persuasions within the umbrella of Islam. One of the most important differences between Muslims, in addition to the well-known division between Shiite and Sunni, lies in their interpretation of the Qur'an. On the one hand lies the modernist Muslim who wishes to take the Qur'an and to interpret it in the light of the twentieth century. The sacred text, the modernist argues, originally written some fourteen hundred years ago, needs adapting to the twentieth century. The Qur'an speaks of a literal creation by God, for example: The modernist would wish to update the concept of creation in the light of twentieth century scientific ideas and would wish to say that Allah created the universe through the process of evolution. One of the founding fathers of modernism was Muhammad Rashid Rida. He made the following comment concerning science and the Qur'an: "Human history contained in the Qur'an is like the natural history of animals, plants, and inanimate objects in it. . . . What is intended by all this is to demonstrate by example the omnipotence of the Creator and His Wisdom and not to set forth in detail the natural sciences or astronomy which God has enabled man to understand through study, contemplation and experiment. . . ."[4] In other words, the Qur'an is to be read not as a scientific text book, as the fundamentalist reads it, but as a religious document revealing religious truth. Similarly the modernist would argue that the Qur'anic requirement that thieves have a limb amputated is a requirement conditioned by its time: Nowadays, such a barbaric punishment is no longer appropriate.

The fundamentalist, on the other hand, would argue that the Qur'an is the literal, absolute, and final Word of God and must therefore be understood just as it stands without interpretation. What Allah said fourteen hundred years ago was said for all time. The concept of the book being interpreted for modern times is alien to the fundamentalist. According to the fundamentalist, the Qur'an is "the supreme norm for human life, the chief source of guidance. This means subordination of all other sources of knowledge to the Divine Revelation."[5] For the fundamentalist, literal creation by Allah means just that, and if the Qur'an demands amputation, then that is what shall be given, for that is what Allah is demanding. Such a literal reading of the Qur'an by fundamentalists results in ideas that are ". . . the product of a highly specific reading of a small range of sources, interpreted politically to favour right-wing, fascist and hypernationalist ideology."[6]

The fundamentalist understanding of the Qur'an has another aspect to it: If it is the direct Word of God to his people and should be interpreted exactly as it stands, then the assumption is that the text can be understood, or at the very least interpreted, directly by each individual Muslim. The fact that no adaptation to modern times is necessary and that the text is in itself plain can have the additional corollary that anyone can interpret the text and can do so directly and correctly. No priest, mullah, or imam needs to interpret the book for the believer: It is in itself directly apprehensible. In this respect commentators have pointed out a similarity between fundamentalist Islam and the ideas of Martin Luther in the Christian rebellion.[7] Dale Eickelman and James Piscatori point out that the concept of each individual Muslim being the interpreter of the Qur'an, this concept of individual access to the divine, means that each individual Muslim is endowed with authority. There is no intermediary necessary between the believer and the Qur'an to say that his interpretation is incorrect. What the Muslim believer interprets directly must be the correct interpretation. The fundamentalist Muslim is therefore, in one sense, his own authority.

In essence, therefore, the fundamentalist Muslim regards the Qur'an as the direct revelation of God. It is to be interpreted by the individual believer exactly as it stands without any need for updating or setting in context.

Fundamentalist Muslims share certain ideas. They are committed to the cause of social action. The Qur'an commands: "Serve God . . . and do good—to parents, kinsfolk, orphans, those in need, neighbors who are near, neighbors who are strangers, the companion by your side, the wayfarer. . . ."[8] When Cairo was hit by an earthquake in 1992, it was the fundamentalist Muslim Brotherhood which provided relief centers in the poor neighborhoods. Similarly in Algeria the Islamic Salvation Front (FIS) earned goodwill when it provided tents and blankets after an earthquake near Tipaza. The Lebanese fundamentalist *Hizbullah* (Party of God) has developed an extensive social welfare system in Lebanon that involves educational, agricultural, medical and housing assistance. In Beirut's Bir al-Abid quarter, it has run a supermarket co-operative, selling produce at below retail cost, and provides scholarships, runs health clinics, and subsidizes housing for the needy. A recent British newspaper report highlighted the charitable works of Muslim fundamentalist groups among North African immigrant families in the poor areas of French cities, including rehabilitation work with drug addicts.[9] Raphael Israeli's study of fundamentalist groups in Palestine paints a similar picture.[10] Such charitable work is done not only for its own sake but also to serve fundamentalist groups' power-seeking strategies in the local and national political arena.

THE LEGITIMACY OF VIOLENCE: DIFFERENCES BETWEEN THE FUNDAMENTALISTS

Although Muslim fundamentalists agree on certain issues, there are some over which they differ. Chief among these differences is their stance toward a non-Muslim government. Fundamentalists agree that the Muslim ideal is a country run according to the precepts of the Qur'an and the *Sunnah* (sayings and deeds of the prophet Muhammad). It means the implementation and application of the law code known as *Sharia*, that is, law derived from the Qur'an and *Sunnah*.[11] In contradistinction to the non-Muslim state, fundamentalists see an Islamic country as one that is in one sense inevitable in that it conforms to the pre-existent divine pattern. Rational argument can be used with little effect to buttress the fundamentalist position, since the whole concept rests purely on divine command. But how should the Muslim fundamentalist react in the face of a government which rejects such an ideal?

The majority of fundamentalists would wish to pursue a peaceful path of progress toward their ideal, a path marked by persuasion and social action. Such a path is one espoused by the moderate fundamentalist Egyptian Muslim Brotherhood. In the West Bank the moderate fundamentalist Sheikh Abdallah Nimr Darwish wants a Muslim state but denounces terrorism as an acceptable means of achieving that end even under Israeli domination. He believes that any struggle with the Israeli government must be undertaken within the limits of Israeli law. Just as most fundamentalists wish to achieve a Muslim state by peaceful means, so most Palestinian fundamentalists wish to see the return of the West Bank and its development into a Muslim state by a similar peaceful process.

On the other hand there are more militant Muslims at the other end of the spectrum who see violence as an acceptable tool. In Egypt groups such as *Takfir wal-Hijra* (Excommunication and Flight), *Jamaat al-Jihad* (Holy War Society) and Salvation from Hell are all prepared to use violence as a means of achieving their ends. At the heart of *al-Jihad's* message and mission is the belief that Egypt has regressed to the state of *Jahiliyya*, the pre-Islamic time of ignorance and unbelief.[12] The only cure the fundamentalist group sees is *Jihad* or Holy War. One of the group's tracts declares, "There is no doubt that the idols of this world can only disappear through the power of the sword."[13] At a conference in 1968, Sheikh Abdullah Ghoshash, Supreme Judge of the Hashemite kingdom of Jordan, pronounced that "[it] is unlawful to give up *Jihad* and adopt peace and weakness. . . . War is the basis of the relationship between Muslims and their opponents unless there are justifiable reasons for peace such as adopting Islam or making an agreement with them to keep peaceful."[14] Similar thoughts were expressed by the Ayatollah Khomeini: "The Qur'an commands: Wage war until all corruption and all disobedience [of divine law] are wiped out! The wars that our prophet—blessed be his soul—waged against the infidels were divine gifts to humanity. Once we have won the war [against Iraq] we shall turn to other wars. . . . We have to wage war until all corruption, all disobedience of Islamic laws cease. . . . A religion without war is a crippled religion."[15]

THE NATURE OF ISLAMIC GOVERNMENT: A LACK OF CLARITY

Just as there is no unanimity concerning the use of violence, so there is a lack of unanimity concerning the nature of Muslim government.[16] The balance between given Divine Law and a democratic procedure, for example, is unclear. The Ayatollah Khomeini was clear concerning his vision: "What the nation wants is an Islamic republic. Not just a republic, not a democratic republic, not a democratic Islamic republic. Just an Islamic republic. Do not use the word 'democratic.' That is Western and we do not want it."[17] Saleh Sirriyah, the mastermind behind the attempted seizure of the Heliopolis Military Academy in Egypt in 1974, offers a similar analysis: "Democracy . . . is a way of life which contradicts Islam's way; for in Democracy the people have the power to legislate and to permit and forbid what they will . . . while in Islam people have no such competence over what is *halal* [permitted by Allah] and what is *haram* [prohibited by Allah], even if they were to achieve total unanimity over the matter. Combining Islam and Democracy is, then, like combining Islam and Judaism. . . ."[18] A document by *Islamic Jihad* in Egypt argues that democracy can never be the correct form of government as it allows equal rights to all citizens, whereas Islam regards Christians and Jews as second-class citizens, having to pay the special *Jizzyah* tax. Non-Muslims would be effectively second-class citizens with limited rights and opportunities.

Other fundamentalists give more weight to a possible democratic procedure within a Muslim state. In Islam there exists the concept of *Ijma*. *Ijma* is the consensus of religious leaders who may decide courses of action, provided they remain within the guidelines set down in the Qur'an and the *Sunnah*, the sayings and deeds of the prophet. *Ijma* should be informed by *Shura*, a process of consultation with the people. In this way fundamentalists can argue that there is a place for at least a limited form of democracy within an Islamic regime. Contrary to popular opinion, such a form of government exists in Iran, where there are democratic elections for the *Majlis* (Parliament) and for the President of the Republic. That having been said, however, all legislation is subject to examination by the Council of Guardians, who can veto measures if they are deemed not to be in conformity with Islam. Some form of democracy has been advocated by the Muslim Brotherhood movements in

Egypt and Jordan, Algeria's Islamic Salvation Front, and Kuwait's *Jamiyyat al-Islah* (Reform Society), among others.

Defining the precise nature of governmental authority using and balancing such concepts as *Sharia* (that is law based on the Qur'an and *Sunnah*),[19] *Ijma* and *Shura* is not easy. One might argue that Islam itself has no fully clear guidelines on the matter: At the very least it lacks clarity. One commentator on religious law has said, concerning *Shura*, "To do any collective work without any prior mutual consultation is not only a way of the ignorant but it is also a clear defiance of the regulation laid down by Allah."[20] What would happen, one might ask, if *Shura* took place, the people were consulted and they pressed for the dissolution of a Muslim state? One critic of fundamentalist Islam comments that much of the Islamic political ideal is little more than a rejection of what it sees as the corrupt Western model. In other words it knows what it does not want, but lacks a coherent picture or vision of what it does want. He concludes that "there is no concrete political . . . model inherent in Islam."[21]

If fundamentalist Islam is not fully clear on what constitutes a truly Muslim government, it is even less clear on the question of economics. According to Olivier Roy the problem with fundamentalist Islamic economics is that it offers no socio-economic analysis and presents nothing in the way of a proper economic system. It concentrates so much on the relationship of the individual Muslim to his God that there is a resulting absence of anything of real substance when it comes to society, either in terms of government or in terms of basic economic policy.[22]

FUNDAMENTALIST ISLAM: PRESENT AND FUTURE

Those of us who remember the days of the Ayatollah Khomeini will remember seeing on our television screen streets full of Iranians demonstrating against the West: The United States was denounced as the "Great Satan" and the crowds chanted "*Allaho Akbar*" ("God is Great"). Amuzegar's study of contemporary Iran concludes that while there is an ingrained faith in Allah, an adulation for the prophet Muhammad, an enthusiasm for some of the Shia religious rites, and a concurrence with many Islamic symbols, there is at the same time a resistance to ecclesiastical coercion, a resentment of Islam's undue infringements on one's private life, and a rejection of thought control. He notes that despite the Islamic dress code with its head covering for the women and tieless, bearded men, there is in some sections of society the regular consumption of alcohol and what some fundamentalists would consider improper partying. Many Iranians listen to broadcasts by the BBC and by CNN rather than listen to their own indigenous networks; there is a black market for modern popular music, CDs and denim jeans.[23]

Discontent among some sections of Iranian society over economic hardship and particularly over activities of the Islamic moral police recently forced authorities to relax a number of fundamentalist measures: Male students may now wear short-sleeved shirts to university, and floral headscarves and raincoats are now tolerated in lieu of the traditional *abayya*, the black, head-to-toe covering for women. Yet the fundamentalists still hold the reins of power: Religious scholars recently pronounced it forbidden for women to ride bicycles because bicycle seats resemble saddles and women should not ride horses; therefore they should not ride bicycles. None of the 1,500 novels sent to censors in the past year have been approved. Uprisings against the fundamentalist regime were crushed in three separate Iranian states in 1996. One Iranian commented, "That is what we have here, a totalitarian country ruled by religious clerics with no idea of how economies work and what people want." The leader of an underground pro-democracy movement made his feelings clear: "The ideals of the revolution have been betrayed. We wanted justice and social equality then. We are back to where we started with this regime."[24]

In that last comment there is a telling sentiment. The pro-democracy leader intimates that the Iranian revolution was supported not just for its Islamic basis, but more for its ability to release the Iranians from an unjust regime. What the people wanted, he implies, was not simply an Islamic regime: They wanted a regime that was more democratic in style and which would do away with the injustices of the Shah. It may be that, for many, support of fundamentalist Islamic movements is given not so much for religious reasons but for reasons of democracy and social justice. When they find that the fundamentalist regime is unpalatable in its religious strictures, they cry out again for what they really wanted in the first place: social justice and a greater measure of democracy. In other words, fundamentalist Islam is accepted by many mainly because it is seen as a vehicle for other things.[25]

It is therefore not surprising that in the recent Iranian presidential election the people voted for a more liberal figure, Mohammed Khatami. Although the reason for his victory was not simply anti-fundamentalist sentiment, it is clear that many Iranian people are not in favor of many of the measures brought in by the leaders of the Islamic republic.[26] Observers will also note the result of the recent Algerian election in which only 6 percent of the population voted for parties who suggested that the fundamentalist FIS should be re-integrated into Algerian politics. While the election was not entirely perfect, the result certainly demonstrated the peoples' lack of motivation for an Islamic state.[27]

Fundamentalist Islam with its punishments that many would confine to the Middle Ages and with its outdated strictures on dress and recreation sits uneasily in the latter part of the twentieth century. As a result many are suggesting that fundamentalist Islam as we have come to know it cannot survive in the longer term. Amuzegar points out that in Iran the rising strength of the middle classes, the development of new forms of communication, especially satellite television, and contacts with foreign nations can only serve to bring the future of the fundamentalist Islamic regime into question. He concludes that "The peoples' free spirit and their instinctive preference for progress and prosperity over retrogression and deprivation are bound to pave the way for the emergence of a more moderate, secular government."[28] Measures such as the Iranian *Majlis'* ban in 1994 on satellite dishes and a similar ban by the Ministry of the Interior in Saudi Arabia cannot keep the twenty-first century at bay forever. Young people in particular are not going to tolerate such retrograde measures, especially when they see the alternative a short distance away in the Mediterranean. Fundamentalist Islam has an "inability to incorporate modernity."[29]

FUNDAMENTALIST ISLAM: A TEMPORARY PHENOMENON

Muslim fundamentalists require that not only their personal beliefs be shaped by their religion but also their government. For the fundamentalist a Muslim government is a necessary part of their belief in the supremacy of Allah and of his revelation in the Qur'an. Despite this they cannot agree on the legitimacy of violence in achieving their objective, on the precise nature of a Muslim government, or on its economic system. In addition there is, in Iran at least, a significant body of Muslim opinion which rejects an Islamic fundamentalist government from the inside.

These disagreements with regard to policy and practice are so significant that we may question the sustainability of fundamentalist Islam in the longer term. If a religion has a directly revealed text which is supposed to require a government determined by that text, it would seem to be a significant source of weakness that its adherents cannot agree on what that text requires. Fundamentalist Muslims have an Achilles heel in their inability to determine the shape of what is a major part of their belief.

It might be pointed out that Christians, for example, are not united with regard to their political beliefs. That is true, but the Christian faith never suggested that there should be the unity of church and state that the fundamentalist Muslim faith requires. Jesus' suggestion that the Christian should render unto Caesar that which Caesar requires, would seem to call for some element of separation between church and state. In fundamentalist Islam there is to be a distinctly Muslim state.

It is therefore concluded that the internal divisions within fundamentalist Islam will weaken it so significantly that it will, in the longer term, cease to be the major force in foreign affairs that it is at present. It would also seem difficult to see how a faith which involves barbaric punishment which might have been accepted in the Middle Ages, can continue in the twenty-first century. It seems difficult to see how a faith that cannot accept many of the ideas of modern science and of modern society can continue for much longer. Aziz Al-Azmeh's study of the various types of movement within Islam suggests that fundamentalism is essentially unreasonable and as such unworthy of the twentieth century. He concludes with the proposition that the use of reason can only have one end in Arab states: the demise of fundamentalist Islam and its replacement by secularism.[30] He sees the establishment of the democratic process as historical, developmental, and highly conflictual: Fundamentalist Islam is just an element in this conflict but one which will eventually succumb to demise. Fundamentalist Islam is "an eminently historical player subject to the ruse of history."[31]

Partly because of these weaknesses, it is difficult to see how fundamentalist Islam can be seen as a long term "threat" to the West. To suggest, as former U.S. Secretary of Defense William Perry suggested, that the spread of Islamic fundamentalism in the Middle East represents a threat to Western survival is an arguable construct at best.[32] Similarly, the comment from former Secretary General of NATO Willy Claes that Islamic fundamentalism "is just as much of a threat to the West as Communism was" is judged to be equally inaccurate.[33]

A more reasonable argument is that Islamic fundamentalism could be better seen as representing steps toward democracy in some of the more authoritarian regimes of the Middle East. As such it could represent a liberating force in many respects.[34] In many areas of the Middle East where free speech is absent, political debate and movement often takes place through professional associations. These include syndicates of doctors, engineers, and teachers—such as Kuwait's University Graduates Society, Qatar's Jassrah Cultural Club, and the United Arab Emirates' Association of Social Professions. Although technically non-partisan, such associations are becoming increasingly politicized, with many being dominated by fundamentalist Muslims. Egypt's medical, engineering, and legal associations had their 1992 elections dominated by the activities of the fundamentalist Muslim Brotherhood. Such groups deserve our support if we are in favor of opening up countries in the Middle East to greater democracy and promoting greater human rights. We should therefore be supporting elements of Muslim fundamentalism rather than blindly campaigning against all of them, particularly when the latter course of action means that we are effectively campaigning for regimes which leave much to be desired in the way of human rights and democracy.[35] However, to support Islamic fundamentalism in the short term as a matter of political expediency should not blind us to the fact that in the long term fundamentalist Islam has only a limited future.[36] The changing world in which we live can only reject a faith that is by its very fundamentalist nature resistant to change.

NOTES

1. Reported in *Daily Telegraph*, 4 October 1996, p. 17.
2. Ibid.
3. For background on the Taliban movement, see K. Clark, "Afghanistan Under the Taliban," *Middle East International*, no. 538 (November 22, 1996), pp. 16–17.

4. Quoted in Aziz Al-Azmeh, *Islams and Modernities* (London: Verso), p. 119.
5. T. B. Irving, K. Ahmad, M. M. Ahsan, *The Qur'an: Basic Teachings* (Leicester, UK: The Islamic Foundation, 1979), p. 27.
6. Al-Azmeh, p. 52.
7. Dale F. Eickelman and James Piscatori, *Muslim Politics* (Princeton, NJ: Princeton University Press, 1996), pp. 70–71; S. J. Al-Azm, "Islamic Fundamentalism Reconsidered: A Critical Outline of Problems, Ideas and Approaches," *South Asian Bulletin*, XIV (1994), pp. 73–88.
8. *Qur'an*, 4:36.
9. See K. Lang, "French Ghettos Breed Guerillas for Islam," *Sunday Times*, 8 December 1996, p. 16.
10. Raphael Israeli, *Muslim Fundamentalism in Israel* (London: Brasseys, 1993).
11. Al-Azmeh contends that in reality no such codified law exists. "The *sharia* itself has evolved in parallel with the [Muslim] societies; and as far as one can tell from an objective examination of History, it is not now—nor has it ever been—a unanimously accepted code, but only a collection of principles and guidelines on what is legal," p. 54.
12. The term *Jahiliyya* was popularized by the radical Egyptian fundamentalist of the mid 1900s, Sayyid Qutb.
13. Quoted in J. L. Esposito, *The Islamic Threat: Myth or Reality* (New York: Oxford University Press, 1992), p. 135.
14. Quoted in J. Laffin, *The Dagger of Islam* (London: Sphere), pp. 54–55.
15. Quoted in A. Taheri, *Holy Terror* (London: Hutchinson, 1987), p. 113.
16. Modernist Muslims would want to challenge the idea that Islam as a way of life necessarily involves an Islamic state. For details and for a bibliography, see Eickleman and Piscatori, pp. 51–57.
17. Quoted in Laffin, p. 125. With regard to the Ayatollah Khomeini, it is interesting that in 1988 he himself suggested in a letter to the then President, Ayatollah Khameini, that the government of Iran, as part of the "absolute vice-regency of the Prophet of God . . . has priority over all other secondary injunctions, even prayers, fasting, and *hajj*. . . . The government is empowered to unilaterally revoke any *Sharia* agreements which it has concluded with the people when those agreements are contrary to the interest of the country or to Islam." Quoted in F. Halliday, *Islam and the Myth of Confrontation* (London: I. B. Tauris, 1996), p. 69. In other words Khomeini says on the one hand that Iran is to be an Islamic country and then says on the other that the government has the power to overrule fundamental Islamic provisions where it deems this to be necessary. It seems that there is an unresolved contradiction here.
18. Quoted in Al-Azm, p. 110.
19. *Sharia* consists of legislation based on the Qur'an and *Sunnah* together with the consensus of opinions of learned judges (*Ijma*), anything deduced by analogy from these (Qiyas), and independent judgement similarly based (*Ijtihad*). See A. R. I. Doi, *Sharia: The Islamic Law* (London: Ta Ha, 1984), Chap. 4.
20. Ibid., p. 17.
21. O. Roy, *The Failure of Political Islam* (London: I. B. Tauris, 1994), p. 195.
22. Ibid., pp. 145–146.
23. Jahangir Amuzegar, "Islamic Fundamentalism in Action: The Case of Iran," *Middle East Policy*, IV (1995), pp. 27–29.
24. A. Malone, "Mullahs Face Struggle to Maintain their Iron Grip," *Sunday Times*, 22 September 1996, p. 15.
25. Fred Halliday sees fundamentalist Islamic politics consisting of a religious "front" for a body of mainly secular political ideals. He maintains that much of the history, development, and future of fundamentalist Islamic movements should be

understood in secular terms using the secular tools of historical, political, and sociological analysis. See F. Halliday, esp. Chaps. 1 and 2.

26. See M. Colvin, "Iran Votes for a Reverse Revolution," *Sunday Times,* 25 May 1997, p. 19; S. Barzin, "Khatami's Shock Victory," *Middle East International,* 551 (May 30, 1997), pp. 5–6; S. Bakhash, "Iran's Remarkable Election," *Journal of Democracy,* 9 (1998), pp. 80–94. For details of Khatami's call for a review of Iran's relationship with the United States, see S. Barzin, "Respect for America," *Middle East International,* 556 (1998), pp. 9–10. For Washington's response, see D. Neff, "Washington's Upbeat Analysis," *Middle East International,* 566 (1998), pp. 10–11.

27. See H. Salen, "A Perfect Election," *Middle East International,* 552 (June 13, 1997), p. 12.

28. J. Amuzegar, p. 32.

29. O. Roy, p. 203.

30. A. Al-Azmeh, p. 58.

31. Ibid., p. 77.

32. Quoted in J. King, "A Clash of Civilizations. Pentagon Rhetoric on the Islamic Threat," *Middle East International,* 495 (March 3, 1995), p. 16.

33. Quoted in ibid. For other representations of an Islamic threat, see F. A. Khavari, *Oil and Islam: The Ticking Bomb* (Malibu: Roundtable, 1990). Part of the problem of seeing fundamentalist Islam as a threat is that it simply substitutes the old communist threat with another. The two are very different and should not be interpreted in the light of each other.

34. See H. A. Hawad, "Islam and the West: How Fundamental Is the Threat?" *Royal United Services' Institute Journal,* 140 (1995); M. Azzam, "Islamism, the Peace Process, and Regional Security"; J. Esposito, *The Islamic Threat*; D. G. Kibble, "The Threat of Militant Islam: A Fundamental Reappraisal," *Studies in Conflict and Terrorism,* 19 (1996).

35. See Clarence J. Bouchat, "A Fundamentalist Islamic Threat to the West," in *Studies in Conflict and Terrorism,* 19 (1996).

36. Supporting Islamic fundamentalism in this way does not mean that we should support it lock, stock, and barrel. We should criticize those elements of it with which we disagree. See D. G. Kibble, "Tomahawks for the Terrorists? A Considered Response to Fundamentalist Islamic Terrorism," *Naval Review,* 85 (1997). But also see F. Halliday, p. 127 ff, who takes a different point of view.

ISSUE 9

INTERNATIONAL CRIMINAL COURT

The Balkan and Central African atrocities that occurred in the mid-1990s renewed the international community's interest in creating an International Criminal Court to bring to justice those responsible for such heinous crimes. The initial response was the establishment, by the United Nations Security Council, of the Yugoslavia War Crimes Tribunal in 1993 and the International Criminal Tribunal for Rwanda in 1994. Given the limited jurisdiction of these tribunals, efforts were subsequently initiated to create a permanent international court, efforts that culminated in the signing in Rome, Italy, in July 1998, of a treaty establishing a permanent International Criminal Court. The treaty was approved with a vote of 120 to 7, with the United States in opposition, along with China, Iran, Iraq, the Sudan, and Libya. Subsequently, President Clinton, on December 31, 2000, in one of his last official acts, reversed American opposition to the Court, just prior to its coming into force. However, on May 6, 2002, President Bush "unsigned" American participation, when, in a letter to Kofi Annan, the Secretary-General of the United Nations, he stated that "the United States does not intend to become a party to the treaty," and that, "[a]ccordingly, the United States has no legal obligations arising from its signature on December 31, 2000."

The first selection for Issue 9, the remarks of Marc Grossman, Under Secretary for Political Affairs, U.S. State Department, presents the objections of the Bush administration to the International Criminal Court. Foremost are the lack of Security Council oversight of the Court's activities, and the prospect of American citizens becoming subject to the Court's jurisdiction over the objection of the U.S. government. In response are the remarks before the Senate of Senator Christopher Dodd (D-CT), challenging the administration's concerns as unreasonable, and the "unsigning" as prejudicial to the cause of pursuing global justice.

DISCUSSION QUESTIONS

As you read the speeches by Under Secretary Grossman and Senator Dodd, consider the following questions:

1. Does the establishment of the ICC represent an unwarranted erosion of national sovereignty?
2. Would the creation of the ICC further promote the cause of human rights?
3. Is the American "unsigning" justified, even at the cost of associating the United States with the other countries which voted against the creation of the ICC?

KEY WEB SITES

For more information on this topic, visit the following Web sites:

Rome Statute of the International Criminal Court
http://www.un.org/icc/romestat.htm

American Society of International Law
http://www.asil.org/iccbib3.htm

Human Rights Watch—ICC
http://www.hrw.org/campaigns/icc

U.S. Foreign Policy and the International Criminal Court

Marc Grossman, Under Secretary for Political Affairs

Center for Strategic and International Studies, Washington, D.C.
May 6, 2002

Good morning. Thank you for that kind introduction.

It's an honor to be here today. I would like to thank CSIS for hosting this discussion of American foreign policy and the International Criminal Court.

Let me get right to the point. And then I'll try to make my case in detail: Here's what America believes in:

We believe in justice and the promotion of the rule of law.

We believe those who commit the most serious crimes of concern to the international community should be punished.

We believe that states, not international institutions are primarily responsible for ensuring justice in the international system.

We believe that the best way to combat these serious offenses is to build domestic judicial systems, strengthen political will, and promote human freedom.

We have concluded that the International Criminal Court does not advance these principles. Here is why:

We believe the ICC undermines the role of the United Nations Security Council in maintaining international peace and security.

We believe in checks and balances. The Rome Statute creates a prosecutorial system that is an unchecked power.

We believe that in order to be bound by a treaty, a state must be party to that treaty. The ICC asserts jurisdiction over citizens of states that have not ratified the treaty. This threatens U.S. sovereignty.

We believe that the ICC is built on a flawed foundation. These flaws leave it open for exploitation and politically motivated prosecutions.

President Bush has come to the conclusion that the United States can no longer be a party to this process. In order to make our objections clear, both in principle and philosophy, and so as not to create unwarranted expectations of U.S. involvement in the Court, the President believes that he has no choice but to inform the United Nations, as depository of the treaty, of our intention not to become a party to the Rome Statute of the International Criminal Court. This morning, at the instruction of the President, our mission to the United Nations *notified* the UN Secretary-General in his capacity as the depository for the Rome Statute of the President's decision. These actions are consistent with the Vienna Convention on the Law of Treaties.

The decision to take this rare but not unprecedented act was not arrived at lightly. But after years of working to fix this flawed statute, and having our constructive proposals rebuffed, it is our only alternative.

HISTORICAL PERSPECTIVE

Like many of the nations that gathered in Rome in 1998 for the negotiations to create a permanent International Criminal Court, the United States arrived with the firm belief that those who perpetrate genocide, crimes against humanity, and war crimes must be held accountable—and that horrendous deeds must not go unpunished.

The United States has been a world leader in promoting the rule of law. From our pioneering leadership in the creation of tribunals in Nuremberg, the Far East, and the International Criminal Tribunals for the former Yugoslavia and Rwanda, the United States has been in the forefront of promoting international justice. We believed that a properly created court could be a useful tool in promoting human rights and holding the perpetrators of the worst violations accountable before the world—and perhaps one day such a court will come into being.

A Flawed Outcome   But the International Criminal Court that emerged from the Rome negotiations, and which will begin functioning on July 1 will not effectively advance these worthy goals.

First, we believe the ICC is an institution of unchecked power. In the United States, our system of government is founded on the principle that, in the words of John Adams, "power must never be trusted without a check." Unchecked power, our founders understood, is open to abuse, even with the good intentions of those who establish it.

But in the rush to create a powerful and independent court in Rome, there was a refusal to constrain the Court's powers in any meaningful way. Proposals put forward by the United States to place what we believed were proper checks and balances on the Court were rejected. In the end, despite the best efforts of the U.S. delegation, the final treaty had so many defects that the United States simply could not vote for it.

Take one example: the role of the UN Security Council. Under the UN Charter, the UN Security Council has primary responsibility for maintaining international peace and security. But the Rome Treaty removes this existing system of checks and balances, and places enormous unchecked power in the hands of the ICC prosecutor and judges. The treaty created a self-initiating prosecutor, answerable to no state or institution other than the Court itself.

In Rome, the United States said that placing this kind of unchecked power in the hands of the prosecutor would lead to controversy, politicized prosecutions, and confusion. Instead, the United States argued that the Security

Council should maintain its responsibility to check any possible excesses of the ICC prosecutor. Our arguments were rejected; the role of the Security Council was usurped.

Second, the treaty approved in Rome dilutes the authority of the UN Security Council and departs from the system that the framers of the UN Charter envisioned.

The treaty creates an as-yet-to-be defined crime of "aggression," and again empowers the court to decide on this matter and lets the prosecutor investigate and prosecute this undefined crime. This was done despite the fact that the UN Charter empowers only the Security Council to decide when a state has committed an act of aggression. Yet the ICC, free of any oversight from the Security Council, could make this judgment.

Third, the treaty threatens the sovereignty of the United States. The Court, as constituted today, claims the authority to detain and try American citizens, even through our democratically elected representatives have not agreed to be bound by the treaty. While sovereign nations have the authority to try noncitizens who have committed crimes against their citizens or in their territory, the United States has never recognized the right of an international organization to do so absent consent or a UN Security Council mandate.

Fourth, the current structure of the International Criminal Court undermines the democratic rights of our people and could erode the fundamental elements of the United Nations Charter, specifically the right to self-defense.

With the ICC prosecutor and judges presuming to sit in judgment of the security decisions of States without their assent, the ICC could have a chilling effect on the willingness of States to project power in defense of their moral and security interests.

This power must sometimes be projected. The principled projection of force by the world's democracies is critical to protecting human rights—to stopping genocide or changing regimes like the Taliban, which abuse their people and promote terror against the world.

Fifth, we believe that by putting U.S. officials, and our men and women in uniform, at risk of politicized prosecutions, the ICC will complicate U.S. military cooperation with many friends and allies who will now have a treaty obligation to hand over U.S. nationals to the Court—even over U.S. objections.

The United States has a unique role and responsibility to help preserve international peace and security. At any given time, U.S. forces are located in close to 100 nations around the world conducting peacekeeping and humanitarian operations and fighting inhumanity.

We must ensure that our soldiers and government officials are not exposed to the prospect of politicized prosecutions and investigations. Our President is committed to a robust American engagement in the world to defend freedom and defeat terror; we cannot permit the ICC to disrupt that vital mission.

Our Efforts   The President did not take his decision lightly. After the United States voted against the treaty in Rome, the United States remained committed and engaged—working for two years to help shape the court and to seek the necessary safeguards to prevent a politicization of the process. U.S. officials negotiated to address many of the concerns we saw in hopes of salvaging the treaty. The United States brought international law experts to the preparatory commissions and took a leadership role in drafting the elements of crimes and the procedures for the operation of the court.

While we were able to make some improvements during our active participation in the UN Preparatory Commission meetings in New York, we were ultimately unable obtain the remedies necessary to overcome our fundamental concerns.

On December 31, 2000, the previous administration signed the Rome Treaty. In signing, President Clinton reiterated "our concerns about the significant flaws in the treaty," but hoped the U.S. signature would provide us influence in the future and assist our effort to fix this treaty. Unfortunately, this did not prove to be the case.

On April 11, 2002, the ICC was ratified by enough countries to bring it into force on July 1 of this year. Now we find ourselves at the end of the process. Today, the treaty contains the same significant flaws President Clinton highlighted.

Our Philosophy   While we oppose the ICC, we share a common goal with its supporters—the promotion of the rule of law. Our differences are in approach and philosophy. In order for the rule of law to have true meaning, societies must accept their responsibilities and be able to direct their future and come to terms with their past. An unchecked international body should not be able to interfere in this delicate process.

For example: When a society makes the transition from oppression to democracy, their new government must face their collective past. The state should be allowed to choose the method. The government should decide whether to prosecute or seek national reconciliation. This decision should not be made by the ICC.

If the state chooses as a result of a democratic and legal process not to prosecute fully, and instead to grant conditional amnesty, as was done in the difficult case of South Africa, this democratic decision should be respected.

Whenever a state accepts the challenges and responsibilities associated with enforcing the rule of law, the rule of law is strengthened and a barrier to impunity is erected. It is this barrier that will create the lasting goals the ICC seeks to attain. This responsibility should not be taken away from states.

International practice should promote domestic accountability and encourage sovereign states to seek reconciliation where feasible.

The existence of credible domestic legal systems is vital to ensuring conditions do not deteriorate to the point that the international community is required to intercede.

In situations where violations are grave and the political will of the sovereign state is weak, we should work, using any influence we have, to strengthen that will. In situations where violations are so grave as to amount to a breach of international peace and security, and the political will to address these violations is nonexistent, the international community may, and if necessary should, intercede through the UN Security Council as we did in Bosnia and Rwanda.

Unfortunately, the current framework of the Rome treaty threatens these basic principles.

We Will Continue to Lead

Notwithstanding our disagreements with the Rome Treaty, the United States respects the decision of those nations who have chosen to join the ICC; but they in turn must respect our decision not to join the ICC or place our citizens under the jurisdiction of the court.

So, despite this difference, we must work together to promote real justice after July 1, when the Rome Statute enters into force.

The existence of a functioning ICC will not cause the United States to retreat from its leadership role in the promotion of international justice and the rule of law.

The United States will

> work together with countries to avoid any disruptions caused by the Treaty, particularly those complications in U.S. military cooperation with friends and allies that are parties to the treaty;
>
> continue our longstanding role as an advocate for the principle that there must be accountability for war crimes and other serious violations of international humanitarian law;
>
> continue to play a leadership role to right these wrongs.

The armed forces of the United States will obey the law of war, while our international policies are and will remain completely consistent with these norms.

[We will] continue to discipline our own when appropriate.

We will remain committed to promoting the rule of law and helping to bring violators of humanitarian law to justice, wherever the violations may occur.

We will support politically, financially, technically, and logistically any postconflict state that seeks to credibly pursue domestic humanitarian law.

We will support creative ad hoc mechanisms such as the hybrid process in Sierra Leone—where there is a division of labor between the sovereign state and the international community—as well as alternative justice mechanisms such as truth and reconciliation commissions.

We will work with Congress to obtain the necessary resources to support this global effort.

We will seek to mobilize the private sector to see how and where they can contribute.

We will seek to create a pool of experienced judges and prosecutors who would be willing to work on these projects on short notice.

We will take steps to ensure that gaps in U.S. law do not allow persons wanted or indicted for genocide, war crimes, or crimes against humanity to seek safe haven on our soil in hopes of evading justice.

And when violations occur that are so grave that they breach international peace and security, the United States will use its position in the UN Security Council to act in support of justice.

We believe that there is common ground, and ask those nations who have decided to join the Rome Treaty to meet us there. Encouraging states to come to face the past while moving into the future is a goal that no one can dispute. Enhancing the capacity of domestic judiciaries is an aim to which we can all agree. The United States believes that justice would be best served in creating an environment that will have a lasting and beneficial impact on all nations across the globe. Empowering states to address these challenges will lead us to a more just and peaceful world. Because, in the end, the best way to prevent genocide, crimes against humanity, and war crimes is through the spread of democracy, transparency, and rule of law. Nations with accountable, democratic governments do not abuse their own people or wage wars of conquest and terror. A world of self-governing democracies is our best hope for a world without inhumanity.

The International Criminal Court

Senator Christopher Dodd

U.S. Senate, Washington, D.C.
May 13, 2002

Mr. President, I wish to take a few minutes to express my deep disappointment at the announcement made last week by Under Secretary of State John Bolton with respect to the "unsigning," as they have called it, of the International Criminal Court. This decision, in my view, is irresponsible, it is isolationist, and contrary to our vital national interest.

Many of our closest allies—in fact, every one of our NATO allies—has put their faith and vision in this new legal instrument, the International Criminal Court. To date, sixty-six nations have ratified the International Criminal Court and over 130 nations have signed on to this particular effort, including those nations I mentioned—all of our NATO allies—countries such as France, Germany, the United Kingdom, and the like. These are governments with deep ties to our Nation. We share a deep sense of common values, a deep sense of democracy, and a deep sense of justice.

It is outrageous that the United States has now put itself in a position of joining only a handful of rogue nations that are frightened to death of the International Criminal Court as we enter the twenty-first century. We should be joining these countries and supporting them in their commitment to making the court work and strengthening international respect for the rule of law. That is what we stand for as Americans. That is what we are trying to export around the world. In addition, we try to export the notion of justice, of fair justice, such as the symbols we see outside this building a block away: the Supreme court, Justice blindfolded with the scales equally divided.

That is what we have stood for as a nation for more than two centuries. What a great shame it is that as we enter the twenty-first century, in an effort to establish an international criminal court of justice, the Bush administration is going to "unsign" a document, a treaty, that I think would have gone a long way to helping us achieve the very goals incorporated in the Treaty of Rome.

We should have been rejoicing that finally with the entry and divorce of the court, any individual who commits genocide, war crimes, and crimes against humanity would be on notice that he or she would be prosecuted for those offenses. I find it disheartening there is a lack of historical perspective when it comes to this issue. Let's remember it was the atrocities of World War II, the Holocaust, that led to the establishment of the Nuremberg Tribunal to bring those who committed such acts of violence and human rights violations to justice, which highlighted the fact that there was a void in the international legal system. Those who participated in the Nuremberg process came to believe strongly that a permanent international criminal court should be established to try future heinous international criminals. The hope was that the existence of such a court would also serve as a deterrent to those who might consider committing such crimes.

Unfortunately, the proposal floundered during fifty years of superpower rivalry, but the United States kept arguing that we ought to do this, through Republican and Democratic administrations. Conservatives, liberals, moderates all suggested and all argued at one time or another for the importance of the establishment of such a court.

I have no doubt that such a court would have been extremely useful had it existed during the last quarter of the twentieth century. It should still be fresh in our minds the fact that the end of the Cold War, and the explosion of ethnic brutality led to the necessity of creating ad hoc tribunals for Rwanda and Yugoslavia, but there was no means available for trying the Idi Amins and Saddam Husseins of this world, or others who have been able to evade their nation's justice. With very few exceptions, the world has stood helpless in the face of such crimes against humanity.

Had the court existed, it just might have deprived these tyrants of the safe havens from prosecution. It just might have deterred some of the worst atrocities and also prevented the U.S. service members from being sent into harm's way to reestablish the rule of law.

President Clinton, to his credit, appreciated that fact, and that is why he signed the treaty. He was not starry-eyed about it. However, he recognized that additional safeguards with respect to the operation of the court were needed in order to reassure those skeptical about the international organization, and he rightly decided that since the court was still a work in progress, and given the role of the United States as a leader in the promotion of the rule of law, that it was in the national interest of the United States to remain engaged with our allies as they moved forward to bring the Rome statute into force.

Some in the United States harbor the unreasonable fear that Americans will be taken before this tribunal on politically motivated charges, fears that I believe are unfounded but fears that have not been dispelled with the erasing of our signature. U.S. men and women in uniform are no safer today than they were before Monday's announcement. In fact, I argue they are in greater jeopardy because the court, as it is presently construed, does have flaws because we disengage from rewriting the court to try to establish better rules—the court is going into existence in a matter of weeks. Whether we signed it or not, it is becoming the international rule of law, and today that court could have been stronger had we decided to remain engaged in helping frame the structure of the institution.

These men and women in uniform may be in some jeopardy, and my hope would be they would not, but had we stayed engaged in this process, we could have eliminated even that slight possibility. Moreover, to the best of my knowledge, what we have done with respect to the ICC, the "unsigning" of a treaty, is without precedent. I am sure there are legal scholars on diplomacy that can correct me if I am wrong, but I cannot find a single example in the more than two centuries of history where an American president has unsigned an agreement. . . .

The fear in Washington is that American soldiers abroad, as I said, would be charged unjustly with war crimes. Such a possibility is very remote. The court already contains strong safeguards that ensure it will deal only with the most serious of international crimes and can take a case only if a nation's own judicial system has declined to carry out a conscientious investigation of the charges.

Does anyone really believe that in this country we would not pursue a person in uniform who had committed heinous crimes to come before a bar of justice?

The Rwandan and former Yugoslavian tribunals, which have rendered fair and reasonable judgments, show that America has little to fear from such a court. The Clinton administration negotiators were able to significantly improve the court's rules. Continued engagement, as I said a moment ago, by the Bush administration could have built upon that record.

One would have thought it was in the interest of the United States not to miss a chance to affect the selection of judges in the definition of new crimes, issues that should matter to us and to our allies. Apparently that is not the case.

A few weeks ago, on April 11, governments gathered in New York to mark what they called the depositing of the sixty-sixth instrument of ratification of the Rome statute, meaning that the international criminal court will come into existence this July. The court is going to exist and, unfortunately, we are going to be on the outside.

We have made further announcements we will not even support or assist the court as it tries to gather information against those who may have committed these dreadful crimes that the court would have jurisdiction over.

I am deeply disturbed by this action. I think it is a huge mistake. What are the implications of this course the Bush administration has set for the United States? The United States no longer can credibly voice its opinion on who should be selected to be the court's judges and prosecutors, nor will we be taken seriously if we attempt to use our seat in the UN Security Council to refer situations to the court, such as the current conflict in Sudan that has already claimed over 2 million lives as a result of war crimes, genocide, and crimes against humanity.

Finally, our words will fall on deaf ears when we purport to act as an unbiased watchdog of the court's integrity having denounced its fundamental purposes. We have also lost the opportunities that ensure the court stays focused on its primary task, that of bringing to justice the world's worst criminals.

I have cited a number of vital American interests that are wrapped up in this institution, the court. Those interests are not going to be erased with the name of the United States gone from the Rome statute. The administration may have struck a responsive cord with a right-wing antimultilateralist constituency with this announcement, but it has jeopardized the interests of all Americans in so doing.

The administration could have taken the higher road, the responsible road, recognizing that there is a constructive and useful role the United States could perform without making a decision at this juncture concerning U.S. ratification. Sadly, President Bush has chosen not to do so.

While some may be cheering the administration's decision, those of us who care deeply about promoting the rule of law are not. The issue has particular significance for me. My father, Thomas Dodd, was an executive trial counsel at Nuremberg in 1945 and 1946. The Nuremberg trials of the leading Nazi war criminals following World War II was a landmark of the struggle to deter and punish crimes of war and genocide, setting the stage for the Geneva and genocide conventions. It was also largely an American initiative.

Today, instead of America being a leader in the pursuit of global justice, we would act to throw up roadblocks toward that goal. Make no mistake about it, today was a setback in the promotion of global justice. Today was a setback for what America is supposed to stand for, and I regret this decision very deeply indeed.

ISSUE 10

CIVIL LIBERTIES

At least since September 11, 2001, the United States has been engaged in a "War on Terrorism." Since the destruction of the World Trade Center, the attack on the Pentagon, and the destruction of American airliners in flight, there is little doubt that America is under attack, and there is a broad consensus that measures must be taken to defend us from further attack. Still, however, many disturbing issues remain. Is there any distinction between an "act of terrorism," an "act of war," and a "criminal act"? Further, what kinds of security measures threaten the fundamental values of democracy itself?

Assuming that terrorism can be defined, and that is not an easy assumption to make, what are the moral responsibilities of democracies when they set out to combat terrorists? Dov Waxman, a visiting researcher at the Moshe Dayan Center for the Study of Middle Eastern and African Studies, Tel Aviv University, Israel, notes that "the fundamental challenge is to reconcile the necessity of combating terrorism with the constitutional, legal, and ethical demands of a democratic state."

Democracies are not necessarily benevolent or merciful. America seems to have no moral qualms about killing thousands of people when a state of war has been declared. Our bombings of Germany in World War II, not to mention Hiroshima and Nagasaki, destroyed many more people than the collapse of the World Trade Center. Does this mean, however, that democracy requires no special moral standards at all? Are democracies not to distinguish themselves from the world's tyrannies and dictatorships? Waxman and most champions of democracy assert that democracy is not merely a type of power structure; it is a moral structure as well. Waxman argues that a war on terrorism holds certain moral perils for democracies. First, in fighting terrorism, we may become indistinguishable from the threats we fight. Second, our quest to find and stop terrorists may threaten the liberties that democracies are established to save.

In the debate that follows, the imperatives of homeland security and preserving democratic freedoms meet head on. First, Attorney General John Ashcroft explains why strong security measures are needed and then discusses some of the security measures being taken and the reasons that he believes they do not threaten America's fundamental freedoms. Then, Representative Lynn C. Woolsey (D-CA) explains her reservations about the new security measures, and expresses concern that they may be abused.

DISCUSSION QUESTIONS

As you read the speeches by Attorney General Ashcroft and Representative Woolsey, consider the following questions:

1. Have the new security measures violated the constitutional freedoms of Americans or resident aliens thus far?
2. Are the security measures likely to be abused in the future?
3. To what extent do the security measures represent a threat to America's fundamental freedoms?

KEY WEB SITES

For more information on this topic, visit the following Web sites:

Center for Democracy and Technology
http://www.cdt.org

The Terrorism Research Center
http://www.terrorism.com

The American Civil Liberties Union
http://www.aclu.org

Center for Justice and Democracy
http://www.centerjd.org

Homeland Security

Attorney General John Ashcroft

U.S. Senate, Washington, D.C.
December 6, 2001

Mr. Chairman, Senator Hatch, members of the Judiciary Committee, thank you for this opportunity to testify today. It is a pleasure to be back in the U.S. Senate.

On the morning of September 11, as the United States came under attack, I was in an airplane with several members of the Justice Department en route to Milwaukee, in the skies over the Great Lakes. By the time we could return to Washington, thousands of people had been murdered at the World Trade Center. One hundred and eighty-nine were dead at the Pentagon. Forty-four had crashed to the ground in Pennsylvania. From that moment, at the command of the President of the United States, I began to mobilize the resources of the Department of Justice toward one single, overarching, and overriding objective: to save innocent lives from further acts of terrorism.

America's campaign to save innocent lives from terrorists is now eighty-seven days old. It has brought me back to this committee to report to you in accordance with Congress's oversight role. I welcome this opportunity to clarify for you and the American people how the Justice Department is working to protect American lives while preserving American liberties.

Since those first terrible hours of September 11, America has faced a choice that is as stark as the images that linger of that morning. One option is to call September 11 a fluke, to believe it could never happen again, and to live in a dream world that requires us to do nothing differently. The other option is to fight back, to summon all our strength and all our resources and devote ourselves to better ways to identify, disrupt, and dismantle terrorist networks.

Under the leadership of President Bush, America has made the choice to fight terrorism—not just for ourselves but for all civilized people. Since September 11, through dozens of warnings to law enforcement, a deliberate campaign of terrorist disruption, tighter security around potential targets, and a preventative campaign of arrest and detention of lawbreakers, America has grown stronger—and safer—in the face of terrorism.

Thanks to the vigilance of law enforcement and the patience of the American people, we have not suffered another major terrorist attack. Still, we cannot—we must not—allow ourselves to grow complacent. The reasons are apparent to me each morning. My day begins with a review of the threats to Americans and American interests that were received in the previous twenty-four hours. If ever there were proof of the existence of evil in the world, it is in the pages of these reports. They are a chilling daily chronicle of hatred of America by fanatics who seek to extinguish freedom, enslave women, corrupt education, and to kill Americans wherever and whenever they can.

The terrorist enemy that threatens civilization today is unlike any we have ever known. It slaughters thousands of innocents—a crime of war and a crime against humanity. It seeks weapons of mass destruction and threatens their use against America. No one should doubt the intent, nor the depth, of its consuming, destructive hatred.

Terrorist operatives infiltrate our communities—plotting, planning, and waiting to kill again. They enjoy the benefits of our free society even as they commit themselves to our destruction. They exploit our openness—not randomly or haphazardly—but by deliberate, premeditated design.

This is a seized al Qaeda training manual—a "how-to" guide for terrorists— that instructs enemy operatives in the art of killing in a free society. Prosecutors first made this manual public in the trial of the al Qaeda terrorists who bombed U.S. embassies in Africa. We are posting several al Qaeda lessons from this manual on our Web site today so Americans can know our enemy.

In this manual, al Qaeda terrorists are told how to use America's freedom as a weapon against us. They are instructed to use the benefits of a free press— newspapers, magazines and broadcasts—to stalk and kill their victims. They are instructed to exploit our judicial process for the success of their operations. Captured terrorists are taught to anticipate a series of questions from authorities and, in each response, to lie—to lie about who they are, to lie about what they are doing, and to lie about who they know in order for the operation to achieve its objective. Imprisoned terrorists are instructed to concoct stories of torture and mistreatment at the hands of our officials. They are directed to take advantage of any contact with the outside world to, quote, "communicate with brothers outside prison and exchange information that may be helpful to them in their work. The importance of mastering the art of hiding messages is self-evident here."

Mr. Chairman and members of the committee, we are at war with an enemy who abuses individual rights as it abuses jet airliners: as weapons with which to kill Americans. We have responded by redefining the mission of the Department of Justice. Defending our nation and its citizens against terrorist attacks is now our first and overriding priority.

We have launched the largest, most comprehensive criminal investigation in world history to identify the killers of September 11 and to prevent further terrorist attacks. Four thousand FBI agents are engaged with their international counterparts in an unprecedented worldwide effort to detect, disrupt, and dismantle terrorist organizations.

We have created a national task force at the FBI to centralize control and information sharing in our investigation. This task force has investigated hundreds of thousands of leads, conducted over 500 searches, interviewed thousands of witnesses and obtained numerous court-authorized surveillance orders. Our prosecutors and agents have collected information and evidence from countries throughout Europe and the Middle East.

Immediately following the September 11 attacks, the Bureau of Prisons acted swiftly to intensify security precautions in connection with all al Qaeda and other terrorist inmates, increasing perimeter security at a number of key facilities.

We have sought and received additional tools from Congress. Already, we have begun to utilize many of these tools. Within hours of passage of the USA Patriot Act, we made use of its provisions to begin enhanced information sharing between the law-enforcement and intelligence communities. We have used the provisions allowing nationwide search warrants for e-mail and subpoenas for payment information. And we have used the Act to place those who access the Internet through cable companies on the same footing as everyone else.

Just yesterday, at my request, the State Department designated thirty-nine entities as terrorist organizations pursuant to the USA Patriot Act.

We have waged a deliberate campaign of arrest and detention to remove suspected terrorists who violate the law from our streets. Currently, we have brought criminal charges against 110 individuals, of whom 60 are in federal custody. The INS has detained 563 individuals on immigration violations.

We have investigated more than 250 incidents of retaliatory violence and threats against Arab Americans, Muslim Americans, Sikh Americans, and South Asian Americans.

Since September 11, the Customs Service and Border Patrol have been at their highest state of alert. All vehicles and persons entering the country are subjected to the highest level of scrutiny. Working with the State Department, we have imposed new screening requirements on certain applicants for nonimmigrant visas. At the direction of the President, we have created a Foreign Terrorist Tracking Task Force to ensure that we do everything we can to prevent terrorists from entering the country, and to locate and remove those who already have.

We have prosecuted to the fullest extent of the law individuals who waste precious law enforcement resources through anthrax hoaxes.

We have offered noncitizens willing to come forward with valuable information a chance to live in this country and one day become citizens.

We have forged new cooperative agreements with Canada to protect our common borders and the economic prosperity they sustain.

We have embarked on a wartime reorganization of the Department of Justice. We are transferring resources and personnel to the field offices where citizens are served and protected. The INS is being restructured to better perform its service and border security responsibilities. Under Director Bob Mueller, the FBI is undergoing an historic reorganization to put the

prevention of terrorism at the center of its law enforcement and national security efforts.

Outside Washington, we are forging new relationships of cooperation
with state and local law enforcement.

We have created ninety-three Anti-Terrorism Task Forces—one in each
U.S. Attorney's district—to integrate the communications and activities of
local, state, and federal law enforcement.

In all these ways and more, the Department of Justice has sought to prevent terrorism with reason, careful balance, and excruciating attention to detail. Some of our critics, I regret to say, have shown less affection for detail.
Their bold declarations of so-called fact have quickly dissolved, upon inspection, into vague conjecture. Charges of "kangaroo courts" and "shredding the
Constitution" give new meaning to the term, "the fog of war."

Since lives and liberties depend upon clarity, not obfuscation, and reason,
not hyperbole, let me take this opportunity today to be clear: Each action
taken by the Department of Justice, as well as the war crimes commissions
considered by the President and the Department of Defense, is carefully drawn
to target a narrow class of individuals—terrorists. Our legal powers are targeted at terrorists. Our investigation is focused on terrorists. Our prevention
strategy targets the terrorist threat.

Since 1983, the U.S. government has defined terrorists as those who perpetrate premeditated, politically motivated violence against noncombatant
targets. My message to America this morning, then, is this: If you fit this definition of a terrorist, fear the United States, for you will lose your liberty.

We need honest, reasoned debate, not fearmongering. To those who pit
Americans against immigrants, and citizens against noncitizens; to those who
scare peace-loving people with phantoms of lost liberty; my message is this:
Your tactics only aid terrorists—for they erode our national unity and diminish our resolve. They give ammunition to America's enemies, and pause
to America's friends. They encourage people of good will to remain silent in
the face of evil.

Our efforts have been carefully crafted to avoid infringing on constitutional rights while saving American lives. We have engaged in a deliberate
campaign of arrest and detention of law breakers. All persons being detained
have the right to contact their lawyers and their families. Out of respect for
their privacy, and concern for saving lives, we will not publicize the names
of those detained.

We have the authority to monitor the conversations of 16 of the 158,000
federal inmates and their attorneys because we suspect that these communications are facilitating acts of terrorism. Each prisoner has been told in advance his conversations will be monitored. None of the information that is
protected by attorney-client privilege may be used for prosecution. Information will only be used to stop impending terrorist acts and save American
lives. . . .

Bill of Rights Cannot Be the Next Victim of Terrorism

Representative Lynn C. Woolsey

House of Representatives, Washington, D.C.
December 12, 2001

Mr. Speaker, the terrorist attacks on September 11 struck fear in the heart of every American. Today, we continue to fight a war against terrorism on two fronts—in the mountains of Afghanistan and on the main streets of the United States. The first is a more traditional war against soldiers and war machinery; the second, a war against domestic terrorism.

Within days of the attacks, Congress passed a Homeland Security Bill that included the so-called "Patriot Act." The Patriot Act allows the government to increase its use of wiretaps and surveillance, and enhances its ability to trace e-mail and Internet usage. I voted against the Patriot Act because it intrudes unnecessarily on our civil liberties. We had adequate police and intelligence systems available to prevent September 11, but they were not used effectively. The inadequate use of these resources is no reason to trample our freedoms.

The Bill of Rights, civil rights, and civil liberties must not be the "other victim" of terrorism. As the domestic war against terrorism continues, my concern is that "increased police power" will encroach on our liberties.

In the past month, Attorney General John Ashcroft issued rules to allow the FBI to eavesdrop on communications between attorneys and their clients who are suspected terrorists, ordered prosecutors to interview over 5,000 young, mostly Middle Eastern men in the United States, and supported a system of secret military tribunals that could be used to try alleged accomplices in the September 11 attacks.

Members of Congress and eight former high-ranking FBI officials have questioned the effectiveness of Attorney General Ashcroft's plan to fight terrorism. The tactics that he is proposing are not new. By interviewing over 5,000 mostly Middle Eastern men to gather information about terrorists, he is merely recycling the same "preventive" intelligence-gathering techniques that were rejected in the late 1970s because they did not prevent terrorism and, in fact, led to abuses of civil liberties.

In the 1950s and 1960s, FBI Director J. Edgar Hoover used "Red Squads" to collect massive amounts of "preventive" intelligence to deter terrorist attacks. The "Squads" were criticized for abusing civil liberties and they were seldom effective. Because the majority of preventive intelligence investigations did not lead to criminal cases, most terrorist activities went unsolved and most of the terrorists were not apprehended. There is no reason to return to a system that didn't work and has a track record of failure and abuse.

Attorney General Ashcroft wants terrorist suspects to be tried by secret military tribunals. Conducting the tribunals in secret with the possibility of imposing capital punishment by a mere two-thirds vote, is an infringement of our civil liberties. It also undermines our system of checks and balances. Our Democracy retains its integrity in large part because no single branch of government overwhelms another. The military tribunals circumvent the role of oversight control granted to Congress in the Constitution, and allow too much power to the Executive branch.

The strength of the United States does not rest entirely on our overwhelming military superiority. Our country's strength lies in its moral authority, its reliance on the rule of law, and its belief in democracy. The ideals stated in our Constitution and Bill of Rights resonate throughout the world. It is our strength as a just, fair, and transparent society that has made us a superpower, and these are the ideals that will ensure our world preeminence in the future.

Just as we cannot win the battle against terrorism in Afghanistan with purely military options, we cannot improve homeland security by infringing on our freedoms. The Bill of Rights cannot be the next victim of terrorism. We will eventually win the military intervention against terrorism, but we cannot lose our national character in the meantime. Fear should not guide our decisions or cloud our judgment. Fear must not muffle the voice of freedom.

ISSUE 11

INTELLIGENCE

Where were you when you first learned of the September 11 terrorist attacks in New York and Washington? For most people these gripping moments are seared deeply in their memories. It was surreal, more like a horror movie than reality. Yet it was all too real, as 2,801 people lost their lives in the World Trade Center towers in New York, as another 189 died at the Pentagon building in Washington, followed by the deaths of 45 passengers and crew onboard a hijacked airliner that crashed in Pennsylvania. Quickly the names of Osama bin Laden and the al Qaeda terrorist network became household words.

But how could nineteen terrorists successfully plan and execute such an elaborate operation without being detected by American intelligence organizations? Foremost among those asking this question are the U.S. House and Senate Intelligence Committees, which in the fall of 2002 held joint hearings on alleged intelligence failures related to the September 11 plot. The first selection presented for Issue 11 is a statement made at these hearings by Kristen Breitweiser, the widow of a man who died in the World Trade Center. She represented a group of persons who suffered similar losses, and she minced few words in charging government intelligence agencies with ineptitude and negligence.

The second selection for Issue 11 is a speech by Robert S. Mueller, the Director of the Federal Bureau of Investigation (FBI), the agency that has primary responsibility for collecting intelligence information within the United States. He recounts his recollections from September 11, notes how the hijackers were able to "stay below our radar," and lays out actions that the FBI is taking to prepare for the future.

Discussion Questions

As you read the speeches by Breitweiser and Mueller, consider the following questions:

1. What role should a nation's intelligence organizations play in combatting international terrorism?
2. Should American intelligence organizations have detected the September 11 plot? Or were these bizarre attacks so far removed from past experience that no intelligence organization could have been expected to foresee them?
3. Are the changes being made in the FBI, as outlined by Mueller, appropriate? Is the Bureau on the correct course?

Key Web Sites

For more information on this topic, visit the following Web sites:

The "War on Terrorism" page of the Central Intelligence Agency
http://www.cia.gov/terrorism/index.html

"War on Terrorism" page of the Federal Bureau of Investigation
http://www.fbi.gov/terrorinfo/terrorism.htm

Terrorism Research Center
http://www.terrorism.com

Joint hearings by House and Senate Intelligence Committees on 9/11 attacks
http://intelligence.senate.gov/hr107.htm#October_2002

The Failure of U.S. Intelligence

Kristen Breitweiser

Family Advocates and Joint Inquiry Staff Statement,
Testimony from September 11
September 18, 2002

September 11 was the devastating result of a catalogue of failures on behalf of our government and its agencies. My husband and the approximately 3,000 others like him went to work and never came home. But, were any of our governmental agencies doing their job on that fateful morning? Perhaps the carnage and devastation of September 11 speaks for itself in answering this question.

Our intelligence agencies suffered an utter collapse in their duties and responsibilities leading up to and on September 11. But their negligence does not stand atone. Agencies like the Port Authority, the City of New York, the FAA, the INS, the Secret Service, NORAD, the Air Force, and the airlines also failed our nation that morning. Perhaps, said more cogently, one singular agency's failures do not eclipse another's. And it goes without saying that the examination of the intelligence agencies by this Committee does not detract, discount, or dismantle the need for a more thorough examination of all of these other culpable parties.

An independent blue-ribbon panel would be the most appropriate means to achieve such a thorough and expansive examination, in large part because it would not be limited in scope or hindered by time limits. An independent blue-ribbon panel would provide the comprehensive, unbiased, and definitive report that the devastation of September 11 demands.

Soon after the attacks, President Bush stated that there would come a time to look back and examine our nation's failures, but that such an undertaking was inappropriate while the nation was still in shock. I would respectfully suggest to President Bush and to our Congress that now, a full year later, it is time to look back and investigate our failures as a nation. A hallmark of democratic government is a willingness to admit to, analyze, and learn from mistakes. And it is now time for our nation to triumph as the great democracy that it is.

The families of the victims of September 11 have waited long enough. We need to have answers. We need to have accountability. We need to feel safe living and working in this great nation.

Specific Threats as to Using Planes as Weapons

On May 17, 2002, National Security Advisor Condoleezza Rice stated emphatically, "I don't think anybody could have predicted that these people would take an airplane and slam it into the World Trade Center . . . that they would try to use an airplane as a missile, a hijacked airplane as a missile."

The historical facts illustrate differently:

- In 1993, a $150,000 study was commissioned by the Pentagon to investigate the possibility of an airplane being used to bomb national landmarks. A draft document of this was circulated throughout the Pentagon, the Justice Department, and to FEMA.
- In 1994, a disgruntled FedEx employee invaded the cockpit of a DC-10 with plans to crash it into a company building in Memphis.
- In 1994, a lone pilot crashed a small plane into a tree on the White House grounds.
- In 1994, an Air France flight was hijacked by members of the Armed Islamic Group with the intent to crash the plane into the Eiffel Tower.
- In January 1995, Philippine authorities investigating Abdul Murad, an Islamic terrorist, unearthed "Project Bojinka." Project Bojinka's primary objective was to blow up eleven airliners over the Pacific, and in the alternative, several planes were to be hijacked and flown into civilian targets in the United States. Among the targets mentioned were CIA headquarters, the World Trade Center, the Sears Tower, and the White House. Murad told U.S. intelligence officials that he would board any American commercial aircraft pretending to be an ordinary passenger. And he would then hijack the aircraft, control its cockpit, and dive it at the CIA headquarters.
- In 1997, this plot resurfaced during the trial of Ramsi Yousef—the mastermind behind the 1993 bombings of the World Trade Center. During the trial, FBI agents testified that "the plan targeted not only the CIA but other U.S. government buildings in Washington, including the Pentagon."
- In September 1999, a report, *The Sociology and Psychology of Terrorism*, was prepared for U.S. intelligence by the Federal Research Division, an arm of the Library of Congress. It stated, "Suicide bombers belonging to Al Qaeda's Martyrdom Battalion could crash-land an aircraft packed with high explosives (C-4 and Semtex) into the Pentagon, the headquarters of the CIA, or the White House."

This laundry list of historical indicators—in no way exhaustive—illustrates that long before September 11 the American intelligence community had a significant amount of information about specific terrorist threats to commercial airline travel in America, including the possibility that a plane would be used as a weapon.

Failure to Make Warnings Public

On March 11, 2002, Director of the CIA George Tenet stated "in broad terms last summer that terrorists might be planning major operations in the United States. But, we never had the texture—meaning enough information—to stop what happened."

On May 8, 2002, director of the FBI, Robert Mueller, stated, "There was nothing the agency could have done to anticipate and prevent the attacks."

Once again, the historical facts indicate differently:

- Throughout the spring and early summer of 2001, intelligence agencies flooded the government with warnings of possible terrorist attacks against American targets, including commercial aircraft, by al Qaeda and other groups. The warnings were vague but sufficiently alarming to prompt the FAA to issue four information circulars, or ICs, to the commercial airline industry between June 22 and July 31, warning of possible terrorism.
- On June 22, the military's Central and European Commands imposed "Force Protection Condition Delta," the highest antiterrorist alert.
- On June 28: National Security Advisor Condoleezza Rice said, "It is highly likely that a significant al Qaeda attack is in the near future, within several weeks."
- As of July 31, the FAA urged U.S. airlines to maintain a "high degree of alertness."
- One FAA circular from late July noted, according to Condoleezza Rice, that there was "no specific target, no credible info of attack to U.S. civil aviation interests, but terror groups are known to be planning and training for hijackings and we ask you therefore to use caution."
- Two counterterrorism officials described the alerts of the early and midsummer 2001 as "'the most urgent in decades."

One thing remains clear from this history. Our intelligence agencies were acutely aware of an impending domestic risk posed by al Qaeda. A question that remains unclear is how many lives could have been saved had this information been made more public.

Airport security officials could have gone over all the basics, again, of the steps needed to prevent hijackings. The policy of allowing passengers to carry razors and knives with blades of up to four inches in length certainly could have come under scrutiny. Indeed, officials could have issued an emergency directive prohibiting such potential weapons in carry-on bags. Finally, all selectees under the Computer Assisted Passenger Pre-Screening System (CAPPS), and their carry-on luggage and checked bags could have been subjected to additional screening. Apparently, none were on September 11, although internal FAA documents indicate that CAPPS selected some of the hijackers.

And how many victims may have thought twice before boarding an aircraft? How many victims would have chosen to fly on private planes? How many victims may have taken notice of these Middle Eastern men while they were boarding their plane? Could these men have been stopped? Going further, how many vigilant employees would have chosen to immediately flee Tower 2 after they witnessed the blazing inferno in Tower 1, if only they had known that an al Qaeda terrorist attack was imminent?

Could the devastation of September 11 been diminished in any degree had the government's information been made public in the summer of 2001?

FAILURE TO INVESTIGATE AND SHARE INFORMATION

On July 5, the government's top counterterrorism official, Richard Clarke, stated to a group gathered at the White House, "Something really spectacular is going to happen here, and it's going to happen soon."

The group included the FAA, the Coast Guard, the FBI, the Secret Service, and the INS. Clarke directed every counterterrorist office to cancel vacations, defer nonvital travel, put off scheduled exercises, and place domestic rapid response teams on much shorter alert.

For six weeks last summer at home and abroad, the U.S. government was at its highest possible state of readiness—and anxiety—against imminent terrorist attack.

A senior FBI official attending the White House meeting on July 5 committed the bureau to redouble contacts with its foreign counterparts and to speed up transcription and analysis of wiretaps obtained under the Foreign Intelligence Surveillance Act (FISA), among other steps.

But when the field agent in Phoenix, Arizona, reported the suspicions of a hijacking plot just five days later, the FBI did not share the report with any other agency. One must ask, why?

That report, written by Agent Kenneth Williams, now well known as the "Phoenix Memo," recommended that the FBI investigate whether al Qaeda operatives were training at U.S. flight schools. Williams posited that Osama Bin Laden's followers might be trying to infiltrate the civil aviation system as pilots, security guards, or other personnel, and he recommended a national program to track suspicious flight school students. Agent Williams was dead-on point.

But, in the summer of 2001, while our nation was at its highest state of alert, his memo was flatly ignored. And, what result if it hadn't been ignored? What if his memo was promptly placed on INTELINK, SIPRNET, or NIPRNET? What if other agents had the same suspicions in Florida, California, Georgia, Ohio, and Nevada? Could the terrorists have been stopped?

On August 15, 2001, an alert civilian instructor at a Minnesota flight school called the FBI and said, "Do you realize that a 747 loaded with fuel can be a bomb?" The next day, Zacarias Moussaoui was arrested. After investigating Zacarias Moussaoui's past, the FBI (with the help of French Intelligence) learned that he had Islamic extremist connections. They also knew that he was interested in flight patterns around New York City, and that he had a strong desire to fly big jets, even though at the time he didn't have so much as a license to fly a Cessna.

And then, what happened?

The FBI office in Minnesota attempted to get a FISA warrant, but they were rebuffed. A crucial mistake, because Zacarias Moussaoui's possessions contained evidence that would have exposed key elements of the September 11 plot.

But why was this request denied? Again, the historical facts must be analyzed.

In March 2001, an internal debate ignited at the Justice Department and the FBI over wiretap surveillance of certain terrorist groups. Prompted by questions raised by Royce C. Lamberth, the Chief Judge of the FISA court, the Justice Department opened an inquiry into Michael Resnick, an FBI official who coordinated the Act's applications. Attorney General John Ashcroft and Robert Mueller (then Deputy Attorney General) ordered a full review of all foreign surveillance authorizations.

Justice Department and FBI officials have since acknowledged the existence of this internal investigation, and said that the inquiry forced officials to examine their monitoring of several suspected terrorist groups, including al Qaeda. And while senior FBI and Justice Department officials contend that the internal investigation did not affect their ability to monitor al Qaeda, other officials have acknowledged that the inquiry might have hampered electronic surveillance of terror groups. The matter remains highly classified.

What is not classified is that in early September a Minnesota FBI agent wrote an analytic memo on Zacarias Moussaoui's case, theorizing that the suspect could fly a plane into the World Trade Center. And, tragically, this, too, was ignored.

Also ignored by U.S. intelligence agencies was the enormous amount of trading activity on the Chicago Exchange Board and in overseas markets. Our intelligence agencies readily use Promts software to analyze these kinds of market indicators that presented themselves in the weeks prior to September 11. Why were these aberrational trades and market swings ignored? We were at the highest state of alert. An attack by al Qaeda was expected to occur at any given moment. And yet, massive amounts of trades occurred on American Airlines, United Airlines, Reinsurance companies, and leaseholders in the World Trade Center and none of our watchdogs noticed?

Perhaps even more disturbing is the information regarding Khalid al-Midhar and Nawaf Alhazmi, two of the hijackers. In late August, the CIA asked the INS to put these two men on a watchlist because of their ties to the bombing of the U.S.S. Cole. On August 23, 2001, the INS informed the CIA that both men had already slipped into the country. Immediately thereafter, the CIA asked the FBI to find al-Midhar and Alhazmi. Not a seemingly hard task in light of the fact that one of them was listed in the San Diego phone book, the other took out a bank account in his own name, and finally, an FBI informant happened to be their roommate.

But, again, our intelligence agencies failed.

WERE THE TERRORISTS ALREADY UNDER SURVEILLANCE?

It was only after the devastation of September 11 that our intelligence agencies seemed to get back on track.

On September 12, 2001, the *New York Times* reported, "On Tuesday *a few hours* (emphasis added) after the attacks, FBI agents descended on flight schools, neighborhoods, and restaurants in pursuit of leads. The FBI arrived at Huffman Aviation at about 2:30 A.M., Wednesday morning. They walked out with all the school's records, including photocopies of the men's passports."

The *New York Times* also reported that students at Embry Riddle Aeronautical University said that *within hours* (emphasis added) of the attacks FBI investigators were seen at their school.

How did the FBI know exactly where to go only a "few hours" after the attacks? How did they know which neighborhoods, which flight schools, and which restaurants to investigate so soon into the case?

The *New York Times* went on to report that "federal agents questioned employees at a store in Bangor, Maine, where five Arab men believed to be the hijackers tried to rent cell phones late last week. Store employees at first refused to sell the phones because the men lacked proper identification, but they gave in after the five offered $3,000 cash, store employees and an airport official said."

The article goes on to state, "The men then phoned Bangor airport trying to get a flight to Boston but were told there was no flight that matched their desired departure time, the authorities said. The men then phoned Portland International JetPort, where two of them apparently made reservations for a flight to Boston on Tuesday morning."

How would this information be gleaned so quickly? How would the FBI know to visit a store in Bangor, Maine, only *hours* after the attacks? Moreover, how would they know the details of a phone conversation that occurred a *week prior* to the attacks? Were any of the hijackers already under surveillance? It has been widely reported that the hijackers ran practice runs on the airline routes that were chosen on September 11. Did our intelligence agents ever shadow these men on any of their prior practice runs?

Furthermore, on September 12, the *New York Times* reported that, "authorities said they had also identified accomplices in several cities who had helped plan and execute Tuesday's attacks. Officials said they knew who these people were and important biographical details about many of them. They prepared biographies of each identified member of the hijack teams and began tracing the recent movements of the men."

How were complete biographies of the terrorists and their accomplices created in such short time? Did our intelligence agencies already have open files on these men? Were they already investigating them? Could the attacks of September 11 have been prevented?

The speed by which the FBI was able to locate, assimilate, and analyze a small amount of information so soon after the attacks—barely one day later, perhaps answers this question for itself. But, if the terrorists were under investigation, then why were they ever permitted to board those planes? Perhaps, even more potently, why, if such an investigation was already underway, why was our nation so late in responding to the emergency that quickly unfolded that day?

TOO MANY QUESTIONS REMAIN

Too many questions remain. Topping the list of unanswered questions are those that involve our nation's coordination, communication, and response to the attacks that morning. The twenty-four hours that presented themselves on September 11 beg to be examined. Questions like:

Why did the New York/New Jersey Port Authority not evacuate the World Trade Center when they had an open phone line with Newark Traffic Control Center and were told that the second plane was bearing down on the South Tower? The New York/New Jersey Port Authority had at least eleven minutes of notice to begin evacuations of the South Tower. An express elevator in the World Trade Center was able to travel from top to bottom in one minute's time. How many lives may have been saved, had the Port Authority acted more decisively or, rather, acted at all.

Were F-16s and Stealth bombers seen and tracked on radar screens at approximately 8:05 A.M. the morning of September 11 in the vicinity of the New York metropolitan area?

Washington Air Traffic Control Center knew about the first plane before it hit the World Trade Center. Yet, the third plane was able to fly "loop de loops" over Washington D.C. one hour and forty-five minutes after Washington Center first knew about the hijackings. After circling in this restricted airspace—controlled and protected by the Secret Service who had an open phone line to the FAA, how is it possible that the plane was then able to crash into the Pentagon? Why was the Pentagon not evacuated?

Why was our Air Force so late in its response?

What, if anything, did our nation do, in a defensive military posture that morning?

Three thousand innocent Americans were killed on September 11, leaving behind families and loved ones like myself and my daughter. There are too many heartbreaking stories to recount. There are too many lost opportunities and futures to be told.

But what can be said to you today is that the families continue to suffer each and every day. All we have are tears and a resolve to find the answers because we continue to look into the eyes of our young children who ask us why? We have an obligation as parents and as a nation to provide these innocent children with answers as to why their mother or father never returned home from work that day.

We need people to be held accountable for their failures. We need leaders with the courage to take responsibility for what went wrong. Mistakes were made and too many lives were lost. We must investigate these errors so that they will never happen again. It is our responsibility as a nation to turn the dark events of September 11 into something from which we can all learn and grow, so that we, as a nation, can look forward to a safe future.

In closing, I would like to add one thought. Undoubtedly, each of you here today, because you live and work in Washington D.C., must have felt that you were in the bull's-eye on September 11. For most of you, there was a relief at the end of that day, a relief that you and your loved ones were in safe hands. You were the lucky ones. In your continuing investigation, please do not forget those of us who did not share in your good fate.

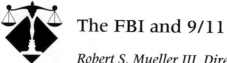

The FBI and 9/11

Robert S. Mueller III, Director, Federal Bureau of Investigation

Commonwealth Club of California, San Francisco
April 19, 2002

Thank you, Roy (Eisenhardt) and good afternoon everyone. It's good to be back home. It brings back a lot of wonderful memories. My years in San Francisco were among the most satisfying and enjoyable of my career. It gave me the opportunity to work with some of the finest criminal justice and law enforcement professionals in the country. They taught me a great deal, and it was an honor to serve alongside them.

As much as I miss San Francisco, I am grateful to have the opportunity to serve in what I believe to be the world's finest law enforcement agency—the FBI. It is particularly rewarding to serve at this unparalleled moment in history, when America is depending on the FBI more than ever, when protecting the homeland from terrorist attacks has taken on new meaning and new urgency.

Like most Americans, I'll never forget the day it all began. I had been on the job exactly one week when word came that a plane had struck the World Trade Center. We rushed down to the FBI's command center, hoping it had been a terrible accident but fearing the worst. Minutes later, we watched in horror as a plane hit the second tower. Then, reality hit even closer to home, when across the Potomac, another plane rammed into the Pentagon.

Not long after learning that the third hijacked airliner had gone down, a controller from the Federal Aviation Administration, who was on the phone with his agency, told us more shocking news. A fourth plane had been hijacked. It was heading straight toward the nation's capitol. And it was just fifteen minutes away.

It was a surreal moment for us all, realizing this plane—this flying bomb—was headed our way, yet not knowing where it might hit: the White House, the Capitol, a schoolyard, or FBI headquarters.

As we all know, Flight 93 never made it to Washington. The brave passengers on board—including many from the San Francisco Bay area—were determined that this flying missile would not reach its target, and they sacrificed their lives to save our city. They are among the true heroes of that day.

From those first moments, we in the FBI, like the rest of the nation, knew that the world had changed. And we knew that our institution would never be the same.

Our first thought was to do what we'd always done after a terrorist attack: set up command centers and start managing the crisis from a law enforcement perspective; get control of the crime scenes and begin gathering evidence; and deploy our vast investigative force to find out everything we could about the attacks.

At the same time, we realized that we had to conduct this investigation somewhat differently. These attacks were not just an act of terror. They were an act of war. The most pressing issue for the FBI and for the nation was to find out who we were at war with, and more importantly, to make sure we were not attacked again.

To do that, the FBI began working in concert with its many partners to find out everything we could about the hijackers and how they pulled off their attacks. We ran down literally hundreds of thousands of leads and checked every record we could get our hands on, from flight reservations to car rentals to bank accounts.

What emerged from our massive investigation was a sobering portrait of nineteen hijackers who carried out their attacks with meticulous planning, extraordinary secrecy, and extensive knowledge of how America works.

The plans were hatched and financed overseas, beginning as long as five years ago. Each of the hijackers came from abroad: fifteen from Saudi Arabia, two from the United Arab Emirates, and one each from Lebanon and Egypt. All nineteen entered our country legally, and only three had overstayed the legal limits of their visas on the day of the attacks.

While here, the hijackers did all they could to stay below our radar. They contacted no known terrorist sympathizers. They committed no egregious crimes. They dressed and acted like Americans, shopping and eating at places like Wal-Mart and Pizza Hut, blending into the woodwork all the while. When four got speeding tickets in the days leading up to September 11, they remained calm and aroused no suspicion. Since none were known terrorists, law enforcement had no reason to question or detain them.

The hijackers also left no paper trail. In our investigation, we have not uncovered a single piece of paper—either here in the United States or in the treasure trove of information that has turned up in Afghanistan and elsewhere—that mentioned any aspect of the September 11 plot. The hijackers had no computers, no laptops, no storage media of any kind. They used hundreds of different pay phones and cell phones, often with prepaid calling cards that are extremely difficult to trace. And they made sure that all the money sent to them to fund their attacks was wired in small amounts to avoid detection.

In short, the terrorists had managed to exploit loopholes and vulnerabilities in our systems, to stay out of sight, and to not let anyone know what they were up to beyond a very closed circle.

The investigation was enormously helpful in figuring out who and what to look for as we worked to prevent attacks. It allowed us to see where we as a nation needed to close gaps in our security. And it gave us clear and definitive proof that al Qaeda was behind the strikes.

At the same time, we were taking other steps to track down any potential associates who might still be out there. We began to identify individuals whom we needed to question. We went to the flight schools to identify associates of the hijackers. We went to those who run a popular travel Web site that several of the hijackers used to make their flight reservations. They showed us the patterns the hijackers followed and identified others who fit a similar profile. And we ran down all leads in the hopes that they might turn up associates of the terrorists.

Through this process, and with the help of state and local authorities, we interviewed thousands of persons to develop a full picture of the hijackers and others associated with them. In the United States, a number of suspects were detained on federal, state, or local charges; on immigration violations; or on material witness warrants. Ultimately, these and other actions with our partners around the world have helped prevent more terrorist attacks.

As the days and weeks went by, though, it became clear that the war on terror had only just begun. Our investigation moved from the events of September 11 to the anthrax attacks, to the foiled shoe bombing on the flight from Paris to Miami, to the kidnapping and murder of a *Wall Street Journal* reporter in Pakistan. Through it all, the FBI had become part and parcel of what is now called "homeland security," a government-wide campaign to protect America from terrorist attacks. And we have been given a critical role to play, one that is redefining much of what we do.

The homeland security effort is being waged on many fronts. The law enforcement component is building cases against terrorists in the court of law. The military component is deploying our armed forces to attack terrorist strongholds overseas. The intelligence component is using information and analysis to anticipate and prevent attacks, and to better understand the enemy. The diplomatic component is building an international coalition against terror. The financial component is drying up the pool of funds used by terrorists. And the public health component is preparing now to save lives and protect our communities.

Today, the FBI is fully integrated into this campaign. We play a leadership role, of course, in the law enforcement arena. At the same time, we are supporting each of the other components of the campaign and each of its players. In this environment, we realize that what we do to help our colleagues is every bit as important as what we do within our own agency.

We are supporting the military, for example, by sharing information and intelligence that we gather in our investigations and in our interviews of prisoners. In some cases, we have also facilitated the capture and arrest of terrorists overseas.

We are supporting the intelligence effort by working more closely than ever with our partners in the intelligence community here and around the world to gather and share information. We are developing new tools to make this process easier and more effective.

To cut off terrorist funding, we've created a financial review group that is working with many other agencies to investigate shady bank accounts and wire transfers and to develop predictive models that can help target suspicious ones in the future. So far, this group has reviewed over 75,000 transactions and helped freeze millions in terrorist funds worldwide.

In the public health area, we continue to investigate any incidents involving biological or chemical agents. Since September 11, we've not only launched a massive investigation into the anthrax attacks, we've also responded to the 16,000 hoaxes and threats that have followed in their wake. We have also stepped up efforts to work more closely with state and local officials, and we continue to coordinate issues, provide training, and stage exercises.

As I'll discuss later, the FBI also plays a role in the diplomatic component through our overseas offices, which work closely with American embassies and foreign governments.

Our role in homeland security builds upon what we have been doing for many years. We're still the lead law enforcement agency for counterterrorism. We're still assessing threats and issuing warnings and advisories to our law enforcement partners and to the American people. We're still leading the multiagency National Infrastructure Protection Center, a key force in protecting our nation's critical physical and electronic infrastructures. And most of all, our top priority is still prevention.

The difference is largely a matter of degree. Terrorists have shown they are willing to go to great lengths to destroy America. We must be willing to go to even greater lengths to stop them. Our worldwide network must be more powerful. Our financial commitment must be stronger. Our techniques and training must be more sophisticated. And our sense of urgency and intensity must be greater.

This reality is driven home to me in a very real way each day. Since the attacks, I have briefed President Bush in the Oval Office each morning. Together with George Tenet, the Director of the CIA, we go over what we call the "threat matrix," a list of every threat directed at the United States in the past twenty-four hours.

During these briefings, the President is not so much interested in who has been arrested or who has been prosecuted. What the President cares about most is what we in the FBI are doing—in concert with our partners—to run down each of these threats. He wants to be absolutely sure that we are aggressively pursuing every angle and every lead, so that America never wakes up to another morning like September 11.

George Tenet calls those meetings "galvanizing." He recognizes, as I do, that you simply cannot walk into that briefing without feeling completely confident that your people are on top of every issue. More importantly, you cannot come back day after day without being sure that your agency is taking every step to make prevention both a priority and a reality.

In the Bureau, we have taken a long, hard look in the mirror to see how we measure up to this mandate. We see some strong counterterrorism capabilities, expertise that has been refined over time and sharpened by experience. But we also see areas where we could do more. And we are moving forward to address them as quickly as possible.

First, we are putting more resources into the fight. As we speak, we are overhauling our counterterrorism operations so that we have twice as many agents focused on prevention. As we hire nearly one thousand new agents this year, we are also recruiting the right mix of skills—primarily computer, scientific, and language—that we need to fight terror.

More resources also means a much stronger presence at major special events. We were out in force, for example, at this week's Boston Marathon. At the Winter Olympics in Salt Lake City, we stationed nearly 1,400 personnel—about five percent of our workforce—to support the many professionals devoted to ensuring the safety of the games.

We are also expanding and improving our analytic capability. The September 11 terrorists spent a great deal of time and effort figuring out how America works. They knew the ins and outs of our systems. We need to have a complete grasp on how terrorists operate as well. Our analysts do some great work, but we need more of them and we need to do more of the kind of strategic thinking that helps us stay one step ahead of those who would do us harm.

Second, we are overhauling our technology. Here in the heart of Silicon Valley, you understand how quickly technology changes and how fast you can be left behind. The fact is, for all the state-of-the-art systems in our lab, for all the high-tech services we provide to law enforcement, the Bureau has simply not kept pace when it comes to the equipment on our desktops. We have computers discarded by other agencies that we took as upgrades. We have systems that cannot talk with other Bureau systems, much less with other federal agencies. We have thirty-four different investigative applications, none of which are easy to use and all of which must ultimately be integrated.

In the wake of September 11, we have accelerated our plans to fix these problems. We will put in place new hardware this year and we will overhaul our key applications by the end of next year. Our goal is a near paperless environment, a development that will put us light years ahead of where we are today.

Technology will also help us share information more quickly and effectively outside the Bureau. We don't have the right systems in place now to make information flow as freely and as seamlessly as we'd like. We're working to create a database—one that sits on top of all the others—that we can use to share information and intelligence with the outside world. We hope to test it later next year.

We're also looking for a way to get information out more quickly and universally. Today, there is no one system—no digital pipeline—that we can use to send advisories and information to all of law enforcement. We have to do it piecemeal and patchwork. We're working hard to find a solution.

Third, effective prevention requires strengthening the defensive infrastructure of the country. This means immigration and customs programs that keep terrorists out, airports that are secure, and seaports that are on alert.

We are supporting these efforts wherever we can. It also means a national program where the FBI joins with state and local law enforcement to form a national antiterror network. There are just over 11,000 Special Agents. There are 650,000 state and local law enforcement officers. An integrated national program that combines our resources and expertise substantially increases the safety of all Americans.

Finally, prevention also means something America has not really focused on before September 11. It means an aggressive—but rigorously lawful—program of disruption abroad and at home. The September 11 terrorists had the luxury of time and tranquility to put the pieces of their plan in place. From the training camps of Afghanistan to the universities of Germany to the flight schools of America, they were able to assemble the components of their plan and pick their moment to execute it. We cannot afford them this operational luxury again. For America, prevention must include an international offensive capability in which the intelligence and law enforcement resources of the global community are integrated into a program to disrupt and attack terrorist operations in their infancy.

It is this international component, as much as any other ingredient, which heralds a new day for the FBI. In a post–September 11 world, partnerships abroad equal security at home.

We are working to build these partnerships through our forty-four overseas offices, what we call Legal Attachés. Today more than ever, they are an important first line of defense against terror. They enable us to build the kind of face-to-face, personal relationships we need to track down terrorists around the globe and root them out of their hiding places.

Last month, working through our Legal Attaché in Manila, a group of twenty-eight senior level government officials from the Republic of the Philippines came to our National Academy in Virginia for a two-week seminar. They wanted to learn how to knock the financial legs out from under terrorists. One of the participants in the class was Jose Calida, the Undersecretary for the Department of Justice in the Philippines. He decided to give the class a name. He came up with the word "Balikatan," which in his native tongue means "shoulder-to-shoulder." Because when he looked out at the class, that's what he saw: twenty-eight leaders sitting shoulder-to-shoulder with each other and with us, united in a common purpose of defeating terror.

Al Qaeda and other international terrorist groups have developed networks around the world. We need the same kind of networks to defeat them. Even in this age of sophisticated technologies and techniques, it is critically important that we be able to sit down with a colleague and develop a rapport that will ultimately help us build a national and international coalition against terror. That is why our overseas offices are so important and why we need even more of them in the days ahead.

As we in the Bureau move through a period of intense change, as we adjust to our new role in homeland security, we must be flexible and open-minded. We can never afford to cling to the status quo. Where our capabilities are strong, they must be stronger. Where problems exist, we must acknowledge them, fix them, and move on.

The reality is, change is never smooth or easy. That is especially true for an agency like the FBI, one that is always on the cutting edge, pioneering new tools and techniques to help us catch an increasingly savvy band of criminals.

In the past, though, the FBI has sometimes made problems worse by ignoring or denying them. That can't be the way we do business going forward. We've got to welcome and even embrace constructive criticism. We have to acknowledge problems and be ahead of the curve in fixing them. That has been our approach in recent months, and it will remain our approach.

Standing behind all the capabilities that we have now and that we are working to build is a cadre of FBI professionals, men and women who exemplify courage, integrity, respect for the law, and respect for others. We are extremely proud of how they have performed over the past seven months. They have worked long days and nights, sacrificing time with their families to get the job done. They have shown grace under fire in difficult and often dangerous situations.

There is one special agent, though, who made the ultimate sacrifice for the FBI and for the country he cared about so deeply. His name is Lenny Hatton, and he is one of the many law enforcement professionals lost on September 11.

Lenny was an exceptional agent and a remarkable man. He was on his way to work on September 11 when he saw the World Trade Center on fire. Instinctively, he went straight to the scene and started working with police and firefighters to evacuate the buildings. He was last seen helping a victim out of one of the buildings, and rushing back in to save more.

Several days later at Lenny's funeral Mass, an individual by the name of Chris O'Connell paid tribute to the fallen agent. Chris talked about how Lenny devoted his life to serving—as a Marine, as a volunteer firefighter, as an FBI Special Agent, as a husband and father—and how Lenny had served until his last breath, trying to save lives.

In tears, Chris O'Connell closed his eulogy by saying: "On September 11, we saw a horrific event in this country and our city. Special Agent Lenny Hatton stood shoulder to shoulder with the finest and the bravest. Until we meet again, my partner, my friend."

Chris O'Connell was Lenny's partner, and Chris O'Connell was and is a detective with the New York Police Department. Lenny and Chris cared for each other like brothers. It didn't matter to them that one worked for the FBI and one worked for the NYPD. They just wanted to get the job done. They were a team.

Lenny Hatton exemplifies what the FBI is really all about: defending freedom through courage, compassion, and cooperation. Just as this tragedy brought out Lenny's best, it is already bringing about a fundamentally better FBI.

Thanks for having me, and God bless.

ISSUE 12

HUMAN RIGHTS

That human rights have affected the course of world politics over the past fifty years is beyond doubt. What that impact has been remains a controversial question. Ever since the 1948 Universal Declaration of Human Rights, and the 1966 Covenants on Political/Civil and Economic/Social/Cultural Rights, the place of human rights in the discourse of global politics has been secure. The promotion of human rights has become an important component of the foreign policy of many countries. Numerous nongovernmental organizations (NGOs) have also appeared on the scene promoting the cause of human rights. All told, voices in support of human rights have become more numerous and more vocal. In light of recent experiences such as "ethnic cleansing," however, the question remains: How effective have these voices been in advancing the cause of human rights?

Lorne W. Craner, Assistant Secretary of State for Democracy, Human Rights, and Labor, in a speech to the Heritage Foundation, lays out the administration's commitment to the promotion of human rights as part of its commitment to promoting democracy. Respect for universal human rights is linked to a country's ability to achieve and maintain political stability, as well as to attain higher levels of economic growth and prosperity. Of particular note is the administration's shift in emphasis in the post–September 11 global environment.

On the other side of the debate, John A. Gentry argues that "excessive human rights are socially divisive and politically costly." While he recognizes the merit of promoting first generation rights guaranteeing political and civil freedoms, he questions the "uncontrolled growth" of second- and third-generation rights which seek to further economic, social, cultural, and group rights. On balance, while he does not necessarily present an unduly pessimistic view, he reminds the reader of the hurdles even a well-intentioned human rights campaign faces.

Discussion Questions

As you read the speech by Craner and the article by Gentry, consider the following questions:

1. Can, as Gentry suggests, the pursuit of human rights go too far, even up to the point of endangering the stability of the entire community?
2. What role should support for human rights play in the foreign policy of the United States? Should they be given more or less emphasis in a post–September 11 world?
3. If not all human rights are equal, which ones deserve primacy?

Key Web Sites

For more information on this topic, visit the following Web sites:

Human Rights Watch
www.hrw.org

Amnesty International
www.amnesty.org

American Association of the Advance of Science—Directory of HR Resources
http://shr.aaas.org/dhr

The Role of Human Rights in Foreign Policy

Lorne W. Craner, Assistant Secretary of State for Democracy, Human Rights, and Labor

Heritage Foundation, Washington, D.C.
October 31, 2001

It is an honor to be invited to speak at the Heritage Foundation, where your guiding principles are free enterprise, limited government, individual freedom, traditional values, and strong defense.

I would like to thank Dr. Kim Holmes for inviting me, and more importantly, for the leadership he has shown in the foreign policy arena. I have read many Heritage Foundation foreign policy publications that have his stamp and am especially aware of his good work on East–West relations.

Also, Heritage Foundation audiences consist of individuals who care passionately about liberty and freedom. Over the years, many of you have probably written editorials, Congressional Record statements, and letters to editors on human rights issues. Some of you may well have been directly involved in helping to build our country's human rights policy in the Reagan or Bush I administrations, and so you know firsthand that the U.S. commitment to human rights has a strong foundation.

Dr. Holmes has asked that I speak today about the role of human rights in the Bush administration. This is a great assignment because I can wholeheartedly attest to the fact that in the Bush administration human rights and democracy work is alive and well.

The world has changed dramatically for all of us since September 11, and some people have expressed the concern that, as a result of the attacks on America, the Bush administration will abandon human rights and democracy work. To those people I say boldly that this is not the case. In fact, maintaining the focus on human rights and democracy worldwide is an integral part of our response to the attack and is even more essential today than before September 11. They remain in our national interest in promoting a stable and democratic world.

As Dr. [Condoleezza] Rice said only a week after the horrific attack, "Civil liberties matter to this president very much, and our values matter to us abroad. We are not going to stop talking about the things that matter to us, human rights, religious freedom, and so forth and so on. We're going to continue to press those things; we would not be American if we did not." In practical terms, we continue to raise human rights issues at the highest levels of governments worldwide and have made it clear that these issues remain important to us.

We do so because there is often a direct link between the absence of human rights and democracy and seeds of terrorism. Promoting human rights and democracy addresses the fear, frustration, hatred, and violence that is the breeding ground for the next generation of terrorists. We cannot win a war against terrorism by halting our work promoting the universal observance of human rights. To do so would be merely to set the stage for a resurgence of terrorism in another generation. As Thomas Jefferson said: "That government is the strongest of which everyone may feel a part."

At the very least, the brutality of the attack on the World Trade Center and the Pentagon and the fact that it was completely unprovoked suggest that models based on what we used to call the "rational actor" are far from fully comprehensive—unless, of course, you are willing to take Clausewitz one step further and suggest that not only is war politics by another means, but so, too, is terrorism. But that would be to give it a legitimacy that it clearly does not merit.

Even so, what drives individuals—not states, but men, individual, independent actors—to assume the cloak of moral or religious rectitude and declare holy war on a country? This is not an attack on armies, but on symbols. Obviously, we need to learn how to fight the perceptions and misperceptions that lie behind all that better than we do. The question that we all are asking ourselves since that terrible day last month is this: How do we, who have the responsibility for promoting and protecting the values that underpin civil society at home and throughout the world, pick our way through all the causes and effects of that and make sure that it does not happen again?

Obviously, there is much we can do: in intelligence-gathering and information-sharing, in civil defense and homeland security, in diplomacy and economic leveraging, in international cooperation and coalition-building, in pressure and in force. All this the administration is doing, and much, much more.

My point is not to venture into the realm of military strategy. That is not my responsibility in this administration. Fortunately for all of us, the president has assembled a very experienced and capable team for that.

This country is not the cause of all the problems of this world—quite the contrary. We spend a great deal of time and effort trying to solve them. But still, we cannot be everywhere at once. We cannot solve every regional dispute and ethnic conflict. And yet, we are the sole superpower. Our reach is global and unprecedented. People look to us. Our power and our potential are immense. We have interests and we have obligations to our friends and allies.

As the head of the bureau charged with advising the president and secretary of state on human rights, I have to worry about the causes and consequences of conflicts wherever they take place, for all of them involve human rights in one way or another—whether in Sudan or Sierra Leone, Indonesia, Macedonia, or the Middle East.

I suspect most of you are looking to hear something about this administration's priorities within the field of human rights, especially after the September 11 attacks. Let me begin by outlining the general principles that I think will guide us.

First, over the past twenty years, both political parties—Republicans and Democrats—have firmly embraced the belief that America has an obligation to advance fundamental freedoms around the world. Thus human rights have the deep and strong backing of both parties, all branches of government, and, most importantly, the American people. This will not change.

In a multilateral sense, the United States has been the unquestioned leader of the movement to expand human rights since the Second World War. We pushed it in the UN Charter, the Universal Declaration of Human Rights, and into the conventions and treaty bodies that have ensued. And when I say "we," I do not just mean the U.S. government. For it was our people, Americans from every walk of life, who gave the international non-governmental organization (NGO) movement so much of its intellectual force, its financial muscle, and its firm commitment to civil society.

This, too, will not change. We in this administration are conscious of our history and are proud to bear the mantle of leadership in international human rights into this new century.

While my first point is the continuity of our policy, the second is the way our approach to human rights policy will shift.

Our policy in this administration, and it is certainly true after September 11, is to focus on U.S. national interests. Lest that sound bloodless to my colleagues in the human rights community, it should be understood that the definition of national interests can never be as narrow as it was through the late 1970s. Indeed, those at high levels of this administration watched during those years as a narrow definition of national interests led us to back the Shah of Iran, Somoza, and others. As Colin Powell writes in his autobiography, "In the end, in Iran, all our investment in an individual, rather than a country, came to naught. When the Shah fell, our Iran policy fell with him. All the billions we spent there only exacerbated conditions and contributed to the rise of a fundamentalist regime implacably opposed to us. . . ."

Our focus on national interests will come by concentration on advancing human rights and democracy in countries important to the United States. Some are obvious—nations of the former Soviet Union, Indonesia, Colombia, and Cuba—but others come to mind, including nations in Africa with a high demonstration value in their respective regions, such as Zimbabwe, Kenya, and Nigeria.

A third characteristic of our democracy policy will be a willingness to take on tough jobs, long-term projects in countries and regions that today appear inhospitable to human rights and democracy. We are working every day to end human rights violations in China, but beneath the surface are developments in terms of rule of law, basic elections at the village level, nascent legislative oversight, and some journalistic independence. These changes are necessitated by economic development, but they are also important blocks in building a democratic society.

Similarly, in the Persian Gulf, Oman is experimenting with an increasingly independent legislature and Qatar will hold local elections, with women voting, in 2003. No one, least of all me, would claim that any of these countries are democracies, and it may be that the end result, many years from now, is not precisely comparable to our democratic system. The point is that the United States is now willing to assist those working to bring pluralism to their countries, even if it may only occur over the long term.

In countries that have already made democratic breakthroughs, a fourth tenet of our policy will be to increase governance assistance. In the 1980s, many believed that elections made a democracy. In the 1990s, we concentrated on the demand side of governance, civil society. We cannot lose our proficiency in helping advance balloting, political parties, and nongovernmental organizations abroad. But the challenge of the third decade of democracy assistance must be helping new democratic rulers govern their countries in a manner that advances democratic practices, an end to the corruption that often afflicts authoritarian nations, and economic well being. The latter is especially important; if those who have lived with tyranny associate democracy with economic dislocation—in other words, losing their jobs—they could well choose to revert to stable authoritarianism.

A component of this effort will be an emphasis on labor rights. This administration does not see globalism as the enemy, just the opposite. Globalism can promote democratic ideas as well as economic growth, but we do believe that it can be made kinder and gentler. Indeed, as I just outlined, an absence of attention to worker rights would lead to dissatisfaction in a developing democracy, and therefore take us back in time.

In a similar vein, one of the areas where I think we in the human rights community can gain some important new leverage is with this country's companies and corporations. In the first place, they are laboratories of innovation, repositories of experience, talent, and, yes, resources. They have relationships that go beyond those we have in government. But more than that, an increasing number of businesses share some of our interest in advancing human rights. Why? Because countries that respect human rights have more open and transparent laws and financial systems, less corruption, better educated workforces, and more stability and security.

I don't want to oversell the idea. Business runs on profits, not on human rights. But more and more companies are beginning to see that they can help themselves by paying close attention to giving back to the communities in which they operate. Companies are also anxious to protect their corporate image and reputations.

That's why my bureau is giving a high priority to working with many companies on issues of corporate responsibility, building on the good work the previous administration did in this domain. We are especially proud of the beginnings of progress made with oil and gas and mining companies, who often operate in very difficult situations in countries riven with conflict and internal tension. By working together with governments and NGOs, companies can strengthen the business and human rights environment that is needed for their success. Changing the face of globalization may require us to change the way that we as members of the global community do business.

An additional area of emphasis for the administration will be in the area of religious freedom, tolerance, and understanding. Our nation was founded on this ideal. I will work to ensure, to a greater degree than has been the case, and particularly in light of the events of September 11, that it receives due consideration in our foreign policy. We will also seek allies abroad in our efforts, for other countries and the United Nations are working to integrate considerations of religious freedom into their diplomacy.

Finally, our core function in DRL, our key legislative mandate, is monitoring and reporting on human rights conditions throughout the world. This process, I believe, is of great value to our country. The monitoring we do, in conjunction with our human rights officers in the field, the media, and the growing human rights NGO community, ensures a steady stream of information will flow throughout our government.

No other country produces anything like our annual reports on country situations, international religious freedom, and now trafficking in human beings. Even the NGOs, who often have occasion to criticize us, have for some time acknowledged their accuracy, integrity, and comprehensive nature. That is a tribute to my predecessors, most notably Harold Koh. The policy of making honest, comprehensive reports on every country in the world is one that both Republicans and Democrats embrace. And because they are available to everyone, via the Internet, they can now reach millions of people across the globe. This reinforces the seriousness with which the United States takes human rights. And so our dedication to the quality, integrity, and inclusiveness of our reporting will not change, even as the number we are asked to prepare keeps growing.

To do all of this more effectively, we will also need partners. We will be looking to work with other organizations, from the private sector, the NGO and faith-based communities, other governments, and the specialized UN agencies. And we will be looking to work with other branches of our government, as well: the U.S. Agency for International Development (USAID), which shares our concern with promoting human rights and democracy programs, the Justice Department, where we cooperate on rule-of-law programs, the Defense Department, where we support the human rights components of programs like Plan Colombia, and last but not least, the Congress, which brought my bureau into existence, and continues to strongly support human rights activities.

Here I will conclude, and again say thank you to all in this room who have ensured that human rights is and will remain a pillar of American foreign policy.

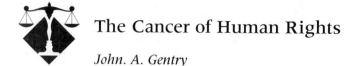

The Cancer of Human Rights

John. A. Gentry

The development of a broad variety of rights is a prominent feature of social and political life in the late second millennium. The establishment of political rights in the U.S. Constitution and its first ten amendments were a radical break from the political norms of the late eighteenth century. The growth and spread of these rights, and the philosophy they embodied, had a profound influence on the development of the United States and on ideas throughout the world.

The notion that good countries grant specific rights to their citizens has evolved to the point that many persons believe that innate "human rights" belong to all people—and that these rights transcend and subordinate national governments and social norms. Governments exist to provide resources to actualize the promises of human rights. Not surprisingly, ostensibly universal rights look much like those that developed in North America and Europe.

Elemental political rights, such as freedoms of speech and religion of the sort embodied in the U.S. Constitution, are political forces that largely define democratic societies. They allow much opportunity for individual growth and personal freedom. Many persons thus see such rights as powerful forces for good. I will not argue differently.

The expansion of rights from beyond elemental guarantees of personal opportunity and protections from state tyranny to much more numerous, tailored rights that guarantee results in narrow aspects of life, however, is causing problems. Rights are costly and dangerous when they disrupt traditional and effective organizational structures, contradict religious and secular moral values, and unbalance previously functional social systems. They render ineffective or incompetent the foreign policies of states led or strongly influenced by strong human-rights adherents. They lead to and prolong conflicts rather than resolve them. The unbridled growth of human rights accentuates differences among persons and groups, threatens internal order and social cohesion, and transforms nations into mere states. In the worst cases the uncontrolled growth of rights, like cancer cells, can kill the hosts that nurture them—and thereby kill themselves.

John A. Gentry researches and writes on defense- and security-related issues. He spent much of 1996 with the U.S. Army in Bosnia.

This article is from *The Washington Quarterly* 22, no. 4 (autumn 1999). Copyright © 1999 by the Center for Strategic and International Studies (CSIS) and the Massachusetts Institute of Technology. Reprinted by permission.

The United States most clearly reflects an advanced development of human rights, both domestically and in foreign policies, but it is not unique. Other countries and a powerful international group of human rights advocates—in and out of national governments—have altered the conduct of international affairs.

COSTS OF U.S. DOMESTIC RIGHTS

The proliferation of rights in the United States is pandemic. Once restricted to the major rights embodied in the Constitution, the legal, regulatory, cultural, and commercial rights of residents of the United States are massive and growing. Creation of rights has accelerated since the 1960s, when Great Society social programs were based in part on rights-based arguments. These benefits are part of the entitlement structure of the U.S. federal government and its mandates on state and local governments. This phenomenon helped generate what is known as an entitlement ethic—the notion that receipt of government services and cash is a right. This view, evident in many ways, permeates U.S. society.[1]

The creation of rights has spread from fundamental political guarantees to economic safety nets, consumption-support programs, government administrative procedures, and trivial matters of personal convenience. The creation of rights has shifted toward narrow functional issues and the assurance of outcomes rather than processes, opportunities, and protections. New legislative, administrative, and court-ordered rights in recent years gave handicapped persons rights to access to public transportation and buildings, often at substantial private and public financial cost. Partners of homosexuals won rights to medical insurance coverage similar to legally married persons in some jurisdictions. The U.S. Congress embodied a second "taxpayer bill of rights" in legislation in 1998 to modestly reform the Internal Revenue Service. Many people argue that respect is an entitlement right, not something that is earned. Commercial firms see the appeal of rights and offer variations of "consumers' rights." The list is long.

The establishment of rights creates high standards for acceptable performance that society and government cannot achieve. Because rights as entitlements are not things to be earned or purchased at market prices, people demand immediate consumption of lots of them. People expect the rights to meet absolute standards of quality and timeliness that usually are not attainable. Resources are scarce. Moreover, some rights grant persons changes in the behavior of people with whom they associate, even casually. As animals with limited intellectual capacities and abundant sociopolitical teachings or prejudices embodied in their cultures, people cannot and often do not want to perform to the standards of contemporary Western idealism.

The complex of alleged rights is internally inconsistent. So many rights exist that all U.S. citizens now are victims of discrimination—the failure of government or society to assure one or more explicit or perceived rights. The United States now has true equality of victimization. Further, the gap between slowly rising resources and more rapidly increasing demands to satisfy rights-rationalized agendas is growing. This amounts to a new variant of the "revolution of rising expectations" that originally referred to the political consequences of the slow realization of economic ambitions.

The proliferation of human rights is a boon for rights-oriented bureaucracies and trial lawyers, but it damages the social fabric that turns groups of people into communities and communities into a nation. Because the only asset any government ultimately has is its legitimacy, the cost of a government's inability to satisfy rights-based demands is overwhelming. That cost rises further when governments, and the political parties that seek to control them, favor some rights over competing claims to please political backers or to curry favor with voters.[2]

Excessive human rights are anathema to nationhood because they denigrate the compromise, discipline, and sacrifice needed for collective work in pursuit of common goals in favor of the immediate gratification of individual desires. With personal desires enshrined as rights through justifications of ideology or theology, there is no need to share them or to compromise on their definition, cost, or speed of actualization. Rights are absolute by definition. With claims to rights clear, the shared community values and goals that helped bond society when rights were fewer and resource constraints more obvious are much less important. There is less need to work together and thus less of the glue of nationhood. Even when nationhood is diminished or destroyed, however, government structures remain to service the rights of individuals and small groups, including the employment rights of bureaucracies and unions built to provide services justified by rights.

Although initially created as individual properties, human rights are easily aggregated to become collective assets of groups of similar individuals. The logical step is small, but the consequences of this action are sometimes very large because group rights are different from and greater than the sum of rights of individuals. Just as individuals have alleged rights of opportunity and sometimes results, activists often claim that the collective ambitions of groups deserve actualization as rights. The variously defined performances of groups in society—be they consumption levels, unemployment rates, or inmate populations—must in aggregate be at least equal to that of other groups without consideration of troublesome distractions such as historical and cultural factors, labor force participation rates, and work ethics. As in Lake Wobegone, everyone must be at least average. Subpar performance by any of a host of measures is allegedly evidence of discrimination.

As for individuals, the rights of groups allegedly are immutable and merit immediate gratification. Because they too are absolute, there is no appropriate compromise among the demands for group rights. The result is proliferation of strident social subgroups of special interests little inclined to work constructively with one another except for reasons of tactical expediency. The degeneration of U.S. society into narrow interest groups further diminishes the nationhood of the United States. Countless commentators have identified symptoms; single-issue groups constitute a growing share of politically active citizens, for example.

Samuel Huntington made the point differently by observing that, in the name of multiculturalism, powerful forces in the United States are accentuating the differences among U.S. residents and encouraging their preservation. By so doing, these persons attack the identity of the United States as a member of Western civilization.[3] Failure to assimilate immigrant groups risks transformation of the United States into what Huntington calls a cleft country, with potentially dire consequences for political stability. This amounts to an attack on the whole in the name of the perceived rights of groups that refuse to assimilate.

Countries that are not nations can survive a long time in the absence of a crisis. They are prone to fail in the face of external threat but may explode, however, if the crisis is internal. They are especially likely to fail if disparate groups, bolstered by the certainty that they hold rights to their goals, strive for self-gratification at the expense of other groups. If groups threaten the perceived vital interests of other groups, including perceived human rights, civil war may result. This happened in Bosnia in 1992 and in Kosovo in 1998. Although not an immediate threat, it could happen in California, too.

A United States that protects and advances under the rubric of rights the parochial interests of discrete but politically powerful groups, including bureaucratic constituencies, must damage the traditional freedoms of small groups and individuals, either absolutely or by relative deprivation compared with favored groups. Disregard for, or subordination of, the rights of the politically weak generates substantial unhappiness among persons and groups personally aggrieved or disillusioned with the failure of the country to honor its promises. Antigovernment groups thus flourish in the late twentieth century in the United States. Timothy McVeigh swore allegiance to the United States as a U.S. Army soldier but became angry enough with its government to attack it physically in Oklahoma City in 1995.

Even in the absence of civil war, part of government in an age of human rights must become impersonal and disconnected from the lives of citizens, that is, the part that through taxation fills the economic trough that feeds people who are transformed from taxpayers to rights holders. Obtuse tax systems enable governments to accomplish this magic by separating the pleasures of receiving baskets of entitlements—and the benevolence of politicians for providing them—from the magnitude and timing of the pain of taxation.

Lee Kuan Yew, prime minister of Singapore from 1959 to 1990, and others have noted the deleterious effects of the proliferation of individual rights in the West in general and the United States in particular.[4] Lee has noted that the proliferation of rights in the United States is dysfunctional because it places the freedom of individuals above the interests of society as a whole. This damages the coherence of society and eventually those same individual freedoms, broadly defined to include freedom of individual action and personal safety.[5]

A key consequence of the proliferation of human rights is the deterioration of personal responsibility. When the government guarantees rights, there is no need for personal responsibility in those aspects of life the rights cover. There is no personal responsibility to pay for rights that states exist to deliver. Thus the idea of a personal payment, denominated in money, time, or blood, for rights-based objectives is offensive. Virtually any price is too high, hence the need for an obtuse, federal fiscal policy. In a world dominated by human rights, humans should expect to get what they want without paying. Rights come without strings. Rights do not bear the symmetrical burdens of duty and responsibility that privileges carry. In a rights-based society, privileges have little value and compel correspondingly modest obligations.

Personal irresponsibility borne in part by the proliferation of human rights has spread to many aspects of life in the United States. The decay of national fiscal responsibility, interrupted temporarily in the late 1990s by a booming economy and a movement toward budget balance, is caused largely by demands on the resources of a distant impersonal state. Many people presume that this state has deep pockets filled with resources that are numerous and free.[6] At the personal level, the penchant to satisfy desires immediately is a major cause of the long-term decline in personal savings at rates that long have been below other industrialized countries and that in late 1998 and 1999 was negative for the first time since the 1930s.[7] Personal irresponsibility aided by lax bankruptcy laws surely is a major cause of the otherwise incongruous surge in personal bankruptcies during the boom years of the late 1990s.

The attitudes of U.S. citizens toward human rights and responsibilities have changed significantly in a relatively short time. Presidents and the citizenry have long felt that something special about the United States makes the advancement of good an ideal that the United States should pay to advance. President John Kennedy eloquently said in his inaugural address that his administration would not permit "the slow undoing of those human rights to which this nation has always been committed, and to which we are committed today at home and around the world. Let every nation know, whether it wishes us well or ill, that we shall pay any price, bear any burden, oppose any foe to assure the survival and success of liberty."[8]

But in recent years, support for human rights has evolved toward carping. The United States has been little inclined to pay much of a tangible price for human rights, even for clear national interests.

A focus on rights, and a collective confidence that the United States knows better than the rest of the world what human rights are and how they are rank-ordered, has led the government to a growing extent to pontificate, cajole, exhort, and extort through sanctions political action from countries around the world. Across the political spectrum, from religious conservatives to radical secular leftists, Americans criticize the performances of foreign governments in those parts of the human-rights spectrum that are their own personal interest. They also criticize U.S. leaders who fail to advocate the brand of ethical imperialism that advances their favorite human rights.

The United States has embodied human rights firmly in the institutional framework of its foreign policy. Human rights are prominent in the national security strategies of presidents. The U.S. Department of State has an assistant secretary who manages issues related to human rights and an ambassador for war crimes. Policymakers both pay lip service to and embody human rights into policy decisions.[9]

Congress, reflecting the activism of constituents with narrow interests across the political spectrum, pushes the executive branch to be yet more active in human-rights arenas. When foreign governments fail to heed their advice, members of Congress increasingly impose economic sanctions to force action. By its own count, Congress through mid-1998 imposed sanctions 104 times since World War II, including 61 times since Bill Clinton became president.[10] State and local governments have jumped on the bandwagon by banning their purchasing agents from buying goods and services from allegedly offending nations ranging from Myanmar to Switzerland. They have ordered government employee pension funds to sell shares of companies doing business in "bad" places. These mini–foreign policies have prompted many legitimate foreign complaints and undoubtedly caused consternation at the State Department.

Americans appear to support strongly such actions in most cases. They evidently care little that economic sanctions rarely change the behavior of foreign governments but regularly damage the well-being of the citizens of target countries. Since 1991, for example, many reputable Western organizations and United Nations agencies estimate that sanction-induced deprivations have killed several hundred thousand Iraqis, mainly children and old people. Advocates for these victims argue without effect that deprivation sponsored by the United States violates their rights. But Americans, if they know the human cost of sanctions, typically claim piously that it is all Saddam Hussein's fault, that all would be well if Saddam only did as Washington properly demands.

COSTS OF PROLIFERATION OF INTERNATIONAL HUMAN RIGHTS

As rights-oriented agendas increasingly dominate the politics and budgets of Western countries, human-rights activism has expanded to exert pressure on nations around the world to assure greater governmental and social compliance with Western human rights standards. Governments and private groups regularly press new rights agendas with mixed success. In some cases they generate internally inconsistent demands that defeat their own goals. Even in temporary failure, however, rights advocates often plant the seeds of new human-rights institutions.

Prompted by large-scale killing in Bosnia, central Africa, and Cambodia, for example, human-rights advocates won signature in July 1998 of a treaty that establishes a permanent international war crimes tribunal at The Hague. The court would have supranational authority to charge alleged violators of human rights.[11] After ratification by sixty countries, the treaty will give indictment powers to the UN and special prosecutors as well as countries.

After initially supporting the new tribunal, the United States opposed it because Washington feared that the court would charge U.S. citizens with war crimes. This reflected an obvious interest in self-preservation; statecraft is often dirty business and no politician wants to be vulnerable to attacks by naive human-rights activists or political opponents using loose international human-rights statutes as political weapons. Like other rogue states, moreover, the United States in recent years regularly flaunted international law when it saw fit. An example is the unilateral 1986 air strikes against Libya that killed Muammar Gadhafi's young daughter. The United States surely wants to continue to do so unimpeded by the opinions of other countries of its actions. The ethical imperialism of the United States, its sometimes crude Realpolitik, and its support for states such as Israel that regularly commit war crimes and violate human rights as defined by Amnesty International and others, have created many enemies. Moreover, the United States clearly prefers to judge others without risk of reciprocal treatment.

Bureaucratic concerns and national ambitions aside, there are fundamental reasons why major parts of the international human-rights agenda make little sense. Warfare in recent decades has changed dramatically toward total warfare of a sort that prominently involves civilians as both targets and participants, which often is in alleged defense of group rights. The 1992–1995 Bosnian war is a classic example. In this conflict, simply put, grievances among three ethnic factions—Bosnian Serbs, Bosnian Croats, and Bosnian Muslims—led to combat whose strategic as well as tactical objectives focused on increasing the size and security of pockets of land held nearly completely by one's own ethnic group. This required expansion of key chunks of ethnically homogeneous land and capture of some strategic locations, which simplified the demographic mosaic of prewar Bosnia.

Pejoratively called ethnic cleansing, the strategy that all three sides employed had at its heart the advancement of the rights of their own group over those of others and the targeting of members of other groups who stubbornly resisted achievement of those goals by refusing to leave their homes. When bombast did not work, the groups used murder and other "atrocities" to move people to other places, either horizontally as corpses or vertically as living beings. This type of warfare both tramples the human rights of victims and fosters alleged rights to personal and group security and self-actualization. Western descriptions, such as victim or war criminal, depend largely on who won and who lost, not on behavior.

This kind of conflict is incompatible with current international rules of warfare that define acceptable actions between groups of fighters called soldiers who are government employees. That is, the 1949 Geneva Conventions and other conventions that regulate by voluntary state compliance the conduct of the armies fighting conventional wars are woefully inadequate to describe, let alone regulate, intrasocietal and intersocietal wars. In a conflict such as Bosnia's in which movement of civilians was a major strategic goal, all significant participants were war criminals by conventional standards because they targeted noncombatants. In societal wars the distinction is often unclear between combatants and noncombatants who provide logistical, intelligence, and other support to people who pull triggers.

With human-rights definitions of war crimes increasingly more stringent through regular new declarations of "crimes against humanity" that satisfy the sensitivities of Western special-interest groups, ever smaller parts of the spectrum of organized combat are not criminal. This trend further limits states that mean well but has no effect on persons, groups, and states that fight to win by any means—including "terrorism." Thus war-crimes standards, rather than being moderating influences on an inherently brutal business, are so naive that they are increasingly irrelevant.

While much of the world focused on the indictments of The Hague tribunal for Bosnian war crimes, Bosnian Federation and Republika Srpska courts indicted hundreds of others, including Bosnian president Alija Izetbegovic.[12] Each used aspects of Western rights-oriented law focused on the rights of individual victims to advance, where possible, the collective interests of its group. Through 1999 the mixed record of implementation of the General Framework Agreement on Peace, or the Dayton agreement of November 1995, reflects the three factions' use of aspects of the rights-oriented Dayton pact, which is both incomplete and internally inconsistent, to derive advantage and deny gains to adversaries.

If the Western world were reasonably objective, and not so blatantly biased against the Serbs, all major Bosnian leaders, military and civilian, might be under international indictment. Postures similar to the decision of Richard Holbrooke, then assistant secretary of state, not to deal with indicted war criminals at Dayton might mean that reaching a genuine peace agreement would be impossible: There might be no leaders to negotiate peace agreements that would be locally legitimate. Pseudolegalistic, human-rights-driven motives of revenge called justice against persons culpable for the unpleasantness of the war thus would be counterproductive.[13]

Excessive focus on doomed efforts to create a multiethnic state in postwar Bosnia that met Western ethical standards sacrificed an opportunity to address regional grievances. The flawed Dayton agreement prompted disappointed Albanian Kosovars to step up activities of the Kosovo Liberation Army. Its attacks spurred the Yugoslav crackdown that in turn led the North Atlantic Treaty Organization (NATO) to attack Yugoslavia.

Moralizing by forced agreement, such as Dayton, thus can damage reconciliation and precipitate other problems, not further nascent peace processes.[14] Moreover, international arrests of indicted war criminals who are also factional leaders are likely to prolong active combat or heighten chances that cease-fires will collapse, not spur political settlements or foster postwar reconciliation. Barring the unlikely achievement of the dream that morally oriented appeals to human rights will end warfare and less formal human conflict, a focus on new rules that reflect little reality serves only to diminish the value of standards that have a chance of ameliorating the horrors of warfare.

In March 1999, NATO attacked Yugoslavia for the explicit purpose of furthering human rights. Canadian prime minister Jean Chretien put the point simply at a NATO summit in April: "Right now in the heart of Europe, NATO is fighting for humanity."[15] Strange logic. NATO chose to destroy and kill for human rights just as U.S. military forces in Vietnam once destroyed towns to "save" them. It killed hundreds of ethnic Albanian refugees in air strikes because it told its pilots to fly so high for their protection that they could not accurately identify targets. As it launched an inept military operation designed more to assure an absence of Western casualties than to influence actions on the ground, it both helped accelerate the atrocities that prompted the war in the first place and risked the coherence of the alliance.[16] At the same time it gave Yugoslav president Slobodan Milosovic incentive to continue the war by promising to prosecute him as a war criminal. The capitulation of Yugoslavia does not alter these facts.

Once again, seemingly good intentions were immediately counterproductive and created significant longer-term threats to regional stability. Excessive use of a human-rights prism to view events in Bosnia and Kosovo has significantly hampered Western understanding of the nature of the conflicts and prevented the West from playing a constructive role in regional reconciliation. The West clearly does not understand the obstacles it has placed in the path to reestablishment of political stability in southeastern Europe. It has been blinded by an excessive focus on human rights and visceral dislike of Milosovic.

The human-rights community is in other ways out of step with reality and is pushing agenda items that are obstacles to the greater good of resolution of international disputes. Again Bosnia offers examples. Annex 7 of the Dayton agreement states that all persons displaced by war are entitled to return to their prewar homes. Displacement was, however, what the war was about. The allegation of a right for all to go home amounts to undoing the results of the war. After a quarter million dead, few Bosnians want to return to the 1992 demographic mix and waste the sacrifices and incomplete gains of combat. All factions instead use Annex 7 to justify moving their people to territory they want while obfuscating if the annex helps another group.

Annex 7 thus complicates the effort to create a new normalcy in Bosnia by holding the factions to standards no group wants while offering no realistic means of achieving the ideal of multiethnic pluralism embodied in the Dayton pact. It damages the peace process as a result. Annex 7 also damages the credibility of the international community, including NATO, which is trying to force a dysfunctional agreement on reluctant Bosnians. Presumably we will see a similarly flawed regime imposed on postwar Kosovo.

Bosnia saw the emergence of a new human-rights organizational form, a nongovernmental organization (NGO) devoted entirely to furthering political goals that prominently feature human rights. Whereas thousands of NGOs, such as CARE and Doctors Without Borders, for many years have worked to ameliorate suffering, the International Crisis Group (ICG) came to Bosnia with an overt political agenda. Well funded, largely by U.S. and British interests, and featuring politically prominent individuals, ICG rapidly achieved prominence. It conducted a sophisticated publicity campaign to shape implementation of the civil aspects of the Dayton agreement and to influence implementation of Dayton by Western governments. It argued publicly that the capture of indicted war criminals and Bosnian Serb leaders Dr. Radovan Karadzic and General Ratko Mladic was worth resumption of the war, an extraordinarily narrow focus on retributional justice not shared by local NATO commanders and surely most Bosnians.

The ICGs of the world have an opening because the wealthy nation states do not have the political will to actively manage major international trouble spots—and increasingly seem incapable of crafting creative solutions that generate lasting, positive results. For many reasons that reflect the widely noted diminution of state power, NATO countries have handed some responsibility to organizations run by people who gain personal satisfaction and bureaucratic standing from doing "good."[17]

The positions of private-rights groups reflect the parochial interests–personal, organizational, and ideological—of human-rights advocates. Organizations compete for money and credit. Personal desires to perform types of public service and change the world in ideologically motivated ways constitute ambition—and success confers psychic income. Personal greed for ideological gratification is like a marbling of fat through the muscle of the ostensible good intentions of human-rights advocacy groups. The groups thus are less than fully altruistic.

This amorphous group moves globally and pontificates with the impunity of the press and its own self-proclaimed rights. It has plentiful funding, a steady flow of idealistic foot soldiers, and often close ties to government officials through former officials such as Jimmy Carter and ICG's George Mitchell. These factors combine to give such groups substantial extragovernmental political power.

Meanwhile, the UN has a High Commissioner for Human Rights with its own human-rights agenda and other subordinate organizations, such as the

UN High Commissioner for Refugees, that are good at humanitarian relief work. However, the UN has been unable to consistently run effective large-scale peacekeeping or peace enforcement operations that foster human rights. This is viewed positively in some quarters—and the UN arguably is set up to move slowly and inefficiently.

In addition, there is a growing list of multilateral, regional, and specially created organizations with limited powers that further fragment international political powers. For example, the Organization for Security and Cooperation in Europe specializes in human rights and sponsorship of elections—and jealously guards its bureaucratic turf. UN Security Council resolutions have created the Office of the High Representative in Bosnia; a series of international civilian police organizations for crisis points around the world when civil order was threatened or when local police were part of the problem, such as in Haiti; and special war crimes tribunals for Bosnia and central Africa. Most of these creations also have open-ended mandates, adding to the proliferation of narrow rights-oriented agencies that also have agendas of bureaucratic survival that undoubtedly will lead to expansion of their activities. The war crimes tribunal created in 1998 will have global jurisdiction indefinitely.

The international press corps, particularly television, has demonstrated a powerful ability to influence short-term human-rights agendas and government policies by showing photographs of suffering. Unable to ignore pathetic images, national governments have become heavily reactionary to press imagery—a phenomenon termed the "CNN effect." Television played prominent roles in U.S. decisions to act in Somalia in 1992 and Bosnia in 1995. A few photographs of a few corpses of ethnic Albanians in Kosovo prompted the West in late 1998 to threaten extensive NATO bombing and to propose a highly intrusive political agenda for all Yugoslavia. By so doing the United States and its allies provided de facto aid to the Kosovo Liberation Army seeking independence from Yugoslavia. In January 1999, reports of a minor massacre at Racak, a human-rights violation, prompted Clinton to decide to push NATO to enter the civil war.[18]

In late 1998 the United Kingdom further damaged the status of states by arresting former Chilean president and serving senator Augusto Pinochet at the request of a mid-level Spanish official who bypassed his national government by using legal, not diplomatic, channels to make his request. A prosecutor wanted to try Pinochet for alleged crimes against Spanish citizens in Chile during and after the 1973 coup that brought then-General Pinochet to power. The United States promptly supported the effort by selectively declassifying and releasing documents about Pinochet. In copycat fashion, people began to call for the extradition of Pinochet to the United States for the murder of Chilean dissident Orlando Letelier and his aide in a 1976 car bomb attack in Washington.[19]

These actions open the way for charges against many sitting and former government leaders for real and imagined crimes.[20] Once used by the left against one of its favorite enemies, the precedent would be available for all to use. U.S. presidents would be vulnerable for the foreign actions of U.S. government employees and their agents—as would Israeli leaders whose operatives routinely murder opponents around the world. President Clinton could be liable for crimes against humanity for his "genocide" against Iraqi civilians or "murder" for his cruise missile diplomacy that has killed civilians in Iraq, Sudan, and Afghanistan. Under modified Nuremburg standards, he as commander-in-chief might be liable for not acting to stop the atrocities in Rwanda that he knew were happening. As former Bosnian prosecutor Richard Goldstone said of Milosovic in 1999, "Even assuming he hasn't given the orders [for atrocities in Kosovo] it would be sufficient that he could have stopped them but didn't."[21] The Pinochet precedent, if generalized, could alter fundamentally the long-standing diplomatic rules that provide immunity from prosecution to diplomats and serving senior government officials. The loss of such protections could have a chilling effect on international relations.

The proliferation of human rights weakens individual states and their leaders, but it contributes to desires for more states. Perceived human rights to self-expression and national self-actualization drive pressures for creation of new states in, for example, the Basque region of Spain; northern Italy; the Kosovo region of Serbia; eastern Indonesia; Quebec; Wales and Scotland in the United Kingdom; Palestine; and the Kurdish lands of Turkey, Iran, and Iraq. Dissolution of tiny Belgium owing to ethnic squabbling is a growing possibility. Human rights are recruiting tools and powerful propaganda weapons in the already lethal arsenals of separatists and revolutionaries.

The differential definitions of human rights in the world contribute to additional conflict. Especially when couched in nationalist terms, human rights are incendiary. Before the rise of modern nationalism, a complex mix of nationalities occupied much of central and eastern Europe. Russian tsars and other rulers purposely sought out German and other workers with skills. The Austro-Hungarian empire centuries ago granted land to Serbs and others in what eventually became Croatia in return for protecting its borders with Ottoman Turkey, contributing to the ethnic mix that exploded in the 1990s.

In the past two centuries, however, and especially in this century, nationalists have acted to increase the ethnic homogeneity of states by war, fragmentation, or expulsion of minorities. Czechoslovakia, the Soviet Union, and Yugoslavia fragmented in the early 1990s to enhance ethnic sovereignty. The states of the former Warsaw Pact systematically for decades after World War II cleansed ethnic Germans from their territory; those with German surnames but unable to speak German found themselves deported with little international consternation. Greece and Turkey expelled the nationals of each other after World War I. Jews invaded Palestine and drove Arabs from what is now Israel. The dissolution in 1947 of British India led to migrations that created Hindu-dominated India and prominently Muslim Pakistan. For the most part this cleansing has enhanced regional stability. Israel is an exception. The departure of some 300,000 Serbs from the Krajina region of Croatia in the 1990s similarly has enhanced the stability of Croatia.[22]

The practice of ethnic cleansing that drew such ire in Bosnia and Kosovo is not new. What is new is the hypocrisy of selective moral outrage that accompanies some human-rights abuses. For many, the expulsion of Serbs from Croatia in 1991–1992 and 1995 was fine because other Serbs drove Muslims from portions of Bosnia in 1992–1995. Expulsions of Palestinians from their homes is acceptable because Jews allegedly have a right to a homeland based on occupation of some of the land two millennia ago; the property and human rights of the grandparents of refugees are subordinate or irrelevant. Although certainly many human-rights partisans are ignorant and others naive, human rights have also become major tactical and sometimes strategic propaganda components of conflict between ethnic groups and nations with territorial and ideological ambitions.

THE WAY AHEAD

Nothing seems to be on the immediate horizon to slow the growth of selective human-rights advocacy or its capacity for destruction. At first glance the proliferation of human rights is good: Human rights seem consistent with the ethical teachings of the major religious groups; they are part of the success of the North Atlantic community; and they sometimes improve conditions in unpleasant prisons. However, the damage to nationhood in the name of individual rights, the Balkanization of countries into smaller states, the fragmentation of states into competing subgroups, the weakening of a country's commitment of resources to back its rhetoric, and the evolution of international relations into a new form of world disorder all threaten the general welfare.

In the United States, federal courts and politicians of both major parties are firmly committed to generating new rights. The Democrats, for ideological reasons and to build tactical coalitions, have been primary manufacturers of rights, but it was Republicans who created a new round of taxpayer rights in 1998. A Senate vote was unanimous in October 1998 to authorize administrations to apply economic sanctions to countries that do not grant adequate religious freedom by U.S. standards. President Clinton wants a new "bill of rights" for recipients of health care and wants to make parents a new interest group with special rights.[23]

To restore balance and protect the interests of all citizens that accrue from social stability, citizens and their governmental representatives must realize that excessive human rights are socially divisive and politically costly, particularly those that are payoffs to domestic pressure groups or satisfactions of wants that are nice to have but nonessential. At the same time, it is essential to distinguish clearly and to protect vigorously the basic rights that are functional and fundamental to Western democratic government. Western governments, especially that of the United States, should therefore do the following:

Realize that not all rights are equal. They have different values and their realization has different costs. Some are essential, whereas others reflect cultural quirks, campaign slogans, special interest politics, and marketing gimmicks. The development of ways to identify and prioritize important rights should lead to decisions to diminish and even quash others. Some should be redefined as goals that wealthy and compassionate societies wish to achieve at some point. Only coherent and just governments can identify and adjudicate among competing claims of rights-hood.

Prohibit state and local governments in the United States from imposing economic sanctions on foreign governments whose policies they dislike. This makes the United States look foolish, violates international trade norms, and complicates the work of the State Department.

Stop pontificating about the alleged human-rights deficiencies in other countries. This irritates people who for good reason are not convinced that Western ideals are universal. Preaching is almost always ineffective and often counterproductive. Malaysian trade minister Rafidah Aziz commented on a speech in Kuala Lumpur in which Vice President Al Gore blasted the alleged lack of democracy in Malaysia: "It was the most disgusting speech I've heard in my life."[24] Others are surely as indignant if more diplomatic. The United States pontificates about human rights, but it bridles in response to the criticisms of other nations of its own human-rights performance. This is transparently hypocritical. Not surprisingly, Lee Kuan Yew, Malaysian prime minister Mahathir Mohamad, Japanese leaders, and others resist U.S. efforts to push on them an obviously flawed value system in favor of Asian values.[25]

Rein in amateur human-rights diplomats, including former President Jimmy Carter, Jesse Jackson, and the International Crisis Group, in favor of coherent foreign policies and use of functional international organizations when appropriate.

Think about the costs of war, and weigh those costs against expected benefits, before launching another inept war in the name of human rights.

Balance Western demands that other governments accept Western definitions of human rights with increased tangible efforts to further humanitarian goals. The United States spends a tiny share of its gross domestic product on foreign aid, popular belief notwithstanding, and most of that goes to countries with big domestic pressure groups, particularly Greece and Israel.

Exercise some self-discipline and control urges to impose sanctions to foster favorite ideological or theological agendas. This also would help further another right that the United States holds dear, the right of all people to conduct their own affairs as they see fit with minimal external interference.

These recommendations require leadership traits and government competence that are rare, especially when politicians reach and hold pinnacles of power by pandering to the human-rights claims of shifting coalitions of pressure groups.

Hardest may be public acceptance that the pandemic of rights is a human creation that has costs as well as benefits. For true believers, any notion that human rights are mortal, with blemishes, is blasphemy, and all who fail to share their beliefs are moral savages. There is little verbiage that will sway this group. The rest of us, however, should be much more sophisticated about managing our political creations and their consequences.

NOTES

1. Traditional welfare payments go to a small share of citizens. But entitlements through the redistributive effects of Social Security (tens of billions of dollars annually in de facto payments through tax exemptions, deductions, and credits) and a host of other programs benefit the vast majority of citizens regardless of social status or need.
2. These predictable costs are exacerbated by the unintended costs of incompetent implementation of rights-generated government programs. There is a now-extensive history of ostensibly well-intended laws, regulations, policies, and programs that have unintended ramifications, including the establishment of new incentives that either prevent achievement of goals or cause other problems.
3. Samuel P. Huntington, *The Clash of Civilizations and the Remaking of World Order* (New York: Touchstone, 1996), p. 305.
4. Fareed Zakaria, "A Conversation with Lee Kuan Yew," *Foreign Affairs* (March/April 1994), 109–126.
5. Excessive personal freedoms damage the ability of social organizations, especially corporations, to create wealth. Social disincentives potentially are numerous, including a host of regulations, taxation, and liability to lawsuits for alleged product or workplace deficiencies.
6. Note that the U.S. federal budget, claims of both major political parties notwithstanding, did not balance in the 1990s except with the help of a large surplus in the Social Security trust fund. Non-Social-Security tax receipts did not match non-Social-Security spending.
7. Commentators have offered many explanations for this phenomenon, including the rise in tax-sheltered investments and the rise in wealth that booming capital markets have provided. The trend of the consistently defined measure of personal savings has been steadily downward for years, however, and is the lowest among all industrialized nations.
8. John F. Kennedy, inaugural address, January 20, 1961, in *Public Papers of the President of the United States: John F. Kennedy*, 1961 volume (Washington, D.C.: Government Printing Office, 1962), p. 1.
9. See, for example, Richard Holbrooke, *To End a War* (New York: Random House, 1998).
10. Gerald E. Seib, "Sanctions Here, Sanctions There: Time to Pause?" *Wall Street Journal*, 17 June 1998, p. A18.
11. Thomas W. Lippman, "Worldwide War Crimes High Court Is Approved," *Washington Post*, 18 July 1998, p. A1.

12. Under the provisions of the Dayton agreement, Bosnia was divided into a Croat-Muslim Federation and a Serb-dominated Republika Srpska that maintain separate court and police systems.

13. Holbrooke, *To End a War*.

14. Recall that Croatian president Franjo Tudjman represented Bosnian Croats. Bosnian Serbs were essentially excluded from the process by an agreement to cede negotiating power to Serbian president Milosovic and Holbrooke's refusal to deal with key Serb leaders.

15. Barton Gellman, "Can NATO Muster Will to Win?" *Washington Post*, 25 April 1999, pp. A1, A29.

16. John A. Gentry, "Military Force in an Age of National Cowardice," *Washington Quarterly* 21, no. 4 (autumn 1998), p. 179–191.

17. Rebecca R. Moore, "Globalization and the Future of U.S. Human Rights Policy," *Washington Quarterly* 21, no. 4 (autumn 1998), pp. 193–212.

18. Barton Gellman, "The Path to War," *Washington Post*, 18 April 1999, p. A1.

19. Lawrence Barcell Jr., "The Case We Made, 22 Years Ago," *Washington Post*, 6 December 1998, p. C3.

20. For a discussion of other costs, see Ricardo Lagos and Heraldo Munoz, "The Pinochet Dilemma," *Foreign Policy*, no. 114 (spring 1999), pp. 26–39.

21. William Branigin, "U.S. Report Details Expulsions, Attacks," *Washington Post*, 11 May 1999, pp. A13, A14.

22. Daniel Pearl, "Why Ethnic Cleansing, Once Under Way, Is so Difficult to Reverse," *Wall Street Journal*, 22 April 1999, p. A1.

23. Charles Babington, "Clinton Seeks Ban on Job Bias against Parents," *Washington Post*, 17 April 1999, p. A1.

24. Mark Landler, "Gore, in Malaysia, Says Its Leaders Suppress Freedom," *New York Times*, 17 November 1998, p. A1.

25. David E. Sanger, "Clinton's Call for Pacific Harmony Meets a Chorus of Criticism from Asians," *New York Times*, 2 May 1994, p. A10.

PART III

ISSUE 13

NUCLEAR WEAPONS

The development of nuclear weapons was judged by *Time* magazine to be the most significant event of the twentieth century. Born of world war and nurtured during the prolonged era of the Cold War, the presence of the atomic bomb altered the calculus by which nations look at and act toward one another. For those nations that came to possess them, nuclear weapons symbolized the high stakes game of international politics and the struggle for power and influence played out by its major protagonists.

Now that the end of the Cold War has considerably reduced the risk of nuclear conflict between the major nuclear weapon states, is there a need for the continued existence of such weapons? Or does their existence represent a risk, and a cost, no longer worth taking?

The first selection for Issue 13, the Goodpaster Committee report, which was sponsored by the Stimson Center Steering Committee for the Project on Eliminating Weapons of Mass Destruction, firmly concludes that, given the changed strategic context of the post–Cold War era, the continued presence of nuclear weapons is more a threat to national security than a guarantor of it. Citing the economic and political costs of maintaining a nuclear arsenal, as well as the inherent risk of accidental or deliberate use, the committee concludes that nuclear weapons are of declining military and political utility and that the "assumed military and political value of nuclear weapons should be weighed against the dangers of continued nuclear reliance." While the report recognizes the continued deterrent function of nuclear weapons and thus does not advocate their unilateral elimination from the U.S. arsenal, it does state that "a world in which no state or group possessed nuclear weapons would be a safer place."

The second selection for Issue 13 contains excerpts from the Nuclear Posture Review, submitted to Congress on December 31, 2001. Contrary to the tenor of the Goodpaster Committee report, the Nuclear Posture Review calls for developing a new mix of nuclear capabilities for U.S. armed forces, and a greater flexibility in planning for their potential use. The Nuclear Posture Review argues that the new threats faced by the United States and its allies require newer, lower-yield weapons to neutralize, or, if necessary, counteract the threat posed by rogue states, or other non-state actors, who would consider using weapons of mass destruction. Responding to this newer threat environment, the Nuclear Posture Review argues that nuclear weapons must remain an integral part of the U.S. defense posture, and should be considered as part of any range of options available to defeat an adversary, even a nonnuclear one.

DISCUSSION QUESTIONS

As you read the Goodpaster Committee report and the Nuclear Posture Review, consider the following questions:

1. Would the development of low-yield, bunker-busting nuclear weapons blur the distinction between nuclear and conventional war? Is that a threshold worth crossing?
2. Are nonproliferation efforts ultimately doomed as long as existing nuclear weapon states maintain their nuclear capability? Does their reluctance, in fact, invite proliferation?
3. Would it be a safer world if no state or group possessed nuclear weapons?

KEY WEB SITES

For more information on this topic, visit the following Web sites:

The Arms Control Association
http://www.armscontrol.org

Center for Strategic and International Studies
http://www.csis.org

Carnegie Endowment for International Peace
http://www.ceip.org

The Declining Utility of Nuclear Weapons

The Goodpaster Committee

For over forty years, nuclear weapons have played a central role in U.S. foreign and defense policies. Throughout the Cold War, the United States relied on nuclear weapons to deter conventional and nuclear attacks by the Soviet Union and China on American territory, certain friendly states, and U.S. forces abroad. The extension of U.S. nuclear security assurances also dampened pressures for proliferation in Germany, Japan, South Korea, and other nations that otherwise might have chosen to seek to preserve their security through the independent possession of nuclear weapons. But the possession of nuclear weapons and reliance on nuclear deterrence also entailed significant costs and risks:

1. *Economic Costs.* The development and maintenance of large nuclear arsenals absorbed tremendous resources in the United States and the Soviet Union, and the final price tag for nuclear activities—especially environmental and safety costs—continues to rise. It is estimated that the United States will spend between $200 and $500 billion on environmental cleanup related to nuclear weapons facilities. The costs of cleaning up the monumentally worse contamination in the former Soviet Union is beyond calculation.[1] During a time of intense competition for budgetary resources, moreover, maintenance of the nuclear weapons infrastructure and currently planned force levels could divert scarce funds from other military programs of greater utility to U.S. national security.

2. *Political Costs.* Throughout the Cold War, the central role of nuclear weapons in U.S. and Soviet policies put the two states at odds with many non-nuclear states over nonproliferation policy and exposed them to increased dangers, particularly in crisis situations. If international support for nonproliferation continues to grow stronger, U.S. reliance on nuclear weapons is likely to be a source of renewed tension in relations with many non-nuclear states.

The Stimson Center Steering Committee for the Project on Eliminating Weapons of Mass Destruction included Andrew J. Goodpaster (chair), Howard Berman, Barry M. Blechman, William F. Burns, Charles A. Horner, James M. Jeffords, Michael Krepon, Robert S. McNamara, Will Marshall, Paul H. Nitze, Janne E. Nolan, Philip A. Odeen, Rozanne L. Ridgway, Scott D. Sagan, W. Y. Smith, John Steinbruner, and Victor Utgoff.
  This article is from *The Washington Quarterly* 20, no. 3 (summer 1997). Reprinted by permission of the Henry L. Stimson Center.

3. *Nuclear Accidents and Incidents.* Although the two nuclear superpowers devoted significant resources to the development of elaborate security and safety systems, both countries suffered a number of near-accidents and false alarms on several occasions. These incidents never resulted in catastrophic consequences and were relatively few in number compared to the total number of nuclear operations. Yet, even an advanced industrial power such as the United States with redundant safety and security arrangements was unable to eliminate these risks entirely. The risk of accident will persist so long as nuclear weapons exist. If an accident ever occurred, the human, environmental, and economic costs would be catastrophic.[2]

4. *Risk of Nuclear Use.* Most importantly, the very existence of nuclear weapons entails a risk that these weapons will be used one day, with devastating consequences for the United States and other nations. The manipulation of nuclear risk in U.S.-Soviet relations, as during the Cuban Missile Crisis and the 1973 Middle Eastern crisis, by its nature implied a danger that a crisis could escalate and end in a cataclysmic nuclear exchange.[3] In the multipolar structure of international relations that characterizes the post–Cold War period, the risks of nuclear use could increase with every new nuclear power.

During the Cold War, the contributions of nuclear weapons to U.S. national security and international stability were believed to outweigh the dangers associated with their integration in foreign and defense policies and, indeed, their very existence. There was no feasible alternative to reliance on nuclear deterrence, in any event. As long as the United States faced a nuclear-armed and implacable foe in Moscow, there was little reason to reconsider the desirability of reliance on nuclear deterrence.

The strategic context that undergirded the Cold War calculus of nuclear risks and benefits has changed fundamentally, however. The dawn of the nuclear age forced policymakers and military strategists to reexamine traditional assumptions about the uses and purposes of military force in interstate relations. In a similar vein, the new strategic situation demands a fundamental reassessment of the assumptions and theories that have guided U.S. nuclear policy for four decades. What is the political and military utility of nuclear weapons in the post–Cold War era? Alternatively, what costs and dangers does continued reliance on nuclear deterrence imply? In particular, what implications, if any, does the U.S. nuclear posture have for international efforts to stem the spread of weapons of mass destruction? These are the key questions that need to be addressed.

In our view, U.S. nuclear weapons are of declining military and political utility in both addressing the residual threats of the Cold War and in countering emerging threats to the security of the United States. There is no need for the United States to use nuclear weapons against a non-nuclear opponent; sufficient U.S. conventional forces can and should be maintained to counter non-nuclear threats. In our view, the only military role of nuclear weapons should be to deter nuclear threats to the population and territory of the United States, to U.S. forces abroad, and to certain friendly states. Although the United States must be concerned about the proliferation of all weapons of mass destruction, a combination of defensive measures and strong conventional forces could neutralize the need for a nuclear retaliatory threat to deter chemical and biological attacks. Moreover, the nuclear deterrent function, the one necessary function in our view, can be preserved at much lower force levels, as long as other states move in tandem with the United States toward smaller nuclear forces. There is no military justification to maintain U.S. and Russian strategic nuclear stockpiles at their current or even planned START II [Strategic Arms Reduction Treaty] levels.

Current rationales for nuclear weapons are primarily political. Perceptions of the political and military utility of nuclear weapons, while changing, have been slow to catch up with the new strategic realities. Given the uncertainties surrounding the Russian reform movement, a certain reluctance to abandon traditional ways of thinking about nuclear weapons is understandable, and will necessarily constrain rapid movement to lower force levels.[4] However, the assumed military and political value of nuclear weapons should be weighed against the dangers of continuing nuclear reliance. In addition to the costs and risks already noted, political upheaval or the weakening of state authority in Russia or China could cripple existing systems for ensuring the safe handling and control of nuclear materials and weapons, increasing the odds of accidents, more widespread proliferation, or nuclear terrorism.

Indeed, the dispersion of nuclear weapons and nuclear weapons material is a major risk of continued nuclear reliance. Only nuclear weapons can destroy the United States as a society and a nation. States in the Middle East and Asia that are unfriendly to the United States already are seeking to acquire nuclear capabilities. While would-be proliferators may be motivated primarily by developments in their immediate regions, the actions and policies of the two largest nuclear powers could affect the health and durability of the nonproliferation regime more generally. A re-emphasis, or even continuing emphasis, on nuclear weapons in U.S. policy, for example, would undermine U.S. ability to persuade other states to cap, to reduce, or to eliminate their nuclear weapon capabilities. Indeed, a world in which no state or group possessed nuclear weapons would be a safer place for the United States.

In the long term, only a policy aimed at steadily curbing global reliance on nuclear weapons—including our own—is likely to progressively eliminate nuclear dangers. Under existing political conditions, the elimination of nuclear weapons is infeasible. But progress toward elimination does not imply the creation of a world government. And much can be done in the current climate to reduce nuclear risks, while working progressively to narrow the roles that nuclear weapons play in U.S. policy and in interstate relations.

NOTES

1. According to one estimate, the United States expended nearly $4 trillion on its nuclear forces over the past fifty years. The ultimate cost to the Soviet Union may be counted even higher, to the degree that the nuclear arms race contributed to Soviet economic stagnation and, eventually, to the dissolution of the Soviet state. For an estimate of the total cost of the U.S. nuclear arsenal, see Stephen I. Schwartz, ed., *Atomic Audit: What the U.S. Nuclear Arsenal Really Cost* (Washington, D.C.: The U.S. Nuclear Weapons Cost Study Project, July 11, 1995), p. 3. For an estimate of the environmental clean-up costs, see Schwartz, p. 21. On the cost to the former Soviet Union, see Alexei G. Arbatov, ed., *Russian Arms Control Compliance and Implementation* (Washington, D.C./Moscow: The Henry L. Stimson Center & The Center for Geopolitical and Military Forecasts, spring 1994).

2. For examples of several incidents involving the nuclear weapons infrastructure in the United States during the Cold War, see Scott D. Sagan, *The Limits of Safety: Organizations, Accidents, and Nuclear Weapons* (Princeton, NJ: Princeton University Press, 1993), Chapters 2–4. Recent reports from the former Soviet Union may indicate that the risks of a nuclear accident are increasing due to the continued weakening of centralized control over nuclear facilities. See for example, Associated Press, "Russian Nuclear Plant Fire Stirs Furor," *New York Times*, 2 September, 1994, p. A8; Associated Press Wire Service, "Russia—Misguided Missile," March 13, 1995; "Unpaid Bill Triggers 15-Minute Power Cut at Plesetsk ICBM Test Site," *Aerospace Daily*, 18 September, 1995; and Oliver Wates, "Russian Brass Apoplectic over Missiles Power Cut," Reuters News Service, 22 September, 1994.

3. In October 1962, the United States believed that there were neither strategic nor tactical nuclear warheads in Cuba. That belief influenced officials who were prepared to recommend to President Kennedy that he authorize an attack on the island. It is now known that at the height of the crisis, Soviet forces possessed approximately 60 strategic and 100 tactical warheads, and Khrushchev, anticipating a U.S. attack, had approved an order to move at least some of the warheads close to their delivery vehicles. Had the United States invaded Cuba, there was a high risk that the Soviets would have chosen to use their nuclear weapons.

4. Robert S. McNamara does not believe "uncertainties surrounding the Russian reform movement" should "necessarily constrain" balanced movement to lower force levels.

Nuclear Posture Review

U.S. Department of Defense

The Nuclear Posture Review (NPR) represents the nuclear analog to the Bottom-Up Review of conventional forces, undertaken in 1993 to address the significant changes in the security environment which face the United States, and the military consequences of those changes. The NPR was the first review of nuclear policy in the post–Cold War world, the first such review in fifteen years, and the first review ever to include policy, doctrine, force structure, command and control, operations, supporting infrastructure, safety, security, and arms control. The decisions made in the NPR process allow DOD to put its nuclear programs on a stable footing after several years of rapid change in the international environment and in DOD's forces and programs, and at the threshold of a decade of further reductions called for by the START I and START II agreements.

Five basic themes of U.S. nuclear strategy emerged from the Nuclear Posture Review:

First, nuclear weapons are playing a smaller role in U.S. security than at any other time in the nuclear age. This fact served as a point of departure for the rest of the review. The Bottom-Up Review and the Counterproliferation Initiative (CPI) are designed to achieve and protect U.S. conventional superiority wherever American defense commitments require it.

The second principal finding is that the United States requires a much smaller nuclear arsenal under present circumstances. Dramatic reductions in U.S. (and, when implemented, former Soviet) forces from Cold War levels are underway.

Third, although the security environment has changed dramatically since the end of the Cold War, there is still great uncertainty about the future, particularly in the New Independent States where the process of denuclearization and reduction is underway but by no means completed. The United States must provide a hedge against this uncertainty. Therefore, the NPR stresses prudence in the face of potential risks while also identifying some new policy departures that reflect changes in the security environment.

Fourth, the United States does not have a purely national deterrent posture; it extends the deterrent protection of its nuclear arsenal to its allies. A very progressive aspect of U.S. nuclear posture is that it is, in part, an international nuclear posture. The NPR strongly supports continued commitment to NATO and Pacific allies.

Finally, the United States will continue to set the highest international standards of stewardship for nuclear safety and security, command and control, use control, and civilian control.

Process

The Nuclear Posture Review was chartered in October 1993 to determine what the role of nuclear weapons in U.S. security strategy should be. A ten-month DOD collaborative effort, the NPR was co-chaired by the Office of the Secretary of Defense (OSD) and the Joint Staff. Working groups were comprised of representatives from OSD, the Joint Staff, the Services, and the unified commands. The Deputy Secretary of Defense and the Vice Chairman of the Joint Chiefs of Staff reviewed and directed the progress of the NPR through issue briefs and the development of a final report, which was presented to the Secretary of Defense and the Chairman of the Joint Chiefs of Staff. Some decisions relating to the NPR were raised through the interagency process, including all relevant agencies of the U.S. government, which had the opportunity to review a wide range of options. The president approved the recommendations of the NPR on September 18, 1994.

Role of Nuclear Weapons in U.S. Security

The U.S. National Security Strategy states: "We will retain strategic nuclear forces sufficient to deter any future hostile foreign leadership with access to strategic nuclear forces from acting against our vital interests and to convince it that seeking a nuclear advantage would be futile. Therefore we will continue to maintain nuclear forces of sufficient size and capability to hold at risk a broad range of assets valued by such political and military leaders." Recent international upheavals have not changed the calculation that nuclear weapons remain an essential part of American military power. Concepts of deterrence and survivability must adapt to the new international environment, yet continue to be central to the U.S. nuclear posture. Thus, the United States will continue to threaten retaliation, including nuclear retaliation, and to deter aggression against the United States, U.S. forces, and U.S. allies.

Alliance relationships are an important element of U.S. security. Through forward basing and power projection capabilities, overseas U.S. military presence—including nuclear capabilities—helped promote regional stability, avert crises, and deter war. In recent years, there has been a dramatic reduction in both the overall size of the U.S. military presence abroad and in the nuclear capabilities deployed overseas. Yet maintaining U.S. nuclear commitments with NATO, and retaining the ability to deploy nuclear capabilities to meet various regional contingencies, continues to be an important means for deterring aggression, protecting and promoting U.S. interests, reassuring allies and friends, and preventing proliferation. Although nuclear capabilities are now a far smaller part of the routine U.S. international presence, they remain an important element in the array of military capabilities that the United States can bring to bear, either independently or in concert with allies to deter war, or should deterrence fail, to defeat aggression. Thus, the United States continues to extend deterrence to U.S. allies and friends.

CONTEXT: LEAD BUT HEDGE

The Nuclear Posture Review considered the size and role of U.S. nuclear forces in a world in which the proliferation of nuclear weapons and other weapons of mass destruction, rather than the nuclear arsenal of a hostile superpower, poses the greatest security risk. One goal for the NPR was to demonstrate U.S. leadership in responding to that risk. Major reductions in U.S. nuclear weapons are already underway, confirming the U.S. commitment to a smaller international role for nuclear weapons. Since 1988, the United States has reduced its nuclear arsenal by 59 percent, and either eliminated, truncated, or never fielded over fifteen nuclear weapons systems. The United States has no new nuclear weapons programs, and has committed to achieving a Comprehensive Test Ban Treaty, extending its testing moratorium in the interim. Program changes of this magnitude help set an example of decreasing dependence on nuclear weapons for military purposes.

U.S. nuclear weapons were for years justified by the potential for a massive conventional attack by the Warsaw Pact through the Fulda Gap which would overwhelm NATO conventional forces. The decisions of the members of the Warsaw Pact to dissolve their alliance and the subsequent transformation of the Soviet Union into independent states removed this potential threat. No equivalent threat to American vital interests can be identified in the post–Cold War era, and for very few of the existing threats are nuclear weapons appropriate responses. The NPR sought to adjust and reduce strategic programs to reflect actual U.S. needs, thereby setting an example for other nuclear powers to consider post–Cold War adjustments of their own.

Moreover, the CPI has as its central tenet the creation and furtherance of conventional responses to the threat or use of weapons of mass destruction. Far from inventing new roles for nuclear weapons in countering WMD, the NPR supports the CPI, because in a potential case of WMD threat or use, senior political and military leaders must have a wide range of responses—especially non-nuclear—from which to choose. Having the conventional capability to respond to WMD threat or use further reduces U.S. dependence on nuclear weapons.

These realities make the indefinite extension of the Nuclear Non-Proliferation Treaty (NPT) all the more important. A failure to codify the reduced role of nuclear weapons in nations' security could result in the creation of additional nuclear powers—a clear reduction in the security of all nations. The Posture Review sought to demonstrate American leadership by reducing the role of nuclear weapons in U.S. security. The combination of the large negotiated reductions embodied in the START I and START II treaties and the further unilateral reductions recommended by the NPR makes tangible the U.S. commitment to Article 6 of the NPT, which calls for the nuclear powers to take steps to reduce their arsenals. Once START II has been ratified, further negotiated reductions can be considered. The notion, however, that nations are motivated by U.S. nuclear forces in making decisions about acquiring nuclear weapons themselves is simply not valid. Potential proliferators are more likely to be driven by concerns about neighbors' capabilities or the desire for prestige or regional hegemony than by decisions America makes about its nuclear arsenal. Extending the NPT indefinitely will therefore do far more to improve individual nations' security than would further declines in superpower weapons stocks.

A major focus of the Nuclear Posture Review was nonstrategic nuclear forces (NSNF) and safety, security, and use control. The United States decided in the NPR to completely eliminate two out of its five types of NSNF, and to augment several aspects of nuclear safety and security. These efforts were discussed with Russian civilian and military leaders in the hope that they would take similar measures to reduce NSNF and improve nuclear safety, security, and use control. The United States is prepared, under the Cooperative Threat Reduction program, to cooperate with and support Russia in these endeavors.

Both the United States and the states of the former Soviet Union have acted quickly and responsibly to ease Cold War tensions. Both sides have decreased their nuclear stockpiles and are eliminating the weapons which most undermine stability. U.S. and Russian weapons have been de-targeted so that they are no longer aimed at any country. With U.S. help and financial aid, Russia is moving in the direction of economic reform and working to consolidate the nuclear arsenal that belonged to the Soviet Union.

These policies have not eliminated the threat posed by the weapons of the former Soviet Union, however. START I has just entered into force; START II has not been ratified by either the United States or Russia. Even after achieving the full reductions called for by both treaties, each side will retain up to 3,500 warheads on strategic offensive systems. While political relations with Russia have changed dramatically in recent years, the United States must retain a nuclear capability adequate to respond to any challenge. Further, most of the strategic nuclear weapons remaining in the former Soviet Union still are deployed and capable of attacking targets in the United States. Russia remains the focus of the Posture Review not because its intentions are hostile, but because it controls the only nuclear arsenal that can physically threaten the survivability of U.S. nuclear forces.

A significant shift in the Russian government into the hands of arch-conservatives could restore the strategic nuclear threat to the United States literally overnight. The removal of weapons located on the territory of Ukraine, Kazakhstan, and Belarus is still incomplete. Other nations not allied with the United States either have declared nuclear arsenals or are capable of developing them. With this kind of instability and uncertainty, the United States must maintain nuclear weapons necessary to deter any possible threat or to respond to aggression, should deterrence fail.

The NPR called for an affordable hedge in which the approved force structure could support weapons levels greater than those called for under START II should major geostrategic changes demand it. This lead and hedge theme reflects the pragmatic partnership between the United States and Russia, in which the United States seeks both to cooperate with Russia wherever such cooperation is possible, and to prepare realistically for possible tensions or disruptions of that relationship.

Reductions in U.S. Nuclear Posture

The deep reductions in nonstrategic and strategic nuclear weapons that have been underway for several years and will continue under START I and START II are clear evidence that the United States is reducing the role that nuclear weapons play in its military posture. Throughout the last several years, nuclear targeting and war planning have undergone several reviews and adjustments to account for the decline of the Warsaw Pact and the Soviet breakup, and will continue to change in response to further developments in international affairs. In fact, there have been significant changes in the U.S. nuclear posture since the end of the Cold War:

> There are no nuclear weapons in the custody of U.S. ground forces.
>
> Naval NSNF are no longer deployed at sea.
>
> Strategic bombers have been taken off day-to-day alert.
>
> The total U.S. active warhead stockpile has been reduced by 59 percent (79 percent by 2003). Deployed strategic warheads have been reduced by 47 percent (71 percent by 2003, when START I and II are implemented).
>
> NSNF weapons have been cut by 90 percent, and the NATO stockpile has been cut by 91 percent.
>
> Nuclear weapons storage locations have been reduced by over 75 percent.
>
> The number of personnel with access to nuclear weapons has been cut by 70 percent.
>
> The Department also is reducing substantially the worldwide airborne command post fleet—reflecting the decline in the likelihood of a superpower confrontation.

Since 1989, the programmatic implications of START I and II, and the two earlier Presidential Nuclear Initiatives on U.S. nuclear programs, also have been quite substantial. Program terminations, or systems that were developed but never became operational, include the small intercontinental ballistic missile (ICBM), Peacekeeper rail garrison, Lance follow-on, New Artillery Fired Atomic Projectile, Tactical Air to Surface Missile and Short Range Attack Missile II. Other programs were truncated, that is, systems were either fielded in fewer numbers than originally envisioned or, in the case of the B-1, will be converted to conventional-only usage. These truncations include

Peacekeeper, B-2, B-1 (which will drop its nuclear role), Advanced Cruise Missile, and the W-88 warhead. There are also a number of nuclear systems that were retired from service and never replaced; these include the Artillery Fired Atomic Projectile, FB-111, Minuteman II, Lance, Short Range Attack Missile-A, Nuclear Depth Bomb, and C-3/C-4 Backfit nuclear-powered ballistic missile submarines (SSBN). In all, spending on strategic nuclear forces, in constant 1994 dollars, dropped from $47.8 billion in 1984 to $13.5 billion in 1994, or 14.0 percent and 5.3 percent, respectively.

STRATEGIC NUCLEAR FORCES

Two basic requirements necessarily guide U.S. planning for strategic nuclear forces: the need to provide an effective deterrent while remaining within START I and II limits, and the need to allow for additional forces to be reconstituted in the event of a reversal of currently positive trends. The Department must hedge against uncertainties while recognizing that no new nuclear systems are under development.

The NPR examined a wide variety of options for strategic nuclear force structures, ranging from ones which increased platforms over those previously planned, to a minimal force that eliminated ICBMs and reduced the number of SSBNs to ten. The Review examined what force levels were needed to handle the most stressing case that could develop—deterring a hostile Russia. The president approved the NPR's recommended strategic nuclear force posture as the U.S. START II force. This force will maintain flexibility to reconstitute or reduce further and assumes that Russia ratifies and implements START II. At this level, the United States would have adequate weapons to:

Deter a hostile Russian government by holding at risk a range of assets valued by its political and military leaders.

Maintain a strategic reserve force to ensure continued deterrence of other nuclear powers.

Account for weapons on systems which are not available due to maintenance and overhaul.

The NPR did not change the total number of warheads the United States planned to retain under START II. However, the Review did identify ways to streamline forces by reducing the number of platforms carrying these warheads. As a result of the NPR, U.S. strategic nuclear force structure will be adjusted to comprise:

Fourteen Trident submarines—four fewer than previously planned—carrying twenty-four D-5 missiles, each with five warheads, per submarine. This will require backfitting four Trident SSBNs, currently carrying the Trident I (C-4) missile, with the more modern and capable D-5 missile system.

Sixty-six B-52 bombers—down from ninety-four planned in 1993—carrying air-launched cruise missiles (AGM-86B) and advanced cruise missiles (AGM-129).

Twenty B-2 bombers—the same number previously envisioned—carrying gravity bombs.

Four hundred and fifty to five hundred Minuteman III missiles, each carrying a single warhead.

In addition, no new strategic nuclear systems are either under development or planned.

The NPR re-examined the concept of a triad of ICBMs, submarine-launched ballistic missiles (SLBMs), and bombers as the basis for a strategic deterrent and determined it remains valid for a START II–size force. Today, the United States relies on fewer types of nuclear weapon systems than in the past. Hedging against system failure of a leg of a triad—either because of technical failure of a delivery platform or warhead, or technological breakthroughs by potential adversaries—is a primary reason to retain a triad. Each leg also has unique characteristics and specific advantages.

SLBMs　　Under START II, the SLBM force will provide about half of the 3,000 to 3,500 accountable warheads that the United States will be permitted to deploy. Because of this increased reliance on the SLBM force and the continued need for survivable weapons to enhance stability, the NPR determined that the conversion of four submarines to carry the more modern D-5 missile was appropriate. Conversion of these four submarines from the older C-4 missile ensures that the U.S. force can remain intact without danger of age-related problems crippling missiles that would carry 40 percent of SLBM warheads.

The SLBM force, which is virtually undetectable when on patrol, is the most survivable and enduring element of the strategic nuclear triad. A significant portion of the SSBN force is at sea at any given time, and all submarines that are not in the shipyard for long-term maintenance can be generated during a crisis. Moreover, the Trident II (D-5) missile—with its improved accuracy, range, and payload relative to previous SLBMs—allows the SLBM force to hold at risk almost the entire range of strategic targets. In order to have adequate, survivable, at-sea weapons to support deterrence, accountable SLBM warhead levels need to be maintained close to the START II limit of 1,750. With the fourteen SSBN option selected by the NPR, the United States will retain a significant capability to hedge against a failure of the START II Treaty or unforeseen changes in the world, because the D-5 missile loaded on the Tridents will carry fewer warheads than the maximum allowed by START Treaty limits. The fourteen-boat force also maintains the security of two-ocean basing, further enhancing operational effectiveness and stability.

ICBMs ICBMs provide the United States a prompt-response capability. START II requires the downloading of ICBMs to one warhead, but does not place a sublimit on the total number of single-warhead ICBMs. Approximately 500 Minuteman IIIs will be retained and downloaded to one warhead apiece. ICBMs also increase the cost ratio to an adversary of attempting a first strike. Retaining approximately 500 single-warhead Minuteman IIIs provides for a reduced but prudent ICBM force.

Bombers There is no START II sublimit on the number of bombers. Because bombers are dual-capable, they fulfill two important functions: They serve as an integral part of the U.S. nuclear deterrent, providing a hedge against a catastrophic failure of either the SSBN or ICBM leg of the triad, and they provide an important conventional capability in MRCs; 100 bombers in a conventional role are tasked for MRCs. Retaining sixty-six B-52s and twenty B-2s will allow the bombers to serve these functions.

Nonstrategic Nuclear Forces

The Nuclear Posture Review affirms that the United States has not only a national deterrent posture, but an international nuclear posture. Indeed, the United States extends the deterrent protection of its nuclear arsenal to its allies. Nowhere is this more evident than in the area of NSNF, which are not covered by START I and START II. For nearly fifty years, the United States has maintained a sizable military presence in regions deemed vital to American national interests.

Alliance commitments and the unique characteristics of nonstrategic nuclear forces were primary considerations in the NPR's consideration of what the NSNF force structure should be. The Nuclear Posture Review considered numerous options, ranging from one more robust than today's structure to elimination of NSNF entirely. As a result of the NPR, the following decisions were made regarding U.S. nonstrategic nuclear force structure:

Eliminate the option to deploy nuclear weapons on carrier-based, dual-capable aircraft.

Eliminate the option to carry nuclear Tomahawk cruise missiles (TLAM/N) on surface ships.

Retain the option to deploy TLAM/N on attack submarines (although none are currently deployed, they could be deployed if needed).

Retain the current commitment to NATO of dual-capable aircraft based in Europe and CONUS and the deployment of nuclear weapons (gravity bombs) in Europe.

These NSNF decisions have the effect of permanently eliminating the capability to deploy nuclear weapons on naval surface ships—a step that could encourage the Russians to reciprocate—while maintaining a nonstrategic nuclear force capable of fulfilling U.S. commitments to allies.

Command, Control, Communications, and Intelligence

Nuclear-related command, control, communications, and intelligence (C^3I) and operations have undergone dramatic changes since the end of the Cold War. For example:

Strategic bombers are off alert.

ICBMs and SLBMs have been de-targeted.

U.S. command post structure has been reduced.

The operating tempo of the worldwide airborne command post structure has been reduced. The National Emergency Command Post, formerly used only for a nuclear role, is now the National Airborne Operation Center and is available to the Federal Emergency Management Agency for civil emergencies.

Systems endurability requirements have been reduced by two-thirds.

The C^3I portion of the DOD strategic nuclear budget has been reduced from $3.4 billion to $2.1 billion.

Nevertheless, to maintain viability, the C^3I structure must maintain capability to carry out key missions: early warning; threat assessment; connectivity of the National Command Authority; dissemination of emergency action messages for the launch of nuclear forces, if necessary; and safe, secure force management. With these considerations in mind, the NPR made the following decisions regarding strategic C^3I:

Continue adequate funding of critical programs.

Correct existing/projected communication system and tactical warning/attack assessment deficiencies.

Support intelligence systems which provide timely information and threat characterization and warning indicators.

Infrastructure

In order to maintain a streamlined and adjusted nuclear posture, DOD must sustain the infrastructure to support U.S. nuclear forces. The Nuclear Posture Review focused its examination of the nuclear infrastructure on two key areas: the industrial base for strategic missiles, reentry systems, and guidance, as well as for bombers; and support by the Department of Energy (DOE), which is responsible for producing and maintaining nuclear weapons for the Department's systems. The NPR made the following infrastructure recommendations:

Replace the guidance system and re-motor those Minuteman IIIs which are retained.

Continue D-5 production past 1995 to maintain the strategic ballistic missile industrial base (this is a secondary advantage of backfitting the fourteen SSBNs to be retained with the D-5 missile).

Fund the sustainment of the guidance and reentry vehicle industrial base.

With regard to bomber infrastructure, no specific funding was found to be necessary, since Stealth and commercial aircraft should keep the industrial base healthy.

Provide the Department of Energy—the supplier of nuclear weapons—with DOD's requirements:

Maintain nuclear weapon capability (without underground nuclear testing).

Develop a stockpile surveillance engineering base.

Demonstrate the capability to refabricate and certify weapon types in the enduring stockpile.

Maintain the capability to design, fabricate, and certify new warheads.

Maintain a science and technology base needed to support nuclear weapons.

With regard to the tritium supply to support weapons (as specified annually by the Department of Defense in its Nuclear Weapons Stockpile Memorandum), DOD and DOE must decide on a source and a production program. In order to have an upload hedge in case events require it, an accelerated decision will be needed.

No new-design nuclear warhead production is required.

SAFETY, SECURITY, AND USE CONTROL

The safety, security, and use controls of nuclear weapons are the solemn responsibility of those nations which possess them. The United States sets the highest international standards for the safety, security, and responsible custodianship of its nuclear arsenal. The dramatic force reductions which already have taken place since the end of the Cold War—U.S. strategic warheads have been cut by 59 percent since 1988; nonstrategic nuclear forces have been cut by 90 percent—have contributed greatly to the increased safety and security of U.S. nuclear weapons. As a result of these reductions, nuclear storage sites have been reduced by 75 percent. The Nuclear Posture Review concerned itself with maintaining the U.S. lead role in nuclear safety and security issues.

The NPR thoroughly reviewed the recommendations of the Fail-Safe and Risk Reduction (FARR) Commission of 1992 and determined that the vast majority of them had been implemented or were well underway. Among the FARR recommendations the NPR singled out for continued implementation were:

Completing the Trident Coded Control Device (CCD) in 1997, providing for system-level CCDs or permissive action links (PALs) on all U.S. nuclear weapons by 1997.

Seeking alternatives to those recommendations that a test moratorium may preclude (for example, protection equivalent to Category F PAL on all new weapons).

The Department of Defense also will re-institute a regular and realistic nuclear procedures exercise program, with participation by senior DOD civilian and military leadership, to ensure thorough understanding of nuclear procedures by this nation's nuclear stewards.

Threat Reduction and Counterproliferation Initiatives

The Nuclear Posture Review made adjustments to the U.S. nuclear posture unilaterally. They are consistent with, but are not required by, any new arms control agreements. There remains hope for Russia to undertake a comparable review, and to make similar adjustments in its strategic force plans, nonstrategic force plans, and ways of ensuring safety, security, and use control. When President Yeltsin came to Washington to meet with President Clinton in September 1994, they had the opportunity to discuss these adjustments, which were made possible in great measure by the new security relationship with Russia—pragmatic partnership.

At the Summit, the presidents made important progress on a number of arms control issues and, in fact, took steps down the road of further reductions and increased cooperation on nuclear issues. The presidents confirmed their intention to seek early ratification of the START II Treaty, once the START I Treaty enters into force, and expressed their desire to exchange START II instruments of ratification at the next U.S.–Russia Summit meeting. Once START II is ratified, the presidents agreed to begin immediately to de-activate all strategic delivery systems to be eliminated under START II. The presidents also instructed their experts to intensify their dialogue to compare conceptual approaches and to develop concrete steps to adapt the nuclear forces and practices on both sides to the changed international security environment, including the possibility, after ratification of START II, of further reductions and limitations on remaining nuclear forces.

In this uncertain environment, traditional arms control concerns of the past are augmented by the more urgent issues of security and control of key elements of the nuclear complex, particularly the warhead, warhead component, and weapon fissile material stockpiles. The potential for loss or theft of fissile material or nondeployed nuclear warheads is a real risk to U.S. security. As such, there is merit in exploring, together with the Russians and others, initiatives that would reduce this risk.

Conclusion

In the Nuclear Posture Review, the Department of Defense has struck a prudent balance between leading the way to a safer world and hedging against the unexpected. In the post–Cold War environment, the United States continues to require a nuclear deterrent. The strategic triad has been streamlined and adjusted, as have nonstrategic nuclear forces, to account for the reduced role nuclear weapons play in U.S. national security. Major force reductions and cost savings are already underway, leading to a smaller, safer, and more secure U.S. nuclear force.

ISSUE 14

MISSILE DEFENSE

Ballistic missile defense has long been the Holy Grail of military strategies. Standing in the way of its realization have been daunting technological challenges, summarized best by the aphorism that an effective missile defense would require *hitting a bullet with a bullet*. This seemingly impossible challenge has not deterred efforts to develop such a capability. From the beginning of the ICBM standoff between the Soviet Union and the United States, both sides sought to acquire the ability to defend their territory from ballistic missile attack. These early efforts proved futile, and the Cold War soon settled down to the acceptance by both sides of mutual assured destruction (i.e., MAD). This status quo of terror came to be symbolized by the 1972 Anti-Ballistic Missile Treaty, which placed severe limits on any future efforts by either party to develop missile defense systems. This agreement was due more to the technical and fiscal limitations such efforts would have entailed than to either side's willingness to accept the logic of MAD. Nevertheless, this basic reality of strategic deterrence remained until the advent of the Reagan administration in 1980, which revived interest in ballistic missile defense with its so-called Star Wars program.

The first of the selections for Issue 14 are two fact sheets issued by the U.S. government, one from the Bureau of Arms Control, the other from the Bureau of Nonproliferation. Both lay out the rationale for the administration's determination to pursue a national missile defense program. They also address the changed strategic relationship with Russia, particularly the impact of the withdrawal of the United States from the 1972 ABM Treaty, and how the administration sees missile defense as complementing its nonproliferation efforts. Both signal the administration's determination to proceed on a broad front to prevent any future attempt to politically coerce or blackmail the United States or its allies through the threat of missile attack.

In the second selection for Issue 14, Senator Robert Byrd of West Virginia casts doubt on the efficacy and viability of the administration's plans.

DISCUSSION QUESTIONS

As you read the U.S. State Department fact sheets and Senator Byrd's speech, consider the following questions:

1. What are the likely impacts of efforts to develop a national missile defense on relations with allies and with potential adversaries?
2. Should missile defense be given the priority and resources it is enjoying in the post–September 11 era?
3. Are efforts to stem the proliferation of weapons of mass destruction compatible with a national missile defense program?

KEY WEB SITES

For more information on this topic, visit the following Web sites:

U.S. Department of Defense
http://www.defenselink.mil

Center for Defense Information
http://www.cdi.org

Federation of American Scientists
http://www.fas.org

National Missile Defense Fact Sheets

U.S. State Department

Bureau of Arms Control, Washington, D.C.
September 1, 2001

MISSILE DEFENSE AND DETERRENCE

Deterrence must and will remain a critical component of our security posture. Yet, many of the conditions and assumptions that long guided the way we thought about deterrence and its supporting strategic force posture have changed fundamentally. Deterrence can involve more than just the threat to retaliate in the event of an attack. It can also be based on the ability to prevent potential adversaries from achieving their objectives thereby deterring them from pursuing such objectives in the first place. The United States is developing a forward-looking strategy that takes into account the changing nature of the threats we face, as well as the full range of capabilities that we can marshal to protect our nation and its vital interests, as well as meet our commitments to friends and allies.

Deterrence Is Our Highest Priority   Maintaining a reliable deterrent against attacks on the United States and our allies is a critical objective of our national security strategy. Our nation always prefers peaceful means to maintain its own security and prosperity, and that of its friends and allies, but maintains the military capabilities needed to deter and defend against the threat or potential use of force by prospective adversaries.

Our deterrence strategy to date has largely relied on our ability to respond to attack with a variety of options, ranging from a devastating retaliation through more selective strikes, and our offensive nuclear forces are and will remain a key component of that capability. No group or nation should doubt that the United States will continue to depend on the certainty of a devastating response to any attack on the United States or its allies to deter attacks by ballistic missiles or other weapons.

Emerging Threats and the Need to Diversify Our Approach to Deterrence   However, given the new threats we all face—especially from weapons of mass destruction and increasingly sophisticated ballistic missiles in the hands of rogue states—our deterrence posture can no longer rely exclusively on the threat of retaliation. We now need a strategy based on an appropriate mix

219

of offensive and defensive capabilities to deny potential adversaries the opportunities and benefits they might hope to realize from the threat or use of weapons of mass destruction against our homeland and forces deployed abroad, as well as those of our allies and friends.

Today, we are confronted with a more diverse, less predictable, and less risk-averse group of hostile states that are aggressively seeking to develop or acquire weapons of mass destruction and longer-range missiles as a means of their delivery. They see such weapons both as operational weapons of war and as coercive tools of diplomacy to preclude us and our partners from assisting friends and allies in regions of vital interest. For such threats, deterrence must take advantage of the contribution of both offensive and defensive forces, working together.

Ballistic missile defenses enhance the traditional deterrence of offensive capabilities by denying rogue states the ability to reliably and predictably inflict mass destruction on other nations. By complicating his calculation of success, these defenses add to a potential aggressor's uncertainty and weaken his confidence. Effective missile defenses may also serve to undercut the value potential aggressor's place on missiles as a means of delivery, thereby advancing our nonproliferation goals. With these considerations in mind, missile defenses can be a force for stability and security.

Moreover, some potential threats, such as accidental or unauthorized launches of ballistic missiles, cannot be deterred by their very nature. They can only be defended against. To counter such contingencies, missile defenses provide an element of insurance that supplements and enhances their deterrent value.

A New Relationship with Russia   We are committed to creating a new strategic and diplomatic relationship with Russia, one founded not on common vulnerabilities, but on common interests and shared objectives. As Secretary of State Colin L. Powell has said: "It is time to change the nuclear equation of mutual assured destruction to a more sensible strategic arrangement." While we seek to persuade Russia to join us in further reducing our nuclear arsenals, we are also prepared to lead by example. Therefore, we are committed to ensuring that this new strategic framework with Russia is characterized by efforts to achieve the lowest levels of nuclear weapons consistent with our present and future national security needs. Our missile defenses will not threaten Russia's deterrent forces.

Missile Defense and China   Our missile defenses will be designed to deter and defend against small-scale attacks from rogue states, as well as from accidental or unauthorized attacks from any source. As a force for stability and security in both the Asian region and the world at large, defense and deterrence working together advance goals of regional peace and stability which we share with China. Missile defense is not intended as a threat to China's deterrent forces.

Summary

Finally, it is worth emphasizing that missile defenses are only one tool among many in maintaining peace, security, and stability, and must be considered within the context of our entire strategic framework. This framework includes offensive nuclear arms as well as our broader diplomatic and security activities, including arms control and nonproliferation efforts. This diversified approach to deterrence is appropriate for the complex and less predictable world in which we live.

Bureau of Nonproliferation, Washington, D.C.
September 1, 2001

Missile Defense and Nonproliferation

Weapons of mass destruction (WMD) and their missile delivery systems pose a direct and serious threat to the national security of the United States, our friends, forces, and allies. President Bush has made clear that we must have a comprehensive strategy to counter this complex and dangerous challenge. This strategy must include strengthening nonproliferation measures (prevention), more robust counterproliferation capabilities (protection), and a new concept for deterring contemporary threats, relying more on defenses and less on offensive nuclear forces.

U.S. Nonproliferation Efforts   Our nonproliferation efforts seek to prevent or slow the spread of nuclear, biological, and chemical weapons and their missile delivery systems. We are working to impede WMD and missile development programs existing in key countries and regions of concern such as Iran, Iraq, Libya, North Korea, and South Asia, and to halt transfers of missiles and missile-related items from countries such as Russia, China, and North Korea. There are four elements of our nonproliferation strategy:

1. Persuade or induce proliferating governments to change course: Engage directly and indirectly with countries of concern to urge them to constrain, halt, or reverse proliferation. This includes renewed engagement with North Korea on its nuclear and missile programs, working through the UN to induce Iraq to accept international inspections, and efforts to persuade India and Pakistan to constrain their nuclear and missile competition.

2. Use positive and negative incentives to demonstrate to proliferators there are benefits to observing nonproliferation norms and costs for disregarding them.

Deny proliferators the supply of equipment, material, or technology from abroad.

Work with other governments to monitor and stop foreign shipments of sensitive WMD and missile-related technologies to countries and programs of concern.

Press countries like North Korea, Russia, and China to behave more responsibly, and assist others to upgrade their export controls.

Craft a United Nations control mechanism to deny Iraq sensitive goods while permitting the Iraqi people to receive the civilian goods they need.

Cut off outside assistance to Iran's nuclear and missile programs.

Reinforce the Missile Technology Control Regime and other suppliers' nonproliferation arrangements, to create rules that member countries and others use to guide their export behavior.

Impose sanctions, when warranted, on countries and specific entities that assist proliferators, to deter would-be suppliers.

3. Use U.S. threat reduction programs to secure or eliminate WMD and missile capabilities left over from the Cold War.

Pursue programs in the New Independent States (NIS)—especially Russia—to help them meet their arms control obligations, and to control and dispose of the massive quantities of WMD and missile materials there.

Ensure former Soviet WMD and missile expertise does not leak out of Russia and the NIS to rogue states.

4. Strengthen existing international nonproliferation treaties, promote new ones that meet U.S. interests, and upgrade the means of verifying them.

Support formal treaties such as the Nuclear Nonproliferation Treaty (NPT), the Chemical Weapons Convention (CWC), and the Biological Weapons Convention (BWC) that set the international "rules of the road" on possession, deployment, or transfer of nuclear, chemical, and biological weapons.

Strengthen the International Atomic Energy Agency's (IAEA) nuclear inspection system.

Press others to bring into force upgraded IAEA safeguards designed to detect Iraq-style clandestine nuclear activities.

Seek to break the international logjam that is blocking negotiation of a treaty to end the production of unsafeguarded nuclear weapons material.

Nonproliferation and Missile Defense   Nonproliferation, deterrence, and missile defense are complementary parts of our overall strategy.

Nonproliferation reduces the threat missile defenses are designed to counter.

The threat posed by WMD and missile proliferation is the driving force behind our desire for missile defense. To the extent this threat is reduced by other means, the magnitude of the threat that must be dealt with by missile defenses also declines.

Missile defense weakens the incentive to develop, test, produce, and deploy missiles.

Rogue states such as Iran, Iraq, Libya, and North Korea are less likely to invest in missiles as a weapon of choice if they know they will face effective defenses.

Missile defense does not mean that we are giving up on deterrence.

Missile defense strengthens deterrence and keeps rogue states from being able to blackmail the United States, its friends, or allies by threatening a missile attack.

For more on nonproliferation, see <http://www.state.gov/t/np>.

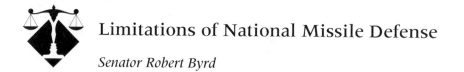

Limitations of National Missile Defense

Senator Robert Byrd

U.S. Senate, Washington, D.C.
June 25, 2001

Mr. President, the president has recently concluded his trip to Europe, where he attempted to convince European leaders of the need for the United States to deploy a national missile defense system. It seems that our friends in Europe still have the same reservations about this apparent rush to a missile shield, and I can understand why. While I support the deployment of an effective missile defense system, there are a number of reasons why I believe it is not as easy to build such a system as it is to declare the intent to build it.

One cannot underestimate the scientific challenge of deploying an effective national missile defense system. The last two antimissile tests, performed in January and July of 2000, were failures. In response to these failures, the Department of Defense did the right thing. The Department of Defense took a time-out to assess what went wrong, and to explore how it can be fixed. The next test, scheduled for July of this year of our Lord 2001, will be a crucial milestone for the national missile defense program. All eyes will be watching to see if the technological and engineering problems can be addressed, or if we have to go back to the drawing board once more.

It must also be recognized that no matter how robust missile defense technology might become, it will always—now and forever—be of limited use. I fear that in the minds of some, a national missile defense system is the sine qua non of a safe and secure United States. But the most sophisticated radars or space-based sensors will never be able to detect the sabotage of our drinking water supplies by the use of a few vials—just a few vials—of a biological weapon, and no amount of antimissile missiles will prevent the use of a nuclear bomb neatly packaged in a suitcase and carried to one of our major cities. We should not let the flashy idea of missile defense distract us from other, and perhaps more serious, threats to our national security.

If deployment of a missile defense system were to be expedited, there is the question of how effective it could possibly be. Military officers involved in the project have called a 2004 deployment date "high risk." That means that if we were to station a handful of interceptors in Alaska in 2004, there is no guarantee—none, no guarantee that they would provide any useful defense at all. Secretary of Defense Donald Rumsfeld has downplayed this problem, saying that an early system does not have to be 100 percent effective. I believe that if we are going to pursue a robust missile shield, that is what we should pursue. I do not support the deployment of a multibillion dollar scarecrow that will not be an effective defense if a missile is actually launched at the United States.

The *New York Times* has printed an article that drives this point home. The newspaper reports on a study by the Pentagon's Office of Operational Test and Evaluation that details some of the problems that a national missile defense system must overcome before it can be considered effective. According to the *New York Times*, the authors of this internal Department of Defense report believe that the missile defense program has "suffered too many failures to justify deploying the system in 2005, a year after the Bush administration is considering deploying one."

The article goes on to state that system now being tested has benefitted from unrealistic tests, and that the computer system could attempt to shoot down inbound missiles that don't even exist. If the Department of Defense's own scientists and engineers don't trust the system that could be deployed in the next few years, this system might not even be a very good scarecrow. Let the scientists and engineers find the most effective system possible, and then go forward with its deployment.

Let us also consider our international obligations under the Anti-Ballistic Missile (ABM) Treaty of 1972. The president has begun discussions with Russia, China, our European allies, and others on revising the ABM Treaty, but so far the responses have been mixed. I suggest that it is because our message is mixed. On one hand, there is the stated intent to consult with our allies before doing away with the ABM Treaty. On the other, the administration has made clear its position that a missile defense system will be deployed as soon as possible.

It is no wonder that Russia and our European allies are confused as to whether we are consulting with them on the future of the ABM Treaty, or we are simply informing them as to what the future of the ABM Treaty will be. We must listen to our allies, and take their comments seriously. The end result of the discussions with Russia, China, and our European allies should be an understanding of how to preserve our national security, not a scheme to gain acceptance from those countries of our plan to rush forward with the deployment of an antimissile system at the earliest possible date.

What's more, Secretary of State Colin Powell said this past weekend that the president may unilaterally abandon the ABM Treaty as soon as it conflicts with our testing activities. According to the recently released Pentagon report on missile defense, however, the currently scheduled tests on antimissile systems will not conflict with the ABM Treaty in 2002, and there is no conflict anticipated in 2003. Why, therefore, is there a rush to amend or do away with the ABM Treaty? Who is to say that there will not be additional test failures in the next two and a half years that will further push back the test schedule, as well as potential conflicts with the ABM Treaty?

There is also the issue of the high cost of building a national missile defense system. This year, the United States will spend $4.3 billion on all the various programs related to missile defense. From 1962 to today, the Brookings Institution estimated that we have spent $99 billion, and I do not believe that for all that money, our national security has been increased one bit.

The Congressional Budget Office in an April 2000 report concluded that the most limited national missile defense system would cost $30 billion. This system could only hope to defend against a small number of unsophisticated missiles, such as a single missile launched from a rogue nation. If we hope to defend against the accidental launch of numerous, highly sophisticated missiles of the type that are now in Russia's arsenal, the Congressional Budget Office estimated that the cost will almost double, to $60 billion.

We have seen how these estimates work. They have only one way to go. That is always up.

However, that number may even be too low. This is what the Congressional Budget Office had to say in March 2001: "Those estimates from April 2000 may now be too low, however. A combination of delays in testing and efforts by the Clinton administration to reduce the program's technical risk (including a more challenging testing program) may have increased the funding requirements well beyond the levels included in this option [for national missile defense systems]." Is it any wonder that some critics believe that a workable national missile defense system will cost more than $120 billion?

Tell me. How does the administration expect to finance this missile defense system? The $1.35 trillion tax cut that the president signed into law last month is projected to consume 72 percent of the non–Social Security, non-Medicare surpluses over the next five years. In fact, under the budget resolution that was passed earlier this year, the Senate Budget Committee shows that the federal government is already projected to dip into the Medicare trust fund in fiscal years 2003 and 2004. The missile defense system envisioned by the administration would likely have us dipping into the Social Security trust funds as well—further jeopardizing the long-term solvency of both federal retirement programs. This is no way to provide for our nation's defense.

I must admit that I am also leery about committing additional vast sums to the Pentagon. I was the last man out of Vietnam—the last one. I mean to tell you, I supported President Johnson. I supported President Nixon to the hilt.

I have spoken before about the serious management problems in the Department of Defense. I am a strong supporter of the Department of Defense. When it came to Vietnam, I was a hawk—not just a Byrd but a hawk. I am not a Johnny-come-lately when it comes to our national defense.

As Chairman of the Appropriations Committee, I find it profoundly disturbing that the Department of Defense cannot account for the money that it spends, and does not know with any certainty what is in its inventory. These problems have been exposed in detail by the Department's own Inspector General, as well as the General Accounting Office. Ten years after

Congress passed the Chief Financial Officers Act of 1990, the Department of Defense has still not been able to pass an audit of its books. The Pentagon's books are in such disarray that outside experts cannot even begin an audit, much less reach a conclusion on one!

Although it does not directly relate to this issue of national missile defense, I was shocked by a report issued by the General Accounting Office last week on the Department of Defense's use of emergency funds intended to buy spare parts in 1999. Out of $1.1 billion appropriated in the Emergency Supplemental Appropriations Act for Fiscal Year 1999 to buy urgently needed spare parts, the GAO reported that the Pentagon could not provide the financial information to show that 92 percent of those funds were used as intended. This is incredible. This Senate passed that legislation to provide that money for spare parts. That is what they said they needed it for. That is what we appropriated it for. Congress gave the Department of Defense over a billion dollars to buy spare parts, which we were told were urgently needed, and we cannot even see the receipt!

If the Department of Defense cannot track $1 billion that it spent on an urgent need, I don't know how it could spend tens of billions of dollars on a missile defense system with any confidence that it is being spent wisely.

As a member of the Armed Services Committee and the Administrative Co-Chairman of the National Security Working Group, along with my colleague, Senator Cochran, who was the author of the National Missile Defense Act of 1999, I understand that ballistic missiles are a threat to the United States. I voted for the National Missile Defense Act of 1999, which stated that it is the policy of the United States to deploy a national missile defense system as soon as it is technologically possible. Now, I still support that act. But I also understand that an effective national missile defense system cannot be established through intent alone. Someone has said that the road to Sheol is paved with good intentions. Good intentions are not enough. I think there might be a way toward an effective missile defense system, and it is based on common sense. Engage our friends, and listen to our critics. Learn from the past, and invest wisely. Test carefully, and assess constantly. But most of all, avoid haste. We cannot afford to embark on a folly that could, if improperly managed, damage our national security, while costing billions of dollars.

ISSUE 15

WMD (WEAPONS OF MASS DESTRUCTION) PROLIFERATION

The development of nuclear weapons began in 1895 when German scientist Wilhelm Konrad Roentgen discovered X rays. Following his discovery, Marie and Pierre Curie discovered polonium in 1896 and radium in 1897. These discoveries gave rise to theories such as Albert Einstein's theory of relativity (1905). In 1921, American chemist H. D. Harkins announced the discovery of neutrons, and in 1933, Hungarian physicist Leo Szilard presented a theory of how a series of neutron collisions could produce a chain reaction that would release an enormous amount of energy. From 1942 to 1945, the first atomic bomb was developed by the secret Manhattan Project at Los Alamos, New Mexico. On August 6, 1945, an atomic bomb destroyed the Japanese city of Hiroshima. The destruction of Nagasaki by a second atomic bomb followed on August 9.

Today, the United States has about 9,600 nuclear weapons, considerably fewer than the 30,000 weapons it had at the height of the Cold War. About 2,600 of the current missiles are awaiting dismantlement. Other nations have thousands more. Although a series of ten major treaties, from the Limited Test Ban Treaty in 1963 to START (Strategic Arms Reduction Treaty) II in 1993, have been signed, the full arms reductions expected after the end of the Cold War have been stalled by a number of events, including the splintering of the former Soviet Union.

In the first selection for Issue 15, Jonathan Schell—the peace and disarmament correspondent for *The Nation* and the Harold Willens Peace Fellow at The Nation Institute—expresses his belief that the threat of nuclear arms will not disappear until all nations agree to renounce them. In the second selection for Issue 15, Ashton B. Carter—Assistant Secretary of Defense for International Security Policy during the Clinton administration—expresses the attitude of the United States toward nuclear proliferation.

DISCUSSION QUESTIONS

As you read the article by Schell and the speech by Carter, consider the following questions:

1. On what rational basis can the United States argue that other countries should reject nuclear weapons when America maintains the largest nuclear force in the world?
2. Are nuclear weapons of any practical use?
3. What is the best strategy for minimizing the proliferation of nuclear weapons to countries around the world?
4. Do Ashton Carter's remarks reveal that he really believes that the United States and its allies should continue to have nuclear weapons while other nations should not?

KEY WEB SITES

For more information on this topic, visit the following Web sites:

Nuclear Files.org (a project of the Nuclear Age Peace Foundation)
http://www.nuclearfiles.org

Nuclear Arms Race
http://www.pbs.org/wgbh/pages/amex/bomb

Nuclear Control Institute
http://www.nci.org

Nuclear Madness

Jonathan Schell

One day early in the month, I heard an astonishing announcement on the radio. I was on my way to get a cup of coffee before teaching a class in Middletown, Connecticut. I noticed that it was a few minutes to nine, and I decided to catch the top of the news. The station was the local NPR outlet, and the first thing I heard was the announcer saying, "At the Nuclear Nonproliferation Treaty conference in New York, the five major nuclear powers have announced their unequivocal commitment to eliminate nuclear weapons." No further detail was offered. Had the great turning point come? Had the United States and the other nuclear powers decided, after fifty-five years of living with the threat of nuclear annihilation, to disburden themselves and the world of this curse without limit?

Skepticism was in order. I went to the Internet, where, strangely, the news was not yet in evidence. Some phone calls revealed that the five would release a statement later in the afternoon. I permitted myself—perhaps a little willfully—a measure of hope. I pictured the five foreign ministers at a press conference announcing their historic change of heart and of policy. Even if the spectacular announcement was mainly rhetorical, I reflected, it would be a helpful benchmark in the coming fight for a world free of nuclear weapons. The news was worthy of the day around me: It was the peak of spring, the sun was shining, a cool breeze was blowing, the flowering trees were in full bloom. Was it possible that we were at last on our way to lifting the shadow that we had cast with our own human hands over all of this, over life on earth itself? And why not? Was it so implausible? Why, as the new century begins and ten years after the end of the Cold War, should we endure any longer the presence among us of 32,000 nuclear weapons, in the hands of growing ranks of nuclear powers? As soon as one imagined that the decision had been made, it all seemed perfectly obvious—a matter of elementary common sense, the bare minimum of sanity and decency.

Well, it turned out, of course, that my imaginings had indeed been dreams. In actuality, the commitment was nothing more than routine lip service at the NPT conference by the five powers, in which they "reiterate" their "unequivocal commitment" to the "ultimate" goals of "a complete

Jonathan Schell is *The Nation*'s peace and disarmament correspondent and the Harold Willens Peace Fellow at The Nation Institute.

This article is from *The Nation* 270, no. 21 (May 29, 2000). Copyright © 2000 The Nation Company L. P. Reprinted by permission.

elimination of nuclear weapons and a treaty on general and complete dis-armament. . . ." The word "reiterate" (signaling "nothing new here"), the in-clusion of the word "ultimate" (the internationally recognized code word for "never") and the coupling of nuclear abolition with the distant goal of "complete disarmament" gave the game away. There had been no change of heart, no change of policy. The nuclear powers were kicking dust in the world's eyes.

If anyone doubts this, they only have to read the language, made known to the world in the current issue of the *Bulletin of the Atomic Scientists*, of the "talking points" given U.S. officials for negotiations with Russia on the U.S. proposal to field a National Missile Defense. The Russians should not worry that NMD will erode their capacity to destroy the United States, the negotia-tor is supposed to say, because "both the United States of America and the Russian Federation now possess, and, as before, will possess under the terms of any possible future arms reduction agreements, large, diversified, viable ar-senals of strategic offensive weapons consisting of various types of ICBMs, submarine-launched ballistic missiles, and heavy bombers."

In other words, as far as the United States is concerned, the "unequivo-cal commitment" to nuclear abolition apparently is to be achieved without the help of "any possible future arms agreements." (The document did not say how the unequivocal commitment would be honored.) The actual U.S. pol-icy, which is in fact to keep its nuclear arsenal indefinitely, was also revealed by the U.S. response to a Russian proposal that in a potential START III agree-ment the sides reduce their arsenals to 1,500 strategic warheads each. No, the United States answered, we require—even in the context of mutual re-ductions—an arsenal of 2,500 nuclear warheads. Two thousand five hun-dred, evidently, is the point at which START stops. In case these statements were not clear enough, Deputy Secretary of Defense John Hamre gave the true U.S. position once and for all in a little-noticed statement he made at Of-futt Air Force Base in Nebraska: "Nuclear weapons are still the foundation of a superpower. That will never change."

It would be too simple, though, merely to accuse the United States of hypocrisy. The disorder is deeper. U.S. nuclear policy since the end of the Cold War has fallen into incoherence. At the root of the problem is the sev-erance of nuclear strategy from connection with any current political reali-ty. The cold war produced nuclear policies that were contradictory and self-destructive (envisioning, as they did, mutual assured destruction as the lodestar of strategy) but not incoherent. Whatever one thought about the policy of nuclear deterrence, it had the virtue of providing, for a time, an agreed-upon framework within which policymakers on both sides of the con-flict could assess the meaning of events—to judge what was "destabilizing" and what was stabilizing, what was provocative and what was reassuring. This consensus was lost with the end of the Cold War, which, of course, was the political context that lent deterrence whatever sense it had.

Now, administration policies are, on the one hand, still guided by deterrence, exactly as if the Cold War were continuing. That is why administration planners say that the reliance of the United States on nuclear weapons "will never change" and refuse even to consider reducing nuclear arsenals below some thousands of weapons. Yet, on the other hand, the administration does know that the Cold War is over, and that is why, with increasing frequency, it at the same time tries to persuade the world of its "unequivocal" commitment to nuclear abolition. It knows, too, that its own half-concealed determination to preserve nuclear arsenals indefinitely is a fatal flaw in U.S. efforts to stop nuclear proliferation, including the incipient arms race in South Asia, and that is another reason that, in public negotiations like the NPT review conference, Washington falsely asserts its readiness to live in a world without nuclear weapons.

Meanwhile, a new, third nuclear strategy, incompatible with both of the administration's contradictory commitments, has arisen. This is the resolve of the majority of Republicans in the Senate to protect the United States from nuclear war by developing antinuclear defenses. The defenses they envision go far beyond the limited protection against "rogue" states that the Clinton administration is trying to convince the Russians to accept by reminding them of Russia's overwhelming deterrent power. In the Republican vision, which harks back to President Reagan's hope for a space-based shield that would protect the United States against the Soviet arsenal, the goal of U.S. policy, in the words of a recent report by the U.S. Space Command called Vision for 2020, should be "dominating the space dimension of military operations to protect U.S. interests and investment" [see Karl Grossman and Judith Long, "Waging War in Space," December 27, 1999]. In such a world, plainly, nuclear deterrence would be a dead letter.

As if all this weren't chaotic enough, the Russians are pursuing a none-too-clear fourth vision. Fearful, after NATO expansion and the Kosovo war, of encroachment by the self-styled "only superpower," they have given nuclear weapons a new salience in their policy.

These four contradictory frameworks—the administration's policy of Cold War deterrence (*sans* Cold War), into which it somehow hopes to incorporate an NMD; the world's expectation and demand for the abolition of nuclear weapons, to which the administration pays lip service; the Republican vision of a solution to nuclear danger through antinuclear defenses, which would upend deterrence entirely; and a weakened Russia's resolve to preserve the nuclear parity won by the Soviet Union—are now on the verge of an incredibly complex multiple collision that has the potential to leave the arms-control agreements of the past forty years a shambles.

One more passage from the leaked American talking points for discussions with Russia on an NMD can serve as an illustration of the sort of unreal and senseless deliberation that is accompanying the slide toward disaster. The U.S. negotiators, having depicted in glowing terms the capacity of Russia to annihilate the United States (but why?), are encouraged to go on to point out to the Russians the great value of a launch-on-warning posture for their forces. "Furthermore," the paper helpfully notes, "it is highly unlikely that any enemy [i.e., the United States] would ever contemplate a first strike, since it would have to assume that Russian ICBMs and submarine-launched ballistic missiles/nuclear-powered ballistic missile submarines in port would be launched after tactical warning, which would neutralize the effectiveness of the assault."

A policy of tactical warning, commonly known as launch-on-warning, is the policy of responding to nuclear attack in the interval between the detection of an attack and the arrival of the bombs. Reliance upon it, by reducing decision time for Russian retaliation to less than five minutes, greatly increases the dangers of accidental attack on the United States. The deterioration of Russian command and control, including loss of some of its early-warning satellites, increases the danger of a mistaken launch. In order to fully grasp the irresponsibility of this advice to Russia, we must recall that NMD is as yet technically unproven. Yet in order to obtain this phantom protection, the administration is willing to recommend to Russia reliance on a hair-trigger posture for missiles that decidedly do exist and have the potential today to erase the United States from the face of the earth.

The mischief does not stop there. The peculiar revelation that the United States is counting on the might of Russia's nuclear forces to nullify the threat of American NMD reveals to the nations now assembled at the NPT conference in New York that U.S. professed interest in full nuclear disarmament is hollow and therefore notably increases the pressures that, since the proliferation in South Asia, have been threatening to tear the whole fabric of the NPT apart.

During the Cold War, the reasons for enduring nuclear peril were at least widely understood. What most characterizes the new nuclear dangers, by contrast, is a sort of cosmic pointlessness. The Clinton administration's unbudgeable devotion to nuclear deterrence with arsenals of thousands of weapons condemns the United States to apocalyptic peril without any political justification. A policy of mutual assured destruction with our avowed friend postcommunist Russia may or may not be as dangerous as mutual assured destruction with the Soviet Union, but it certainly is crazier. The missile defenses insisted upon by the Republican Senate are a $60 billion solution that doesn't work to a problem that doesn't exist. The new Russian emphasis on nuclear forces represents the attempted substitution of the baseless and useless image of a superpower for the lost reality of being one. The diplomatic clash of these fantasies is, however, producing dangers that are immense and real—dangers of accidental nuclear war, of uncontrolled nuclear proliferation, of multiple new arms races.

The only vision that offers serious hope of heading off these gratuitous disasters is the simple, clear, sensible goal now being advocated in New York by most of the 182 countries that, under the terms of the Nuclear Nonproliferation Treaty, have renounced nuclear weapons. That is also a goal to which the nuclear powers gave mere lip service in the rhetorical commitment that briefly brightened my day in Connecticut. Until that commitment is real—but not until then—nuclear danger is destined to increase.

Counterproliferation Initiative

Ashton B. Carter, Assistant Secretary of Defense for International Security Policy

Conference on Nuclear, Biological, and Chemical Weapons Proliferation
Washington, D.C.
May 23, 1996

I welcome this conference on nuclear, biological, and chemical [NBC] weapons proliferation. We must never fail to remember that these weapons pose the most serious challenges to the security of the United States—a fact that the ordinary citizen can easily overlook, since the headlines seem to be monopolized by other international security problems of fundamentally lesser importance. But NBC have the capacity to sweep everything else off the front page with a single incident.

Secretary of Defense [William J.] Perry signaled DOD's recognition of this fact with the recent publication of "Proliferation: Threat and Response." Like its Cold War predecessor, "Soviet Military Power," this publication provides authoritative unclassified information on the paramount security problem of its time. "Proliferation: Threat and Response" goes one step further: It also describes DOD's responses to this threat, from counterproliferation military capabilities to Cooperative Threat Reduction.

I am particularly pleased that this conference is honoring two pioneers of what Secretary of Defense Perry has termed "defense by other means" or "preventive defense"—Senators Sam Nunn and Dick Lugar.

I also applaud the inclusion of chemical weapons and above all biological weapons in the scope of the conference. Nuclear proliferation justifiably receives a lot of attention. But to those of us who must plan against the threats that are clearly here and now, the existence of CW [chemical weapons] and BW [biological weapons] programs in most theaters where U.S. forces would go into action and their ease of access to terrorists command equal attention. BW, in particular, are the great sleeping dragon.

Finally, I also applaud the soup-to-nuts coverage of this conference, with panels ranging from "denying access to technology" to "consequence management." This is very much in the spirit of counterproliferation, which seeks to address head-on the question, "What if proliferation?"

The theme of my presentation on DOD efforts can be summarized in two sentences: If you don't think the U.S.G. [U.S. government] is doing anything to combat NBC proliferation and terrorism, then you don't know what's going on. But if you think it's enough, you don't know the gravity of the threat and how much more could be done.

The topic of this panel is "Management of Crises Involving NBC." I will divide my remarks among three crises: war, terrorism, and the breakup of the former Soviet Union.

Our job in DOD is to fight and win wars should that become necessary. Therefore, our approach to NBC begins there—a DOD mission we term counterproliferation. The Counterproliferation Initiative grew out of the Bottom-up Review, which reoriented U.S. defense strategy from Cold War to major regional contingencies.

We realized that our likely opponents in MRCs possess NBC and ballistic missiles—not with some probability sometime in the future, but with probability here and now. Our duty to the taxpayer and our troops in this era is to ensure to the best of our ability that our forces will be able to prevail in future MRCs as handily as we prevailed against Saddam Hussein even if our opponents possess and use NBC and ballistic missiles. Doing so requires us to have conventional capabilities to deter and defeat proliferators—recognizing that our nuclear deterrent will always be a factor but should not be the only arrow in our quiver.

Let me be clear that preparing to deal with proliferation on the battlefield does not imply any downgrading in our efforts to prevent proliferation in the first place. Prevention is and will remain the top priority. And DOD is deeply involved in prevention, as I will detail below. But counterproliferation recognizes that prevention is not successful in all places at all times. Let me also be clear that our counterproliferation capabilities are being devised for winning MRCs, not for preemptive attack on proliferators, as some academics have speculated.

These counterproliferation capabilities range from better BW detectors to better protective suits and medical protection; from earth-penetrating munitions to theater missile defenses—our highest priority in our ballistic missile defense program; and from hardware to the vital exercising, training, and doctrine development without which this military mission cannot be accomplished.

If we are successful, the result of the CPI over time will be the enhancement of two capabilities: a war-winning combat capability for MRCs and a closely related capability for civil response to NBC that can be used to protect rear areas in a theater of conflict, the populations of coalition partners, or populations threatened by or affected by NBC terrorism. Deputy Secretary of Defense John White has recently established a counterproliferation council to coordinate all DOD counterproliferation activities.

In building these capabilities, we must rely on a strong technology base in the NBC fields. Our nuclear technology base is superb, largely because we still retain a nuclear deterrent that supports a solid base. In CW, our knowledge and technology base is shrinking after the end of the U.S. offensive CW program, though the costly program to eliminate CW stocks helps support a cadre of knowledgeable people, including local emergency response authorities. I am most concerned about our BW technology base, which is high in quality but small in size, since it supports only a defensive program.

DOD's NBC capabilities, especially those associated with the civil response capability—equipment, trained personnel, technical experts—can and will be made available for terrorist response. Overseas, DOD would follow the lead of the Department of State; domestically, DOD would follow the lead of the Department of Justice (normally through the FBI). The procedures for doing this are well worked out, and DOD provides for CW and BW threats the functional equivalent of the much publicized nuclear [emergency search] teams, as well as a much broader counterterrorism capability. We are working with the CIA and FBI to make our terrorism response teams better equipped and trained and to sensitize and train the broader counterterrorism community (and its vital intelligence support) to the particular problems posed by BW and CW.

Specifically, for crisis management, Special Operations Command can provide its special mission units to resolve terrorist incidents. These units are always on alert, are very familiar with BW and CW agents and effects, have state-of-the-art protective suits and masks, are immunized against some BW agents and are trained to render safe and dispose of BW and CW agents.

These SOCOM units are supported by a specialized chem/bio response unit consisting of an Army Technical escort unit providing search, sampling, disposal, and transportation of agents; and on-call teams from the Army's and Navy's laboratories and CW/BW commands for expert knowledge on the scene. For consequence management, DOD would provide through FEMA [Federal Emergency Management Agency] the capabilities of Army NBC defense units, together with military medical care capabilities and supplies. A number of initiatives exist for upgrading these capabilities as well as for strengthening their links to civilian first responders and foreign governments.

The breakup of the former Soviet Union has the potential to be the single most significant event in proliferation history. Two farsighted senators, both present at this conference, gave the U.S. government a valuable tool with which to confront this emergency: the Cooperative Threat Reduction, or Nunn-Lugar, program.

Congress has made available in the defense budget over $1.5 billion for CTR, dwarfing all other cooperative activities with the former Soviet Union, and today American project leaders, contractors, and their Russian, Ukrainian, Kazakstani and Belarusan colleagues are executing over thirty large engineering programs that directly reduce the threat to the United States. Two examples from many will suffice.

In two weeks, Secretary of Defense Perry and I will travel to Pervomaysk, Ukraine, where we will view the site of an SS-19 silo that Secretary Perry, Russian Defense Minister [Pavel] Grachev and Ukrainian Defense Minister [Valeriy] Shmarov blew up in January. The site will be planted with sunflowers—a local cash crop and a national flower of Ukraine—like the fields around it. In a short time, Ukrainian territory will be free of the 1,900 strategic nuclear weapons designed to destroy the United States with which it began its existence as an independent state.

In late 1994, a DOD-DOE [Department of Energy] team secretly packaged 600 kilograms of highly enriched uranium [HEU] in Kazakstan, loaded it aboard C-5 transports at Ust-Kamenogorsk airfield and flew with continuous midair refueling to Dover AFB [Air Force Base], Delaware. There, the HEU was transferred to special transports and driven to Oak Ridge, Tennessee, for safe and secure storage in a vault. Only in the last day of this eight-month effort did the leaks occur and the project become known to the public just a few hours before Secretaries Perry, [Secretary of State Warren] Christopher, and [Secretary of Energy Hazel] O'Leary announced it at the Pentagon.

Managing large engineering projects at U.S. taxpayers' expense in the strange and understandably chaotic environment of the newly independent [ex-Soviet] states was a task that DOD had never before undertaken and which took some learning. In January 1993, when I first had the opportunity to review the CTR program, it had been on the books for some time and had accumulated a bank account but little in the way of on-the-ground technical activity.

Interagency committees met and pronounced, but the tough job of working out cooperative programs that our NIS counterparts were willing to share in and then getting the necessary technical activity under way—including contracting according to the usual cumbersome rules—remained. I am pleased to say that DOD now knows how to execute these programs. We use integrating contractors. We contract in-country when doing so is competitive. Today, this vast program conducts hundreds of actions a day involving thousands of persons throughout the many time zones of the NIS.

None of this would be possible without the cooperation of our counterparts in Russia, Ukraine, Kazakstan, and Belarus. We have superb working relationships with almost all the involved ministries in the four countries. I would cite as an example our relationship with the Russian ministry of defense, responsible for warhead protection, control, and accounting, a vitally important and rapidly growing CTR program.

Despite the sensitivity of nuclear weapons and the understandable security consciousness of MOD officials, our relationship is mutually respectful and beneficial. The WPC&A program is embedded in a broader MOD-DOD relationship that extends to other, deadly serious joint pursuits like peacekeeping in Bosnia.

Finally, our ability to pursue CTR projects—and to pursue all the other programs discussed by panelists today—depends on the overall political relationship between the United States and the NIS, relationships which are very different from those of the early years of the program. The days of "I've come from Washington to assist you" are over. We are adapting accordingly.

I caution American commentators on threat reduction and materials protection, control, and accounting that money, good intentions and strong will on the part of the U.S. government are not enough: These are not our countries or our weapons and materials, and cooperation can be the scarce resource when it comes to getting results.

Finally, none of this is possible without the support of Congress and the American people. I must say that personally it is a puzzle to me why a program of such self-evident security value to the United States and which has such strong support from DOD and the administration requires such strong advocacy. But it does.

Many wrongly liken it to foreign aid, discounting its benefit for our security as well as for the security and benefit of the cooperating NIS countries. Others wish to hold threat reduction hostage to the resolution of other issues we have with Russia. Others seem to assume that the dangers addressed by CTR belong to the Cold War and will simply disappear by themselves. It is a great tribute to Senators Nunn and Lugar that they have so resolutely refuted these misapprehensions and that CTR continues to grow and strengthen.

CTR is busy reducing the threat, but there is more threat out there than we are now addressing. Let me therefore close by citing some examples of areas where growth and expansion of the U.S. effort through CTR or other programs would be valuable.

First and foremost, much more remains to be done on MPC&A with Russia's MINATOM [ministry of atomic energy]. Second, we have begun to broaden our focus from nuclear weapons to chemical and biological weapons, but our BW and CW threat reduction programs should grow. Third, efforts to stem smuggling and terrorism could usefully grow both in scale and in geographic scope. Fourth, we hope the START [Strategic Arms Reduction Talks] II treaty will be ratified by Russia's Duma [parliament] in coming months. Prompt implementation of that agreement is in the interests of both Russia and the United States.

I am grateful to the organizers of this conference and to Senators Nunn and Lugar for their attention to these possibilities for CTR in the future.

Issue 16

NATO Expansion

Military alliances seldom outlive the purpose behind their formation. The North Atlantic Treaty Organization [NATO] was formed in response to the threat Western democracies faced from the spreading influence of communism in the post-World War II era. As a collective security organization, committed to the mutual defense of its membership, the end of the Cold War seemingly brought its raison d'etre to an end. How ironic is it that NATO's mutual defense obligations have been called upon only once, in response to the September 11 attacks on the United States? NATO, whose security role seemed diminished in the mid-1990s, was given a new lease on life as it was seen as a vital partner in the new war on terrorism.

The rationale for the continued existence and expansion of NATO is laid out in the remarks of President George W. Bush on November 20, 2002, just prior to the beginning of the NATO Prague Summit, where membership was extended to seven new countries: Bulgaria, Estonia, Latvia, Lithuania, Romania, Slovakia, and Slovenia. Citing the traditional objective of promoting a strong and more united Europe, and the more recent need to resolutely face new dangers, President Bush endorsed the expansion of NATO as vital to the continued peace and prosperity of all democratic nations. Unstated was perhaps the strongest argument in support of NATO's continuance and its expansion. If not NATO, then what? As nature abhors a vacuum, many difficult questions of European security would need to be addressed if NATO were to depart from the scene.

Representative Dana Rohrabacher (R-CA) succinctly states the opposite side of the argument. NATO did its job. The communist threat to Europe is over. Let it die an honorable death rather that try to extend its mandate beyond what its membership is willing to unanimously accept. Employing

NATO as a social club to further promote the political and economic integration of Europe is both too costly and counterproductive to future U.S. and European interests.

Discussion Questions

As you read the speeches by President Bush and Representative Rohrabacher, consider the following questions:

1. Should NATO have a new role beyond its traditional one of guaranteeing the security of Europe? Specifically, what might its role be in the war against terrorism?
2. Has NATO expansion reached its limits? Should Russia ultimately be extended a membership invitation?
3. Does the United States need NATO to help advance its foreign and security objectives in the immediate future?

Key Web Sites

For more information on this topic, visit the following Web sites:

The Atlantic Council of the United States
http://www.acus.org
The North Atlantic Treaty Organization
http://www.nato.int
Institute on Global Conflict and Cooperation (IGCC)
http://www.igcc.ucsd.edu

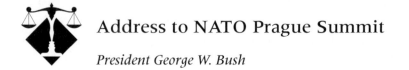

Address to NATO Prague Summit

President George W. Bush

Prague, Czech Republic
November 20, 2002

Thank you all very much for that warm welcome. It's an honor to be here in Prague, home to so much of Europe's history and culture, and the scene of so much courage in the service of freedom. . . .

. . .

This NATO summit that convenes tomorrow will be the first ever held at the capital of a Warsaw Pact. The days of the Warsaw Pact seem distant—they must seem to you; after all, the Warsaw Pact ended a half a lifetime ago for you. It was a dark and distant era. The years since have brought great challenge and great hope to all of the countries on this continent. And tomorrow in Prague we will have reached a decisive moment, and historic moment. For, tomorrow, we will invite new members into our alliance. It's a bold decision—to guarantee the freedom of millions of people.

At the summit, we'll make the most significant reforms in NATO since 1949—reforms which will allow our Alliance to effectively confront new dangers. And in the years to come, all of the nations of Europe will determine their place in world events. They will take up global responsibilities, or choose to live in isolation from the challenges of our time.

As for America, we made our choice. We are committed to work toward world peace, and we're committed to a close and permanent partnership with the nations of Europe. The Atlantic Alliance is America's most important global relationship. We're tied to Europe by history; we are tied to Europe by the wars of liberty we have fought and won together. We're joined by broad ties of trade. And America is bound to Europe by the deepest convictions of our common culture—our belief in the dignity of every life, and our belief in the power of conscience to move history.

And this city and town squares across the Czech Republic are monuments to Jan Hus who said this: "Stand in the truth you have learned, for it conquers all and is mighty to eternity." That ideal has given life to the Czech Republic, and it is shared by the republic I lead.

America believes that a strong, confident Europe is good for the world. We welcome the economic integration of Europe. We believe that integration will extend prosperity on both sides of the Atlantic. We welcome a democratic Russia as part of this new Europe, because a free and peaceful Europe will add to the security of this continent. We welcome the growing unity of

Europe in commerce and currency and military cooperation, which is closing a long history of rivalry and violence. This continent, wounded by Nazism and communism, is becoming peaceful and secure and democratic for the first time. And now that the countries of Europe are united in freedom they will no longer fight each other and bring war to the rest of the world.

Because America supports a more united Europe, we strongly support the enlargement of NATO, now and in the future. Every European democracy that seeks NATO membership and is ready to share in NATO's responsibilities should be welcome in our Alliance. The enlargement of NATO is good for all who join us. The standards for membership are high, and they encourage the hard work of political and economic and military reform.

And nations in the family of NATO, old or new, know this: Anyone who would choose you for an enemy also chooses us for an enemy. Never again in the face of aggression will you stand alone.

A larger NATO is good for Russia, as well. Later this week I will visit St. Petersburg. I will tell my friend, Vladimir Putin, and the Russian people that they, too, will gain from the security and stability of nations to Russia's west. Russia does not require a buffer zone of protection; it needs peaceful and prosperous neighbors who are also friends. We need a strong and democratic Russia as our friend and partner to face the next century's new challenges.

Through the NATO–Russia Council we must increase our cooperation with Russia for the security of all of us. Expansion of NATO also brings many advantages to the Alliance, itself. Every new member contributes military capabilities that add to our common security. We see this already in Afghanistan—for forces from Romania, Bulgaria, Estonia, Lithuania, Slovakia, and others have joined with sixteen NATO allies to help defeat global terror.

And every new member of our Alliance makes a contribution of character. Tomorrow, NATO grows larger. Tomorrow, the soul of Europe grows stronger. Members recently added to NATO and those invited to join bring greater clarity to the purposes of our Alliance, because they understand the lessons of the last century. Those with fresh memories of tyranny know the value of freedom. Those who have lived through a struggle of good against evil are never neutral between them. Czechs and Slovaks learned through the harsh experience of 1938, that when great democracies fail to confront danger, greater dangers follow. And the people of the Baltics learned that aggression left unchecked by the great democracies can rob millions of their liberty and their lives.

In Central and Eastern Europe the courage and moral vision of prisoners and exiles and priests and playwrights caused tyrants to fall. The spirit now sustains these nations through difficult reforms. And this spirit is needed in the councils of a new Europe.

Our NATO Alliance faces dangers very different from those it was formed to confront. Yet, never has our need for collective defense been more urgent.

The Soviet Union is gone, but freedom still has enemies. We're threatened by terrorism, bred within failed states; it's present within our own cities. We're threatened by the spread of chemical and biological and nuclear weapons which are produced by outlaw regimes and could be delivered either by missile or terrorist cell. For terrorists and terrorist states, every free nation—every free nation—is a potential target, including the free nations of Europe.

We're making progress on this, the first war of the twenty-first century. Today more than ninety nations are joined in a global coalition to defeat terror. We're sharing intelligence. We're freezing the assets of terror groups. We're pursuing the terrorists wherever they plot and train. And we're finding them and bringing them to justice, one person at a time.

Today the world is also uniting to answer the unique and urgent threat posed by Iraq. A dictator who has used weapons of mass destruction on his own people must not be allowed to produce or possess those weapons. We will not permit Saddam Hussein to blackmail and/or terrorize nations which love freedom.

Last week Saddam Hussein accepted UN inspectors. We've heard those pledges before and seen them violated time and time again. We now call an end to that game of deception and deceit and denial. Saddam Hussein has been given a very short time to declare completely and truthfully his arsenal of terror. Should he again deny that this arsenal exists, he will have entered his final stage with a lie. And deception this time will not be tolerated. Delay and defiance will invite the severest of consequences.

America's goal, the world's goal is more than the return of inspectors to Iraq. Our goal is to secure the peace through the comprehensive and verified disarmament of Iraq's weapons of mass destruction. Voluntary, or by force, that goal will be achieved.

To meet all of this century's emerging threats from terror camps in remote regions to hidden laboratories of outlaw regimes, NATO must develop new military capabilities. NATO forces must become better able to fight side by side. Those forces must be more mobile and more swiftly deployed. The allies need more special operations forces, better precision strike capabilities, and more modern command structures.

Few NATO members will have state-of-the-art capabilities in all of these areas; I recognize that. But every nation should develop some. Ours is a military alliance, and every member must make a military contribution to that alliance. For some allies, this will require higher defense spending. For all of us, it will require more effective defense spending, with each nation adding the tools and technologies to fight and win a new kind of war.

And because many threats to the NATO members come from outside of Europe, NATO forces must be organized to operate outside of Europe. When forces were needed quickly in Afghanistan, NATO's options were limited. We must build new capabilities and we must strengthen our will to use those capabilities.

The United States proposes the creation of a NATO response force that will bring together well-equipped, highly ready air, ground, and sea forces from NATO allies—old and new. This force will be prepared to deploy on short notice wherever it is needed. A NATO response force will take time to create and we should begin that effort here in Prague.

Yet, security against new threats requires more than just new capabilities. Free nations must accept our shared obligations to keep the peace. The world needs the nations of this continent to be active in the defense of freedom; not inward-looking or isolated by indifference. Ignoring dangers or excusing aggression may temporarily avert conflict, but they don't bring true peace.

International stability must be actively defended, and all nations that benefit from that stability have a duty to help. In this noble work, America and the strong democracies of Europe need each other, each playing our full and responsible role. The good we can do together is far greater than the good we can do apart.

Great evil is stirring in the world. Many of the young here are coming up in a different world, different era, a different time, a different series of threats. We face perils we've never thought about, perils we've never seen before. But they're dangerous. They're just as dangerous as those perils that your fathers and mothers and grandfathers and grandmothers faced.

The hopes of all mankind depend on the courage and the unity of great democracies. In this hour of challenge, NATO will do what it has done before: We will stand firm against the enemies of freedom, and we'll prevail.

The transatlantic ties of Europe and America have met every test of history, and we intend to again. U-boats could not divide us. The threats and stand-offs of the Cold War did not make us weary. The commitment of my nation to Europe is found in the carefully tended graves of young Americans who died for this continent's freedom. That commitment is shown by the thousands in uniforms still serving here, from the Balkans to Bavaria, still willing to make the ultimate sacrifice for this continent's future.

For a hundred years place names of Europe have often stood for conflict and tragedy and loss. Single words evoke sad and bitter experience—Verdun, Munich, Stalingrad, Dresden, Nuremberg, and Yalta. We have no power to rewrite history. We do have the power to write a different story for our time.

When future generations look back at this moment and speak of Prague and what we did here, that name will stand for hope. In Prague, young democracies will gain new security; a grand Alliance will gather a strength and find new purpose. And America and Europe will renew the historic friendship that still keeps the peace of the world.

Thank you for your interest. May God bless you all.

NATO Deserves to Pass On

Representative Dana Rohrabacher

U.S. House of Representatives, Washington, D.C.
November 7, 2001

Mr. Speaker, I rise . . . in opposition to the underlying legislation. . . .

Now let us talk about NATO. NATO will not be missed. NATO has done its job. NATO deserves to pass on, because NATO accomplished its mission and now it deserves to dissolve.

We called on this organization, we created this organization back when there was a major Soviet threat to invade Western Europe. Thus we created NATO in order to deter war, not to waste money, because that money was necessary at the time. But instead, to deter a Soviet invasion of Western Europe. It did its job, and it did its job well.

During the Cold War, it served to stand guard and to deter attack and that attack was deterred; and it saved lives and it helped us come to the end of the Cold War. But the Cold War is over. The price we paid for NATO in the tens of billions of dollars was worth it back then. It is not worth it now.

In fact, what NATO today is is nothing more than a subsidy for the defense of Western Europe and in Europe as a whole. They can afford, our European friends can afford to pay for their own defense now. When NATO was first created, they were coming out of World War II, their economies were in a shambles; and yes, we stepped forward to protect the world against communism, just as we stepped forward to protect the world against Japanese militarism and Nazism. We can be proud of that, and we can be proud of the role NATO played. But today, the purpose NATO was created for has passed away, and the Europeans can afford to pay for their own defense. By staying in NATO, we are going to continually be involved in missions like those in Kosovo and Bosnia, right in our European friends' backyard, and we end up paying a major portion of that battle in Kosovo and Bosnia. That makes no sense.

Our European friends are richer than we are. The European governments have many, many more services for their people than we have for our own people, because we are spending that money trying to police the world. By keeping NATO going, it just reinforces that policy that the United States is going to be the policeman of the world.

Furthermore, by expanding NATO the way this bill is proposing, we are slapping Russia in the face. Come on. Come on, now. NATO was established to counter the Soviet Union, and now the Russians have done what we always wanted them to do: Cast off this dictatorship. And what do we do? We try to expand this military alliance right into their front yard. That is wrong.

Russia has disbanded the Warsaw Pact; it is trying to be democratic. President Putin is making efforts. In fact, he was the first one to call President Bush to offer his help when America was attacked on September 11. We should not be putting that type of pressure on a democratic Russia. We should, instead, be reinforcing that we are their friends and no longer consider Russia a threat. If Russia ever goes back to its old ways, we can reconfigure that. I would just say NATO is not helping us as much as they should in this current crisis, so why should we continue subsidizing our European friends?

PART IV

INTERNATIONAL POLITICAL ECONOMY

ISSUE 17

PROTEST MOVEMENTS AND THE WTO

When the World Trade Organization (WTO) met in Seattle in November of 1999, Mike Dolan and several thousand associates were ready to protest. Dolan, Field Director of Global Trade Watch, a branch of Ralph Nader's Public Citizen organization, spent a lot of time and energy talking to groups of disaffected individuals throughout the Seattle area, trying to find allies in his quest to get WTO's and the public's attention in an attempt to change WTO policies. What is the WTO and why is Dolan unhappy with it?

The WTO is an international organization comprised of national governments that, at least in theory, is dedicated to creating new opportunities for international trade. The Seattle meeting hosted nearly 5,000 delegates from about 150 countries who came together to discuss such issues as global investment by corporations, eliminating subsidies that give companies in some countries advantages over companies elsewhere, and reducing tariffs, which are taxes applied to goods as they cross international boundaries. Despite problems, the WTO and its predecessor have traditionally supported the goal of free trade because it increases economic competition, which drives down prices, and ends up creating more jobs than it eliminates.

Why, then, are Dolan and his fellow protesters unhappy? According to Dolan, the WTO creates arrangements that benefit large transnational corporations at the expense of everyone else. On a binge of greed, it is argued, these corporations destroy the environment while leaving the economies of developing nations in shambles. Among the groups most actively involved in the protest are longshoremen and other labor unions, Greenpeace and other environmental organizations, and socialists and other opponents to capitalism from around the world. Armed with smoke bombs and spray paint, the protesters were hoping for an opportunity to bring their case before the world via the news media.

In the first selection for Issue 17, Joseph S. Nye, Jr., Dean of Harvard University's Kennedy School of Government, attempts to find a way to resolve disputes about globalization and to establish means of mitigating the injustices it creates. The second selection for Issue 17 is a statement by Public Citizen (an advocacy group) that explains the protesters' demands and objectives.

DISCUSSION QUESTIONS

As you read the articles by Nye and Public Citizen, consider the following questions:

1. Who is helped most by globalization? Who is hurt most?
2. To what extent is globalization inevitable?
3. Can globalization be controlled, and can its negative effects be mitigated?

KEY WEB SITES

For more information on this topic, visit the following Web sites:

World Trade Organization
www.wto.org

Protest.net
http://www.protest.net

WTO Action.org
http://www.wtoaction.org

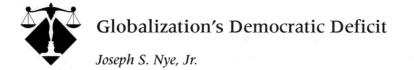

Globalization's Democratic Deficit

Joseph S. Nye, Jr.

Seattle; Washington, D.C.; Prague; Quebec City. It is becoming difficult for international economic organizations to meet without attracting crowds of protesters decrying globalization. These protesters are a diverse lot, coming mainly from rich countries, and their coalition has not always been internally consistent. They have included trade unionists worried about losing jobs and students who want to help the underdeveloped world gain them, environmentalists concerned about ecological degradation and anarchists who object to all forms of international regulation. Some protesters claim to represent poor countries but simultaneously defend agricultural protectionism in wealthy countries. Some reject corporate capitalism, whereas others accept the benefits of international markets but worry that globalization is destroying democracy.

Of all their complaints, this last concern is key. Protest organizers such as Lori Wallach attributed half the success of the Seattle Coalition to "the notion that the democracy deficit in the global economy is neither necessary nor acceptable." For globalization's supporters, accordingly, finding some way to address its perceived democratic deficit should become a high priority.

IT'S A SMALL WORLD

Globalization, defined as networks of interdependence at worldwide distances, is not new. Nor is it just economic. Markets have spread and tied people together, but environmental, military, social, and political interdependence have also increased. If the current political backlash against globalization were to lead to a rash of protectionist policies, it might slow or even reverse the world's economic integration—as has happened at times in the past—even as global warming or the spread of the AIDS virus continued apace. It would be ironic if current protests curtailed the positive aspects of globalization while leaving the negative dimensions untouched.

Joseph S. Nye, Jr., is Dean of Harvard University's Kennedy School of Government. This article draws on his address to the March 2001 meeting of the Trilateral Commission in London and on his work with Robert O. Keohane in the recent book *Governance in a Globalizing World*.

This article is from *Foreign Affairs* 80, no. 4 (July/August 2001). Reprinted by permission of *Foreign Affairs*. Copyright 2001 by the Council on Foreign Relations, Inc.

Markets have unequal effects, and the inequality they produce can have powerful political consequences. But the cliche that markets always make the rich richer and the poor poorer is simply not true. Globalization, for example, has improved the lot of hundreds of millions of poor people around the world. Poverty can be reduced even when inequality increases. And in some cases inequality can even decrease. The economic gap between South Korea and industrialized countries, for example, has diminished in part because of global markets. No poor country, meanwhile, has ever become rich by isolating itself from global markets, although North Korea and Myanmar have impoverished themselves by doing so. Economic globalization, in short, may be a necessary, though not sufficient, condition for combating poverty.

The complexities of globalization have led to calls for a global institutional response. Although a hierarchical world government is neither feasible nor desirable, many forms of global governance and methods of managing common affairs already exist and can be expanded. Hundreds of organizations now regulate the global dimensions of trade, telecommunications, civil aviation, health, the environment, meteorology, and many other issues.

Antiglobalization protesters complain that international institutions are illegitimate because they are undemocratic. But the existing global institutions are quite weak and hardly threatening. Even the much-maligned World Trade Organization (WTO) has only a small budget and staff. Moreover, unlike self-appointed nongovernmental organizations (NGOs), international institutions tend to be highly responsive to national governments and can thus claim some real, if indirect, democratic legitimacy. International economic institutions, moreover, merely facilitate cooperation among member states and derive some authority from their efficacy.

Even so, in a world of transnational politics where democracy has become the touchstone of legitimacy, these arguments probably will not be enough to protect any but the most technical organizations from attack. International institutions may be weak, but their rules and resources can have powerful effects. The protesters, moreover, make some valid points. Not all member states of international organizations are themselves democratic. Long lines of delegation from multiple governments, combined with a lack of transparency, often weaken accountability. And although the organizations may be agents of states, they often represent only certain parts of those states. Thus trade ministers attend WTO meetings, finance ministers attend the meetings of the International Monetary Fund (IMF), and central bankers meet at the Bank for International Settlements in Basel. To outsiders, even within the same government, these institutions can look like closed and secretive clubs. Increasing the perceived legitimacy of international governance is therefore an important objective and requires three things: greater clarity about democracy, a richer understanding of accountability, and a willingness to experiment.

WE, THE PEOPLE

Democracy requires government by officials who are accountable and removable by the majority of people in a jurisdiction, together with protections for individual and minority rights. But who are "we the people" in a world where political identity at the global level is so weak? "One state, one vote" is not democratic. By that formula, a citizen of the Maldive Islands would have a thousand times more voting power than would a citizen of China. On the other hand, treating the world as a single global constituency in which the majority ruled would mean that the more than 2 billion Chinese and Indians could usually get their way. (Ironically, such a world would be a nightmare for those antiglobalization NGOs that seek international environmental and labor standards, since such measures draw little support from Indian or Chinese officials.)

In a democratic system, minorities acquiesce to the will of the majority when they feel they are generally full-fledged participants in the larger community. There is little evidence, however, that such a strong sense of community exists at the global level today, or that it could soon be created. In its absence, the extension of domestic voting procedures to the global level makes little practical or normative sense. A stronger European Parliament may reduce the "democratic deficit" within a union of relatively homogeneous European states, but it is doubtful that such an institution makes sense for the world at large. Alfred, Lord Tennyson's "Parliament of man" made for great Victorian poetry, but it does not stand up to contemporary political analysis. Democracy, moreover, exists today only in certain well-ordered nation-states, and that condition is likely to change only slowly.

Still, governments can do several things to respond to the concerns about a global democratic deficit. First, they can try to design international institutions that preserve as much space as possible for domestic political processes to operate. In the WTO, for example, the procedures for settling disputes can intrude on domestic sovereignty, but a country can reject a judgment if it pays carefully limited compensation to the trade partners injured by its actions. And if a country does defect from its WTO trade agreements, the settlement procedure limits the kind of tit-for-tat downward spiral of retaliation that so devastated the world economy in the 1930s. In a sense, the procedure is like having a fuse in the electrical system of a house: Better the fuse blow than the house burn down. The danger with the WTO, therefore, is not that it prevents member states from accommodating domestic political choices but rather that members will be tempted to litigate too many disputes instead of resolving them through the more flexible route of political negotiations.

CLEARER CONNECTIONS

Better accountability can and should start at home. If people believe that WTO meetings do not adequately account for environmental standards, they can press their governments to include environment ministers or officials in their WTO delegations. Legislatures can hold hearings before or after meetings, and legislators can themselves become national delegates to various organizations.

Governments should also make clear that democratic accountability can be quite indirect. Accountability is often assured through means other than voting, even in well-functioning democracies. In the United States, for example, the Supreme Court and the Federal Reserve Board respond to elections indirectly through a long chain of delegation, and judges and government bankers are kept accountable by professional norms and standards, as well. There is no reason that indirect accountability cannot be consistent with democracy, or that international institutions such as the IMF and the World Bank should be held to a higher standard than are domestic institutions.

Increased transparency is also essential. In addition to voting, people in democracies debate issues using a variety of means, from letters to polls to protests. Interest groups and a free press play important roles in creating transparency in domestic democratic politics and can do so at the international level as well. NGOs are self-selected, not democratically elected, but they too can play a positive role in increasing transparency. They deserve a voice, but not a vote. For them to fill this role, they need information from and dialogue with international institutions. In some instances, such as judicial procedures or market interventions, it is unrealistic to provide information in advance, but records and justifications of decisions can later be disclosed for comment and criticism—as the Federal Reserve and the Supreme Court do in domestic politics. The same standards of transparency should be applied to NGOs themselves, perhaps encouraged by other NGOs such as Transparency International.

The private sector can also contribute to accountability. Private associations and codes, such as those established by the international chemical industry in the aftermath of the Bhopal disaster, can prevent a race to the bottom in standards. The practice of "naming and shaming" has helped consumers hold transnational firms accountable in the toy and apparel industries. And although people have unequal votes in markets, the aftermath of the Asian financial crisis may have led to more increases in transparency by corrupt governments than any formal agreements did. Open markets can help diminish the undemocratic power of local monopolies and reduce the power of entrenched and unresponsive government bureaucracies, particularly in countries where parliaments are weak. Moreover, efforts by investors to increase transparency and legal predictability can spill over to political institutions.

NEW DEMOCRATS

Rather than merely rejecting the poorly formulated arguments of the protesters, proponents of international institutions should experiment with ways to improve accountability. Transparency is essential, and international organizations can provide more access to their deliberations, even if after the fact. NGOs could be welcomed as observers (as the World Bank has done) or allowed to file "friend of the court" briefs in WTO dispute-settlement cases. In some cases, such as the Internet Corporation for Assigned Names and Numbers (which is incorporated as a nonprofit institution under the laws of California), experiments with direct voting for board members may prove fruitful, although the danger of their being taken over by well-organized interest groups remains a problem. Hybrid network organizations that combine governmental, intergovernmental, and nongovernmental representatives, such as the World Commission on Dams or UN Secretary-General Kofi Annan's Global Compact, are other avenues to explore. Assemblies of parliamentarians can also be associated with some organizations to hold hearings and receive information, even if not to vote. In the end, there is no single answer to the question of how to reconcile the necessary global institutions with democratic accountability. Highly technical organizations may be able to derive their legitimacy from their efficacy alone. But the more an institution deals with broad values, the more its democratic legitimacy becomes relevant. People concerned about democracy will need to think harder about norms and procedures for the governance of globalization. Neither denying the problem nor yielding to demagogues in the streets will do.

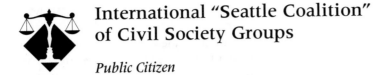

International "Seattle Coalition" of Civil Society Groups

Public Citizen

The international "Seattle Coalition" of civil society groups are launching a new global campaign to demand transformational changes to the international trade system and the corporate economic globalization that it is fueling. We are seeking to restore *checks and balances* among the international institutions and rules that are shaping the version of globalization we now face—one that serves special interests at the expense of the public interest. Currently, the pro-corporate dictates of the so-called "Bretton Woods" institutions (World Trade Organization, International Monetary Fund and World Bank) simply trump the pro-people rules of *existing* international labor, environmental, human rights, health, and other public interest standards.

After accomplishing the first half of its Seattle agenda of "WTO: No New Round, Turnaround," the Seattle Coalition is launching a new initiative to turn around the WTO's corporate managed trade rules so as to fight for a better set of comprehensive global rules that balance the public interest with commercial interests. To get this balance right, some of the existing rules and institutions need to be curbed, while others need to be bolstered. Our own system of government is based on such checks and balances, ensuring that no one special interest or branch of government is able to impose its will against the interests of the majority.

The fact is that there already is broad international agreement on the substance of labor, environmental, health, and human rights rules. The WTO must be cut back so that these already-agreed public interest standards can serve as a floor of conduct that no corporation can violate if it wants the benefits of global trade rules and market access. For instance, the International Labor Organization has core labor standards. There are over 300 multilateral environmental agreements on issues from toxics to air and water pollution to biodiversity and waste dumping. The World Health Organization conventions and the UN Charter on Human Rights provide many guarantees regarding access to medicine and food security. But, the WTO's backwards terms TRUMP all of these good international rules.

What we want is for countries to be free to prioritize these other values and goals. And, as long as a country treats domestic and foreign goods and investors the same, it's up to the country to decide the values it seeks for its domestic policies. So, if the United States bans child labor here then it must have the right to also forbid imported products made with child labor. If India decides that it wants to prioritize the World Health Organization treaty on access to essential medicines above the WTO's intellectual property rules to ensure lifesaving drugs are available, so be it—as long as it treats foreign firms the same way it treats its domestic firms.

This is a campaign about what we are FOR. We are a global movement for democracy and diversity. We believe that the people living with the results must make the decisions important to their lives and families. Inherently, this means that there will be differences in priorities and choices depending on the local values and cultures of different people and the level of development of their country. Yet, corporate globalization attempts to force us all worldwide to accept the same subjective, value-based priorities and policies. We are for internationalism—where *different* cultures, countries, and people trade and exchange goods and ideas and work together toward common goals—not for corporate economic globalization which imposes a one-size-fits-all model of economic and social policy worldwide.

This new campaign demands eleven transformational changes from the WTO. The strategy is quite straightforward: The WTO is like a crazed pro-corporate, anti-environment, anti-worker octopus hiding under the name of "free trade." The WTO has its many damaging arms prying into our domestic food safety, worker, environmental, and health safeguards and imposing on us and the whole world one-size-fits-all dictates on how our economy, social services, taxes, and more should be shaped. If the legitimate international trade rules—setting tariff levels for instance—are to be saved from the excesses of the WTO, then the WTO's excesses must be cut back.

Either the WTO will be forced to bend, or the WTO will be broken. We must separate the traditional trade principles that are appropriate for an international commercial regime from the WTO's new social and worker policy impositions. For instance, we must restore the right to decide for ourselves how much food safety protection we want or if we want to keep child labor products out of our market. As long as we enforce these values equally on domestic and foreign goods, there is no real trade issue. But, under current WTO rules, setting strong food safety standards or banning child labor products are *declared* to be illegal trade barriers. We must cut out these rules through which the WTO steps out of the trade bounds and tries to force us to change our values and policies to better suit big corporations. Unless we cut back WTO, it will unacceptably override our democracy and smother the diversity and differences in our world.

What sorts of changes are we demanding: Certain things should simply be kept outside of global commercial rules: WTO commodifies and provides for trade in everything from our essential social services to our very human genetic material. If a country decides it is against its morals or religion to patent life forms, then who is the WTO to override those values?

Now the WTO trumps all other international agreements. This must be reversed by adding a "savings clause" which makes clear that the International Labor Organization core labor standards, the Multilateral Environmental Agreements, the World Health Organization's treaties, for instance on access to essential medicines, and other internationally agreed public interest standards take precedent over WTO terms.

The WTO must allow countries to set their own level of food safety and environmental protection.

Over 1,000 citizen, labor, consumer, environmental, religious, women's, and development groups from 77 countries have signed on to the new campaign. The Turnaround Agenda espoused in the "WTO: Shrink or Sink" statement demands eleven fundamental changes to WTO's procedures and substantive rules. It was developed by hundreds of NGOs from many countries.

This approach is doable—if there is political will. Instead of adding new, controversial items to the WTO, we call for the WTO's most extreme excesses to be cut back. Despite six years of campaigning by the international labor movement, there has been fierce opposition by many developing country governments to adding labor and other standards to the WTO. With powerful China—a strong foe of labor standards in WTO—entering the WTO imminently, any hope for the previous approach is lost. In addition, the international environmental and consumer movements have not favored the "social charter" approach. They argue that it is unwise to concentrate too much power in any one institution and especially in one like WTO whose only purpose is to remove all "barriers" to commerce. Many citizens' movements in the rich and poor countries could work together on this approach.

The WTO's establishment dramatically expanded the issues covered by international commercial rules to include domestic policy on food and product safety, environmental protection, human rights, and government procurement. As a result, the WTO undermines nations' control of value-based decisions and the ability to set development and economic priorities and the *level* of health and environmental protection. It is this effective shift of decision making on non-trade matters away from democratically elected domestic bodies to the WTO that fuels the opposition.

"The WTO imposes a one-size-fits-all policy favored by corporations. It is essential to use this moment as an opportunity to change course and develop an alternative, humane, democratically accountable, and sustainable system of commerce that benefits all," the agenda states. "This process entails rolling back the power and authority of the WTO.

The WTO: "Shrink or Sink" coalition demands that their governments successfully push for eleven fundamental changes to the WTO:

1. Prioritize international agreements on labor and social rights and the environment.
2. No WTO expansion into new areas like investment, competition, government procurement, biotechnology, or tariff liberalization.

3. Protect basic social rights and needs by removing WTO constraints on policies critical to human or planetary welfare, such as WTO rules on constraining even non-discriminating government action concerning public access to food, water, social services, and regarding health and safety and animal protection.

4. Protect basic social services by excluding health, education, energy, and other basic services from international free trade rules.

5. Restore national patent protection by removing inappropriate corporate protection such as the Trade Related Intellectual Property Rights (TRIPS) Agreement from the WTO.

6. No patents on life, meaning WTO rules allowing patents of human cells, seeds, animal and plant varieties must be eliminated.

7. Food is a basic human right that should exempt measures to promote and protect food security and sovereignty, subsistence farming, humane farming, and sustainable agriculture from international free trade rules.

8. No forced investment liberalization or speculation enforcement by eliminating the Trade Related Investment Measures Agreement from the WTO to ensure policy options such as local content rules that allow increases in local capacity of productive sectors.

9. Fair Trade: special and differential treatment rights for developing countries must be recognized, expanded, and put into operation in the world trading system.

10. Democratize decision making by requiring the decision-making process in international commercial bodies to be democratic, transparent, and inclusive.

11. Dispute the dispute settlement system of WTO that enforces an illegitimate system of unfair rules using undemocratic procedures. Transformation of WTO requires more than transparency: The substantive rules and enforcement system also must be changed.

ISSUE 18

INTERNATIONAL MONEY LAUNDERING

For some people or organizations, it is useful to conceal the source of money that they have or want to transfer to another. Often this is money obtained through illegal activity or intended for an illegal purpose—perhaps involving drug runners, terrorist organizations, or dictators in developing countries who are draining the national treasury for their personal gain.

The process of concealing the source of such funds—known as "money laundering"—usually involves the transfer of funds from one country to another, often from one currency to another, and therefore becomes an international issue. To successfully launder money, it is crucial that the bank receiving funds from abroad maintain absolute confidentiality of transactions with the foreign client and not divulge the source of the money, particularly to law enforcement officials in the client's home country. For a bank to maintain this high level of confidentiality it is necessary, first, that the bank's home government permit such transactions and, second, that the government not cooperate with investigations by foreign governments.

Banking practices and government policies in some countries have been well suited to protecting bank clients. In the past, Swiss banks were famous for having accounts in which depositors could choose to be identified only by numbers—not names—and account information was divulged to no one. Some Caribbean and Pacific islands have been especially hospitable to money launderers. Government officials, sometimes profiting from the scheme personally, have permitted banking secrecy and have shielded their banks from law enforcement officials in other countries.

In recent years considerable international pressure has been directed toward these governments to force them to prohibit practices conducive to money laundering. In the first article for Issue 18, William F. Wechsler, a former U.S. Treasury official, describes the problem and the status of international efforts against money laundering, efforts that he strongly supports. The second article for Issue 18 is written by a banker in Antigua, a Caribbean island that has had a reputation as a tax haven and money-laundering center. The author, Brian Stuart-Young of Swiss American Bank Ltd., details recent actions that the Antigua government has taken, under threat of international sanctions, to halt questionable banking practices. In his account, previous money laundering techniques become apparent, as does resentment toward "arbitrary, unilateral, and high-handed" actions by industrialized nations to force countries like Antigua to become less inviting as targets of money launderers.

Discussion Questions

As you read the articles by Wechsler and Stuart-Young, consider the following questions:

1. What measures are necessary to substantially eliminate international money laundering?
2. Is eliminating or restricting money laundering worth the potential cost?
3. Is privacy in banking doomed?

Key Web Sites

For more information on this topic, visit the following Web sites:

Moneylaundering.com
www.moneylaundering.com

International Money Laundering Information Network
www.imolin.org

United Nations Office for Drug Control and Crime Prevention, Global Programme against Money Laundering
www.undcp.org

Follow the Money: Secrets and Lies

William F. Wechsler

As the international financial system has expanded, so too have financial abuses—money laundering, tax evasion, and rogue banking. Globalization is now changing the nature of these age-old problems, threatening to undermine U.S. diplomatic, economic, and even strategic interests. Multilateral efforts have begun to combat these abuses and have already achieved some impressive results. But time is running short for the Bush administration to act, and its decisions now will determine whether these multilateral efforts will continue.

Financial abuses have been around for as long as there have been finances to abuse. Money laundering and tax evasion are often viewed as complicated, boring matters hinging on the minutiae of tax codes and regulatory laws. But that image masks a destructive, often bloody reality. Drug cartels, arms traffickers, terrorist groups, and common criminal organizations use banks to launder their dirty money, making it appear as the product of legitimate business. Tax evaders structure transactions to hide their wealth from legitimate authorities, weakening national tax bases. Corrupt government officials exploit banks to facilitate their own misdeeds, breeding a lawless business culture and undermining public confidence in national financial systems. And the underregulated banking systems that facilitate these abuses have sparked financial meltdowns around the world.

The United States and many of its economic allies have long understood these threats and know that "following the money" can unearth big vulnerabilities in criminal syndicates. Over the years, their governments—remembering that Al Capone was put behind bars for tax evasion rather than murder—developed legal and regulatory regimes to help detect and deter financial abuses. Banks and other financial-service providers were regulated and supervised. Money laundering and tax evasion were criminalized, banks were required to identify and report suspicious transactions, company-incorporation and trust-formation laws were passed to encourage transparency, and law enforcement agencies developed specialized investigative skills.

As criminal organizations began to operate across international borders, national regulators and law enforcement agencies began to share information.

William F. Wechsler was Special Adviser to the U.S. Secretary of the Treasury from 1999 to 2001. He previously served as Director for Transnational Threats on the staff of the National Security Council and as Special Assistant to the Chairman of the Joint Chiefs of Staff.

This article is from *Foreign Affairs* 80, no. 4 (July/August 2001). Reprinted by permission of *Foreign Affairs*. Copyright 2001 by the Council on Foreign Relations, Inc.

In recent decades, international standards for financial transparency were established through such multilateral organizations as the Financial Action Task Force (FATF) and the Basel Committee on Banking Supervision. But these efforts were not truly global. For the most part, only wealthy countries with well-developed financial systems participated; smaller and less-developed countries were mainly absent from these discussions. This did not seem a problem, however, because most of the world's funds routinely passed through a small number of highly developed economies. In comparison, the banking systems in the developing and then-communist nations were exceedingly small and not globally integrated.

Even among nations with well-developed financial systems, however, a few countries took different approaches. Switzerland and the Cayman Islands, for example, were notoriously reluctant to disclose information on their secret bank accounts. Moreover, they shared certain features that made their banks attractive to money launderers and tax evaders: Both possessed stable political and economic environments, professional work forces, and—most important—physical proximity to more tightly regulated financial centers. A banker in London or Frankfurt needed only to take a brief plane ride with a suitcase full of cash to a colleague in Zurich. Similar trips were regularly made from New York City or Miami to Grand Cayman Island.

These services were enormously profitable. The Cayman Islands, with 35,000 inhabitants, saw its banking assets eventually exceed $670 billion. It became home to 570 banks and trust companies, 2,240 mutual funds, 500 captive insurance firms, and 45,000 offshore businesses. Switzerland, meanwhile, became preeminent in global asset management, controlling up to $2.3 trillion under management, more than half from foreign customers.

Under international pressure in recent years, however, Switzerland and the Cayman Islands have begun restricting their bank secrecy regimes. The Caymans also have begun (albeit slowly) to cooperate with foreign law enforcement, particularly with the United States. Switzerland still refuses to cooperate on international tax matters but is steadily improving its efforts against money laundering. Indeed, Swiss measures to combat money laundering are now superior to U.S. approaches in some areas.

But this is not the end of the story. Just as the international consensus among the leading financial centers began making real progress in the 1990s, another force emerged that undermined those efforts and raised a whole new set of problems: globalization.

MONEY FOR NOTHING

Thanks to globalization and advances in banking technologies, distant countries are now just a mouse-click away. The bank next door may be doing business halfway around the world. This development has opened up great opportunities for nations that were once too small, too bereft of natural resources, or too physically remote from the rest of the world to benefit significantly from the global economy. A remote, poor country can now make easy money by following the example of Tuvalu, a South Pacific nation that sold its Internet suffix ".TV" to an American company for $50 million (as well as a 20 percent stake in future revenues) and leases its telephone prefix, 688, to a telephone-sex operator for $1.5 million per year.

The lure of quick wealth has generated other ideas as well. For money launderers and tax evaders, the proximity of Switzerland and the Caymans to major financial centers is not as important as it once was. Other countries soon figured out that they too could attract dirty money just by passing a few laws. These laws included provisions to establish strict bank secrecy, criminalize the release of customer information, and bar international law-enforcement cooperation. Other laws involved licensing "brass plate" banks (which have neither physical presence nor personnel) and allowing the creation of anonymous companies and asset-protection trusts, some of which can give ownership to whomever happens to be holding the relevant documents at that moment. Some countries also created offshore regimes with special rules, including tax advantages, that are available only to foreign customers. Others established "economic citizenship" programs, which sell passports to anyone who can afford them, and Internet gambling licenses, which provide convenient cover to those who wish to move large amounts of money. These nations then worked to help their banks set up relationships with established banks elsewhere—an easy matter given modern banking and communications technologies. All that was left was to set up Internet sites touting the advantages of offshore banking, sit back, and watch the registration and licensing fees accumulate. Not surprisingly, almost none of these countries bothered to establish the financial supervisory institutions or examination mechanisms that even approached international standards.

The result was a vast proliferation of rogue banking. In the 1990s, remote South Pacific island nations including Nauru, Niue, and Vanuatu took this path to quick wealth. Small Caribbean nations such as Dominica, Antigua and Barbuda, and Grenada also joined in. From the Seychelles in the Indian Ocean to Bahrain in the Persian Gulf, a new breed of underregulated financial centers moved from the fringes of the international banking system to full integration into the global economy. Even wealthier countries such as Panama, Israel, Cyprus, and the Philippines—nations that had long-standing aspirations for international banking but inadequate measures to prevent money laundering—found themselves awash in questionable funds.

At the same time, many emerging markets were receiving previously unimaginable influxes of legitimate foreign investment, much of which was channeled through underregulated banking systems. Local financial markets were expanding wildly and attracting international bankers, for whom the prospective returns far outweighed the risks of doing business with such shaky institutions. The growth of international criminal organizations, drug cartels, and terrorist groups also strongly contributed to the proliferation of rogue banking. In turn, these underregulated financial institutions became prime conduits for funds flowing out of developing countries struggling with economic transition, crime, and corruption. Nowhere was this more evident than in the post-Soviet states. Funds from organized crime, government kickbacks, widespread tax evasion, the rape of natural resources, and old-fashioned legal capital flight all went to banks promising secrecy. Technological advances allowed rogue banking to flourish in a globalized world, but demand for no-questions-asked financial services drove the supply.

HIDE AND SEEK

Over time, U.S. officials realized that these developments presented a growing threat to American interests. Weak banking systems and poor supervision have long been recognized as an underlying cause of financial crises and economic downturns around the world. But not until the 1997 Asian financial crisis did policymakers begin to ask difficult questions about underregulated financial centers. These questions touched not only on the structural weaknesses revealed by the crisis—such as lack of transparency, distortions in resource allocations, and endemic corruption—but on the scale and direction of capital outflows once the crisis had emerged. Policymakers also wondered whether financial abuses might undermine the credibility and efficiency of the international financial system. This subject was put high on the agenda of the Financial Stability Forum (FSF), which the G-7 group of rich industrialized nations established after the 1997 crisis to help promote international financial stability, improve the functioning of markets, and reduce systemic risk.

The International Monetary Fund (IMF) and the Organization for Economic Cooperation and Development (OECD) have also begun to assess the extent and damage of financial abuses. For example, IMF Managing Director Michel Camdessus estimated in 1998 that money laundering represented two to five percent of global GDP—that is, between $800 billion and $2 trillion per year—an amount large enough to merit the attention of policymakers. Among the deleterious effects of such abuses, he noted, are inexplicable changes in money demand, greater risks to bank soundness, contamination of legal financial transactions, and greater volatility of international capital flows and exchange rates. The OECD came to similar conclusions that year, pointing out that harmful tax practices can distort trade and investment, erode national tax bases, and undermine the fairness of tax structures. Oxfam, an international antipoverty organization, has estimated that developing nations alone lose $50 billion each year in taxes due to these practices.

Because of globalization, even the strong U.S. economy can be affected by global financial abuses. Experts estimate that the U.S. Treasury loses $70 billion annually through offshore tax evasions by individuals. The result is a disproportionate tax burden on law-abiding citizens and fewer resources available for public spending or tax cuts. The 1999 scandal involving $7.5 billion of Russian funds moving illegally through the Bank of New York—with the complicity of senior bank officials—demonstrated that financial abuses from abroad can corrupt important U.S. institutions. And even without insider wrongdoing, U.S. banks are more vulnerable to abuse if wire transfers of dirty money have been bounced through underregulated jurisdictions before entering the United States—something increasingly easy to do.

As important as these economic effects are, however, they pale in comparison with the problems that global financial abuses present to U.S. law enforcement and national security. The Colombian black market peso exchange, for instance, is estimated to transmit $5 billion in drug money each year from the United States to Colombian drug traffickers through a complex series of trade and financial transactions. Domestic investigations of criminal finances are normally difficult enough, often requiring forensic accountants to sift through reams of bank transactions. But when a criminal's financial trail leads back to a foreign country that categorically refuses to share information, the investigation can end right there. With the globalization of the international banking system and the proliferation of underregulated foreign jurisdictions, U.S. law enforcement increasingly runs into this brick wall. Given their limited resources and previous bad experiences, U.S. investigators sometimes may not even attempt to seek information from some foreign countries.

Multinational crime networks rely increasingly on international financial mechanisms. In December 2000, U.S. intelligence and law enforcement agencies published the first *International Crime Threat Assessment*, which stressed the growing importance of "safe havens" for international criminal networks. Along with their utility in money laundering, these safe havens are especially useful as staging or transit areas for drugs, arms, and illegal immigrants. In Europe, German intelligence has identified Liechtenstein as a safe haven that some judges, politicians, bank managers, and investment advisers use for illegal financial transactions. Although Liechtenstein has vociferously denied these charges (published in 1999 in *Der Spiegel*) and successfully refuted some of the specific points made by the Germans, many experts believe that the report's general conclusions remain sound.

The value of safe havens has not been lost on terrorists such as Osama bin Ladin, who rose to prominence due not to his military exploits but to his ability to raise, manage, and move money for Afghan rebels in the 1980s. He still derives much of his authority and influence from the money under his control. He is said to have inherited about $300 million, and his Al-Qa'ida organization maintains legal and illegal enterprises, collects donations from supporters, and illicitly siphons funds from donations to Muslim charitable organizations. The funds are moved through a variety of mechanisms, including underregulated banks in the Middle East and elsewhere, then often transferred into better regulated institutions after the funds' origins have been suitably obscured. In the trial of those accused of bombing the U.S. embassies in Kenya and Tanzania, witnesses described Al-Qa'ida bank accounts in such disparate places as Dubai, Malaysia, Hong Kong, and London.

Financial abuses are also affecting regime changes around the world. Corruption has always been unpopular among voters. But recently, revelations of secret accounts held in underregulated banks have helped topple governments. In the Philippines, for instance, President Joseph Estrada was impeached and driven from office this past January after it was revealed that he had opened a $10 million trust account under the assumed name of "Jose Velarde." In Peru, President Alberto Fujimori tried to remain in office even as his intelligence chief and adviser, Vladimiro Montesinos, was caught bribing political officials before becoming a fugitive from justice. Fujimori even led a search team through the Peruvian jungle for the benefit of television cameras. It was only after Swiss authorities announced last November that they had found and frozen $70 million linked to Montesinos that Fujimori had to flee. In Europe, too, financial abuses are undermining politicians. Revelations of secret political slush funds in Liechtenstein ruined former German Chancellor Helmut Kohl's reputation; it seems almost everyone associated with the late French President François Mitterrand is now reeling from investigations into slush funds involving the formerly state-owned oil company Elf Aquitaine.

Rogue banking can even affect key U.S. strategic interests, such as Russian economic and political development. According to the Russian Central Bank, $74 billion was transferred from Russian banks to offshore accounts in 1998, the year of the ruble devaluation and the Russian financial meltdown; $70 billion of that went to accounts at banks chartered in Nauru. The following year, newspapers reported that Nauru's banks were involved in the $7.5 billion that illegally moved from Russia through the Bank of New York. A single bank registered in Nauru was identified as the ordering party for more than $3 billion of those funds. Only a few years earlier, Nauru had been less than a footnote in the global banking system—and suddenly it became a factor in U.S.-Russian relations.

Or take sanctions, one of Washington's most important tools for dealing with states such as Iraq and Yugoslavia. The proliferation of rogue banking has made it harder to enforce these measures. Iraqi leader Saddam Hussein has found enough ways around UN sanctions to keep his regime intact more than a decade after the Persian Gulf War, often using foreign banks that choose to look the other way. Former Yugoslav President Slobodan Milosevic, himself a former banker, used a complex web of financial safe havens (especially in Cyprus) to create offshore companies and accounts that helped him evade the bite of sanctions. One of Milosevic's schemes involved moving more than $1 billion through a single account in a Cypriot bank between 1991 and 1995—money that helped fund his war machine and cause untold misery.

To be certain, New York, London, and other highly developed, well-regulated financial centers are no strangers to money laundering. It is unavoidable that much of the world's dirty money flows through these financial centers, given their size, the architecture of the international banking system, and the desirability of placing criminal funds where they can be of most use. But the United States and its partners have long recognized this problem and have been taking increasingly aggressive actions to curb money laundering and other financial abuses. The new problem lies in clamping down on underregulated jurisdictions and the new threats they pose to U.S. interests—and that requires a new strategy.

THE NAME (AND SHAME) GAME

The Clinton administration realized that any new approach had to focus on stemming the proliferation of underregulated jurisdictions and tackling those jurisdictions that were already established. The strategy also had to recognize the limits of traditional law-enforcement and regulatory channels as well as the relative ineffectiveness of previous diplomatic efforts. Furthermore, any strategy had to be global and multilateral, since unilateral actions would only drive dirty money to the world's other major financial centers. Yet Washington could not afford to take the "bottom-up" approach of seeking a global consensus before taking action; if the debate were brought to the UN General Assembly, for example, nations with underregulated financial regimes would easily outvote those with a commitment to strong international standards. Finally, the strategy had to be politically tenable, given the varied U.S. interests in many nations with underregulated financial sectors.

Led by Treasury Secretary Lawrence Summers, the Clinton administration worked with its allies to develop a three-pronged strategy focused on rogue banking, money laundering, and tax evasion. Three multilateral organizations—the G-7's FSF, the FATF, and the OECD—were asked to address these issues separately but to proceed on similar timetables so that they could conclude their work before the G-7 summit in July 2000. The objective was to "name and shame" those nations that had developed underregulated financial centers and threaten appropriate countermeasures if the pressure was not sufficient. The three efforts each followed a "top-down" approach in which nations committed to regulatory and law enforcement regimes would establish international standards and evaluative criteria before engaging with those who lacked the commitment.

The FSF comprised finance ministers, central bankers, and supervisory officials from eleven nations with advanced financial systems. Also represented were international institutions such as the IMF and the Bank for International Settlements, regulatory bodies such as the Basel Committee on Banking Supervision and the International Organization of Securities Commissions, and committees of central bank experts such as the Committee on

Payment and Settlement Systems. The FSF aimed to compile a list of under-regulated offshore centers, decide how to respond to new international developments, and assess their potential to contribute to instability. To these ends, the FSF created a survey that asked banking, insurance, and securities supervisors in both onshore and offshore centers about offshore laws and supervisory practices, the level of resources devoted to supervision and international cooperation, and the degree of cooperation. The FSF then grouped offshore jurisdictions into three categories, from high quality to low quality.[1] Its most significant conclusion was that "offshore financial centers that are unable or unwilling to adhere to internationally accepted standards for supervision, cooperation, and information-sharing create a potential systemic threat to global financial stability." Finally, the FSF identified key supervisory standards, recommending that the IMF take charge of deciding how to assess adherence to these standards and proposing ways to enhance compliance.

For its part, the FATF was responsible for reviewing the countries that resisted global efforts to combat money laundering, both offshore and onshore. This was an expanded mandate for the group, which the G-7 had established in 1989 to set and evaluate international standards against money laundering and which has since grown to include twenty-nine members. The FATF developed twenty-five criteria for identifying uncooperative nations, focusing on bank regulation, customer identification, the reporting of suspicious activity, international cooperation, and the criminalization of money laundering. It then began to analyze the laws and practices of the twenty-nine nations identified as meriting review. In turn, these nations were allowed to provide their own input and to challenge FATF assessments. In June 2000, the FATF issued a concluding report that identified systemic problems in fifteen "noncooperative" jurisdictions and deficiencies in another fourteen.[2]

Meanwhile, the OECD was responsible for investigating tax evasion and establishing a consensus—ultimately opposed by only Switzerland and Luxembourg—on how to tackle harmful tax practices. The organization then set out to identify the tax havens that undermine other nations' tax bases. These havens, according to the OECD, shared four key factors: lack of transparency, lack of effective exchange of information, "ring-fencing" regimes (whereby foreign customers are subject to rules different from those applied to citizens), and no or low effective tax rates. (On the last point, however, the OECD made clear that low taxes alone do not make a country a tax haven. Low taxes are problematic only when combined with harmful tax practices.) Like the FATF, the OECD permitted the countries being reviewed to have their say in the assessment process. In June 2000, the OECD announced that six jurisdictions under review—Bermuda, the Cayman Islands, Cyprus, Malta, Mauritius, and San Marino—had committed to eliminate harmful tax practices by the end of 2005 and to embrace international tax standards. Others did not, however, and by the end of the month the OECD released a list of these tax havens.[3]

In July 2000, the G-7 finance ministers met and endorsed the recommendations of all three initiatives. More pointedly, they also issued formal advisories to their domestic financial institutions, informing them of the FATF actions against money-laundering havens and calling on those institutions to scrutinize transactions involving the nations on the FATF list. This unprecedented step was, in essence, a warning light from the ministers. They also threatened that if listed countries did not take immediate steps to fight money laundering, the G-7 would consider additional measures, such as restricting financial transactions with those jurisdictions and conditioning support from international financial institutions.

WINNING FRIENDS AND INFLUENCING PEOPLE

The G-7's threat was credible and the global reaction was immediate. Markets responded first: The day the FATF released its list, for instance, Standard & Poor's downgraded its rating for a top Liechtenstein bank. An industry reaction followed, as banks from G-7 nations began to review their relationships with banks from many of the listed countries. Numerous reports emerged of old ties being broken and new relationships being abandoned. Finally, there was a diplomatic reaction: Some of the listed countries started complaining about new difficulties in processing international wire transfers and in balancing accounts by settling their daily dollar transactions. After the initial predictable denunciations of the "naming and shaming" initiatives, many of the targeted countries began to make politically difficult pledges to bring their regimes up to international standards. More countries began to cooperate with the OECD. By the beginning of 2001, 32 of the 35 listed tax havens had sought further dialogue with the OECD. The Isle of Man, the Netherlands Antilles, and the Seychelles took the next step and signed commitments to eliminate harmful tax practices; others were working with the OECD to follow suit. The IMF and other international institutions also incorporated anti–money laundering measures into some of their country reviews and assessments.

Steeled by this reaction, key nations began to apply additional pressures where they held special influence. The French came down particularly hard on Monaco, and the British stepped up pressure on their dependencies in the Caribbean and in the English Channel. The European Union began difficult discussions with Luxembourg and Switzerland about their refusal to cooperate on tax matters. The United States abstained from a vote on an IMF program for the Philippines, which Manila interpreted as a sign of increasing concerns about money laundering. Washington also got tough on Panama. After Peru's Montesinos fled there, Panama told the United States that it would give him asylum only if the United States would rescind its anti–money laundering advisory—a deal that the United States quickly rebuffed.

As a result of this pressure, the short period since the report's publication has seen substantial progress. By this February, seven of the fifteen targets of FATF action—the Bahamas, the Cayman Islands, the Cook Islands, Israel, Liechtenstein, the Marshall Islands, and Panama—had completely reinvented their approaches to combating money laundering. For the first time ever, money laundering is a crime in Israel and customer identification is mandatory in the Cayman Islands. Rogue banks have been closed and new law enforcement investigations have begun. Although full implementation of the new laws is yet to be confirmed in most cases, many listed nations have already cooperated more in assisting investigations.

This policy's success offers several important lessons. First, multilateral efforts can be productive globally without requiring global consensus. Coalitions of the willing can successfully influence and enforce international standards, especially if the coalition partners have a predominant interest in and influence over the subject at hand. In this case, the coalition that drove the FATF, FSF, and OECD process represented the dominant players in the global financial system, so it could effectively set the rules. Second, globalization and the integration of world financial markets give policymakers new abilities to influence events on a global scale. When governments are able to harness market forces, they can incite foreign private actors to lobby their own governments to take action. Third, such multilateral actions are most effective when no special favors are given. During this process, some of the targeted countries urged the United States to protect their interests; at times, divisions emerged within the U.S. government about how Washington should handle sensitive cases such as Israel, Panama, and Russia. In the end, thanks primarily to Deputy Treasury Secretary Stuart Eizenstat, the United States played no diplomatic favorites. This fairness made it much easier for France and the United Kingdom to be equally tough. And fourth, the initiative showed that U.S. leadership was essential even in a multilateral setting. With perhaps the sole exception of France, no other country could apply anywhere near the same degree of diplomatic efforts and legal and regulatory resources to this project.

A WAY FORWARD

The work is far from over. The IMF and the World Bank still need to better incorporate measures to combat financial abuses into their regular programs. The OECD is working with its targeted countries to bring them closer into compliance with international standards—and it must decide what to do about countries that do not respond. The FATF is working to determine which countries have made enough progress toward full reform to be taken off the list; it is also reviewing additional countries to determine whether any should be added. Finally, both the FATF and the G-7 will have to confront the issue of countermeasures.

As successful as this process has been, not every targeted country has responded constructively. For instance, the United States received a letter from the president of Nauru soon after the FATF list's publication. He charged that, because Nauru was the "victim" of adverse publicity, business had taken a turn for the worse. Before Nauru could proceed with reforming its offshore financial regime, he concluded, it would need compensation for its losses—$10 million, to be exact.

Countries such as Nauru are primary targets for multilateral countermeasures. In February, the FATF identified three other states, along with Nauru, that had thus far done little or nothing of substance to improve their anti–money laundering regimes: Lebanon, the Philippines, and Russia. Lebanon has since rushed through new laws, and Russia has now introduced new legislation (after vetoes by former President Boris Yeltsin and broken promises by President Vladimir Putin). But the Bush administration must determine before the next G-7 summit in July whether it wants to support multilateral penalties if that progress is not adequate. These penalties could range from strengthened advisories to bilateral actions such as denying visas or withholding loans. They could even involve outright economic sanctions such as the wholesale restriction of financial transactions.

A number of other initiatives remain necessary to build on the success so far. The United States should continue to improve its own anti–money laundering regime, balancing law enforcement and privacy interests, so that it can continue to lead the world's efforts. All U.S. financial institutions, not just banks, should be brought into the U.S. anti–money laundering regime. Pockets of domestic underregulation, such as Delaware's loose oversight of company incorporation, need additional scrutiny. Overly burdensome regulations, such as the blanket requirement to report cash transactions over $10,000 (a level that has not changed since the 1970s), should be relaxed to balance stronger requirements elsewhere. Most important, Washington should find a better way to share its information on criminal foreign banks with the domestic financial industry to help prevent U.S. banks from being abused.

The United States and its allies should also begin engaging strategically important developing countries such as China, India, and South Africa on this subject. The G-7 should do much more to coordinate action to track funds stolen by former kleptocrats such as Nigeria's Sani Abacha and Indonesia's Suharto. The FATF has already begun to review and improve international standards against money laundering. This review should address tough questions: Should tax fraud formally be an offense under the money-laundering statutes? How can anti–money laundering provisions be applied to the growing Islamic banking system and underground banking mechanisms such as the hawala system, which caters to Middle Eastern and South Asian populations around the world? Lastly, the United States and other interested nations should view the "naming and shaming" efforts of the FATF, the FSF, and the OECD as models for other policy areas.

A Bush Backtrack?

It is perhaps too early to know how the Bush administration will confront abuses in the global financial system. But initial signs indicate that George W. Bush may be less interested in multilateral approaches and strong regulatory actions than his predecessors. Some law enforcement experts are already worried about the views of Bush's chief economic adviser, Lawrence Lindsey, who has long opposed the legislative foundations of the U.S. anti–money laundering regime. In a 1999 article in the *Financial Times*, for example, he challenged the regime's very constitutionality, arguing that the "current money-laundering enforcement practices are the kind of blanket search that the writers of the Constitution sought to prohibit."

Lindsey is correct on one point: the need to balance law enforcement interests against concerns over privacy. In recent years, several good proposals have emerged for modifying U.S. laws and regulations to better address legitimate privacy concerns—something moderates on both sides of this debate should embrace. Otherwise, Lindsey's positions are far from mainstream. He ignores the fact that efforts to balance enforcement and privacy interests have always been integral to U.S. banking laws and regulations. That understanding has resulted in a steady tradition of bipartisan support for efforts to prevent money laundering. Richard Nixon signed the Bank Secrecy Act in 1970 and established the modern regulatory framework. Ronald Reagan signed legislation in 1986 making money laundering a federal crime and expanding Nixon's framework. And George H.W. Bush led the G-7 initiative to create the FATF and established the Treasury Department's Financial Crimes Enforcement Network. Indeed, the same principles that concern Lindsey are central tenets of the international standards that the United States has been urging the rest of the world to adopt. If Washington backtracked from those tenets now—as Lindsey has advocated—it would seriously undermine a successful bipartisan effort.

Lindsey's views are not the only ones that cause concern, however. During his first two meetings with his G-7 counterparts in February and April, Treasury Secretary Paul O'Neill retreated from the previous U.S. position of strong support for the FATF and OECD initiatives, insisting they were now "under review." Then in May, he wrote in the *Washington Times* that he shares "many of the serious concerns that have been expressed recently about the direction of the OECD initiative" and that "the project is too broad and it is not in line with this administration's tax and economic priorities." He left the other finance ministers publicly questioning whether the United States would go along with the critical next step in these efforts: multilateral countermeasures against the most egregious havens for financial abuses.

In taking these positions, O'Neill was reflecting the views of a vocal, well-financed minority of Americans who oppose any multilateral discussions of tax issues for fear of an imaginary "global tax police"—the financial equivalent of UN black helicopters. These ideologues have targeted the

OECD initiative to combat harmful tax practices, arguing that it would somehow prevent the United States from lowering taxes at home. But nothing could be further from the truth. The OECD initiative clearly allows countries to lower taxes—indeed, to zero if they desire. Otherwise, places such as the Cayman Islands would have been listed as tax havens.

Meanwhile, O'Neill's insistence on a lengthy "review" of the OECD initiative has already seen predictable diplomatic consequences. Many countries on the OECD list immediately adopted a new confrontational approach. Rather than working with OECD technical experts to address clear concerns about transparency and information sharing, they now, in the words of one Antiguan official, "seek a global tax forum to resolve these issues, rather than one dominated by the OECD." Of course, if a "global forum" such as the UN General Assembly became the venue for establishing international standards, the votes of underregulators would easily carry the day. Money launderers and tax evaders around the world would then breathe a deep sigh of relief. This July, at the annual G-7 summit in Italy, the Bush administration's official approach will become clear. Notwithstanding Lindsey's previous positions or O'Neill's early statements, the Bush administration could still decide to continue the successful multilateral approach to combating money laundering, tax evasion, and rogue banking. Such a decision would be a victory of good policy over bad politics. But if the United States weakens or withdraws its support, the entire effort will be grievously—perhaps irreparably—harmed. If G-7 decisions about countermeasures are delayed in July, much of the diplomatic momentum will be lost. If no effective sanctions are imposed at all against the worst offenders, the credibility of the entire effort will be put in doubt. Those who would look to the Bush administration to take tough measures against international money laundering and tax evasion would then likely have to wait—at least until the next big money laundering scandal emerges.

NOTES

1. The FSF's "high quality" category included Dublin (Ireland), Guernsey, Hong Kong, the Isle of Man, Jersey, Luxembourg, Singapore, and Switzerland. The "middle quality" jurisdictions were Andorra, Bahrain, Barbados, Bermuda, Gibraltar, Labuan (Malaysia), Macau, and Monaco. The "low quality" group comprised Anguilla, Antigua and Barbuda, Aruba, the Bahamas, Belize, the British Virgin Islands, the Cayman Islands, the Cook Islands, Costa Rica, Cyprus, Lebanon, Liechtenstein, the Marshall Islands, Mauritius, Nauru, the Netherlands Antilles, Niue, Panama, St. Kitts and Nevis, St. Lucia, St. Vincent and the Grenadines, Samoa, the Seychelles, Turks and Caicos, and Vanuatu.
2. The FATF list of "noncooperative" jurisdictions included the Bahamas, the Cayman Islands, the Cook Islands, Dominica, Israel, Lebanon, Liechtenstein, the Marshall Islands, Nauru, Niue, Panama, the Philippines, Russia, St. Kitts and Nevis, and St. Vincent and the Grenadines. The jurisdictions that the FATF also reviewed were Antigua and Barbuda, Belize, Bermuda, the British Virgin Islands, Cyprus, Gibraltar, Guernsey, the Isle of Man, Jersey, Malta, Mauritius, Monaco, St. Lucia, and Samoa.

3. The OECD found the following jurisdictions to be tax havens: Andorra, Anguilla, Antigua and Barbuda, Aruba, the Bahamas, Bahrain, Barbados, Belize, the British Virgin Islands, the Cook Islands, Dominica, Gibraltar, Grenada, Guernsey, the Isle of Man, Jersey, Liberia, Liechtenstein, the Maldives, the Marshall Islands, Monaco, Montserrat, Nauru, the Netherlands Antilles, Niue, Panama, Samoa, St. Lucia, St. Kitts and Nevis, St. Vincent and the Grenadines, the Seychelles, Tonga, Turks and Caicos, the U.S. Virgin Islands, and Vanuatu.

Meeting International Standards: Antigua Restructures Its Offshore Financial Sector

Brian Stuart-Young

Offshore Financial Centres (OFCs) have been under intense pressure by several governments. These governments claim that the OFCs are a threat to the integrity of their economies because of money laundering including tax evasion. As a result, the G7 countries have initiated various types of reviews of several offshore centers. While the process has been arbitrary, unilateral, and high-handed, it has caused several jurisdictions to address the concerns expressed about their offshore financial sectors and to ensure that they comply with the highest international standards for banking and money laundering prevention policies.

Antigua and Barbuda is one of the countries that has paid serious attention to G7 reviews through the OECD programme on "harmful tax" and the FATF review of non-cooperating jurisdictions for the prevention of money laundering. Antigua had added impetus to address the concerns of these G7 programmes because in April 1999, the U.K. and U.S. governments imposed Financial Advisories on banking transactions from the offshore banks located in Antigua. The Advisories were imposed because both governments claimed that, in November 1998, Antigua introduced legislation which weakened its existing money laundering preventions laws.

Since the Advisories were imposed, Antigua and Barbuda has transformed its laws, strengthened its regulatory and supervisory machinery, and improved its capacity for law enforcement with regard to financial crimes. Indeed, it is true to say that today Antigua and Barbuda stands far ahead of many jurisdictions worldwide, including the U.K. and the United States, in terms of its laws and practices with respect to combating money laundering and other financial crime.

BACKGROUND

The original legislation governing the Antigua offshore jurisdiction is the International Business Corporations (IBC) Act of 1982. The first offshore financial institution to be established was Swiss American Bank, in 1983. Within fifteen years the number of offshore banks registered in Antigua exceeded fifty institutions. Regrettably, the legislation and regulatory infrastructure to

Brian Stuart-Young is the Managing Director of Swiss American Bank Ltd.

This article is from the Web site of the High Commission for Antigua and Barbuda <http://www.antigua-barbuda.com/financeinvstmnt/bodyoffshoresector.html>. Reprinted by permission.

govern banks did not keep pace with the Sector. In 1998 the government of Antigua and Barbuda undertook a major exercise to overhaul legislation for banking and money laundering prevention. The task was challenging and the closure of more than thirty offshore banks indicates the depth of the major re-organisation that took place.

Offshore banks are still licensed under the original IBC Act, but amendments to this Act as well as to the Money Laundering (Prevention) Act (MLPA) in 1999 and again in early 2000 have created a regulatory and compliance environment equal to, or stronger than, most international financial centres. The Government of Antigua and Barbuda received the support and cooperation of most of the private sector, which is generally committed to meeting or surpassing the international standards set for the Sector.

Regulatory Control

The original Act provided for the office of a Director to regulate IBCs, including those licensed for banking, trust, and insurance services. A senior civil servant in the Ministry of Finance, who already had a heavy burden of other responsibilities, usually carried out the function of regulator. To focus supervision more closely, the Government established a statutory authority in 1998, known as the International Financial Sector Authority (IFSA) and charged it with responsibilities to supervise and develop the sector. Concerns were later raised, however, that the IFSA depended upon the private sector for assistance. In response, the Government amended the legislation, to separate the IFSA's functions for supervision from any promotional activity. It also provided for a new International Financial Sector Regulatory Authority (IFSRA) that is fully independent of the private sector. The current board comprises senior public servants drawn from the Solicitor General's office, law enforcement, and foreign affairs.

Know Your Customer

Entrenched in the amended IBC Act, are strong "know your customer" requirements to govern the conduct of banks and their clients. No anonymous accounts can be established. Each account application must provide evidence of identity, place of residence, and other current banking relations. Also, customers cannot hide behind corporate veils. Banks require disclosure of true beneficial ownership and the true identity of directors and shareholders. It is the responsibility of banks to know their customers, so that in the event the Supervisory Authority requires information under the law, it can be made available.

Banking Secrecy

The confidentiality afforded to clients by banks will not provide a safe harbour to criminals. In fact, subject to the provisions of the Constitution, the provisions of the MLPA will stand as the governing Act, notwithstanding any obligation to secrecy or other restriction regarding the disclosure of information by any law or otherwise. Bank clients need not to be concerned with this issue. It is only relevant to those who are the subject of a criminal investigation involving the offense of money laundering and when the Court in Antigua has, on application by the competent Antiguan authority, ordered the disclosure of information. In other words, the privacy of customers' banking information remains fully confidential unless it can be established in a Court of competent jurisdiction that a crime has been committed.

NO CASH DEPOSIT

In April 1999, Antigua and Barbuda became the first, and possibly only, jurisdiction to ban the acceptance of cash or bearer negotiable instruments in any amounts. Antigua demonstrated its commitment to be pro-active against money laundering. Given that money laundering begins with the conversion of currency, and one of the concerns expressed has been that anonymous and illicit funds can be returned to their financial systems via correspondents for offshore banks, the Antigua prohibition is a positive and innovative action. And, while it does not prevent money laundering by other means of fund transfers, such other means allow for full identification of the transaction details.

TRANSACTION RECORD KEEPING

The IBC Act as amended requires banks to maintain full details of all transactions in relation to deposits and withdrawals, and to retain the information obtained by the regulation for a period of five years. As no offshore bank may serve as originator or recipient in the transfer of funds on behalf of a person who is not an account holder, all transactions should be easily traceable in the event of an enquiry by the Supervisory Authority or from a correspondent bank.

SUSPICIOUS ACTIVITY REPORTS

In keeping with international standards, offshore financial institutions are required under the MLPA as amended, to pay special attention to all complex, unusual, or large business transactions, whether completed or not, and to all unusual patterns of transactions and to insignificant but periodic transactions, which have no economic or lawful purpose. On reasonable suspicion that a transaction could institute or be related to money laundering, the bank is obligated to promptly report the suspicious transaction to the Supervisory Authority. The Act also requires banks to pay attention to relations and transactions with persons, including business and other financial institutions, from countries that have not adopted a comprehensive anti–money laundering programme.

INTERNATIONAL COOPERATION

In 1995, Antigua was amongst the first countries in the Caribbean region to sign a maritime law enforcement counter drug agreement and an updated extradition treaty with the U.S. Mutual Legal Assistance Treaties in criminal matters were signed with both the United States and the U.K. in 1996. The jurisdiction is a member of the Caribbean Financial Action Task Force (CFATF) and, as recently as March 2000, showed that it is in full compliance with all its requirements. Also in March 2000, Antigua became the first country to sign a commitment letter to the principals of the UN Offshore Forum (UNOF), which confirmed its government's agreement to adhere to the UN's minimum performance standards relating to banking practices, transparency rules, and international cooperation.

The cooperation provided under these various agreements and treaties is also supported under the MLPA. It allows for the Court or the Competent authority in Antigua to cooperate with the Court or other competent authority of another state, and to take appropriate measures to provide assistance in matters concerning money-laundering offences, provided the measures are in accordance with the MPLA and within the limits of their respective legal systems. Assistance includes providing original or certified copies of relevant documents and records, save that no information related to a client account held by a financial institution shall be disclosed unless the client is the subject of a criminal investigation involving the offense of money laundering and the Court has, on application by the competent authority, ordered the disclosure of the information.

Antigua has successfully cooperated with the authorities of the United States, the United Kingdom, Switzerland, Canada, Belgium, and Ukraine in enforcing the law against money laundering and drug traffickers. The role of the authorities in Antigua has been publicly acknowledged and praised by the governments of the United States, Belgium, Canada, and the Ukraine.

In the fiercely competitive environment of offshore centers, Antigua has placed emphasis on ensuring that the reputation of its centre and the quality of its regulation meet international standards. The various steps taken to address the concerns of the international community will benefit the offshore financial institutions and their clients, as well as their correspondent relations with other banks. The G7 countries are trying through various strategies to push a number of countries out of the competition in the international financial market. They will succeed only if these countries choose not to establish legal and regulatory frameworks that will prevent money laundering and other financial crimes. Antigua has made the decision to remain a strong competitor in the international financial market by maintaining a well-regulated sector in which financial institutions are committed to providing a secure environment for their clients, with full compliance to international standards.

ISSUE 19

CONDITIONALITY

"Conditionality" refers to changes in economic policy that national governments must agree to make in order to receive financial assistance from the International Monetary Fund (IMF) or World Bank. The guiding principle of this approach is that the economy should be driven by market forces, free of distorting government interference. This perspective on economic growth and development embodies what came to be known as the Washington Consensus, a view that developing countries should carefully control budget deficits, broaden the tax base, encourage foreign investment, and adopt similar free market policies. To find out more about the basic purposes of conditionality and how it functions in practice, go to the IMF Web site <www.imf.org> and consult the following IMF paper: *Conditionality in Fund-Supported Programs—Policy Issues*.

The first article for Issue 19 comes from the IMF and is an overview of the IMF's philosophy regarding conditionality. It not only sets out the basic principles by which that organization makes loans or restructures lending agreements, but also poses a number of questions regarding its efforts, in response to some of its critics, to streamline the process and make it less onerous on borrowing countries.

The second article for Issue 19, by Sidhesh Kaul, represents a perspective that regards the issue of conditionality as evidence of the continuing "economic subjugation" of borrower countries to the interests of international financial institutions. According to this argument, the economic policies that governments seeking assistance are compelled to adopt do not correct problems. Rather, these measures severely curtail the government's ability to manage its economy in the interests of its own people.

Discussion Questions

As you read the IMF article and the article by Kaul, consider the following questions:

1. Is Sidhesh Kaul correct in arguing that the monetary and budgetary conditions imposed on governments by the IMF and World Bank generally carry unacceptable social costs?
2. Has the IMF taken adequate measures recently to soften the criticism of its past practices?

Key Web Sites

For more information on this topic, visit the following Web sites:

International Monetary Fund
www.imf.org

World Bank
www.worldbank.org

Global Policy Forum
www.globalpolicy.org

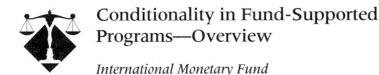

Conditionality in Fund-Supported Programs—Overview

International Monetary Fund

Policy Development and Review Department,
February 20, 2001

I. INTRODUCTION

1. The Fund's conditionality has been an important element in recent proposals to reform the international financial system. In particular, the Managing Director's intention to focus and streamline conditionality and give greater scope for national ownership—a central feature of his vision for the institution—was welcomed by the International Monetary and Financial Committee at its September 2000 meeting. The staff have prepared a set of papers on conditionality as the basis for a discussion by the Executive Board; their scope and coverage is set out in the Appendix to this paper. The present paper presents a brief overview of the issues: Section II reviews the expansion of conditionality over the past several years, and Section III discusses approaches to streamlining.

II. EXPERIENCE WITH CONDITIONALITY

2. Conditionality—the link between the approval or continuation of the Fund's financing and the implementation of specified elements of economic policy by the country receiving this financing—is a salient aspect of the Fund's involvement with its member countries. This link arises from the fact that the Fund's financing and policy adjustments by the country are intended to be two sides of a common response to external imbalances. Conditionality is intended to ensure that these two components are provided together: It provides safeguards to the Fund to ensure that successive tranches of financing are delivered only if key policies are on track, and assurances to the country that it will continue to receive the Fund's financing provided that it continues to implement the policies envisaged.

3. Conditionality has evolved substantially over the history of the Fund. Some element of policy conditionality has been attached to Fund financing since the mid-1950s, but the scope of conditionality has expanded, particularly since the early 1980s. In the process, tensions arose between the desire

to cover aspects of policy central to program objectives and the importance of minimizing intrusion into national decision-making processes. Against this background, the 1979 Guidelines on Conditionality underscored the principle of parsimony and the need to limit performance criteria to the minimum number needed to evaluate policy implementation. They also stressed that the Fund should pay due regard to the country's social and political objectives, economic priorities, and circumstances.[1]

4. The period since the Guidelines—and especially the past decade—has seen a major expansion of conditionality, particularly in the structural area. While structural measures were rarely an element in Fund-supported programs until the 1980s, by the 1990s almost all programs included some element of structural conditionality. The expansion of structural conditionality was also reflected in increasing numbers of performance criteria, structural benchmarks, and prior actions.[2]

5. These changes were the result of several forces. First, the Fund has over time placed increasing emphasis on economic growth as a policy objective, with the recognition that raising growth on a sustainable basis requires strengthening the supply side through structural reforms. This emphasis is reflected in the 1974 Board decision to establish the Extended Fund Facility (EFF) to address the situation of "an economy experiencing serious payments imbalance relating to structural maladjustments . . . or an economy characterized by slow growth and an inherently weak balance of payments position which prevents pursuit of an active development policy."[3] Growth became increasingly prominent as an objective in the 1980s, against the background of the poor growth record of the heavily indebted countries and mounting criticisms that Fund programs had focused excessively on austerity.

6. Second, the Fund became increasingly involved with different groups of countries in which structural reforms were viewed as a particularly important part of an overall policy package. In particular, with the establishment of the Structural Adjustment Facility (SAF) and later the Enhanced Structural Adjustment Facility (ESAF) in the 1980s, the Fund became increasingly involved in lending to low-income countries. The explicit purpose of these facilities was "the alleviation of structural imbalances and rigidities" in low-income developing countries, "many of which [had] suffered for many years from low rates of economic growth and declining per capita incomes."[4]

In addition, the Fund became extensively involved in assisting the transition economies after the breakdown of Communism in Europe in the early 1990s: In these countries, too, major structural reforms were at the heart of the economic agenda. In both these groups of countries, both external adjustment and growth were impeded by massive structural distortions, and it was believed—especially in light of early experience—that attempting to transfer resources to these countries without tackling these distortions would be largely futile. Structural reforms were also important in the Asian crisis countries for another reason: While these countries had achieved impressive growth, serious financial sector vulnerabilities were at the root of their financial crises, so reforms aimed at addressing these vulnerabilities were key to the restoration of confidence on a sustainable basis.

7. A third factor behind the expansion of structural conditionality was an increasing awareness that the monetary and fiscal policy objectives that are key to macroeconomic adjustment often themselves depend critically on structural conditions—including the removal of extensive market distortions and the establishment of the institutional underpinnings for effective policy making in a market economy. In many cases, this awareness reflected bitter experience with macroeconomic policy adjustments that failed to take root, or had adverse side effects, due to weak structural underpinnings. As a related point, an increasing body of experience began to suggest that fiscal sustainability depends on the composition of fiscal adjustment, and more fundamentally on reforms to strengthen revenue performance and remove various drains on the budget. The need for structural reforms to underpin macroeconomic policies is partly reflected in the fact that a large share of the Fund's conditionality has been in the core areas of fiscal policy, the financial sector, and the exchange and trade system, and that these areas account for much of the increase in structural conditionality over the past decade. Other areas in which conditionality has expanded, public enterprise reform and privatization and social security reform, also frequently have important implications for fiscal sustainability.

8. This change in the policy content of programs has gone hand in hand with a change in the modalities by which the Fund monitors policies. The 1979 Conditionality Guidelines envisaged that program monitoring would be mainly through performance criteria: A performance criterion is a condition that must be met for the Fund's financing to continue, unless the Board grants a waiver. The other main tool of conditionality, program reviews, was seen mainly as an occasion to set performance criteria beyond the first year of a program, and in rare cases to monitor policies where uncertainties precluded the setting of performance criteria. In recent years, however, program reviews have increased in importance as an opportunity for both backward- and forward-looking assessments of program implementation.

9. The increasing importance of reviews reflects, in part, greater uncertainty about key macroeconomic relationships in a world of high capital mobility; these circumstances exacerbate the difficulty of specifying a path of performance criteria a year ahead.[5] It also reflects the increasing role of structural reforms, which are often difficult to characterize quantitatively or even qualitatively with sufficient precision to be suitable as performance criteria. Moreover, many key structural reforms take considerable time to implement, making it important to find some way of tracking progress toward the ultimate objective. This has been done in many cases by using a set of structural benchmarks to map out a series of steps toward an overall policy result. A structural benchmark is different from a performance criterion in that failing

to achieve it would not by itself interrupt the Fund's financing. Performance relative to such benchmarks does, however, help inform the Board's assessment of progress on structural reforms during reviews and is bound, therefore, to influence the Board's decision on whether to complete a review. The increasing role of structural benchmarks is reflected in the fact that, behind the overall expansion of conditionality is a proliferation of structural benchmarks, and to a lesser extent of prior actions, compared with a much more modest increase in the number of performance criteria.

10. Along with this shift in monitoring techniques has come an increasing lack of clarity with regard to the boundaries of conditionality. Conditionality is that part of the authorities' policy program that is being monitored as the basis for decisions on the use of Fund resources: The defining question is, "If it's not done, can that stop the Fund's financing?" But in many cases, conditionality has been applied (or has been construed as applying) to reforms that are not really critical to the Fund's decision on whether to continue its financing. Moreover, a Letter of Intent (LOI) is often used to lay out the authorities' entire policy program; and in some cases, it even includes technical assistance advice and the policy priorities of other international financial institutions, regardless of whether the Fund has any intention to make these conditions for its financing.

11. Such murkiness on the boundaries gives the misleading impression that conditionality is all-encompassing. In some cases, this lack of clarity may serve the purposes of the authorities, Fund staff, and/or other international financial institutions, by lending the Fund's imprimatur to elements of the policy agenda whether or not they are at the core of the Fund's concerns; but this comes at the cost of hindering the emergence of a healthy policy debate within the country and of understanding of the role of each international institution in the country. The lack of clarity of the boundaries also has implications for the application of conditionality: In particular, unless the scope of program reviews is precisely delineated, it may not be clear, even within the Fund, which elements of the Letter of Intent can directly affect the completion of a review.

12. Both the increasing structural content of Fund-supported programs and the changing approach to program monitoring has taken place, at least in part, for good reasons. Nevertheless, it has prompted legitimate concerns: In particular, that the Fund is overstepping its mandate and core area of expertise, using its financial leverage to promote an extensive policy agenda and short-circuiting national decision-making processes. Moreover, the expansion of conditionality raises issues regarding its effectiveness. If conditionality is too comprehensive, it may undermine the authorities' assurances of purchase, since it increases the chance of failing to meet all conditions even when the policies that are critical to program objectives are actually on track. A proliferation of measures also has the potential to blur the Fund's focus on what is essential to ensuring that the program fulfills its purposes.

13. Concerns have also been voiced about whether recent Fund-supported programs have taken adequate account of the authorities' ability to muster political support for a multitude of policy changes at one time, as well as their capacity to implement these reforms. In some cases, these concerns may simply point to a need to provide technical assistance and/or elicit support from other international institutions, to guide the implementation of policies that are needed for the program to succeed. In other cases, however, conditionality may have been established on policies that were unlikely to be delivered, calling into question the realism of program design. In instances in which the minimum set of policies required to make a program viable may be beyond the authorities' political and administrative capacity to deliver, saying "no" may be a better choice, albeit often a very difficult one.

14. Finally, there are concerns that overly pervasive conditionality may detract from implementation of desirable policies by undermining the authorities' ownership of the program. It is the authorities who must implement policies, and it is mainly they and their citizens who live with the consequences of either action or inaction. Policies are not likely to be implemented in a sustainable way unless the authorities accept them as their own and unless the policies command sufficiently broad support within the country. Conditionality that is too pervasive may galvanize domestic opposition to the program as well as blurring the authorities' focus on what is essential. Experience suggests that the link between conditionality and program ownership is a complex one; in particular, there are cases in which high program ownership has gone hand in hand with extensive conditionality, as a government wishes to use a Fund program to strengthen its commitment to an ambitious set of domestically owned reforms. Nonetheless, the strong likelihood that a more focused approach to conditionality will enhance country ownership is an important motivation for streamlining.

III. Streamlining Conditionality

15. The issues highlighted in the previous section set the stage for consideration of how to streamline the Fund's conditionality. Streamlining requires:

Reassessing the scope of conditionality—i.e., *what* policies are to be covered by the Fund's conditionality—particularly in the structural areas

Choosing the appropriate degree of detail of conditionality—i.e., *how* these policies are to be monitored

Clarifying the boundaries between what is covered by conditionality and what is not, as well as between the Fund's conditionality and that of other institutions

16. There are two main approaches to curtailing the scope of structural conditionality. First, a higher threshold of relevance could be applied in deciding whether a particular policy action should be covered by conditionality in a

particular instance. The existing Guidelines on Conditionality prescribe that performance criteria should be limited to those needed to ensure the achievement of program objectives. In principle, this is a stricter test than, for instance, the macroeconomic relevance test applied in the context of surveillance.[6] It can also be compared with the criterion established for the Fund's involvement in governance issues—which is to be "guided by an assessment of whether poor governance would have significant current or potential impact on macroeconomic performance in the short and medium term."[7] But in practice, the test of macroeconomic criticality has been applied with considerable latitude. Accordingly, the Interim Guidance Note on Streamlining Structural Conditionality stresses the need to limit conditionality to those measures that are critical for the achievement of the program's macroeconomic objectives. The intention in applying a relatively strict criterion for the application of the Fund's conditionality is to change the mindset with which the staff, management, and the Board consider whether certain structural measures should be covered under conditionality, shifting from a presumption of comprehensiveness to a presumption of parsimony, and thus putting the burden of proof in each case on those who would argue for the inclusion of additional measures under conditionality.

17. A second aspect of streamlining is establishing a better division of labor with the World Bank and other involved multilateral and bilateral institutions and agencies. In the past, the Fund's cooperation with these institutions has not generally contributed to streamlining: On the contrary, in many cases policy measures important to these institutions' objectives have been included in the authorities' Letters of Intent and sometimes established as structural benchmarks or even performance criteria. Steps are now underway to establish a more efficient division of labor. Under the Poverty Reduction Strategy Paper (PRSP) framework for low-income countries supported by the Fund's Poverty Reduction and Growth Facility (PRGF), the Fund and Bank work closely together to support the implementation of a common country strategy and to focus their efforts on their respective areas of responsibility. Under this framework, the Fund will not normally establish conditionality outside its mandate and expertise except where these are essential to the country's fiscal and/or external targets. Instead, these structural and social areas will be covered by complementary World Bank–supported programs. The Bank's recent establishment of the Poverty Reduction Support Credit (PRSC) will facilitate this demarcation of responsibilities, *inter alia*, by better aligning the time-lines of the two institutions' financing. No such framework yet exists for middle-income countries, but greater efforts are being made to improve coordination between the Fund and the Bank in these operations, including through upstream consultation between the two staffs on emerging structural issues in individual programs. Where the Fund's conditionality still needs to cover some measures outside its core areas of competence, it is essential that the

authorities receive adequate advice (from the Bank or from other relevant institutions) on how to implement the agreed measures.

18. Another important aspect of streamlining is with regard to the degree of detail with which policies are monitored. Much of the proliferation of conditionality reflects the practice of mapping out a series of steps toward a particular policy outcome, in some instances using tools of conditionality such as structural benchmarks, in others by listing the individual steps in a policy matrix. For instance, in one case the introduction of a value-added tax involved nineteen structural benchmarks. In many cases, the intention has been to help guide policy implementation or to clarify the extent of progress that will be required in order to complete a review. But this degree of detail of conditionality creates the perception that the Fund is trying to micromanage the authorities' policy program, hampering their flexibility in choosing a different yet viable road to an agreed destination.

19. One solution to the perception of micromanagement would be to rely to an increasing degree on results-based conditionality: making the Fund's financing conditional on the achievement of specified outcomes—such as bank recapitalization, or improved tax enforcement, or foreign exchange market liberalization—rather than on the steps toward those outcomes. The main argument for this approach is that it would give the authorities greater flexibility in choosing the appropriate method of achieving agreed objectives. If the steps taken by the authorities fail to lead to the desired outcome, the program would need to be reassessed before the Fund's financing would be made available. Such a strategy would undermine the country's assurance of being able to draw on the Fund's resources, but would make the authorities responsible for adapting policies to changing circumstances to achieve the intended results. The Fund's traditional macroeconomic conditionality is already somewhere on the spectrum between actions- and results-based conditionality, as it involves intermediate targets—such as ceilings on central bank credit to government—whose outturns in practice reflect economic developments as well as the actions taken by the authorities.

20. While results-based conditionality may have greater applicability than at present, its main limitation is that many structural as well as macroeconomic results take considerable time to achieve. For instance, there are cases in which policy adjustments in a particular area are essential to program objectives, but are not likely to come to fruition until close to the end of the program or even later; in this instance, *ex post* conditionality would not safeguard the Fund's resources unless the Fund's financing were heavily back-loaded—which would bring it out of line with the country's financing needs.[8] This is the motivation for basing the Fund's financing on some assessment of progress toward key policy objectives, in the context of a review.

21. This raises the issue of what guides the Fund's assessment of progress in a review. Here, there are two main models: One is to establish a series of structural benchmarks that are intended to inform the process of assessing

progress at the time of a review. An alternative is a more free-form assessment, albeit based on considerations that should be discussed with the authorities *ex ante*. The latter approach gives the authorities greater flexibility in devising their own path toward an objective that is agreed to be essential, while also giving the Fund greater flexibility in deciding what information is relevant to its assessment of progress; its main drawback is that it gives the authorities less assurance of the conditions on which they will be able to use the Fund's resources. While recognizing this tradeoff, it is worth considering whether the current balance is the right one—or whether a more sparing use of structural benchmarks would be desirable.

22. There are two further issues in the use of structural benchmarks. First, even when an overall policy objective is critical to program objectives, there are cases in which fewer benchmarks would suffice to indicate the path that the authorities would be expected to follow: Each benchmark should pertain to a policy action that, while not decisive in itself, is nonetheless a significant and representative step. Second, there is a need for greater prioritization in the areas of policy covered by structural benchmarks: Conditionality should not be encumbered with structural benchmarks in cases in which the overall outcome is not critical to the program. Of course, the staff may offer useful advice in many areas (perhaps in the context of technical assistance) while eschewing any impression that the Fund's financing hinges on the authorities' acting on this advice.

23. As noted earlier, the scope of program reviews has seen substantial evolution since the 1979 Guidelines on Conditionality. It is particularly important to clarify and delineate the boundaries of these reviews. These reviews should be used for both backward- and forward-looking assessments of policies in areas that are essential to program objectives. But, there may be a need to adjust policies to achieve the objectives agreed at the start, reviews should not become an opportunity to move the goalposts. Moreover, it is important to clarify up front, to the extent possible, the areas to be covered in reviews and the basis on which policies will be assessed, otherwise reviews have the potential to be catch-all assessments of policy implementation.

24. It is also important to clarify the role of the Letter of Intent. An LOI is not a commitment to the Fund, but a statement of the policies the authorities intend to implement. In many cases, the LOI presents the full sweep of the authorities' policy program; in such cases, the Fund's financing is conditional on only some of these policies. But in many cases, there has been a blurring of the boundaries of the part of the authorities' program covered by conditionality. While in some cases this lack of clarity may have served the purposes of the authorities and the Fund staff—for instance in presenting the program to the public and the markets—it has contributed to a misleading impression that conditionality is all-encompassing. A solution would be either to limit the LOI to those policies that are being monitored by the Fund, or ensure that LOIs include a section that delineates precisely which aspects of the

authorities' program actually constitute conditionality. Moreover, it may be desirable simply to end the practice of including detailed matrices of policy actions in LOIs; in most cases, the Fund's financing hinges on only a small subset of the measures in such matrices.

25. These considerations should be carried forward in revising the 1979 Conditionality Guidelines. Some elements of the Guidelines—notably the emphasis on limiting conditions to those needed to monitor policies essential to program objectives—remain appropriate although, as noted, they have not been observed. Other elements of the Guidelines—notably the circumscribed role envisaged for program reviews—should be revised to reflect the changing environment in which Fund-supported programs are framed. It is proposed that, in light of Board discussion of the present set of papers, as well as comments received from outside the institution, the staff would return with a proposal for revising the guidelines following the Spring meetings.

. . .

NOTES

1. See *Selected Decisions and Selected Documents of the International Monetary Fund*, Twenty-Fourth Issue, Washington D.C., 1999, pages 137–139.
2. In contrast, there was virtually no change in the number of quantitative macroeconomic conditions during this period.
3. See Decision No. 4377-74/114, in *Selected Decisions and Selected Documents of the International Monetary Fund*, Twenty-Fourth Issue, Washington, D.C. 1999, pp. 150–154.
4. *The Chairman's Summing Up at the Conclusion of the Discussion on the Structural Adjustment Facility—Review of Experience*, EBM/87/93, June 19, 1987 (BUFF/87/118).
5. For instance, in the area of monetary policy, the Board agreed in January 2000 to authorize an approach whereby program reviews would be used to assess whether monetary policies remained on track to achieve an inflation target. See *Inflation-Targeting Implications for Conditionality* (SM/99/296).
6. See *Biennial Review of the Implementation of the Fund's Surveillance Policy and of the 1977 Surveillance Decision* (SM/00/40), February 2000.
7. See *The Role of the Fund in Governance Issues—Guidance Note*, July 2, 1997. The note indicates, however, that conditionality in this area should be limited to "policy measures . . . that are required to meet the objectives of the program."
8. The 2000 Review of Fund Facilities found that, on the contrary, financing needs are if anything more front-loaded than the usual schedule of uniform purchases and repurchases.

"Conditionalities" Choke Republic of Indonesia's Recovery

Sidhesh Kaul

This is the first of two articles on the relationship between international institutions and Indonesian government. Brazil, Peru, India, Somalia, Rwanda, Bangladesh, Vietnam, Bolivia, Russia, Turkey, Bosnia-Herzegovina and, of course, Indonesia: This is a list of some of the selected and prize medals that decorate the International Monetary Fund's proud chest.

The hand of an IMF-driven recovery has touched all of them and a comparative study reveals a familiar pattern. It appears that there is indeed some method in IMF's madness.

The pattern of economic subjugation prescribed by the IMF-led International Financial Institutions (or IFIs) foretells a bleak picture for Indonesia whose sovereign obligations far outstrip the capacity to repay.

Recently, in the wake of the new wave of politico-economic instability, the IFIs have joined voices in a chorus urging the embattled government of President Abdurrahman Wahid to stick to the several "conditionalities" that the several IFIs have prescribed for the country.

Subservience to the demands of the IMF is well worth the effort. The choice is between getting Indonesian assets to perform productively and efficiently overnight, a task of Herculean proportions given the current chaos, and agreeing to a few conditions.

The vital tools in the hands of IFIs, led by the IMF, for reigning in an economically embattled country are broadly described as "conditionalities."

These "conditionalities" come attached to the loan agreements and ostensibly serve the purpose of re-directing macro-economic policy but in fact serve the narrow interests of the IFIs.

For a developing country, which has borrowed from the IFIs, there is little choice but to synchronize the nation's debt management policy with the IMF-driven macro-economic reform that is warranted under the strict "conditionalities" regime.

The straitjacket of the "conditionalities" ensures that the country continues to abide by its financial obligations.

Sidhesh Kaul is a commentator on regional economic and political issues based in Jakarta, Indonesia.

Debt management typically comprises deferring principal payments and swapping of debt for equity whilst keeping the interest payment current. Often the country has to borrow "new monies" to pay interest arrears (so that the country can avoid a default). This new burden of borrowings comes along with stricter conditionalities.

The cycle carries on and very soon the crippled nation reaches a state where it becomes a net exporter of capital, that is the country pays more in terms of interest than the "new monies" that flow in.

Bowing to the dictates of the "conditionalities" opens the doors to the Paris and London Clubs, commercial banking institutions, and bilateral donors whilst non-compliance brings in its wake obstacles in rescheduling the debt, difficulties in obtaining new developmental assistance, and blockages in short-term credit (that would have the effect of crippling exports and paralyzing debt servicing capacities even further). An errant borrower would soon face isolation.

The IMF–World Bank's "conditionality"-driven remedy begins with a short-term macro-economic stabilization process (read as devaluation, price liberalization, and budgetary austerity) that is followed up with a dose of more fundamental and structural reforms.

The country's exchange rate is an important instrument of macro-economic reform and the IMF–World Bank's short-term macro-economic stabilization programs play a key political role in pushing for devaluation.

Devaluation brings into play the supply-demand interactions within an economy and affects the real prices paid to direct producers as also the real value of wages and leads to a real contraction in those industries and sectors that are heavily reliant on imported inputs (including capital) but whose markets are domestic.

Earnings are compressed and the dollar value of government expenditures falls drastically, which in turn facilitates the release of state revenues toward external debt servicing.

Then there is the social cost to bear. With the contraction in the domestic sector and the subsequent effect this has on real prices for consumer goods, the common man finally begins to feel the pinch. Demands for an increase in real wages to counter this effect fall on deaf ears.

The first symptom after a round of devaluation is spiraling inflation and the "dollarisation" of domestic prices and at this stage the IMF is quick to prescribe its standard "anti-inflationary" program—at best a diversionary tactic.

The program has little to do with the devaluation (the actual impetus for the inflation and an aspect that has met with staunch denial from the IMF historically) but instead focuses on a contraction of demand—reduction in public expenditure, cuts in social sector programs, and deindexation of wages.

Decreases in government expenditure, as a direct consequence of these measures, succeed in diverting state revenues toward debt servicing.

In addition, the IMF prescribes a tight control on money supply as a means of combating inflationary pressures.

The IMF's tight control over money supply would be impossible without a pliant Bank Indonesia. The IMF's constant refrain for "independence of Bank Indonesia from political power" (Is it more than a coincidence that Bank Indonesia's senior officials are former staff members of the IFIs?) is actually an effort at shoring up their tactics to control money creation.

The government thus has very little control over domestic monetary policy and the implication is that the country would have little choice but to depend on international sources of funding for real economic development.

Traditionally, the IMF is not going to settle for anything other than total control over a country's monetary policy.

The domain of public finances too is subjected by the IFIs to across-the-board austerity measures. The social sectors are also not spared and the IFI's advocate programs on the basis of economic feasibility (read as cost recovery) and the gradual withdrawal of state funding from basic health and educational services. Social sector funding is limited to targeted "vulnerable groups."

The entire thrust of the IFIs is to ensure that the government's cuts in public expenditure can bolster the repayment scheme to international creditors. State investment in public infrastructure projects is curtailed, thus leading to a slowing down of the rate of capital formation. The government is basically denied the right to muster its domestic resources for deployment in any major project.

Concessions are made by the IFI's for "essential" projects in the form of soft loans and under the watchful aegis of a set of binding procedures.

The new rules of the game ensure that whilst the state's burden increases, the interest payments keep flowing back to the IFIs.

The explosion of social problems that follows the curtailment of public expenditure has another important side effect—the ensuing destabilizing forces erode the legitimacy of the government in the eyes of the public and make it even more dependent on IFI-driven quick fixes.

The government is pressured to lift subsidies on fuel and utilities. The net effect is a foregone conclusion—domestic prices spiral upwards in the market and the effect is sharpened by the fact that there is a squeeze on real income. Cost structures for both production as well as distribution get affected and domestic producers find that their local markets have been surgically incised.

The Indonesian government is under severe pressure to forego the subsidy on fuel and that too at a time when the country is being wracked by social and political instability.

Whilst the government has managed to stave off increases in fuel prices for the common man till later in October of this year, industries (the major consumers of fuel) have been hit by the increases immediately—the increased costs in a market that is experiencing a second round of currency devaluation is detrimental to growth.

Whilst this situation is an impetus for industries to seek export markets, it spells death for those industries that cater exclusively to the domestic market.

Indonesia has little choice but to swallow the bitter pill of an IMF-driven regime of "macro-economic stabilization" policies.

But this is only the first phase of remedies and the treatment does not end here. What follows next is a phase that entails the implementation of "necessary" structural reforms.

PART V

OTHER GLOBAL CHALLENGES

ISSUE 20

GLOBAL WARMING
AND THE KYOTO TREATY

The words "global warming" in and of themselves do not conjure an imminent threat. They almost sound benign. Warmer winters come to mind: lower heating bills, less snow to shovel. For the decade of the 1990s, global warming meant in fact little more than this to policymakers worried about any possible disruption to the nation's economy. Since 1999, however, scientists have become increasingly unified in their view that the warming of the earth's atmospheric temperatures is likely not only to continue, but also to present an array of threats to the quality of life for humans and animals alike. Among the most severe effects of even incremental warming will be the raising of ocean levels, which may flood the coastal cities in which a large proportion of the world's population lives.

Some environmentalists believe that President Bush is more concerned about short-term economic gains than about the long-term welfare of the nation. Noting that the state of the economy normally plays a critical role in presidential elections, they fear that the president is unwilling to place his political career in jeopardy by advocating policies that may have only long-term economic benefits. True presidential leadership, they insist, requires taking stands that involve changing habits that infuse the daily lives of Americans, and, having taken these stands, accepting the responsibility for global leadership by influencing other nations around the world to do the same. Instead, environmentalists see President Bush as doing just the opposite. They point out that some developing nations, such as China, are currently planning to build coal-burning plants and other environmentally dangerous facilities. By rejecting the recently negotiated Kyoto protocols, by which many nations agreed to adjust their policies to accommodate global warming, President Bush has retreated from his leadership obligations.

294

In the first selection for Issue 20, the United Nations Environment Programme (UNEP) and the Climate Change Secretariat (UNFCCC) explain in laymen's terms the causes and consequences of global warming and why the Kyoto Protocol, an international treaty established in 1992, helps to solve the problem. In the second selection for Issue 20, Representative Dana Rohrabacher (R-CA) explains his opposition to the treaty.

DISCUSSION QUESTIONS

As you read the article by the UNEP and UNFCCC and the speech by Representative Rohrabacher, consider the following questions:

1. Now that a scientific consensus is emerging over the rate of global warming, are the economic costs of reducing emissions worth the investment?
2. Are the proposals made by the Kyoto Protocol too costly or unreasonable?
3. Should the developing world be given a grace period to allow it to achieve higher levels of development before being required to take measures to reduce their greenhouse gas emissions?
4. Should President Bush's administration play a stronger role in providing environmental leadership? How should he do this?

KEY WEB SITES

For more information on this topic, visit the following Web sites:

The U.S. Global Change Research Information Office (GCRIO)
http://www.gcrio.org

Committee for the National Institute for the Environment
http://www.cnie.org

Center for International Earth Science Information Network
http://www.ciesin.org

Understanding Climate Change

UNEP / UNFCCC

FIRST ACT: THE CONVENTION

A giant asteroid could hit the earth! Something else could happen! The global temperature could rise! Wake up!

The last several decades have been a time of international soul-searching about the environment. What are we doing to our planet? More and more, we are realizing that the Industrial Revolution has changed forever the relationship between humanity and nature. There is real concern that by the middle or the end of the twenty-first century human activities will have changed the basic conditions that have allowed life to thrive on earth.

The 1992 United Nations Framework Convention on Climate Change is one of a series of recent agreements through which countries around the world are banding together to meet this challenge. Other treaties deal with such matters as pollution of the oceans, dryland degradation, damage to the ozone layer, and the rapid extinction of plant and animal species. The Climate Change Convention focuses on something particularly disturbing: We are changing the way energy from the sun interacts with and escapes from our planet's atmosphere. By doing that, we risk altering the global climate. Among the expected consequences are an increase in the average temperature of the earth's surface and shifts in worldwide weather patterns. Other—unforeseen—effects cannot be ruled out.

We have a few problems to face up to.

Problem No. 1 (The Big Problem)   Scientists see a real risk that the climate will change rapidly and dramatically over the coming decades and centuries. Can we handle it?

A giant asteroid did hit the earth—about 65 million years ago. Splat. Scientists speculate that the collision threw so much dust into the atmosphere that the world was dark for three years. Sunlight was greatly reduced, so many plants could not grow, temperatures fell, the food chain collapsed, and many species, including the largest ever to walk the earth, died off.

Published by the United Nations Environment Programme (UNEP) and the Climate Change Secretariat (UNFCCC). Revised in July 2002. Reprinted by permission. For more information, contact the Climate Change Secretariat, Box 260124, D-53153 Bonn, Germany <secretariat@unfccc.int>, or UNEP's Information Unit for Conventions (UNEP/IUC), International Environment House (Geneva), Box 356, 1219 Châtelaine, Switzerland <iuc@unep.ch>.

That, at least, is the prevailing theory of why the dinosaurs became extinct. Even those who weren't actually hit by the asteroid paid the ultimate price.

The catastrophe that befell the dinosaurs is only one illustration, if dramatic, of how changes in climate can make or break a species.

According to another theory, human beings evolved when a drying trend some 10 million years ago was followed around three million years ago by a sharp drop in world temperature. The ape-like higher primates in the Great Rift Valley of Africa were used to sheltering in trees, but, under this long-term climate shift, the trees were replaced with grassland. The "apes" found themselves on an empty plain much colder and drier than what they were used to, and extremely vulnerable to predators.

Extinction was a real possibility, and the primates appear to have responded with two evolutionary jumps—first to creatures who could walk upright over long distances, with hands free for carrying children and food; and then to creatures with much larger brains, who used tools and were omnivorous (could eat both plants and meat). This second, large-brained creature is generally considered to be the first human.

Shifts in climate have shaped human destiny ever since, and people have largely responded by adapting, migrating, and growing smarter. During a later series of ice ages, sea levels dropped and humans moved across land bridges from Asia to the Americas and the Pacific islands. Many subsequent migrations, many innovations, many catastrophes have followed. Some can be traced to smaller climatic fluctuations, such as a few decades or centuries of slightly higher or lower temperatures, or extended droughts. Best known is the Little Ice Age that struck Europe in the early Middle Ages, bringing famines, uprisings, and the withdrawal of northern colonies in Iceland and Greenland. People have suffered under the whims of climate for millennia, responding with their wits, unable to influence these large events.

Until now. Ironically, we humans have been so remarkably successful as a species that we may have backed ourselves into a corner. Our numbers have grown to the point where we have less room for large-scale migration should a major climate shift call for it. And the products of our large brains—our industries, transport, and other activities—have led to something unheard of in the past. Previously the global climate changed human beings. Now human beings seem to be changing the global climate. The results are uncertain, but if current predictions prove correct, the climatic changes over the coming century will be larger than any since the dawn of human civilization.

The principal change to date is in the earth's atmosphere. The giant asteroid that felled the dinosaurs threw large clouds of dust into the air, but we are causing something just as profound if more subtle. We have changed, and are continuing to change, the balance of gases that form the atmosphere. This is especially true of such key "greenhouse gases" as carbon dioxide (CO_2), methane (CH_4), and nitrous oxide (N_2O). (Water vapour is the most important greenhouse gas, but human activities do not affect it directly.) These naturally occurring gases make up less than one tenth of one percent of the total atmosphere, which consists mostly of oxygen (21 percent) and nitrogen (78 percent). But greenhouse gases are vital because they act like a blanket around the earth. Without this natural blanket the earth's surface would be some 30°C colder than it is today.

The problem is that human activity is making the blanket "thicker." For example, when we burn coal, oil, and natural gas, we spew huge amounts of carbon dioxide into the air. When we destroy forests the carbon stored in the trees escapes to the atmosphere. Other basic activities, such as raising cattle and planting rice, emit methane, nitrous oxide, and other greenhouse gases. If emissions continue to grow at current rates, it is almost certain that atmospheric levels of carbon dioxide will double from preindustrial levels during the twenty-first century. If no steps are taken to slow greenhouse gas emissions, it is quite possible that levels will triple by the year 2100.

The most direct result, says the scientific consensus, is likely to be a "global warming" of 1.4 to 5.8°C over the next 100 years. That is in addition to an apparent temperature increase of around 0.6°C over the twentieth century, at least some of which may be due to past greenhouse gas emissions.

Just how this would affect us is hard to predict because the global climate is a very complicated system. If one key aspect—such as the average global temperature—is altered, the ramifications ripple outward. Uncertain effects pile onto uncertain effects. For example, wind and rainfall patterns that have prevailed for hundreds or thousands of years, and on which millions of people depend, may change. Sea levels may rise and threaten islands and low-lying coastal areas. In a world that is increasingly crowded and under stress—a world that has enough problems already—these extra pressures could lead directly to more famines and other catastrophes.

While scientists are scrambling to understand more clearly the effects of our greenhouse gas emissions, countries around the globe have joined together to confront the problem.

How the Convention Responds   It recognizes that there is a problem. That's a significant step. It is not easy for the nations of the world to agree on a common course of action, especially one that tackles a problem whose consequences are uncertain and which will be more important for our grandchildren than for the present generation. Still, the Convention was negotiated in a little over two years, and some 185 states have ratified and so are legally bound by it. The treaty took effect on March 21, 1994.

It sets an "ultimate objective" of stabilizing "greenhouse gas concentrations in the atmosphere at a level that would prevent dangerous anthropogenic (human-induced) interference with the climate system." The objective does not specify what these concentrations should be, only that they be at a level that is not dangerous. This acknowledges that there is currently no scientific certainty about what a dangerous level would be. Scientists believe it will take about another decade (and the next generation of supercomputers) before today's uncertainties (or many of them) are significantly reduced. The Convention's objective thus remains meaningful no matter how the science evolves.

It directs that "such a level should be achieved within a time frame sufficient to allow ecosystems to adapt naturally to climate change, to ensure that food production is not threatened and to enable economic development to proceed in a sustainable manner." This highlights the main concerns about food production—probably the most climate-sensitive human activity—and economic development. It also suggests (as most climatologists believe) that some change is inevitable and that adaptive as well as preventive measures are called for.

Again, this leaves room for interpretation in the light of scientific findings and the trade-offs and risks that the global community is willing to accept.

Problem No. 2 If the consequences of a problem are uncertain, do you ignore the problem or do you do something about it anyway?

Climate change is a threat to mankind. But no one is certain about its future effects or their severity. Responding to the threat is expected to be complicated and difficult. There is even some remaining disagreement over whether any problem exists at all: While many people worry that the effects will be extremely serious, others still argue that scientists cannot prove that what they suspect will happen will actually happen. In addition, it is not clear who (in the various regions of the world) will suffer most. Yet if the nations of the world wait until the consequences and victims are clear, it will probably be too late to act. What should we do?

The truth is that in most scientific circles the issue is no longer whether or not climate change is a potentially serious problem. Rather, it is how the problem will develop, what its effects will be, and how these effects can best be detected. Computer models of something as complicated as the planet's climate system are not far enough advanced yet to give clear and unambiguous answers. Nevertheless, while the when, where, and how remain uncertain, the big picture painted by these climate models cries out for attention.

For example:

- Regional rain patterns may change. At the global level, the evapo-transpiration cycle is expected to speed up. This means that it would rain more, but the rain would evaporate faster, leaving soils drier during critical parts of the growing season. New or worsening droughts, especially in poorer countries, could reduce supplies of clean, fresh water to the point where there are major threats to public health. Because they still lack confidence in regional scenarios, scientists are uncertain about which areas of the world risk becoming wetter and which drier.

But with global water resources already under severe strain from rapid population growth and expanding economic activity, the danger is clear.

- Climate and agricultural zones may shift toward the poles. Increased summer dryness may reduce mid-latitude crop yields, and it is possible that today's leading grain-producing areas (such as the Great Plains of the United States) would experience more frequent droughts and heat waves. The poleward edges of the midlatitude agricultural zones—northern Canada, Scandinavia, Russia, and Japan in the northern hemisphere, and southern Chile and Argentina in the southern hemisphere—might benefit from higher temperatures. However, in some areas rugged terrain and poor soil would prevent these countries from compensating for reduced yields in today's more productive areas. A warming of more than 2.5°C could reduce global food supplies and contribute to higher food prices.

- Melting glaciers and the thermal expansion of sea water may raise sea levels, threatening low-lying coastal areas and small islands. The global mean sea level has already risen by around 10 to 20 centimetres during the past century, and global warming is expected to cause a further rise of about 9 to 88 cm by the year 2100. The most vulnerable land would be the unprotected, densely populated coastal regions of some of the world's poorest countries. Bangladesh, whose coast is already prone to devastating floods, would be a likely victim, as would many small island states such as the Maldives.

These scenarios are alarming enough to raise concern, but too uncertain for easy decisions by governments. The picture is fuzzy. Some governments, beleaguered by other problems and responsibilities and bills to pay, have understandably been tempted to do nothing at all. Maybe the threat will go away. Or someone else will deal with it. Maybe another giant asteroid will hit the earth. Who knows?

How the Convention Responds   It establishes a framework and a process for agreeing to specific actions—later. The diplomats who wrote the Framework Convention on Climate Change saw it as a launching pad for potential further action in the future. They recognized that it would not be possible in the year 1992 for the world's governments to agree on a detailed blueprint for tackling climate change. But by establishing a framework of general principles and institutions, and by setting up a process through which governments meet regularly, they got things started.

A key benefit of this approach is that it allowed countries to begin discussing the issue even before they all fully agreed that it is, in fact, a problem. Even skeptical countries have felt it is worthwhile participating. (Or, to put it another way, they would have felt uneasy about being left out.) This created legitimacy for the issue, and a sort of international peer pressure to take the subject seriously.

The Convention is designed to allow countries to weaken or strengthen the treaty in response to new scientific developments. For example, they can agree to take more specific actions (such as reducing emissions of greenhouse gases by a certain amount) by adopting "amendments" or "protocols" to the Convention. This is what happened in 1997 with the adoption of the Kyoto Protocol.

The treaty promotes action in spite of uncertainty on the basis of a recent development in international law and diplomacy called the "precautionary principle." Under traditional international law, an activity generally has not been restricted or prohibited unless a direct causal link between the activity and a particular damage can be shown. But many environmental problems, such as damage to the ozone layer and pollution of the oceans, cannot be confronted if final proof of cause and effect is required. In response, the international community has gradually come to accept the precautionary principle, under which activities that threaten serious or irreversible damage can be restricted or even prohibited before there is absolute scientific certainty about their effects.

The Convention takes preliminary steps that clearly make sense for the time being. Countries ratifying the Convention—called "Parties to the Convention" in diplomatic jargon—agree to take climate change into account in such matters as agriculture, energy, natural resources, and activities involving seacoasts. They agree to develop national programmes to slow climate change. The Convention encourages them to share technology and to cooperate in other ways to reduce greenhouse gas emissions, especially from energy, transport, industry, agriculture, forestry, and waste management, which together produce nearly all greenhouse gas emissions attributable to human activity.

The Convention encourages scientific research on climate change. It calls for data gathering, research, and climate observation, and it creates a "subsidiary body" for "scientific and technological advice" to help governments decide what to do next. Each country that is a Party to the Convention must also develop a greenhouse gas "inventory" listing its national sources (such as factories and transport) and "sinks" (forests and other natural ecosystems that absorb greenhouse gases from the atmosphere). These inventories must be updated regularly and made public. The information they provide on which activities emit how much of each gas is essential for monitoring changes in emissions and determining the effects of measures taken to control emissions.

Problem No. 3 It's not fair. If a giant asteroid hits the earth, that's nobody's fault. The same cannot be said for global warming.

There is a fundamental unfairness to the climate change problem that chafes at the already uneasy relations between the rich and poor nations of the world. Countries with high standards of living are mostly (if unwittingly) responsible for the rise in greenhouse gases. These early industrializers—Europe, North America, Japan, and a few others—created their wealth in part by pumping into the atmosphere vast amounts of greenhouse gases long before the likely consequences were understood. Developing countries now fear being told that they should curtail their own fledgling industrial activities—that the atmosphere's safety margin is all used up.

Because energy-related emissions are the leading cause of climate change, there will be growing pressure on all countries to reduce the amounts of coal and oil they use. There also will be pressure (and incentives) to adopt advanced technologies so that less damage is inflicted in the future. Buying such technologies can be costly.

Countries in the early stages of industrialization—countries struggling hard to give their citizens better lives—don't want these additional burdens. Economic development is difficult enough already. If they agreed to cut back on burning the fossil fuels that are the cheapest, most convenient, and most useful for industry, how could they make any progress?

There are other injustices to the climate change problem. The countries to suffer the most if the predicted consequences come about—if agricultural zones shift or sea levels rise or rainfall patterns change—will probably be in the developing world. These nations simply do not have the scientific or economic resources, or the social safety nets, to cope with disruptions in climate. Also, in many of these countries rapid population growth has pushed many millions of people onto marginal land—the sort of land that can change most drastically due to variations in climate.

How the Convention Responds   It puts the lion's share of the responsibility for battling climate change—and the lion's share of the bill—on the rich countries. The Convention tries to make sure that any sacrifices made in protecting our shared atmosphere will be fairly shared among countries—in accordance with their "common but differentiated responsibilities and respective capabilities and their social and economic conditions." It notes that the largest share of historical and current emissions originates in developed countries. Its first basic principle is that these countries should take the lead in combating climate change and its adverse impacts. Specific commitments in the treaty relating to financial and technological transfers apply only to the very richest countries, essentially the members of the Organization for Economic Cooperation and Development (OECD). They agree to support climate change activities in developing countries by providing financial support above and beyond any financial assistance they already provide to these countries.

Specific commitments concerning efforts to limit greenhouse gas emissions and enhance natural sinks apply to the OECD countries as well as to twelve "economies in transition" (Central and Eastern Europe and the former Soviet Union). Under the Convention, the OECD and transition countries were expected to try to return by the year 2000 to the greenhouse gas emission levels they had in 1990 (as a group they succeeded).

The Convention recognizes that poorer nations have a right to economic development. It notes that the share of global emissions of greenhouse gases originating in developing countries will grow as these countries expand their industries to improve social and economic conditions for their citizens.

It acknowledges the vulnerability of poorer countries to the effects of climate change. One of the Convention's basic principles is that the specific needs and circumstances of developing countries should be given "full consideration" in any actions taken. This applies in particular to those whose fragile ecosystems are highly vulnerable to the impacts of climate change. The Convention also recognizes that states which depend on income from coal and oil would face difficulties if energy demand changes.

Problem No. 4 If the whole world starts consuming more and living the good life, can the planet stand the strain?

As the human population continues to grow, the demands human beings place on the environment increase. The demands are becoming all the greater because these rapidly increasing numbers of people also want to live better lives. More and better food, more and cleaner water, more electricity, refrigerators, automobiles, houses and apartments, land on which to put houses and apartments. . . .

Already there are severe problems supplying enough fresh water to the world's billions. Burgeoning populations are draining the water from rivers and lakes, and vast underground aquifers are steadily being depleted. What will people do when these natural "tanks" are empty? There are also problems growing and distributing enough food—widespread hunger in many parts of the world attests to that. There are other danger signals. The global fish harvest has declined sharply; as large as the oceans are, the most valuable species have been effectively fished out.

Global warming is a particularly ominous example of humanity's insatiable appetite for natural resources. During the last century we have dug up and burned massive stores of coal, oil, and natural gas that took millions of years to accumulate. Our ability to burn up fossil fuels at a rate that is much, much faster than the rate at which they were created has upset the natural balance of the carbon cycle. The threat of climate change arises because one of the only ways the atmosphere—also a natural resource—can respond to the vast quantities of carbon being liberated from beneath the earth's surface is to warm up.

Meanwhile, human expectations are not tapering off. They are increasing. The countries of the industrialized "North" have 20 percent of the world's people but use about 80 percent of the world's resources. By global standards, they live extremely well. It's nice living the good life, but if everyone consumed as much as the North Americans and Western Europeans consume—and billions of people aspire to do just that—there probably would not be enough clean water and other vital natural resources to go around. How will we meet these growing expectations when the world is already under so much stress?

How the Convention Responds   It supports the concept of "sustainable development." Somehow, mankind must learn how to alleviate poverty for huge and growing numbers of people without destroying the natural environment on which all human life depends. Somehow a way has to be found to develop economically in a fashion that is sustainable over a long period of time. The buzzword for this challenge among environmentalists and international bureaucrats is "sustainable development." The trick will be to find methods for living well while using critical natural resources at a rate no faster than that at which they are replaced. Unfortunately, the international community is a lot farther along in defining the problems posed by sustainable development than it is in figuring out how to solve them.

The Convention calls for developing and sharing environmentally sound technologies and know-how. Technology will clearly play a major role in dealing with climate change. If we can find practical ways to use cleaner sources of energy, such as solar power, we can reduce the consumption of coal and oil. Technology can make industrial processes more efficient, water purification more viable, and agriculture more productive for the same amount of resources invested. Such technology must be made widely available—it must somehow be shared by richer and more scientifically advanced countries with poorer countries that have great need of it.

The Convention emphasizes the need to educate people about climate change. Today's children and future generations must learn to look at the world in a different way than it was looked at by most people during the twentieth century. This is both an old and a new idea. Many (but not all!) preindustrial cultures lived in balance with nature. Now scientific research is telling us to do much the same thing. Economic development is no longer a case of "bigger is better"—bigger cars, bigger houses, bigger harvests of fish, bigger doses of oil and coal. We must no longer think of human progress as a matter of imposing ourselves on the natural environment. The world—the climate and all living things—is a closed system; what we do has consequences that eventually come back to affect us. Tomorrow's children—and today's adults, for that matter—will have to learn to think about the effects of their actions on the climate. When they make decisions as members of governments and businesses, and as they go about their private lives, they will have to take the climate into account.

In other words, human behaviour will have to change—probably the sooner the better. But such things are difficult to prescribe and predict. People will need stronger signals and incentives if they are to do more for the good of the global climate. That leads to . . .

SECOND ACT: THE PROTOCOL

The 1992 Convention was a good start. But as the years passed, and the scientific evidence continued to accumulate, people naturally asked, "What's next?"

In 1997, governments responded to growing public pressure by adopting the Kyoto Protocol. A protocol is an international agreement that stands on its own but is linked to an existing treaty. This means that the climate protocol shares the concerns and principles set out in the Climate Convention. It then builds on these by adding new commitments—which are stronger and far more complex and detailed than those in the Convention.

This complexity is a reflection of the enormous challenges posed by the control of greenhouse gas emissions. It is also a result of the diverse political and economic interests that had to be balanced in order to reach an agreement. Billion-dollar industries will be reshaped; some will profit from the transition to a climate-friendly economy, others will not.

Because the Kyoto Protocol will affect virtually all major sectors of the economy, it is considered to be the most far-reaching agreement on environment and sustainable development ever adopted. This is a sign that the international community is willing to face reality and start taking concrete actions to minimize the risk of climate change. The Protocol's negotiators were able to take this important step forward only after facing up to some tough questions.

Problem No. 5   Emissions are still growing. Isn't it time to take some serious action?

Three years after the Climate Change Convention was adopted at the Rio Earth Summit, the Intergovernmental Panel on Climate Change (IPCC) published its second major assessment of climate change research. Written and reviewed by some 2,000 scientists and experts, the report was soon famous for concluding that the climate may have already started responding to past emissions. It also confirmed the availability of many cost-effective strategies for reducing greenhouse gas emissions. (The IPCC's third assessment was published in 2001.)

Meanwhile, although emissions in some countries stabilized, emissions levels continued to rise around the world. More and more people came to accept that only a firm and binding commitment by developed countries to reduce greenhouse gases could send a signal strong enough to convince businesses, communities, and individuals to change their ways.

Finally, there was the practical matter that the year 2000 was fast approaching, and with it the Convention's non-binding "aim" for industrialized countries—to return emissions to 1990 levels by the year 2000—would expire. Clearly, new steps were needed.

How the Protocol Responds It sets legally binding targets and timetables for cutting developed country emissions. The Convention encouraged these countries to stabilize emissions; the Protocol commits them to reducing their collective emissions by at least 5 percent. Each country's emissions levels will be calculated as an average of the years 2008–2012; these five years are known as the first commitment period. Governments must make "demonstrable progress" toward this goal by the year 2005.

These arrangements will be periodically reviewed. The first review is likely to take place in the middle of the first decade of the new century. At this time the Parties will take "appropriate action" on the basis of the best available scientific, technical, and socio-economic information. Talks on targets for the second commitment period must start by 2005.

The Protocol will only become legally binding when at least 55 countries, including developed countries accounting for at least 55 percent of developed countries' 1990 CO_2 emissions, have ratified it. This should happen some time in 2003.

The Protocol addresses the six main greenhouse gases. These gases are to be combined in a "basket," so that reductions in each gas are credited toward a single target number. This is complicated by the fact that, for example, a kilo of methane has a stronger effect on the climate than does a kilo of carbon dioxide. Cuts in individual gases are therefore translated into "CO_2 equivalents" that can be added up to produce one figure.

Cuts in the three major gases—carbon dioxide, methane, and nitrous oxide—will be measured against a base year of 1990 (with exceptions for some countries with economies in transition). Cuts in the three long-lived industrial gases—hydrofluorocarbons (HFCs), perfluorocarbons (PFCs), and sulphur hexafluoride (SF_6)—can be measured against either a 1990 or 1995 baseline.

Carbon dioxide is by far the most important gas in the basket. It accounted for over four-fifths of total greenhouse gas emissions from developed countries in 1995, with fuel combustion representing all but several percent of this amount. Fortunately, CO_2 emissions from fuel are relatively easy to measure and monitor.

Deforestation is the second largest source of carbon dioxide emissions in developed countries. Under the Protocol, targets can be met in part by improving the ability of forests and other natural sinks to absorb carbon dioxide from the atmosphere. Calculating the amount absorbed, however, is methodologically complex. Governments must still agree on a common approach.

The second most important gas covered by the Protocol is methane. Methane is released by rice cultivation, domesticated animals such as cattle, and the disposal and treatment of garbage and human wastes. Methane emissions are generally stable or declining in the developed countries and their control does not seem to pose as great a challenge as carbon dioxide.

Nitrous oxide is emitted mostly as a result of fertilizer use. As with methane, emissions from developed countries are stable or declining. Nitrous oxide and methane emissions are also similar in being relatively difficult to measure.

One major group of greenhouse gases that the Protocol does not cover is chlorofluorocarbons. This is because CFCs are being phased out under the 1987 Montreal Protocol on Substances that Deplete the Ozone Layer. Thanks to this agreement, atmospheric concentrations of many CFCs are stabilizing and expected to decline over the coming decades.

However, the Protocol does address three long-lived and potent greenhouse gases that, like CFCs, have been created by industry for specialized applications. The use of HFCs and PFCs threatens to go up dramatically in part because they are being adopted as ozone-safe replacements for CFCs. Governments are now working to make sure that the incentives and controls for ozone depletion and global warming are compatible.

The third man-made gas, sulphur hexafluoride, is used as an electric insulator, heat conductor, and freezing agent. Molecule for molecule, its global warming potential is thought to be 23,900 times greater than that of carbon dioxide.

The Protocol recognizes that emissions cuts must be credible and verifiable. Ensuring that governments comply with their targets will be essential to the Protocol's success. Each country will need an effective national system for estimating emissions and confirming reductions. Standardized guidelines must be crafted to make figures comparable from one country to the next and the whole process transparent.

The Protocol allows governments that cut emissions more than they are required to by their national target to "bank" the "excess" as credits for future commitment periods. But what happens if a country's emissions are higher than what is permitted by its target? Non-compliance provisions still need to be developed. Clearly, though, the best approach both politically and environmentally will be to start by helping governments to comply rather than emphasizing punitive or confrontational measures.

Problem No. 6   How can we make our behavior and our economies more climate-friendly?

Minimizing greenhouse gas emissions will require policymakers to make some tough decisions. Every time a subsidy is added or removed, and every time a regulation or reform is put in place, somebody says "ouch." Even though the economy as a whole stands to benefit from well-designed, market-oriented policies for reducing emissions, action—or inaction—by government always helps create winners and losers in the marketplace.

The challenge for policymakers is to design policies that fully engage the energies of civil society. Their goal must be to open the floodgates of industrial creativity. Experience shows that companies often respond rapidly and positively to incentives and pressures. Given the right policy environment, the business sector will roll out low-emissions technologies and services faster than many now believe possible.

Schools, community groups, the media, families, and consumers also have a crucial role to play. Individuals can make a real difference by changing their habits and making thoughtful purchases and investments. If consumers are convinced that the rules of the game are changing, they will start taking the myriad small decisions that, when added together, can have a dramatic impact on emissions.

If large segments of society are willing to make these changes, we can expect an early transition to more energy-efficient, technologically innovative, and environmentally sustainable societies. The trick is getting started.

How the Protocol Responds   It highlights effective domestic policies and measures for reducing emissions. National governments can build a fiscal and policy framework that discourages emissions. They can phase out counter-productive subsidies on carbon-intensive activities, and they can introduce energy-efficiency and other regulatory standards that promote the best current and future technologies. Taxes, tradable emissions permits, information programmes, and voluntary programmes can all contribute.

Local and urban governments—which often have direct responsibility for transport, housing, and other greenhouse gas-emitting sectors of the economy—can also play a role. They can start designing and building better public transport systems and creating incentives for people to use them rather than private automobiles. They can tighten construction codes so that new houses and office buildings will be heated or cooled with less fuel.

Meanwhile, industrial companies need to start shifting to new technologies that use fossil fuels and raw materials more efficiently. Wherever possible they should switch to renewable energy sources such as wind and solar power. They should also redesign products such as refrigerators, automobiles, cement mixes, and fertilizers so that they produce lower greenhouse gas emissions. Farmers should look to technologies and methods that reduce the methane emitted by livestock and rice fields. Individual citizens, too, must cut their use of fossil fuels—take public transport more often, switch off the lights in empty rooms—and be less wasteful of all natural resources.

The Protocol also flags the importance of conducting research into innovative technologies, limiting methane emissions from waste management and energy systems, and protecting forests and other carbon sinks.

The Protocol encourages governments to work together. Policymakers can learn from one other and share ideas and experiences. They may choose to go further, coordinating national policies in order to have more impact in a globalized marketplace. Governments should also consider the effects of their climate policies on others, notably developing countries, and seek to minimize any negative economic consequences.

Problem No. 7   How should we divide up the work—while sharing the burden fairly?

The Climate Change Convention calls on the rich countries to take the initiative in controlling emissions. In line with this, the Kyoto Protocol sets emission targets for the industrialized countries only—although it also recognizes that developing countries have a role to play.

Agreeing how to share the responsibility for cutting emissions amongst the forty or so developed countries was a major challenge. Lumping all developed countries into one big group risks ignoring the many differences between them. Each country is unique, with its own mix of energy resources and price levels, population density, regulatory traditions, and political culture.

For example, the countries of Western Europe tend to have lower per capita emissions than do countries such as Australia, Canada, and the United States. Western Europe's emissions levels have generally stabilized since 1990—the base year for measuring emissions—while other developed countries have seen their emissions rise. Japan made great strides in energy efficiency in the 1980s, while countries such as Norway and New Zealand have relatively low emissions because they rely on hydropower or nuclear energy. Meanwhile, the energy-intensive countries of Central and Eastern Europe and the former Soviet Union have seen emissions fall dramatically since 1990 due to their transition to market economies. These differing national profiles make it difficult to agree on a one-size-fits-all solution.

How the Protocol Responds   It assigns a national target to each country. In the end, it was not possible to agree in Kyoto on a uniform target for all countries. The resulting individual targets were not based on any rigorous or objective formula. Rather, they were the outcome of political negotiation and compromise.

The overall 5 percent target for developed countries is to be met through cuts of 8 percent in the European Union (EU), Switzerland, and most Central and East European states; 7 percent in the United States (although the United States has stated that it is no longer committed to the Kyoto Protocol); and 6 percent in Canada, Hungary, Japan, and Poland. New Zealand, Russia, and Ukraine are to stabilize their emissions, while Norway may increase emissions by up to 1 percent, Australia by up to 8 percent, and Iceland 10 percent.

The EU has made its own internal agreement to meet its 8 percent target by distributing different rates to its member states, just as the entire developed group's 5 percent target was shared out. These targets range from a 28 percent reduction by Luxembourg and 21 percent cuts by Denmark and Germany to increases of 25 percent for Greece and 27 percent for Portugal.

The Protocol offers additional flexibility to the countries with economies in transition. In particular, they have more leeway in choosing the base year against which emissions reductions are to be measured. They also do not share the commitment of the richer developed countries to provide "new and additional financial resources" and facilitate technology transfer for developing country Parties.

It also reconfirms the broader commitments of all countries—developed and developing. Under the Convention, both developed and developing countries agree to take measures to address emissions and adapt to future climate change impacts; submit information on their national climate change programmes and emissions levels; facilitate technology transfer; cooperate on scientific and technical research; and promote public awareness, education, and training. These commitments are reaffirmed in the Protocol, which also sets out ways of advancing their implementation.

The issue of emissions targets for developing countries, and the broader question of how commitments should evolve in the future given continuing growth in global emissions, has generated a great deal of intense debate. A proposal that the Protocol should establish a procedure whereby developing countries could take on voluntary commitments to limit (that is, reduce the rate of increase in) their emissions was not accepted in Kyoto. Many developing countries resist formal commitments, even if voluntary, that would put an upper limit on their emissions, noting that their per capita emissions are still low compared to those of developed countries. Once developed countries start to convincingly demonstrate that they are taking effective actions to achieve their emissions targets, the debate on how new countries might eventually be brought into the structure of specific commitments may be revived.

This is in keeping with the step-by-step approach of the intergovernmental climate regime. The Kyoto Protocol is not an end result, and can be strengthened and built on in the future. What's more, although developing countries are not currently subject to any specific timetables and targets, they are expected to take measures to limit the growth rate of their emissions and to report on actions they are taking to address climate change. There is a good deal of evidence that many developing countries are indeed taking steps that should help their emissions grow at a slower rate than their economic output. This is particularly true in the field of energy.

Problem No. 8   I don't want to spend more money on this than is absolutely necessary!

People are keen to combat climate change because they fear it may be destructive and costly. At the same time, they naturally want to buy their "climate insurance" at the lowest price possible.

Fortunately, the costs of climate change policies can be minimized through "no regrets" strategies. Such strategies make economic and environmental sense whether or not the world is moving toward rapid climate change. For example, boosting energy efficiency not only reduces greenhouse gas emissions but also lowers the cost of energy, thus making industries and countries more competitive in international markets; it also eases the health and environmental costs of urban air pollution. At the same time, the precautionary principle and the expected net damages from climate change justify adopting policies that do entail some costs.

Calculating the costs of climate change policies is not easy. How quickly power plants and other infrastructure are replaced by newer and cleaner equipment, how interest rate trends affect corporate planning and investment, and the way businesses and consumers respond to climate change policies are just a few of the variables to consider.

Costs can also vary from place to place. In general, the costs of improving energy efficiency should be lower in countries that are the most energy inefficient. Countries in the early stages of industrialization may offer cheaper opportunities for installing modern environmentally friendly technologies than do countries whose industrial plant is already developed. And so on.

How the Protocol Responds　　The Protocol innovates by giving Parties credit for reducing emissions in other countries. It establishes three "mechanisms" for obtaining these credits. The idea is that countries that find it particularly expensive to reduce emissions at home can pay for cheaper emissions cuts elsewhere. The global economic efficiency of reducing emissions is increased while the overall 5 percent reduction target is still met. The Protocol stipulates, however, that credit for making reductions elsewhere must be supplementary to domestic emissions cuts.

Governments must still decide just how the three mechanisms for doing this will function. The rules they adopt will strongly influence the costs of meeting emissions targets. They will also determine the environmental credibility of the mechanisms—that is, their ability to contribute to the Protocol's aims rather than opening up "loopholes" in emissions commitments.

An emissions trading regime will allow industrialized countries to buy and sell emissions credits amongst themselves. Countries that limit or reduce emissions more than is required by their agreed target will be able to sell the excess emissions credits to countries that find it more difficult or more expensive to meet their own targets. The rules, however, have not yet been decided on.

Some observers are concerned that the Kyoto targets of some countries are so low that they can be met with minimal effort. These countries could then sell large quantities of emission credits (known as "hot air"), reducing pressure on other industrialized countries to make domestic cuts. Governments are debating the best way to ensure that emissions trading does not undermine incentives for countries to cut their own domestic emissions.

Joint implementation (JI) projects will offer "emissions reduction units" for financing projects in other developed countries. A joint implementation project could work like this: Country A faces high costs for reducing domestic emissions, so it invests in low-emissions technologies for a new power plant in Country B (very likely an economy in transition). Country A gets credit for reducing emissions (at a lower cost that it could domestically), Country B receives foreign investment and advanced technologies, and global greenhouse gas emissions are reduced: a "win-win-win" scenario.

Not only governments, but also businesses and other private organizations will be able to participate directly in these projects. Some aspects of this approach have already been tested under the Convention through a voluntary programme for "Activities Implemented Jointly." Reporting rules, a monitoring system, institutions, and project guidelines must still be adopted. Not only must this infrastructure establish the system's credibility, but it must ensure that JI projects transfer appropriate and current technology, avoid adverse social and environmental impacts, and avoid distorting the local market.

A Clean Development Mechanism will provide credit for financing emissions-reducing or emissions-avoiding projects in developing countries. This promises to be an important new avenue through which governments and private corporations will transfer clean technologies and promote sustainable development. Credit will be earned in the form of "certified emissions reductions."

Whereas joint implementation and emissions trading merely shift around the pieces of the industrial countries' overall 5 percent target, the CDM involves emissions in developing countries (which do not have targets). This in effect increases the overall emissions cap. Verification is therefore particularly important for this mechanism.

The Protocol already details some of the ground rules. The CDM will be governed by the Parties through an Executive Board, and reductions will be certified by one or more independent organizations. To be certified, a deal must be approved by all involved parties, demonstrate a measurable and long-term ability to reduce emissions, and promise reductions that would be additional to any that would otherwise occur. A share of the proceeds from CDM projects will be used to cover administrative expenses and to help the most vulnerable developing countries meet the costs of adapting to climate change impacts. Again, the operational guidelines must still be worked out.

Conclusion: The Twenty-First Century and Beyond

Climate change would have lasting consequences. One giant asteroid came along 65 million years ago, and that was it for the dinosaurs.

In facing up to man-made climate change, human beings are going to have to think in terms of decades and centuries. The job is just beginning. Many of the effects of climate shifts will not be apparent for two or three generations. In the future, everyone may be hearing about—and living with—this problem.

The Framework Convention takes this into account. It establishes institutions to support efforts to carry out long-term commitments and to monitor long-term efforts to minimize—and adjust to—climate change. The

Conference of the Parties, in which all states that have ratified the treaty are represented, is the Convention's supreme body. It met for the first time in 1995 and will continue to meet on a regular basis to promote and review the implementation of the Convention. The Conference of the Parties is assisted by two subsidiary bodies (or committees), one for scientific and technological advice and the other for implementation. It can establish other bodies as well, whether temporary or permanent, to help it with its work.

It can also strengthen the Convention, as it did in Kyoto in 1997. The Protocol's 5 percent cut may seem a modest start, but given the rise in emissions that would otherwise be expected—and remember that emissions in a number of developed countries have risen steadily since the 1990 base year—many countries are going to have to make a significant effort to meet their commitment.

The Kyoto Protocol makes an important promise: to reduce greenhouse gases in developed countries by the end of the first decade of the new century. It should be judged a success if it arrests and reverses the 200-year trend of rising emissions in the industrialized world and hastens the transition to a climate-friendly global economy.

Support for Bush's Policies

Representative Dana Rohrabacher

U.S. House of Representatives, Washington, D.C.
May 10, 2001

Mr. Speaker,

. . . Now I do have my presentation tonight, which I have on global warming, especially considering that President Bush has come under severe attack for his refusal to bow before the pressure of a very well-organized effort that they are trying to pressure him to accept the idea that the world is in peril because it is becoming more and more warm because of industrialization. It is vital that the public understand that what is going on in this attack against President Bush is about a political agenda; that global warming is not a scientific imperative. It is a politically driven theory.

Those espousing global warming are building on public fear and apprehension. Young people in particular are being lied to about the environment and about global warming. Global warming, of course, is one of the worst falsehoods that they talk about. When I meet with student groups, it is clear they are being told false things about a lot of areas of the environment.

In fact, when I meet every student group from my district that comes to Washington, D.C. I always ask them the same question: How many of them believe that the air today in Southern California is cleaner or worse than it was when I went to high school in Southern California thirty-five years ago? Consistently, 95 percent of these students who live in Southern California who are coming to my office say they believe that the air quality today is so much worse than it was when I went to high school and how lucky I was to live in an era, in the early 1960s, when we had such clean air in Southern California.

This, of course, is 180 degrees wrong. These young people have been systematically lied to about their environment. They are being told they are being poisoned by the air. But, in fact, the air quality in Southern California is better than it has ever been in my lifetime. They cannot believe it when they hear it.

They also cannot believe that the quality of the Potomac River, the water quality around us, is better, even the quality of the soil. Even the number of trees and forests that we have has increased. They have been lied to time and again about the environment, and again the global warming theory is the worst of all.

These lies are being used to justify to Americans of all ages, to justify a centralization of power in Washington, D.C., and a centralization of power in global government through the United Nations and other institutions that are run by unelected and unaccountable authorities.

Let us get into what global warming is all about. Global warming is a theory that carbon fuel, coal, oil, gas, et cetera, that this carbon-based fuel is putting CO_2 into the atmosphere, and CO_2 is causing the temperature to rise, which will cause a drastic change in the weather, the ice flows, animal life, plant life on our planet.

First and foremost, let us recognize this: All of the recent scientific reports agree that there may, or may not, be a minor change in the planet's average temperature over this last 100 years. There is no conclusive proof that man is the cause of that perhaps minor change.

That is not what we are being told. The American public is being told all of these scientific reports are claiming that global warming is absolutely a fact and there is no arguing with it. One reads those reports and they will find that there are weasel words and there are all sorts of caveats in these reports that suggest the scientific community cannot say this.

Climate science seems to be a very recent entry into the pantheon of scientific study. Prior to 1980, there was only a handful of climatologists. Now they seem to be everywhere. Try to find a researcher on global warming who is not in some way tied to some sort of research contract by the federal government. Now, could it be that the reason for the increase in the numbers of global warming advocates has something to do with the access to government funding for research?

Eight years ago, when President Clinton took over the executive branch, he saw to it that there would be no one getting scientific research grants from our government unless they furthered the global warming theory.

We were tipped off to this when the lead scientist, and I would say the Director of Energy Research for the Department of Energy, Mr. Will Happer, was precipitously fired from his position because he did not agree with the global warming theory and did not believe that it had been proven. He wrote a little article about it, and Vice President Gore came down on him like an iron fist and he was out of that job.

Dr. Happer, I might add, is now a professor of physics at Princeton University. But his removal as the director of research at the Department of Energy sent a message, clearly heard throughout the scientific community: You do not agree with global warming, you are not going to get the contract. This has gone on for eight years.

There does not appear to be much information on global climate change prior to the mid-1980s. What we have been able to find out, prior to that time period, is that generally people in those times, the scientists, were arguing that we were on the edge of a new ice age. It was not global warming. Then it was global cooling.

In fact, in the span of twenty years, climate models have gone from predicting our eminent demise by freezing to death in a new ice age, to being baked in an oven to death in a global furnace. Interestingly enough, some of the leading proponents of global warming used to be the same advocates for global cooling.

Now, historically speaking we know that the globe and its climate have different ebbs and flows, and there have been ice ages in the past and there have been tropical ages in the past, without interference from man. That is even before man came on the scene.

In the last 1,000 years, for example, we have witnessed, even since man has been on the scene, in this last 1,000 years, we have witnessed a huge temperature swing over much of the world. Early in the last millennium, Lief Erickson established a colony on Greenland, and that colony on Greenland was free of snow for over half a year every year. In less than 100 years, 100 years later, that colony had to be abandoned because the climate had grown so much colder and the snow so much thicker that a new ice age appeared and apparently was on the way, a mini–ice age, not making Greenland hospitable to human habitation anymore.

I wonder in the current climate of scientific investigation what would have been predicted had scientists been available then to chart the course of what direction the world was going. We probably would have been told then that the Earth was on its way to an environment in which only the Eskimos would survive, and all of this was due to, who can tell? Certainly humankind had very little influence on the weather and temperatures then. No one could argue that.

Of course, that trend and lower temperatures reversed itself. Yes, it was getting cooler; but it then reversed itself, because at some point the Earth naturally has a way to adapt to cooler or warmer temperatures.

This historical recollection gives us a reason for concern about some of the trend lines. You take a trend line going in one direction and launch it way out into the future to see that that may not be accurate. It may not be accurate because the world can adapt.

If, in fact we have a minuscule trend toward warming, it could be that we are in fact emerging. Right now, instead of having the trend line being ominous, all it could mean is a trend line of minuscule warming, 1 degree in 100 years. It could mean that we are just emerging from a cooling period, from a period that is a little bit cooler.

Now, none of us should forget our lessons that we learned in sixth grade about those huge glaciers. Remember that? The huge glaciers once covered all of North America. In fact, it happened three or four times. The glaciers would come down, go back, and most of North America and Europe were covered. In fact, the Great Lakes were, if I remember what I was taught, were gouged out by these glaciers; and when the glaciers receded, these lakes were filled with water.

Well, when the glaciers moved forward, it represented a major change in the global climate toward global cooling. When the glaciers retreated, and we are now in a time period when the glaciers are retreating, that must mean that the Earth is getting a little bit warmer. Well, to use that as some sort of scientific basis to say that humankind is creating a warming trend on our planet that threatens and puts our planet in peril is nonsense. The one thing that those glaciers going back and forth did not indicate was that human beings had anything to do with the global weather change that was taking place. Nor did human beings have anything to do with the fact that all the dinosaurs were killed off by this global change in weather.

It seems to me that to understand climate change, we need hundreds of thousands of years' worth of observation and far more types of data than are currently available. Instead of serious scientific investigation and debate, most of those currently clamoring about climate change are looking at unbelievably shallow evidence and rushing to the conclusion that human beings are the cause of this change. But human beings were not around when these other traumatic changes happened in weather and temperature, which occurred in our distant past.

Recently, we have been treated to yet another spectacle of media climate-change hype. As I say, our president is under attack. Our new president, George W. Bush, made it clear that the United States will not be bound by the so-called Kyoto Protocol.

The liberal media and academic establishment went berserk. Just think of it, the president of the United States is calling into question the validity of man's impact on the global climate. Again, elitists have arrogantly labeled an American president as some kind of a moron. Well, they did the same thing to Ronald Reagan when he tried to end the Cold War, and they were dramatically wrong then, too.

George W. Bush is intelligent, and he has common sense. A few days ago the American people were presented something to make them believe that George W. Bush was not so intelligent. They were presented with a National Academy of Science report on climate change.

Now, if you read your newspaper about a week ago or saw the network news coverage, you would think that the president had been dressed down by the scientific community and that, once again, the experts had solidly, solidly, rallied behind the contention that global warming is here and it is a result of human action and that that determination is irrefutable. Well, that is what you would believe by the news reports.

Dan Rather, let us take a look at Dan Rather's report in particular. Dan Rather on CBS news was perhaps the worst in terms of his bias and inaccuracy of the presentation of that report. His lead to the story stated uncategorically that the report had proved global warming was here and that humans were the cause. How many listeners noted that after three minutes of Dan Rather's report, that at the end of that report, Dan Rather's own correspondent stated that the National Academy had not stated that humans were the cause of the temperature increase, and that temperature increase was 1 degree over 100 years?

Now, how many people noticed that? You had Dan Rather leading into his report that the report stated unequivocally that there had been the global warming and that humans were the cause. Yet at the end of the report, his own reporter put a little tag on that that they could not absolutely say that it was caused by human actions and human activity.

The National Academy of Science report is filled with weasel words and caveats. That was true of many of the other scientific investigations. Almost every one of the scientific investigations, the findings about global warming were not conclusive enough to make any solid statement other than words to the effect that further research is necessary.

Just like Dan Rather, it totally misportrayed what that report was all about. Over and over and over again, the American people have heard about reports that global warming is absolutely here, and it has been misportrayed to them. That is not what those reports have said. Sometimes reports have said that, and you go back to who did the reports, just a very small group of radicals who are not respected by the scientific community in those reports. Yet we hear about the reports all the time, and we see these same misquoted reports as being used to justify dramatic headlines and very frightening reports over the broadcast news media.

For the record, I will be submitting two documents highlighting some of the caveats and some of the weasel words, you might say, in the NRC report that indicates that the NRC is not making that conclusive and unequivocal decision that global warming is here and that humans caused that, which is what we heard on CBS news and read in the newspapers throughout this country and were used to beat our president up. Falsehoods. That is what was used to beat our president up. I will submit this for the record.

By the way, the report states that the temperature on Earth, again, let me state this, may or may not be, may or may not be, 1 degree warmer than it was 100 years ago. One degree change over 100 years. Think about that. A 1-degree change? These experts cannot predict the weather one day in advance. How can they predict and calculate and analyze the weather back 100 years ago, when they did not have any of the scientific equipment that was available to them, that is available to them today? How can anyone give credibility and be given credibility claiming a minuscule temperature change that supposedly has taken place across the face of this enormous planet?

Remember, 100 years ago they did not have any satellites; they did not even have telephone communications in most of the world. But across the face of this planet, that it was cooler then by a whole 1 degree? Can anyone listen to that with a straight face? Give me a break. Give the American people a break.

Well, one remembers just a few years ago President Clinton was so committed to proving this theory that he invited hundreds of climatologists who agreed with global warming to the White House. These were people who he thought were sympathetic to the global warming theories. During that time in the White House, I understand a major storm broke out in Washington and was just drenching the entire area; and well, what happened is that of all those hundreds of climatologists that came to the White House to reconfirm global warming, only three of them thought ahead enough to bring umbrellas.

So, what does that tell you? These are the people who are going to decide who can guide us down the path of accepting global warming, which then would lead us to dramatic changes in our lives because we would be giving power and centralization of authority away from what we have it today.

What is essential to the global warming theory, of course, is not just that the temperature is on the rise, but that human beings, especially western civilization, and particularly those of us who live in America, we are at fault; the Americans, the people who live in western civilization and human beings in general, we are the ones at fault for global warming.

Okay, so let us concede before we get into that that the Earth may or may not be 1 degree hotter than it was 100 years ago. That, however, is not necessarily a catastrophe. If the Earth is 1 degree warmer now than it was 100 years ago, that may be a good thing. It may be baloney; it may be a good thing. I do not know. It may be a good thing, especially if that 1 degree warmer is a nighttime temperature in the northern hemisphere in the fall or winter. That would be a very wonderful thing, to have it a little bit warmer during that time.

In fact, some of the people claiming to believe in the global warming theory are in fact saying that is how our temperature increases, it is 1 degree in the northern hemisphere, and I do not think that that is such a big calamity.

Issue 21

AIDS

In a travel program on television, the backpacking film crew crossed the border into a country in South-Central Africa. A large sign stared down at everyone entering this country: "Warning! 1 in 7 young people in [this area] has AIDS." The World Health Organization reports that in some African countries the infection rate is even higher. Moreover, increasingly, AIDS is becoming a worldwide problem.

Several years ago eight organizations affiliated with the United Nations pooled resources in a concerted effort to combat AIDS throughout the world. The result was the creation of the Joint United Nations Programme on HIV/AIDS (UNAIDS), an agency focused exclusively on the international HIV/AIDS problem. The first selection for Issue 21, a report by UNAIDS and the World Health Organization (WHO), recounts the sad facts. AIDS is decimating the populations of many countries in Africa and other developing areas. Babies are born with AIDS contracted from infected mothers. Children are becoming orphans after the deaths of their parents. As an official of World Vision, a private relief organization, told a Congressional committee, "I personally visited two districts of Uganda: Rakai and Masaka. There I saw families with no breadwinners. The 20-to-45 age group has been decimated, leaving behind a disproportionate number of small children and old people who are all dependents. This scenario was repeated in village after village. . . ."

In many of these countries, the AIDS problem is compounded by continual warfare, with marauding soldiers spreading the infection through rape and prostitution.

Over time the world community has accepted responsibility for helping developing countries cope with the AIDS crisis. But is adequate outside assistance getting through to the countries most affected? Leaders of many of these countries say that it is not, and they place primary blame on industrialized nations for failure to provide sufficient resources.

In the face of such criticism, what has the United States done to help? The second selection for Issue 21 is taken from a study of efforts by the U.S. Foreign Aid Agency (USAID) to help developing countries combat AIDS. The study describes specific programs and concludes that the United States is offering effective assistance. This study was done by the General Accounting Office, which reports to Congress, not to the administration. Its positive assessment of American anti-AIDS programs thus has more credibility than had the evaluation been made by the aid agency itself.

DISCUSSION QUESTIONS

As you read the articles by UNAIDS/WHO and USAID, consider the following questions:

1. Suppose you were given $100,000 to spend in fighting AIDS in Kenya. What would you do with this money?
2. On balance, how effective have efforts of the world community been in fighting AIDS in developing countries? Are the right programs being undertaken?
3. Why should the United States feel obligated to help countries in far-away Central Africa fight AIDS?

KEY WEB SITES

For more information on this topic, visit the following Web sites:

The Joint UN Programme on HIV/AIDS

http://www.unaids.org

British Broadcasting Corporation, "AIDS Around the World"

http://news.bbc.co.uk/hi/english/static/in_depth/world/2001/aids/default.stm

General Board of Global Ministries [Methodist], "AIDS in Africa"

http://gbgm-umc.org/programs/aidsafrica

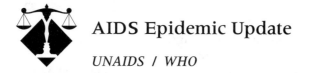

AIDS Epidemic Update

UNAIDS / WHO

United Nations
December 2002

INTRODUCTION

The AIDS epidemic claimed more than 3 million lives in 2002, and an estimated 5 million people acquired the human immunodeficiency virus (HIV) in 2002—bringing to 42 million the number of people globally living with the virus.

As the world enters the third decade of the AIDS epidemic, the evidence of its impact is undeniable. Wherever the epidemic has spread unchecked, it is robbing countries of the resources and capacities on which human security and development depend. In some regions, HIV/AIDS, in combination with other crises, is driving ever-larger parts of nations toward destitution.

The world stood by as HIV/AIDS swept through these countries. It cannot be allowed to turn a blind eye to an epidemic that continues to expand in some of the most populous regions and countries of the world.

PROGRESS TOWARD REALIZING
THE DECLARATION OF COMMITMENT

The Declaration of Commitment on HIV/AIDS is a potential watershed in the history of the HIV/AIDS epidemic. Adopted by the world's governments at the Special Session of the United Nations General Assembly on HIV/AIDS in June 2001, it established, for the first time ever, time-bound targets to which governments and the United Nations may be held accountable.

UNAIDS and its cosponsors have established a set of yardsticks for tracking movement toward those targets. Work on the first report measuring progress against these indicators starts in 2003, and will be based on progress reports provided in March 2003 by the 189 countries that adopted the declaration.

Already, though, there is substantial evidence of progress. More countries are recognizing the value of pooling resources, experiences, and commitment

---

This report was prepared by the Joint United Nations Programme on HIV/AIDS (UNAIDS) and the World Health Organization (WHO) for the United Nations in December of 2002.

by forging regional initiatives to combat the epidemic. Examples are multiplying, among them the following:

> The Asia Pacific Leadership Forum is tasked with improving key decision makers' knowledge and understanding of HIV/AIDS and its impact on different sectors of society.
>
> Members of the Commonwealth of Independent States have developed a regional Programme of Urgent Response to the HIV/AIDS epidemic, which government leaders endorsed in May 2002.
>
> In mid-2002, the Pan-Caribbean Partnership against HIV/AIDS signed an agreement with six pharmaceutical companies as part of wider-ranging efforts to improve access to cheaper antiretroviral drugs.
>
> In sub-Saharan Africa, forty countries have developed national strategies to fight HIV/AIDS (almost three times as many as two years ago), and nineteen countries now have National AIDS Councils (a six-fold increase since 2000).

Additional resources are being brought to bear by the new Global Fund to Fight AIDS, Tuberculosis, and Malaria, which has approved an initial round of project proposals, totalling U.S. $616 million, about two-thirds of which is earmarked for HIV/AIDS. Governments and donors have pledged more than U.S. $2.1 billion to the fund.

But the world lags furthest behind in providing adequate treatment, care, and support to people living with HIV/AIDS. Fewer than 4 percent of people in need of antiretroviral treatment in low- and middle-income countries were receiving the drugs at the end of 2001. And less than 10 percent of people with HIV/AIDS have access to palliative care or treatment for opportunistic infections.

In many countries, especially in sub-Saharan Africa and Asia, competing national priorities inhibit allocation of resources to expand access to HIV/AIDS care, support, and treatment. Unaffordable prices remain the most commonly cited reasons for the limited access to antiretroviral drugs. Insufficient capacity of health sectors, including infrastructure and shortage of trained personnel, are also major obstacles to health service delivery in many countries.

In Eastern Europe and Central Asia, the number of people living with HIV in 2002 stood at 1.2 million. HIV/AIDS is expanding rapidly in the Baltic States, the Russian Federation, and several Central Asian republics.

In Asia and the Pacific, 7.2 million people are now living with HIV. The growth of the epidemic in this region is largely due to the growing epidemic in China, where a million people are now living with HIV and where official estimates foresee a manifold increase in that number over the coming decade. There remains considerable potential for growth in India, too, where almost 4 million people are living with HIV.

In several countries experiencing the early stages of the epidemic, significant economic and social changes are giving rise to conditions and trends that favour the rapid spread of HIV—for example, wide social disparities, limited access to basic services, and increased migration.

Best current projections suggest that an additional 45 million people will become infected with HIV in 126 low- and middle-income countries (currently with concentrated or generalized epidemics) between 2002 and 2010—unless the world succeeds in mounting a drastically expanded global prevention effort. More than 40 percent of those infections would occur in Asia and the Pacific (currently accounting for about 20 percent of new annual infections).

Global Health

USAID

USAID has focused its HIV/AIDS prevention activities in sub-Saharan Africa on three interventions that have been proven to be effective in the global fight against the epidemic: behavior change communications, condom social marketing, and treatment and management of sexually transmitted infections. USAID missions and regional offices in sub-Saharan Africa targeted their HIV/AIDS prevention activities to high-risk groups, such as commercial sex workers and interstate truck drivers. USAID maintains that a targeted approach remains the best way to reduce the number of new infections in the general population and to allow for more efficient use of limited HIV/AIDS prevention funds. Because of the difficulty obtaining accurate information on incidence and prevalence, however, USAID must rely on proxy indicators to measure the impact of its HIV/AIDS programs.

USAID promotes behavior change through voluntary counseling and information campaigns to heighten awareness of the risks of contracting HIV/AIDS and spreading it to others. Specifically, these activities are to help motivate behavior change, heighten the appeal of health products and services, and decrease the stigma related to purchase and use of condoms. For example, the mission in Nigeria reported supporting an information campaign among sex workers, transport workers, and youth to increase condom use. In addition, the mission in Malawi supported voluntary HIV testing and counseling services in two cities, Lilongwe and Blantyre.

Ten USAID missions and one regional office that conducted behavior change communication activities reported increased knowledge and awareness about HIV/AIDS, to measure the effectiveness of these types of programs. For example, six missions and one regional office provided information that showed an increase in knowledge of condoms as a means of preventing HIV infection among people surveyed. The mission in Ghana reported that there was an increase in the proportion of people who knew that a healthy-looking person could have HIV (from 70 percent of women and 77 percent of men in 1993 to 75 percent and 82 percent, respectively, in 1998) but reported no change in the proportion who were aware of mother-to-child transmission (82 percent of women and 85 percent of men in 1993; 83 percent and 85 percent, respectively, in 1998). Moreover, surveys conducted for the mission in Tanzania showed that, between 1994 and 1999, the percentage of women who could name three ways to avoid getting HIV/AIDS increased from 11.4 percent to 24.2 percent. In the same country, the increase for men was from 22.6 percent to 28.6 percent.

USAID has also attempted to measure the effectiveness of behavior change communication activities to help change sexual behavior. In seven countries where USAID undertook such prevention programs, surveys suggested reductions in risky sexual behavior. For example, in Senegal, more men and women who were surveyed reported having used a condom in 1999 than in 1992. More male youth surveyed reported that they were using condoms with their nonregular sex partners in 1998 than in 1997. The same sexual behavior survey of female commercial sex workers showed an increased use of condoms with regular clients; however, female commercial sex workers also reported less frequent use of condoms with their nonregular partners. Also in Senegal, a greater percentage of girls reported in 1998 that they had never had sex compared to a prior survey conducted in 1997. However, there was no change for boys. In Zambia, more sexually active women who were surveyed in 1998 reported having ever used a condom than in a similar survey in 1992, and in 1998, fewer married men in Zambia's capital city reported having had extramarital sex than in a survey conducted eight years earlier.

Condom social marketing, which relies on increasing the availability, attractiveness, and demand for condoms through advertising and public promotion, is another intervention that USAID supports at the country level. It is well established that condoms are an effective means to prevent the transmission of the HIV virus during sexual contact. The challenge for HIV/AIDS prevention then is one of expanded acceptance, availability, and use by high-risk groups. USAID projects in sub-Saharan Africa encourage production and marketing of condoms by the private sector to ensure the availability of affordable, quality condoms when and where people need them.

USAID uses sales of condoms marketed through its program as a measure of the results of its condom promotion activities. USAID missions in fifteen of nineteen countries and one of three regional offices reported increased condom sales, with decreased sales reported in Malawi and Uganda. According to a USAID contractor, sales of condoms promoted under USAID's program decreased in Malawi because of an economic downturn in that country and because another donor was providing free condoms. Sales in Uganda were affected by the introduction of a competing brand of condoms distributed by another donor. Between 1997 and 1999, the number of condoms sold more than doubled in Benin, from 2.9 million to 6.5 million, and increased in Zimbabwe from 2 million to 9 million. Condom sales in the Democratic Republic of the Congo grew more than 800 percent, from about 1 million in 1998 to 8.4 million in 1999. The number of sales outlets carrying socially marketed condoms also increased in Benin, Guinea, Malawi, and Mozambique. In addition to male condom marketing, five missions conducted social marketing of female condoms. Between 1998 and 1999, female condom sales increased in three of the four countries for which data were available but decreased in Zambia.

Management of sexually transmitted infections through improved prevention, diagnosis, and treatment is another important component of USAID's HIV/AIDS efforts, because the risk of HIV transmission is significantly higher when other infections, such as genital herpes, are present. USAID has continued to support standardized diagnosis and treatment of sexually transmitted infections. For example, in Madagascar, USAID's program supported improved diagnosis and treatment by targeting interventions to high-risk populations. USAID has also worked to integrate the teaching of how to prevent sexually transmitted infections into its existing reproductive health and outreach activities.

As a way to measure the impact of its activities to improve management of sexually transmitted infections, USAID tracks the number of people trained in prevention, diagnosis, and treatment in that area. Seven USAID missions in sub-Saharan Africa reported assisting in the expansion of services for management of sexually transmitted infections. For example, USAID reported that it worked in ten primary health facilities in Kenya to develop guidelines for diagnosing symptoms typical of sexually transmitted infections, and to develop health worker training materials. A total of 1,112 outreach workers and 55 health care providers were trained in sexually transmitted disease case management. In addition, the mission in Ghana stated that in 1999 it trained more than 200 medical practitioners and a total of 502 health care workers in public health facilities in the management of sexually transmitted infections. In Ghana's police services, USAID trained 12 health care providers to recognize symptoms of sexually transmitted infections, trained 65 police peer educators, and helped establish an HIV/Sexually Transmitted Disease Unit at the police hospital.

In addition to these three main prevention interventions, USAID missions also implemented activities in other areas. A few missions had activities aimed at improving the safety of blood for transfusions. In 2000, for example, the mission in Tanzania began collaborating with the U.S. Centers for Disease Control and the Tanzanian Ministry of Health to improve blood safety and clinical protocols. The mission in Ethiopia continued programs that are directed at strengthening the capacity of nongovernmental organizations in the region to provide HIV services, while other missions worked to promote community involvement in providing care to those persons living with HIV.

Twelve USAID missions and two regional offices promoted host government advocacy for improved HIV/AIDS policy environments. Some missions, such as Malawi, conducted workshops with key decision makers focusing on specific policy issues such as HIV testing and drug treatment for AIDS patients. The mission in Ghana sought to improve policies for reproductive health services through advocacy and policy development. According to USAID, its advocacy and policy development activities in Ghana led to the development of a national AIDS policy, which at the time of our review was available for parliamentary approval. Also, the mission in Nigeria indicated that its advocacy work on behalf of orphans and vulnerable children led the Nigerian president to announce in 2000 his intention to pursue free and compulsory education for them. The mission in Nigeria also reported helping establish three regional networks of people with HIV/AIDS that later served as the precursor for a national HIV/AIDS support network.